We the Jury...

Great Jury Trials of History

We the Jury...

The Impact of Jurors on Our Basic Freedoms

GODFREY D. LEHMAN

Prometheus Books

59 John Glenn Drive
Amherst, NewYork 14228-2197

Published 1997 by Prometheus Books

01 00 99 98 97   5 4 3 2 1

Library of Congress Cataloging-in-Publication Data

Lehman, Godfrey D.
    We the jury— : the impact of jurors on our basic freedoms / Godfrey D. Lehman.
        p.   cm.
    Includes bibliographical references and index.
    ISBN 1–57392–144–0 (cloth : alk. paper)
    1. Jury—United States. 2. Justice, Administration of—United States. 3. Law and
politics. I. Title.
KF8972.L44   1997
347.73′752—dc21   97–11435
                                                                           CIP

Printed in the United States of America on acid-free paper

*T*his book is dedicated to the Fully Informed Jury Association (FIJA), both to the organization itself and to individual members for their dedication to keeping alive the grand bulwark of all liberty, trial by jury. The primary goal of FIJA is to educate American citizens about their roles as jurors in the survival of the American constitutional republic; members, too numerous to name individually here, have placed their bodies on the firing line to stand against the tyranny in the courtroom that would oppress and destroy this great bulwark.

Out of respect for every citizen who has ever served with honor upon a jury, FIJA has proclaimed September 5 each year since 1991 as National Jury Rights Day. It was on that date in 1670 when twelve English citizens, pulled randomly off the streets of London, succeeded in putting down a panel of judges who had inflicted horrible tortures upon them, to advance eight basic tenets of the American Constitution, including freedoms of religion, speech, and peaceable assembly; protection from arbitrary trial by barring the attaint and ensuring habeas corpus; and establishing the superior power of trials by jury as guaranteed three times in the Constitution, by the Sixth and Seventh Amendments and in the judiciary article. The consciences of the twelve would not allow them to succumb to pressures of the court to convict a youthful Quaker, William Penn, of the "crime" of leading a "dissident" form or worship against the official state religion of Anglicanism. Every one of the jurors stood firmly by his position that: "Every person has a right to worship according to his own conscience," in effect formulating our First Amendment over a century before it was written down.

Although the Penn case is unique in its particulars, it is representative of conscience-driven juries that have served ever since.

5

CONTENTS

FOREWORD

*F*rom this time forward, the history of trial by jury shall be divided into two distinct eras which shall be known as the BOJ period and the AOJ period. The acronyms stand for, respectively, the time Before Orenthal J. Simpson and the time after he crashed into our collective consciousness during that eventful summer of 1994. While all of us were aware that in the background of our national life there existed the concept of "trial by jury," few paid much attention to it unless they were directly involved.

The AOJ period is characterized by our having divided ourselves into two camps. One side takes the position that the jury is a ridiculous notion and should be rejected completely because it has been obvious from the start that Simpson committed the crimes of which he was accused, and how could those idiots have let him go. Without a jury getting in the way, he would have been locked up in just a day or two. On the other side may be less virulent individuals who believe they know that the first verdict was correct and that the outcome of the second trial (the civil suit) proved what a mess our trial system really is.

The controversy became aggravated because hardly had the O. J. trial faded from the spotlight before we witnessed the spectacles of the Oklahoma City bombing, Theodore Kaczynski, and many more. Most of us had already known what the verdicts *should* be; it was just a matter of time before we learned if these juries were as inane as O. J.'s.

Except for one thing. When we find fault with a jury verdict, we are not assessing the jury's failure rate; we are expressing our personal prejudices. We are not really talking about the jury system so much as how it is misused, for if our prejudices were correct, there would be no need for a jury trial at all. We could just announce the verdict at the very start of an investigation. Yet, reflecting further, this is the way things have been since earliest days; people have always taken sides, and through nine centuries, and probably longer, the jury has survived. Why?

The history of the human race is long and sad, characterized mostly by tragedy; it is the story of wars, massacres, pogroms, tortures, and tyrannies. Yet interspersed we find moments of great glory, shining moments which demonstrate that perhaps there may exist within the human soul a natural nobility. We read of the great and the good whose nobility was honored in their time for their accomplishments in the sciences, the arts, and human leadership. We do not often read of the less than famous whose deeds were less spectacular, although nonetheless significant. Though suppressed, hidden, ignored or unrecognized, their nobility is revealed in times of crisis or unusual pressure and appears in contrast to more dominant and ignoble traits, often within the same personality.

David Rieff, reporting from Bosnia for *The New Yorker* magazine in September 1995, expressed this internal conflict: "Most of us have an inner policeman, some kind of internalized restraint," which controls our baser drives. That this restraint is close to universal is revealed by its consistency throughout history, unrelated to time or geography, race, culture, gender, nationality, literacy, intellectual capacity, age, social status or any other factor.

There seems to be concealed within an overwhelming number of us an inborn sense of what is right, of justice, if you will; an unconscious sensitivity toward one another, a feeling of mutual responsibility driven by conscience. It shows itself when we who are ordinarily without power find ourselves thrust into positions where we control the fate and welfare of other persons. It is most evident when we hold that power for a short time only, a power that we share on an equal basis with others—then it is gone. How we handle that power, how deeply we sense our responsibility, evokes caution. Perhaps the driving force is no more than wanting to look good, or at least not wanting to look bad, before our companions; perhaps it is because we apprehend possible retaliation if we fall under the control of others; or fear of being burdened by a heavy sense of guilt if we mishandle the power. (Our inner policeman on patrol!)

This suggests a modification of the axiom created by Lord Acton, (but inserting a portion popularly dropped from the original): "Power *tends to* corrupt, and absolute power corrupts absolutely." When power is not absolute, when it is not held exclusively, it influences us in a surprising way: "Power shared equally with others, all strangers to it and held briefly, tends to ennoble."

This ennobling experience is manifested at its highest through the institution being condemned, AOJ style. When we serve on a jury, power and responsibility are thrust upon us without our expecting it, without our seeking it, and without our being prepared to handle it. We are likely to become awed and intimidated, but are comforted because we are not alone, because other people are there to share the blame with us if things go wrong.

Critics of the trial jury will find fault with me for praising so highly a system that condemns as many innocent defendants to prison and even death as ours does. They will recount scores of tragic anti-libertarian verdicts by juries. I will respond by citing more cases of bad—very bad—verdicts by "juries" gone astray which, on the surface, justify skepticism.

How do I "apologize" for (if that is the proper term) or at least explain the numerous jury disasters? I began my decades-long research on juries with a somewhat negative view of these groups, and great respect for the judiciary. I disdained the concept that the stereotypical "man-on-the-street" could be capable of deciding fundamental issues—not so much of law, perhaps, as of justice. Is not this a specialized talent confined to an elite class of trained professionals? Thus I required strong proof to convince me to reverse my position and regard juries positively and the judiciary a bit more skeptically.

The more extensively I studied, the more thoroughly I was convinced that the jury is indeed "the grand bulwark of all liberty" as assessed by the eighteenth-century English jurist William Blackstone, not despite the miscarriages but because of them, or more precisely, because of the conditions that made them. I discovered a common theme in these disasters. As the following chapters show, where a "jury" errs, it is practically always because the panel has fallen under the influence or domination of the judge or another outside force;

hence the verdict is not the true, conscience-driven decision delivered by an *independent* panel. It is not a true jury! One example is a case where the judge would not allow the jury to deliver a verdict at all; he usurped the prerogative and delivered the verdict himself. Yet the historical record shows this as a "jury" verdict, to make it appear as if a jury had gone astray!

In another case, important evidence was withheld from the jury which received a distorted view and delivered what was shown later to be a false verdict. The jurors were angered when they learned they had been deceived. There is a case where jurors were intimidated by rioting crowds threatening physical harm—even murder—if they did not deliver the "proper" verdict; a case where during jury selection the panel members were painstakingly examined by the prosecution in collusion with a corrupt judge to ensure before-the-fact convictions; and the opposite when the handpicked jury proved immune to manipulation.

Conversely, there are numerous examples of jurors, just plain folks like you and me, whose consciences would not let them forsake basic rights to appease the tyrannies that would seize them, even though appeasement meant escaping the torture the tyrannies imposed upon them.

The greater wonder is that jurors resisted at all and as often as they did, rather than that they succumbed when pressures were too extreme.

I am certainly not the first to concede an extraordinary character to the jury, or to place so high an assessment on it. Every jury historian I have read exalts the institution. The earliest histories go back no further than a century and a half, and there were two (one by Lysander Spooner, the other by William Forsyth) coincidentally and independently published in 1852. Each was unstinting in its praise of how their fellow men (no women jurors at their period of history)— everyday on-the-street or behind-the-plow citizens—would rise to such heights under conditions foreign to most of them. William Forsyth wrote in his *History of Trial by Jury*: "There is no doubt that the jury in any shape, *if left to itself*, is antagonistic to arbitrary power" (italics added). His key phrase "*if left to itself*" implies the necessity for *independence*. Lysander Spooner advised in *An Essay on the Trial by Jury*: "The object of this trial by the people in preference to trial by the government, is to guard against every species of oppression by the government."

Four decades earlier, English philosopher-judge Jeremy Bentham wanted to publish not a history but an analysis of how judges would try to reshape freedom-defending juries in their respective images through techniques of jury selection he considered corrupt. The risk was so great for Bentham and his publisher that they dared not bring his *On the Art of Packing Special Juries,* written in 1810, to light for eleven years. Juries, Bentham's experience had taught him, consistently challenged judicial arbitrariness, a threat intolerable to autocrats.

French historian A. Esmein, who wrote *A History of Continental Criminal Procedure* in 1914, found French juries to be shining examples of justice despite heavy encumbrances placed upon them, such as allowing majority instead of unanimous verdicts and biased evidence. And Russian historian Maurice Baring, writing in *The Mainsprings of Russia* in 1914, found juries in Russia so threatening to the power of the czar that the monarch had to abolish the institution to save his throne. Late-twentieth-century historians include such astute observers as University of Hawaii law professor Jon Van Dyke (*Jury Selection: Our Uncertain Commitments to Representative Panels,* 1978), who faults selection practices which result in unrepresentative panels; and University of Santa Clara, Calif., professor Alan Scheflin, who declared that "the right [of a jury] to nullify on the basis of conscience in the name of the community, [is] essential to a restoration of the vaunted stature the judicial system should occupy."[1] Thomas Allen Green of the University of Chicago reviewed in *Verdicts according to Conscience*[2] six centuries of English jury verdicts from 1200 to 1800, which led him to the conclusion that when juries follow conscience instead of current law, they are indeed the preservers of liberty and defenders of the helpless against oppression.

Green's major theme is jury nullification, which he defines as "the exercise of jury discretion in favor of a defendant whom the jury nonetheless believes to have committed the act with which he is charged. Historically, some instances of nullification reflect the jury's view that the act in question is not unlawful, while in other cases the jury does not quarrel with the law, but believes that the prescribed sanction is too severe."[3]

Harry Kalven and Hans Zeisel, also of the University of Chicago, conducted seminal research on how criminal juries operate. Their book, *The American Jury,*[4] shows that jurors require higher levels of proof than do judges to be convinced of guilt. Greenville, South Carolina, attorney J. Kendall Few published an uninhibited accolade to juries in his two-volume work titled *In Defense of Trial by Jury.*[5]

In all these studies there is the consistent theme that juries in every age tend to respond to conscience in determining their verdicts in the face of established law—but they must be able to act as free agents. Green tells us[6] that trial by jury began to be "the primary means for determining guilt or innocence in prosecutions for felony" starting about 1220, shortly after the Magna Charta was signed. That document in 1215 awarded the jury an honorable status by guaranteeing trials "by the lawful judgment of his [i.e., the defendant's] equals or by the law of the land" (Article 39). So effectually did the jury perform under extreme pressure and against great odds that five centuries later, Blackstone was convinced that:

> Trial by jury is a privilege of the highest and most beneficial nature and our most important guardian both of public and private liberty. Our liberties cannot but subsist so long as this palladium remains sacred and inviolate: not only from all open attacks, but also from all secret machinations which may sap and undermine it.

Thomas Jefferson said: "I consider trial by jury as the only anchor ever yet imagined by man, by which a government can be held to the principles of its constitution." James Madison rated the constitutional guarantees to trial by jury as "the grandest in the whole list" of rights intended to be secured to the people. The persistence of nullification, Green concludes, has impacted "through time on the substantive law, on the administration of the law, and on the ways in which Englishmen—officials, jurists, and laymen—thought about both the jury and the law,"[7] and thus proved to be the most effective control over government excess.

But what do we mean by "jury," and what exactly makes a "trial by jury"?

There are many different interpretations of what a jury is. Let us quickly dispose of the term when used to describe a body of persons, often experts, selected to award prizes or make judgments in a contest or competition. That kind of "jury" is outside our province, and indeed the word in that sense is misleading. The jury we are talking about is composed of nonexperts.

Let us also dispose of "grand jury." This is an investigative, indicting body, and although it has a joint origin with the trial jury it functions very differently. Its duty is to receive complaints and accusations in criminal cases, hear the evidence adduced on the part of the state, and issue bills of indictment when they are satisfied a trial ought to take place. The term "grand" is often misread as "exalted," as if it were of greater significance than our trial or "petit" jury. Actually, they are French terms meaning "large" and "small," respectively, in reference to the size of the jury panel, and have nothing to do with the group's importance. Don't be misled into thinking that the Anglicized pronunciation of "petit" as "petty" is synonymous with "insignificant." This "petty" jury is what Madison called the "grandest." Again it would be better if there were a term other than "jury" to refer to the larger body whose role it is to determine if someone's actions warrant being bound over for trial.

My *Unabridged Webster's* defines "jury"—trial jury that is—as "a number of qualified persons, selected in a manner prescribed by law, empaneled and sworn to inquire *into the facts* in a law case, and to give a decision *on the evidence given them* in the case" (italics added). *Bouvier's Law Dictionary* is much the same: "A body of men who are sworn to *declare the facts* of a case as they are delivered from the evidence placed before them" (emphasis added). *Black's Law Dictionary* includes "women" among those "selected according to law, and sworn to inquire of certain matters of fact and declare the truth upon evidence laid before them." This body, *Black's* adds, and I emphasize, "*is bound to accept and apply . . . the law applicable to the case*" as stated to them by the judge.

Despite my general respect for dictionaries, particularly of the caliber of these three, I find their definitions unsatisfactory, inaccurate, and disturbing. Beyond that, misleading. They do not recognize the independence of the jury, or that a true jury must be "left to itself."

An imprecise "definition" appearing in the 1992 edition of the *Encyclopaedia Britannica* describes the jury as "a group of laymen that decides factual issues in criminal and civil trials. . . . Historically the jury has been composed of twelve members, and unanimity was required in deciding cases. These characteristics have been altered. . . ."

The definition (author not identified) cautions that "The jury trial is always overseen by a judge who decides (to a certain extent) what evidence is appropriate for the jury to hear. Also, if the evidence does not leave a question of fact to be answered, the judge may take the case from the jury. The judge instructs the jury in laws that are applicable. . . ." If that view of the jury prevailed, we would be reducing the panel to so much furniture, tolerated on the premises only to satisfy the pesky demands of the Sixth and Seventh Amendments and Article III, Section 2, Clause 3 of the Constitution that there be such things as juries. It would be an automaton. That every *Encyclopaedia Britannica* analyst peers through glasses tinted by a law school education and not from the jury box may account for the dispiriting view.

There is one wishy-washy exception in the later edition. Collaborating on a definition under the heading of "Procedural Law," law professors Peter Herzog of the University of Syracuse and Mario E. Occhialino of the University of New Mexico advised first that "the function of the jury is to determine the facts of the case, whereas the function of the judge is to determine the applicable law," and "It is the obligation of the judge at the conclusion of the trial, to instruct the jury as to the applicable law governing the case in order to guide it in arriving at a just verdict. . . ." But a few paragraphs later they acknowledge ambiguously: "Most frequently the jury will be requested to return a general verdict—that is, a decision merely stating in general terms the ultimate conclusion that it has reached. . . . This form of verdict gives considerable leeway to the jury and permits, if it does not encourage, some deviation from a strictly logical and technical application of the law to the facts." But the very definition of "general verdict" is, per *Bouvier's,* "one by which the jury pronounces at the same time on the facts *and the law* . . ." (italics added).

Herzog and Occhialino apologize for their presumed heresy by suggesting an "alternative that offers *greater control* over the decision-making process" (italics added). That alternative is the "special verdict," which restricts the jury only to the facts; the judge then determines the general verdict based on jury-found facts. This limits the jury effectually to determining only, for example, whether the defendant actually wrote certain words; whether those words were libelous, without regard to their truth or falsity, would be decided by the judge. The special verdict reduces the jury to mere ciphers.

We are saved from the disasters of special verdicts because, the two law professors conclude, it "is cumbersome." But if the objective is "greater control," why stop there? Why not carry it all the way to total control? Why not eliminate all doubt of not being "guided in arriving at a just verdict" by arranging for the verdict to be arrived at judicially?

Professors Kalven and Zeisel, despite their earlier encomia for the jury, seem almost to have reversed themselves when they write in the *Encyclopaedia,* under "Judicial and Arbitrational Systems," that "the letter of the law confines the jury to 'finding the facts,' " but "the deviations from the judge are mostly due to the jury's subtle, and not always conscious. injecting its sense of justice" against severe punishment, or out of concern for overly harsh criminal laws. Which is exactly what Thomas Green tells us has been going on with juries since at least the days of the Magna Charta.[8] Also, no "letter of the law" can confine a properly informed jury.

Kalven and Zeisel's comments are less stringent than what Chief Judge Charles E. Clark of the U.S. Court of Appeals in New Haven, Connecticut, wrote in the 1956 edition of the *Encyclopaedia*: "In practice [the jury] is largely controlled by the judges," because the judges determine the admissibility of evidence. This tends to "fetter to some extent the independence or limit the chances of error of the jury." For want of clarification of what "error of the jury" means, we must suppose that it occurs when jurors slip out from under judicial control. Which again raises the question of ridding trials permanently of error by dispensing with error-prone juries in favor of inerrant judicial oracles.

The *Encyclopedia Americana* (1992 ed.) tells us, under the heading "Petit Jury," that "Although the jury's role and powers are considerable, they are limited by the judge's powers," which include withholding evidence from the jury. It is also his "province" to instruct the jury on the law.

The *Encyclopedia Americana* does acknowledge the "general verdict," but softens its heretical quality by holding the jury to applying "to the facts as it finds them the legal principles given to it by the judge, thus in essence deciding the ultimate issue of who wins." However, when the jury delivers only a special verdict and the judge a general verdict, the judge applies "the law to the facts," which makes the definition of "special verdict" given above ambiguous. A "special" verdict is based on fact alone.

The *World Book Encyclopedia* (1995 ed.), in a short article, avoids the law-fact dispute, saying only that the petit jury "is a group of citizens" which "determines what it believes is the truth."

The common thrust of these analyses is to pour the jury into a mold shaped by legislative enactment and judicial edict, in opposition to the freer formation ideal prescribed by constitutional and common law mandates. They submit to judicial pretensions; they consign to oblivion the evidence that juries have historically not operated according to their definitions; that juries resist molding. They reveal ignorance of jury history, for had they studied history at all they would know their definitions do not apply.

The law fraternity depends upon the authoritative pronouncements of the encyclopedic statement of the principles of American law known as the *Corpus Juris Secundum* (CJS). There are many pages devoted to "juries," but our interest centers on the CJS definition of a jury (1997 edition) "as a body of persons [formerly "men"] who are sworn to declare the facts of a case as they are proved from the evidence placed before them, or as a body of persons [changed from "twelve men"] duly summoned, sworn, and impaneled for the trial of issues joined between litigants in civil actions, or for the determination of facts adduced for and against accused in criminal cases."

Regarding the jury's function, CJS says that the "term imports a trial of issues of fact by persons . . . under the direction of a competent court, and sworn to render an impartial verdict according to the law and the evidence; and proceeding in their deliberations in the presence and under the superintendence of a judge empowered to instruct them on the law and to advise them on the facts, and, except on acquittal of a criminal charge, to set aside their verdict if in his opinion it is against the law and evidence." To support this estimation, CJS cites many scores of authoritative opinions expressed by—who else?—judges who would do the superintending! The direct inheritors of the censors of Jeremy Bentham! Once again, why bother with error-prone juries when we end up going to infallible judges to straighten out the mess jurors make?

The legal profession's general view of jurors is that they are addle-headed juveniles to be given paternal pats on the head, and sent off for periods of supervised play at being grown-ups by making guesses at "the truth" gleaned from the limited evidence surviving the censoring wisdom of the black-clad judge monitoring their behavior. By controlling the evidence, this grown-up leads the youngsters in the direction he desires. Curiously, all these lawyer-based analyses contravene and ignore the authoritative pronouncements of Forsyth, Spooner, Blackstone, Jefferson, Madison, Esmein, Baring, Van Dyke, Scheflin, Green, Kalven, Zeisel, and others quoted above, and show that the corruption Bentham complained of not only has not changed, but has been endorsed as official legal policy.

When the kids at play rebel (and they often do), their monitor declares them devoid of sense by "overturning" their decisions—unless they have frustrated him with an acquittal, in which case he sits there in stunned silence. (There are noteworthy exceptions, of course, to this as to any generalization.)

There is an element of flexibility to judicial domination. Another legal compendium, *Words and Phrases,* grants that a jury "is composed of the peers or equals of the person whose *rights it is selected or summoned to determine*" (emphasis added). Which means freedom to determine if the law under which the trial is held is the actual offender of rights, and if the jury so determines, to overturn the written law as applied to that case.

Words and Phrases is the only official view of the jury that conforms with basic constitutional philosophy—that the people are sovereign, that all power emanates from the people, and that powers not expressly delegated to the government by the people remain with the people. Thus the jury, mandated by common law and constitutionally supported to represent the whole body of people, retains the powers of sovereignty, which means they are not to be dominated by their less-than-sovereign servants in black uniforms—and that means power to say when any law "becomes destructive . . . [to] their safety and happiness," as expressed in the Declaration of Independence. Therefore, from this view, the jury can, at its sole discretion, render verdicts that veto, nullify, throw out, or deny the existence of any law regardless of how many or how highly placed or how pompous the judicial protesters.

Indeed, proclaims the Declaration of Independence, "it is their right, it is their duty to throw off such government, and to provide new guards for their future security." Such is the authority of twelve just plain folks in *unanimous* agreement. While the jury's power is not limited in the matter before them (other than what might be called "decorum"), its authority does not extend beyond the case at hand, or else it, too, could tend to become abusive. The key to judicious use of power is that it is confined to prescribed boundaries. For, like fire, when it escapes beyond those boundaries—beware!

Consider a few historical examples:

In early-nineteenth-century England, the punishment for forging a bank check was hanging. The jurors, knowing that to convict an obviously guilty defendant before them would mean his death, registered their protest against so harsh a punishment by acquitting. By jury decree, the law did not operate in this one case, but the statute remained on the books.

A second case arose; that jury, entirely independent of the first, also acquitted, followed by a third, a fourth, a score, a hundred. It took most of a decade during which there was hardly a conviction before the message was driven home to Parliament, which then reduced the severity of the penalty for forgery. The jury had effectively invoked a new law before that law was written.

This supervisory power of the sovereign people over government is known as *jury nullification,* and it is one way the governed express their consent or lack of it to their governors. In whatever way encyclopedias, dictionaries, and CJS may define "jury," the "body of men" and women is *not* a true jury unless its members are fully informed of their power to act *independently.* The judge may give legal *advice* about the law and the penalties prescribed therein, but he cannot "instruct" (in the sense of "ordering") the jurors to act in any way but by conscience. A "body of men" not so informed, or not sensing this, is not a true jury and cannot properly be defined as such; it is a puppet body, an organ of the court.

A *true* jury is "left to itself." When the *Encyclopaedia Britannica* describes the jury as "largely controlled by the judges," it is describing exactly what the jury is not; it is describing a subservient body that would have no useful function, the Machiavellian form without substance, as prescribed for the notorious Borgias and de Medicis to subjugate the people. If this were the way the jury acted, Blackstone would never have found service on a jury to be "a privilege of the highest and most beneficial nature and our most important guardian" of liberty. The forgery cases given above are but one example showing that juries have never operated in all history according to the *Black's, Encyclopaedia Britannica, Encyclopedia Americana,* and CJS model, unless they have been tricked.

The following chapters show that when jury panels become subservient to judges, the results are disastrous. But when jurors throw off judicial shackles, verdicts invariably advanced the people's liberties. In other words, when jurors stand up for total independence, when they recognize their authority to judge the law and reject or "nullify" any law they find wanting, they prove that the jury is the grand bulwark of all liberty.

No other force or institution can match it. It is the essence of constitutional republicanism. Indeed, it *is* the living constitutional republic. It is the great defender of the people's liberties, operating peacefully, without bloodshed.

Spooner wrote eloquently about this a century and a half ago, and I cannot improve upon his words:

> For more than six hundred years—that is, since Magna Charta in 1215—there has been no clearer principle of English or American constitutional law, than that . . . it is not only the right and duty of jurors to judge what are the facts, what is the law, and what was the moral intent of the accused; *but that it is also their right, and their primary and paramount duty, to judge of the justice of the law, and to hold all laws invalid, that are, in their opinion, unjust or oppressive, and all persons guiltless in violating, or resisting the execution of such laws.*
>
> Unless such be the right and duty of jurors, it is plain that instead of juries being a "palladium of liberty" (quoting Blackstone)—a barrier against the tyranny and oppression of the government—they are really mere tools in its hands, for carrying into execution any injustice and oppression it may desire to have executed.
>
> But for their right to judge of the law, *and the justice of the law,* juries would be no protection to an accused person, *even as to matters of fact*: for, if the government can dictate to a jury any law whatever . . . it can certainly dictate what evidence is admissible, and what inadmissable, *and also what force or weight is to be given to the evidence admitted.* And if the government can thus dictate to a jury the laws of evidence, it can not only make it necessary for them to convict on a partial exhibition of the evidence rightfully pertaining to the case, but it can even require them to convict on any evidence whatever that it pleases to offer them.[9] (Italics in original)

William Pinkney, a member of the Maryland convention to ratify the Constitution, a vigorous opponent of slavery, attorney general of the United States from 1812 to 1814, and later a U.S. senator, addressed a jury in 1815 in defense of John Hodges, who had been charged with treason:

> The best security for the rights of the individual is to be found in the trial by jury. But the excellence of this institution consists in its exclusive power. The jury are here judges of the law and fact and are responsible only to God, to the prisoner, and to their consciences.
> It is my right to tell the jurors they are judges of the law.

The court in this instance acknowledged that while it was "bound to declare the law wherever called upon in civil or criminal cases, it was also their [i.e., the justices'] duty to inform the jury that they were not obliged to take their direction as the law."

The jury acquitted Hodges.[10]

Not all judges have been so forthright in how they "instruct" jurors. In 1994 a California jury, although agreeing that the defendant was guilty of a bodily attack, was troubled by a description that his victim had suffered "serious bodily injury." In the jurors' view, according to a note written to the trial judge, "our feelings don't follow this. Do we, as a jury, have the option to give the lesser crime of 'Assault'?" Their question, although the jurors were not aware of it, involved the discretionary use of nullification. The trial judge disposed of the issue with a curt "No."

On appeal, presiding judge S. J. Stone of a California Appellate Court, readily admitted that the jury does have the "power to nullify a verdict," although he said: "Here we hold that the trial court did not have to advise the jury of its power to nullify a verdict. . . ." However, the trial judge's response to the jurors' question was erroneous since the jury did have "the option to give the lesser crime." Stone suggested that the trial judge should have responded by reading to the jurors the applicable jury instructions, which Stone put into the trial record. In one short paragraph, the instruction protested against nullification *six times*: first: "It is my duty to *instruct you on the law*. . . ." Second: "You must *base your decision on the facts and the law.*" Third: "You must *apply the law that I state to you*. . . ." Fourth: "You must *accept and follow the law as I state it to you,* whether or not you agree with the law. . . ." Fifth: "You must *follow my instructions.*" Sixth: "Both the People [i.e., the prosecution] and the defendant have a right to expect you will conscientiously consider and weigh the evidence, *apply the law,* and reach a just verdict regardless of the consequences" (italics added).

Stone cited the 1969 case of *U.S.* v. *Moylan* (417 F2d 1002): "A jury has the 'undisputed power' to acquit, even if its verdict is contrary to the law instructed upon by the court and contrary to evidence." Nonetheless, he said, "few states still give [*sic*] juries the power to judge both law and fact," ignoring the fact that the power to nullify does not originate from legislature or judiciary but is an attribute of the people's sovereignty. He reversed the positions of jury and government: "A juror's duty," he concluded, quoting another case, "includes the obligation to follow the instructions of the court . . ." (*People* v. *Fernandez,* 26 Cal App 4th 710 31 Cal Rptr 2d 677).

The factors that ensure jury independence are several: principally, the jury's understanding of its authority to judge the law, jury size, unanimous verdicts in criminal trials, receiving all relevant evidence, no jury packing, and the ability to deliver verdicts based on conscience.

To consider size, smaller panels are less capable of resisting judicial desire to dominate; larger panels are cumbersome and do not permit participation by all members. More important than the formal trial in developing juror understanding is the interchange in the jury room. Discussion and deliberation give the jurors time to interact with each other away from the public eye. They serve as checks against individual biases and extremes; they hold each other to account for their respective positions and to conscience; they overcome bluff and bravado; they sift through the testimony and compare views, often cutting through the histrionics, strategy, and theatrics of the courtroom. Their varying personalities restrain emotional responses and tend to demand self-examination and honesty. In a sense they evoke each other's inner policeman.

With respect to the size of a jury, what is the ideal balance? Ten? Fifteen? Twenty? Any figure is arbitrary, but twelve has generally worked so well for so long there is no reason to change, certainly not downward. How twelve became the number is lost in history, but there is a certain magic and completeness to the figure, as, for example, twelve months in the year or twelve "daytime" and "nighttime" hours. Any attempt to cut jury panel size to eight, six, or even ten conceals the malice of reducing juries to subservience. Combined with judge-written "Rules of Court" so devious as to confuse twelve into delivering false verdicts, larger panels—fifteen perhaps—suggest greater protection. That is how the Scotch have believed for centuries. But smaller—*never*!

The ancient Athenians saw size as protection against corruption, and in doing so carried it too far, defeating themselves. A small jury-style panel known as a "dikastery" consisted of sixty-one "dikasts." The largest had 2,001. When the philosopher Socrates was tried for corrupting the youth of Athens, his "jury" consisted of 501 members. So large a number may have discouraged individual tampering, but it prevented interchange. After each trial, the dikasts deposited marked ballots in designated boxes. Verdicts were based on simple majorities, even as small as one no matter how many votes were cast. With Socrates, the division was fewer than thirty votes; had there been interchange, he probably would have been saved, as only about fifteen hesitant switches would have rescued him.

The requirement for unanimity in criminal trials is based on the doctrine that guilt must be established "beyond reasonable doubt" and that it is better to acquit ten guilty defendants than convict one innocent. Verdicts in civil trials are based on a "preponderance" of the evidence, and a three-fourths or greater majority is often accepted. In criminal trials, less than unanimity brings the jury under the heel of the court, and, as long as a single juror remains unconvinced, "reasonable doubt" is trashed. The split or hung criminal jury indicates that reasonable doubt exists, which even the rules of court respect. In many situations a hung jury protects the minority from majority tyranny. By one estimate, despite unanimity, there are more convicted innocents in the nation's jails today than "pigeons in the park." (See the Afterword.)

Split verdicts may make for quicker, faster decisions, but they will be uncertain, and the number of wrongfully convicted will increase. "Jury reform" is a cover-up term for "jury control," to feed a passion for convictions for convictions' sake. The "reform" needed is to replace "strategy," trickery, and deception with honesty, which we do not see much of; to withhold nothing from the jurors; to inform them fully about their rights and powers; and to stop abusing them by showing greater respect, which means, among other things, paying them decently. (Except perhaps for better pay, none of this is on the agenda of would-be "reformers.")

When jurors do not receive all the evidence, they will have difficulty delivering equitable verdicts, as Andrew Hamilton advised in the freedom-of-the-press trial of John Peter Zenger in New York in 1735: "The suppressing of evidence ought always to be taken for the strongest evidence." Movies have made us familiar with dramatic cries of attorneys gesturing wildly: "I object" to testimony from the other side as being "irrelevant" and "immaterial," and judges hammering with gavels to "sustain" the objection. When a judge does this, he injects his bias into the trial and takes control: it now becomes a trial by judge. How arbitrary his decision to sustain is, is evidenced by another judge in the same circumstance "overruling" and "permitting" the jury to hear the evidence. I have attended seminars sponsored by such organizations as the California Trial Lawyers Association, where panels of judges are always disagreeing about "points of law" to prove that it comes down to which judge is controlling things, not to jury review. If the jury is capable of delivering the verdict, it is capable of determining relevance and materiality without judicial interference. Not to let the jury make these determinations is an example of regarding the jurors as juveniles.

The evidence that is filtered out, the secret huddles between judge and counsel out of range of juror hearing, raise a suspicion about what it is that one side so desperately doesn't want the jury to learn. Which means that that evidence is the very evidence the jury must receive, per Hamilton. The jurors should demand to receive it!

Another factor of independence is the degree to which the jury panel represents the whole people. The Constitution mandates the jury to be "a body truly representative of the community," as defined by Supreme Court Justice Frank Murphy (*Glasser* v. *U.S.* 315 US 60, 1941); and that it "necessarily contemplates an impartial jury drawn from a cross-section of the community . . . without systematic and intentional exclusion of any" group (*Thiel* v. *Southern Pacific,* 328 US 217, 1946).

The Federal Jury Selection and Service Act of 1968 declares that it is a "fundamental right" that the jury be composed of "a fair cross-section"; the American Bar Association, agreeing with the Jury Commissioners Association of the California Court Administrators, advises that the jurors be "selected at random . . . from the broadest possible spectrum of the citizens. . . ." Murphy also offered the caveat that:

> Tendencies, no matter how slight, toward the selection of jurors by any method other than a process which will insure a trial by a representative group are undermining processes, weakening the institution of the jury trial, and should be sturdily resisted.

Such high-sounding phrases, however, are not respected in practice by American courts and the legal profession. No sooner are the sentiments expressed than they are breached by procedures that aim to pack the jury. Beyond the usual attempts by attorneys on both sides to select jurors who are thought to be sympathetic to their position, a new occupation was conceived during the 1970s and dedicated to the proposition that every person called for jury service is automatically deprived of her or his humanity, and yields all rights otherwise protected by the Constitution. This new vocation is that of jury consulting which attempts to offer scientific screening processes to select suitable jurors and to weed out those likely to be unfavorable to one's case. Judge David Scott DeWitt, then of the 42nd Judicial Circuit Court of Michigan, summed up official disdain for jurors by writing a letter to a junior candidate in 1978: "You have no constitutional rights in this area," as if our supreme law were a weapon against the people.

Judicial disrespect for jurors is virtually standard operating procedure, per the intrusions used in jury selection. Judges often put up a façade of protection for the accused by "demanding" that jurors respond to lengthy questionnaires that delve deeply into their private lives. For O. J.'s criminal trial, Judge Lance Ito presented each juror with a booklet containing 294 questions, but never bothered to tell the jurors that they were constitutionally—indeed, *inherently*—protected from responding to any of them. Judge Ito shielded his action, alleging that the court was making every effort to seek "a fair and impartial jury" and "to protect your [juror] privacy" (page 3 of the questionnaire).

"It is not our intent to embarrass anyone," the questionnaire declared, when any of the questions was potentially embarrassing. For example, the court's questions focused on marital status; the number of divorces; which partner initiated the divorce; employment status, including details for the previous ten years (how the juror got the job and details about every employer); educational level, including the names of schools attended; future educational plans; favorite and least favorite subjects at school and why; military service and any involvement with a court martial; "Did you ever see someone being killed or [know someone] who had been killed"; and similar information about a spouse "or partner." Similar information was also requested about parents and siblings, followed by "Have you or any member of your family ever been arrested?" and "Please describe the charge(s)" and the trial. Were there other courtroom disputes to which the juror was a party? Had the juror ever had previous jury experience? In most other situations, if such questions were asked, the person to whom they were directed would be free to offer information voluntarily but not so in the case of jury selection.

Less than one-fourth of the way through the questionnaire comes the classic query: "Both the People [i.e., the prosecution] and the defendant have a right to expect that you will conscientiously consider and weigh the evidence [and] *apply the law*. . . . Are you willing to follow this instruction?" (p. 15). Next comes a series of questions about reading habits—requesting the juror to identify every newspaper, book, magazine, radio and TV station the juror reads, subscribes to, and listens to. Also, how many hours per day are spent before the TV or radio? Personal opinions are solicited about some of the participants in the trial.

At about mid-point the focus of the court's questions turns to possible domestic violence in the prospective juror's own home, and asks for full exposure of embarrassing details. Then come questions regarding interrace relationships and on the person's knowledge of DNA. At the two-thirds point, the inquiry turns to personal politics, such as party affiliation (a private matter) and voting experience; "Have you ever provided a urine sample to be analyzed for any purpose?" and "Do you believe it is immoral or wrong to do an amniocentesis to determine whether a fetus has a genetic defect?" (but the medical term is not defined). The next series of questions is about medicine, science, or biology courses studied at school, with more interest in the reading habits of the juror. Then the juror is asked about his interest in professional sports, favorite teams, and so on.

What is left? What remains of the Fourth Amendment's caveat regarding "The right of the people to be secure in their persons, houses, papers, and effects against unreasonable searches and seizures" without a warrant issued "upon probable cause supported by oath or affirmation and particularly describing the place to be searched and the persons or things to be seized"? Note the term "particularly describing"! Where is the particularization in Ito's questionnaire? Where is the probable cause? What oath or affirmation was offered regarding over nine hundred California citizens? And what has happened to the Fifth Amendment's protection against a person being "a witness against himself, nor be deprived of life, liberty, or property [privacy is also property] without due process of law . . ."?

During the formal trial of O. J. Simpson, so much evidence was withheld as to make it difficult for the jurors to render a fair evaluation, the suppressed evidence carrying the most weight. The jurors have a right to ask for the evidence.

The offenses committed in the Simpson trial and less blatantly in others are the same as those committed during the time of Bentham and Spooner. The latter observed that "there are probably no juries appointed in conformity with the principles of common law": the way Judge Ito handled jury selection shows that the practice has become more aggravated. In 1852 Spooner wrote:

> Since 1285, seventy years after Magna Charta, the common law right of all free British subjects to eligibility as jurors has been abolished, and the qualifications of jurors have been made a subject of arbitrary legislation. In other words, the government has usurped the authority of selecting the jurors that were to sit in judgment upon its own acts. This is destroying the vital principle of the trial by jury itself, which is that the legislation of the government shall be subjected to the judgment of a tribunal, taken indiscriminately from the whole people without any choice by the government, and over which the government can exercise no control. If the government can select the jurors, it will, of course, select those who it supposes will be favorable to its enactments. And an exclusion of any of the freemen from eligibility is a selection of those not excluded. . . .
>
> Any infringement or restriction of the common law right of the whole body of the freemen . . . to eligibility as jurors was legally an abolition of the trial by jury itself.[11]

This theme was expressed by Bentham, with which Forsyth and Van Dyke concur. In his *History of Trial by Jury,* Forsyth wrote that since the jury is antagonistic to arbitrary power, "in all continental nations where it has been introduced, the governments have endeavored to retain some influence over its decisions by entrusting the formation of the primary lists of the jurors, out of whom the particular twelve are to be selected to their own officers." It is no different in the United States. To argue that both sides try to control jury composition is to say "two wrongs make it right."

Openly, unabashedly, the practitioners of the misbegotten new profession of jury or trial consulting, in conspiracy with the government, work with trial lawyers to get around the Sixth and Seventh (jury mandating) Amendments, bypass the Fourth (search and seizure) and Fifth (witness against oneself) Amendments, consign the First (free speech) to oblivion, and raise many other constitutional questions.

There are enough examples of constitutional offenses for a separate discussion (which I have published elsewhere), but a single instance will suffice here. Jury consultant Noelle Nelson, whose offices are in Santa Monica, California, published a book titled *A Winning Case*.[12] She advises lawyers to understand that *voir dire* is a "frightening experience" for most jurors, but attorneys should frighten them anyway, since potential jurors apparently lost their constitutional protections, according to Michigan judge DeWitt, when they were assigned to the jury pool.

Bypassing the Sixth Amendment's declared guarantees to impartiality, Nelson guides her clients into "weeding out those who are not sympathetic to your case and keeping those who are. . . ." It is important to "establish rapport" by "asking prospective jurors about their feelings on any given point [to] elicit more information about their biases and attitudes," such as what magazines and newspapers they read; their private thoughts and opinions; and family secrets, all of which are extensions of questionnaires such as those dispensed by Judge Ito. The objective is to "get the jury you want," which hardly seems possible to reconcile with constitutional impartiality, let alone justice.

Jury and trial "consulting" thus dedicates itself to constitutional destruction by attempting to manipulate the system. If one side "gets the jury it wants," the opposing side, as a consequence, is forced to accept the jury it doesn't want. Which side deserves Nelson's before-the-fact "winning case" and which the losing case? Is Spooner, except for some archaic phraseology, writing as much for the late twentieth century as he did for the mid-nineteenth?

These professionals charge very high prices, which would reduce "justice" to a marketable commodity that can be purchased only by the well off. Justice would then become marketable if the consultant can guarantee his client a winning case. With opposing consultants in competition, which guarantee is likely to be met? Is winning based on the cost of one's consultant? Ironically, even when such consulting services are used the jury principle is so valid that even "packed" panels will deliver fair verdicts often enough to demonstrate the futility of consultants dedicated to destroying the impartial jury. This has been demonstrated many times in history, as this book will show.

Our nation's founders clearly wanted to protect the jury from assault: despite the clarity of Article III, Section 2, Clause 3 of the Constitution that the "trial of all crimes, except in cases of impeachment, shall be by jury," this was not considered strong enough for the likes of Patrick Henry. Before the states would accept the Constitution, they insisted upon adding the Sixth and Seventh Amendments guaranteeing both criminal and civil jury trials respectively. A total of 161 words devoted to trials by jury, more than to any other single subject. In addition, indirect references appear in the Fifth and Fourteenth Amendments in which the phrase "due process of law" is often invoked as a guarantee to trials by jury.

We cannot fault our Founding Parents because current "reformers" are wily enough to find paths around the guarantees. If we are to save trials by jury, which means saving our republic for our posterity as our Founders established it for us, We, the People, are responsible for holding firm against such "reformers." The government will not.

The tyrant knows that his most serious obstacles are trials by panels of fully informed jurors, and he lives in fear that they will learn the full extent of their power. Therefore, he must employ any device to keep juries subservient.

Each of the twelve chapters in this book deals with an organized, sophisticated, polished judiciary in contest with a panel of unorganized, guileless, naive, and often bewildered jurors, unfamiliar with their surroundings and awed by the burdens thrust upon them. Although it is the constitutional duty of judges to act impartially, all too often the presiding authorities in the cases we shall examine have tried to subvert the course of justice by influencing the jury. In each case where the jurors, naive as they were, stood for individual rights against great pressure, they advanced the people's liberties.

Each account is historically accurate and supported by the record. These trials demonstrate better than anyone can say how fully informed juries represent our greatest single defense of freedom, and are the essence of the constitutional republican government our Founders intended to create for us, their posterity. It is our responsibility to maintain and pass this legacy on to our posterity!

NOTES

1. Alan Scheflin, "Jury Nullification: The Right to Say No," *Southern California Law Review* 45 (1972): 168, 224.

2. Thomas Allen Green, *Verdicts according to Conscience* (Chicago: University of Chicago Press, 1985).

3. Ibid., p. xiii.

4. Harry Kalven and Hans Zeisel, *The American Jury* (Boston: Little, Brown and Co., 1966).

5. J. Kendall Few, *In Defense of Trial by Jury* (American Jury Foundation, 1993).

6. Green, *Verdicts according to Conscience,* p. 3.

7. Ibid., p. xiii.

8. Ibid.

9. Lysander Spooner, *An Essay on the Trial by Jury* (1852).

10. *American State Trials,* 10: 170.

11. Spooner, *An Essay on the Trial by Jury.*

12. Noelle Nelson, *A Winning Case* (Englewood Cliffs, N.J.: Prentice-Hall, 1991).

Part 1

JURIES ASSERT THEIR POWER OVER ROYAL EXCESSES

1

THE FATHER OF OUR COUNTRY

*H*is name was Edward Bushell, and because of, rather than in spite of, his obscurity, he was the father of our country. Not literally to be sure, having died eighty-two years before the signing of the Declaration of Independence; but spiritually and philosophically because during ten tortured weeks in London in 1670 he valued conscience over security, liberty above comfort, and honesty more than safety. And if he had not done so, there might never have been a Declaration of Independence or a United States Constitution.

We live in a republic, or what was intended to be a republic. According to the Constitution: "The United States shall guarantee to every State in this Union a *republican* form of government. . . ." It does not guarantee "a democratic form of government."

We pledge allegiance to the flag, and "to the republic for which it stands. . . ." When Benjamin Franklin was asked what those fifty-five men had been doing when they had been convoked to "revise the Articles of Confederation" during the blistering summer of 1787, he replied: "We have given you a *republic*," adding the caveat, "if you can keep it." He did not say, "We have given you a democracy," because a democracy is not quite the same thing. A democracy operates on the principle of majority rule. Whatever 50.01 percent of the people vote for will be forced upon the other 49.99 percent, however reluctant they may be to accept it. That is one reason why slavery was able to exist for so long. A white majority could overrule a black minority.

In a republic, that cannot happen. The majority might be as great as 99.9 percent, but it cannot prevail over that last point alone. A republic respects minorities; it does not believe in theft whether by a single gunman holding you up in the dark, or by a majority approving a law authorizing the government to plunder the property of an unwilling minority, no matter how "legal" such action may appear. A democracy can impose the majority's views of morality or good sense, "political correctness," or other ethical standards on a nonapproving minority, which is nothing less than coercion; whereas a republic makes room for nonconformity as long as there is no injury to another person.

Whether a republic is able to survive depends on its people. It makes little difference what is written down as the supreme law if we, the people, don't keep that law supreme. The Constitution and liberties are secure only as the people (we) are willing to keep them secure; to the extent we do not give in to fear or favor at the price of yielding liberty, and to the extent we will stand up and say no to whatever tyranny would be forced upon us.

Frederick Douglass, born in slavery, understood this. "The limits of tyrants are prescribed by the endurance of those whom they oppress," he wrote in 1857. "Find out just what people will submit to, and you have found out the exact amount of injustice and wrong which will be imposed upon them."

We cannot rest our hopes for liberty in constitutions, Judge Learned Hand advised. "Liberty lies in the hearts of men and women; when it dies there, no constitution, no law, no court can ever do much to help it. While it lies there it needs no constitution, no law, no court to save it." The written law might sound high toned, but it has no effect until we shout "hold, enough." The Declaration of Independence is very clear: ". . . mankind are more disposed to suffer while evils are sufferable."

Edward Bushell became the philosophical father of our country because he sensed how much evil was sufferable. He, together with eleven colleagues, laid down the boundary lines. Together they set the limits to tyranny. The limits they set exist today, safeguarded by other groups of twelve.

Bushell was born outside London in 1621 to a Puritan schoolmaster too poor to provide enough heat or food for his family. He was so frail as a teenager that an uncle, upon dying, named him executor of his will to let the boy enjoy the inheritance as soon as possible, believing he would not survive for long. But Edward did survive and was determined not to put his family through a similar ordeal. In this respect he succeeded extremely well. He went into shipping, and somewhere along the line dispatched a younger brother, John, to the tiny island of Barbados in the Caribbean to raise sugar. With his ships Edward embarked upon a triangular trade between Barbados, Portugal, and England, and through his shipping and "business of sugars," a phrase diarist Samuel Pepys used in reference to him, Bushell became very wealthy.

Success in raising sugar in those days depended largely upon slavery, which was unusually harsh because there could be no escape from the tiny island. And it may have been that slave discontent on brother John's plantation was the cause of the disastrous Bridgetown fire of 1668 which had started in his own warehouses. Nonetheless, when fate selected Edward for a pivotal confrontation with tyranny two years later, he stood up to it—and the concept of Constitutional republicanism was born.

On Wednesday, August 31, 1670, while Edward was on the streets of London, several armed bailiffs swooped down upon him and carried him off to sit as a juror in the Old Bailey, site of criminal trials then and now. It was common in those days to pick juries by "impressment," or random seizure (sometimes still practiced today). In such a manner were fifty or sixty brought in, examined, and, by day's end, all except the fated twelve, which, fortunate for our history included Edward Bushell, were dismissed. These twelve were ordered to report to the court at seven the next morning, Thursday, September 1.

London's Old Bailey had tiered seating circling the pit below, where barristers, prosecutors, and magistrates held court. A capacity crowd of about five hundred excited persons filled the gallery that morning. A rumor had spread that a rebellious boy from a family prominent enough to be within King Charles II's own circle was to be charged again, although he had already been censured and imprisoned for writing a seditious pamphlet "not fit for everybody to read," lengthily titled "The Sandy Foundations Shaken—or Those Doctrines of God Subsisting in Three Distinct and Separate Persons; the Impossibility of God's Pardoning Persons by an Imputative Refuted from the Authority of Scriptures, Testimonies, and Right Reason, Etc."

The Lord Mayor of London, Sir Samuel Starling, doubled as presiding judge over the ten-judge court. He ordered the crier to open the session with the traditional cry: "Oyez, oyez, Hear ye, hear ye. Silence in Court. The Central Criminal Court is now in session. The jurors will answer 'present' to their names as called," and the clerk polled the jury.

"Bring the prisoners William Penn and William Mead to the bar," Starling commanded, and the clerk read the indictment: "That William Penn, gentlemen, and William Mead, linen draper, with divers other persons to the jurors unknown, to the number of 300 on the 14th day of August in the 22nd year of the king, in the street called Gracechurch Street, did unlawfully and tumultuously assemble and congregate themselves together, to the disturbance of the peace of the Lord the King; that the aforesaid William Penn, in conspiracy with and abetted by William Mead, did then and there preach and speak to the persons there assembled; by reason whereof a great concourse and tumult of people then and there a long time did remain in contempt of the Lord the King, and of his law; to the great terror and disturbance of many of his liege people, his crown and his dignity."

In sum, the indictment was charging Penn and Mead with the "crime" of preaching Quakerism. Parliament had previously passed "the Conventicle Act," intended to establish the Church of England as the only legal form of worship. This was in retaliation against the now crushed Puritan tyranny of the Cromwells. All other forms of worship were outlawed, except a dispensation was made for the Jews; punishment was severe. "Every person who shall neglect to worship in the manner prescribed . . . shall ipso facto be deprived of all his spiritual promotions, and that from thenceforth it shall be lawful to present or collate to them as though the person or persons so offending or neglecting were dead."

The clerk then addressed the defendants: "What say you, William Penn and William Mead? Are you guilty as you stand indicted, both in manner and form, or not guilty?"

Penn resisted. "It is impossible that we should be able to remember the indictment, and therefore we desire a copy of it, as is customary on like occasions."

Thomas Howell, Recorder of London, played the role of judicial sycophant: "You must first plead to the indictment before you can have a copy of it."

Penn would not be taken in by this illogic. He would demand no more than a full and fair hearing before twelve of his countrymen. "I am unacquainted with the formality of the law. Therefore, before I shall answer directly I request two things of the court: First that no advantage may be taken against me, nor deprived of any benefit which I might otherwise have received; secondly that you will promise me a fair hearing, and liberty of making my defense, and that the court would be my counsel."

"No advantage shall be taken against you," the mayor assured him, but too dryly to make anyone believe he meant it. "You shall have liberty; you shall be heard. This is an indictment for trespass; therefore you may have what counsel you please."

"Then I plead not guilty in manner and form."

The clerk then addressed Mead, who demanded "the same liberty as is promised William Penn."

"You shall have it," the mayor responded, and Mead also pleaded "not guilty in manner and form."

Starling at once became arbitrary. Instead of proceeding with the trial, he ordered the bailiffs to "stand the prisoners aside." He then called for several other trials for the balance of the day, holding the defendants and the twelve jurors in court for the purpose of wearying them.

By day's end he dismissed them all, directing that they reassemble at 7:00 A.M. on Saturday the 3rd. Why he skipped Friday the 2nd is not clear, unless it was to mark the fourth anniversary of the disastrous fire of London of 1666 when he and several judges/aldermen had lost their homes.

At the time of this trial, Penn was a rebellious youth of twenty-five in almost constant conflict with his conservative father, the senior William Penn, who, as admiral in the king's navy, bore the title "Sir." At age forty-nine, Sir William was ailing, and would survive only a few days after the trial. It was ten years before the younger Penn would bring his Quakers across the sea to found the colony of Penn's Sylvania and the City of Brotherly Love.

With the jury assembled on Saturday, Penn and Mead, some twenty years older than Penn, entered the court carrying their hats. When they approached the bar, Starling attempted to discredit them before the jury: "Sirrah. Who bid you put off your hats?" and ordered the bailiffs to "Put their hats on again." When they had, the mayor charged: "Do you know where you are?"

"Yes, we do," Penn replied.

"Don't you know it is the king's court?"

"I know it to be a court, and I suppose it to be the king's court."

"Do you know there is respect due to the court?"

"Yes, we do."

"You don't show it. Why do you not pull off your hats?"

Penn and Mead were astounded. "Because I do not believe that to be any respect."

"Well, the court sets forty marks apiece upon your heads as fine for contempt of court."

"I desire it might be observed that we came into court with our hats off—that is, taken off in respect for the king's court, and if they have been put on since it was by order from the bench; and therefore not we but the bench should be fined."

"Don't be so insolent," the mayor shouted. "It's you who wear the hats which is a great affront to the honor of His Majesty's court, and in doing so dare the court to trial."

"I have a question to ask the recorder," Mead interrupted. "Am I fined also?"

"You are."

Mead passed over the court and addressed the jury directly. "I desire the jury and all the people to take notice of this injustice of the recorder, who ordered me to put on my hat. Yet this selfsame one has put a fine on my head. Oh, hear the Lord and dread of his power, for He is not far from every one of you."

"Cease your insignificant canting," commanded Starling, and to the clerk: "Swear the jury."

The clerk read the oath: "You shall well and truly try and true deliverance make betwixt our sovereign Lord the King and the prisoners at the bar, according to your evidence, so help you God." Each juror responded: "I do."

"Kiss the Bible," and the clerk ordered it to be passed around. Alderman/Judge John Robinson had been acquainted with Bushell for several years and knew him to be an independent thinker. Fearing that Bushell might dominate the jurymen, he was anxious to discredit him in advance. "That Bushell. He did not kiss the book. Will you disgrace this court again?"

Bushell was astounded. "I bring no disgrace, for I did kiss the book, My Lord."

"Do not insult this court again," Robinson raved. "You say you are a juryman of much tenderness and conscience; yet I saw that you did not kiss the book and require that you be sworn again. Clerk, swear him again; swear him again." And the ritual was repeated. The clerk then turned to the mayor: "The jury is present and sworn, My Lord."

"Call the first witness," ordered Starling.

"Call Lieutenant James Cook into court. Give him the oath. Lt. Cook, lay your hand on the Bible. Do you swear the evidence you shall give to the court betwixt our sovereign the king and the prisoners at the bar shall be the truth, the whole truth and nothing but the truth, so help you God?"

"I do." Cook kissed the Bible.

"What do you know of this case?" the mayor quizzed the witness.

"I was sent for, from the Exchange. To go and disperse a meeting in Gracechurch Street, where I saw Mr. Penn speaking to the people and tried to stop him. But he obeyed me not, and continued speaking. I could not hear what he said because of the noise. I endeavored to make my way to take him, but I could not get to him for the crowd of people. Upon which Captain Mead came to see me and desired me to let him go on, for when he had done, he said he would bring Mr. Penn to me." The reference to Mead as a captain, although now a "linen draper," was to his services more than twenty years earlier in the army of the first Charles, father of the present king.

Penn had been leading the services upon the street, which took its name from the Quaker's Grace Church, because soldiers had ringed the church, preventing them from entering. Preaching nonviolence, these "men of peace" would not rush the soldiers, but it was Sunday, August 14, the "Lord's Day," and they were determined to honor the Lord "upon His day." If they could not do it inside their "Meetinghouse," then they would do it upon the steps or as close as they could come to it.

"Did Mr. Mead bring Mr. Penn to you?"

"He did not, and at length I was forced to take Mr. Penn and Mr. Mead myself, and many others. To call for reinforcements to do it."

"What number do you think might be there?"

"About three or four hundred people."

"You say you tried to stop him?"

"Before he spoke I made entreaties that he do not go on, and that he disperse the people. But to no avail, for he would speak and attract a great concourse of people there."

"Do you know what he said?"

"I could not hear for the noise, but I did not like the tenor of it."

"That is enough. You may go." Cook saluted and left, leaving Penn astounded, for he had intended to cross-examine.

"Call the Constable Richard Read. Give him the oath."

Read was sworn and related his view (probably rehearsed): "My Lord, I was sent for, and went to Gracechurch street where I found this great crowd of people; and I heard Mr. Penn preach to them; and I saw Captain Mead speaking to Lt. Cook, but what he said I could not tell. I endeavored with my watchmen to get at Mr. Penn to pull him down, but I could not, the people kicking my watchmen and myself on the shins."

"What did William Penn say?"

"There was such a great noise that I could not tell what he said."

The attending crowd was almost universally supportive of Penn, and very vocal about it. We might imagine that in their passion they shouted back something like: "So great a din hath come from within thy head" and ridiculed the witness with mocking laughter. They would know that Quakers would remain still and silent while Penn spoke, and would never kick anyone.

Mead addressed the jury. "Jury, observe this evidence. He said he heard him preach, and yet, faith, he does not know what he said. Jury, take notice. He swears a clean and contrary thing to what he swore before the mayor when I was committed. For now he swears that he saw me in Gracechurch Street, and yet swore before the mayor when I was committed that he did not see me there. I appeal to the mayor himself if this is not true."

Starling would not respond; instead he continued to quiz the constable. "What number do you think might be there?"

"About four or five hundred."

Fearing he would not be allowed to conduct a cross-examination, Penn interrupted. "I desire to know of him what day it was."

"The 14th day of August."

"Did he speak to me, or let me know he was there? For I'm very sure I never saw him."

Starling would permit no cross-examination. "This is of no import and serves only to waste the court's time. He saw you there, he has testified, and heard you preach. That is sufficient. Whether you saw him is not. Note that, jurymen. 'Tis enough it was a tumult and he was speaking unlawfully. Call the next witness. You are excused."

Constable Henry Whiting was summoned. "My Lord, I saw a great number of people, and Mr. Penn was speaking. I see him make a motion with his hands and heard some noise but could not understand what he said."

"Was Captain Mead there?"

"But for Captain Mead, I did not see him there."

"What say you, Mr. Mead?" Howell demanded. "Were you there?"

Mead retorted by heralding our yet-to-be-born Fifth Amendment: "It is a maxim of your law that no man is bound to accuse himself. Why do you offer to ensnare me with such a question? Does this not show malice? Is it like a judge that ought to be counsel for the prisoner at the bar?"

"Sirrah, hold your tongue," Howell snapped. "I did not go about to ensnare you."

"We who are Quakers know well this Henry Whiting, for when he was beadle to the Bridgeward he was notorious to us as a person very diligent in arresting the Friends, which is his great delight. His testimony against us is false and prejudiced, and thus should be impeached."

"I desire that we may come more close to the point," Penn would begin his cross, "and that silence be commanded in court." He continued. "We confess ourselves to be so far from recanting or declining to vindicate the assembling of ourselves to preach, pray, worship the eternal, holy just God that we declare to all the world that we do believe it to be our indispensable duty to meet incessantly upon so good an account; nor shall all the powers upon earth be able to divert us from reverencing and adoring our God who made it."

Judge/Alderman Sir Richard Browne offered a comment: "You are not here for worshipping God but for breaking the law. You do yourselves a great deal of wrong in going on in that discourse."

Penn responded: "I affirm I have broken no law, nor am guilty of the indictment that is laid to my charge."

"Not guilty?" Browne would dictate the jury's verdict. "The evidence is clear as ever was offered to any jury. Two witnesses have proved the fact against both, and you confess the whole matter in effect. You justify yourselves, and declare you will do the like again, whatsoever laws the king and Parliament can provide against such action. Oh, confident arrogancy! Surely both king and Parliament will soon take notice of your arrogance in the next session."

Mead came to Penn's defense. "What are you doing there on this court? You are no justice to sway the jury. Come down off the bench."

"Sir, I am a justice and you are an impudent fellow."

"No," repeated Penn. "I am not guilty of the indictment, and to the end that the bench, the jury and myself, with these above us that hear us, may have a more direct understanding of this procedure, I desire you would let me know by what law it is you prosecute me, and upon what law you ground your indictment."

Recorder Howell responded: "The indictment is grounded upon the common law."

"Where is that common law?"

"You must not think that I am able to run up so many years and over so many adjudged cases, which we call common law, to answer your curiosity."

"This answer, I am sure, is so very short of my question, for if it be common it should not be so hard to produce."

Starling lectured Penn: "It is called common law to distinguish it from statute law. Now common law is common right, or *lex rationis*. It is imprinted in every man's understanding. The public peace is the law's darling, and every great assembly of people endangers the public peace. Therefore, the law esteems unlawful assemblies, unless they have a warrant for their assembling."

"Is any assemblage more righteous than the worship of God according to one's own conscience?" Penn asked.

"Sir, speak to the indictment and do not digress therefrom. You are not upon the matter of fact, which fact you have just heard proved against you. You are to answer to it. If the fact be found against you, you may speak to the matter of law in arrest of judgment, and you shall be heard."

"Shall I plead to an indictment that has no foundation in law? If it contains that law you say I have broken, why should you decline to produce that law, since it would be impossible for the jury to determine or agree to bring in their verdict who do not have the law produced by which they should measure the truth of this indictment and the guilt, or contrary, of my facts?"

Howell struck back. "You are a saucy fellow. Speak to the indictment. You have been told if the fact be found against you, it is time then to dispute the law. The question now is whether you are guilty of the indictment."

"I say it is my place to speak to the matter of law," Penn replied. "I am arraigned a prisoner; my liberty, which is next to my life itself, is now concerned. You are many mouths and ears against me, and if I must not be allowed to make the best of my case, it is hard. I say again, unless you show me and the people the law you ground your indictment upon, I shall take it for granted your proceedings are merely arbitrary."

"You have been told that if the fact be found against you it is then time to dispute the law. The question now is whether you are guilty of this indictment."

"The question is not whether I am guilty of this indictment, but whether this indictment be legal."

Penn continued: "The indictment is too general and imperfect an answer to say it is the common law, unless we knew both where and what it is. For where there is no law there is no transgression; and that law which is not in being is so far from being common that there is no law at all."

"You are an impertinent fellow," Howell screamed at him. "Will you teach the court what the law is? It's *lex non scripta*—unwritten law—that which many have studied thirty or forty years to know, and you would have me tell you in a moment?"

"Certainly. If the common law be so hard to understand, it is far from being common. But if my lord Coke in his *Institutions* be of any consideration, he tells us that common law is the Great Charter's privilege."

"Sir, you are a troublesome fellow, and it is not for the honor of this court to suffer you to go on."

"I have asked but one question and you have not answered me, though the rights and privileges of every Englishman are concerned with it."

"If I should suffer you to ask questions until tomorrow morning you would never be the wiser."

Penn demolished Howell. "That is according as the answers are."

Mayor Starling rushed to Howell's rescue. "You have been answered your question. It will be time to dispute the point of law if you are found guilty of the fact. But your design is to affront the court and amuse the people. You have not confided enough to deny the fact so plainly proved against you; but you have the impudence to abuse the court by your unseasonable discourse."

(What the court was trying to do by emphasizing "fact" was to influence the jury to deliver a "special verdict," meaning limiting their verdict to the obvious, that Penn had indeed preached on the street. Then the court would be able to deliver the broader "general verdict" covering both fact and law by declaring that he had violated the Conventicle Act. Understanding this, Penn and Mead wanted to combine fact and law together and urge the jurors to deliver the general verdict themselves. This would mean that if the jury did not like the Conventicle Act, they could find the defendants "not guilty" anyway. Since "to preach" of itself was no crime, the jury would be nullifying the act, which would be to place themselves above Parliament, the courts and king by declaring their law null and void. Thus Penn's insistence that "where there is no law there is no transgression.")

Penn replied to Starling: "I design no affront to the court but to be heard of my just plea. I must plainly tell you that if you deny me a hearing of that law which you suggest I have broken, you do at once deny me an acknowledged right, and make it evident to the whole world that you are resolved to sacrifice the privileges of Englishmen to your sinister and arbitrary and unjust designs."

Howell interceded. "Take him away, my lord. If you do not take some course with this pestilent fellow to stop his mouth, we shall not be able to do anything tonight." And the mayor echoed to the bailiffs, "Take him away. Take him away."

The bailiffs seized Penn, who at first shook them off and continued lecturing. "These are but so many vain explanations. Is this justice or true judgment? Must I therefore be taken away because I plead for the fundamental laws of England?" He appealed to the jurors. "However, this I leave upon your consciences, you who are of the jury, and my sole judges. These ancient and fundamental laws relating to liberty and property are not limited to particular persuasions in matters of religion, and must be indispensably maintained. The Lord of heaven and earth will judge between us and this matter."

"Be silent there," Howell called out, but Penn would not be silenced. "I am not to be silent in a case wherein I am so much concerned, and not only myself but many ten thousand families besides." The bailiffs threw him into the "bale dock," a depressed cell below the floor, and Mead came forward: "You men of the jury; here I do now stand to answer the indictment against me, which is a bundle of stuff, full of lies and falsehoods. There was a time when I had freedom to use a deadly weapon, and then I thought I feared no man. But now I fear the living God, and dare make use of no weapon nor hurt no man.

Nor do I know that I have demeaned myself as a tumultuous person. Therefore it is a very proper question that William Penn demanded in this case—a hearing of the law in which our indictment is grounded."

"I have made answer to that already," protested Howell, but Mead ignored him. "You men of the jury, who are my judges: if the recorder will not tell you what makes a riot, a rout or an unlawful assembly, then he that once they called called Lord Coke tells us. A riot is when three or more men are met together to beat a man, or to enter forcibly into another man's land, to cut his grain, his wood or to break down his property."

The mayor would not let him go on and ordered the bailiffs to throw Mead into the bale dock. Over continued protests from the now imprisoned defendants, Starling lectured the jury: "You have heard the evidence presented here; you have heard Lt. Cook, Constable Reed, and Constable Whiting testify to the great tumult in Gracechurch Street, and that Penn was speaking there in great agitation, waving his arms about and inciting them against the king, his peace and his dignity. You have heard Captain Mead was there, yet not stopping that prating fellow. The evidence is very clear that they did disrupt the king's peace. They would not yet be stopped, if they were not removed, but would go into the night. For what do they care what inconveniences or danger to your health they cause, as long as they can continue their silly canting and mad raving. They should be imprisoned for contempt. Therefore go to the jury room and agree quickly to bring in guilty that we may be done with this tiresome matter. Bailiffs, take the jurors up."

With such heavy pressure placed upon the jurors, most if not all of whom being unfamiliar with court procedures, we should now expect them to follow the most frequent scenario by returning to the court within the fifteen minutes allotted with guilty verdicts for each. Most likely they would not have been made aware of the great power they held inherent in the very character of the jury. The exclusive power of the verdict, a general verdict if they chose to deliver it, rested with them, and until and unless the jurors pronounced "guilty," neither the court nor the government could take any action against the defendants. A verdict of "not guilty" would require release regardless of how it might anger the autocracy.

But the price of conscience was very high. The jurors probably did know something about court abuse of those who did not conform. Jurors rebelling against the royal will often lost their entire estates, seized by order of court or king. Their homes might be burned, their families turned out and reduced to destitution. But their verdicts held! Weighing on their minds were the long imprisonments, high fines, and other tortures inflicted upon them for committing the offense of honesty.

There were other pressures applied by autocratic courts: it would now be about five in the afternoon. The court had been in session since seven in the morning; in order to break the independent jury presumably guaranteed since 1215 by Magna Charta, the common practice was not to allow the jurors anything to eat or drink; no convenience or respite of any kind from the start of the trial until they had delivered their verdicts. Most arduous, they were denied access to even a chamber pot, so that by the time they were given the case, the urgency to relieve themselves would be so great that they would rush to deliver any verdict dictated to them, quite independently of anything else.

One of the better known one-liners coined by the fictional Mr. Dooley of nineteenth-century British farce is that many an innocent was sent to hang so jurors may dine.

But this jury did not return in fifteen minutes. Nor did they return in twenty or thirty. After three-quarters of an hour, the court grew impatient, and after one hour was so greatly disturbed they talked of pulling the jurors down to the courtroom. That would have caused a forced separation and delayed the verdict even longer.

After an hour and a half, eight jurors returned on their own, and the bailiffs were sent to bring down the other four. Upon their return the judges railed at them. "What means this unseemly delay? If the jury does not show respect for this court you shall all be fined and denied your dinners. You will have your noses slit and tongues cut out" and "many other unworthy threats," as recorded by an anonymous observer attending the trial.

Howell turned upon Bushell. "Sir, you are the cause of this disturbance and manifestly show yourself to be an abettor of faction. I shall put a mark upon you, sir, and you shall be carted about the city."

Robinson also attacked. "Mr. Bushell, I have known you near these fourteen years. You have thrust yourself upon this jury because you think there is some service in it for you. I tell you, you deserve to be indicted more than any man that has been brought to the bar this day."

Bushell tried to deny this by stating there were "three score before me, and I would willingly have got off but could not."

Alderman/Judge Bloodworth whined: "I said when I saw Mr. Bushell he would never yield; and what I see has come to pass. But no one would listen to me. And yet he does not yield. Mr. Bushell, we know what you are." Then, to quote our unknown reporter, "the justices continued their menacing language, behaving very imperiously as persons not more void of justice than sober education." When they had grown weary, Sir Samuel demanded to know if the jurors had reached a verdict. Their foreman, Thomas Veer, rose to respond: "No, My Lord, we have not."

The mayor exploded. He delivered a scathing lecture to the jurors for wasting the court's time and keeping them from their dinners without returning with the guilty verdict as commanded. He ordered the jurors taken up again.

Perhaps another half hour passed before the jury came back. And what a half hour of wrangling it must have been, judging from what happened next. After the clerk had called the roll, Starling demanded: "Are you agreed upon your verdict?"

The jurors shouted in unison: "We are."

"Who shall speak for you?"

"Our foreman, Thomas Veer."

The clerk addressed Veer: "Look upon the prisoners at the bar. How say you? Is William Penn guilty of the matter whereof he stands indicted in manner and form, or not guilty?"

Veer called back: "Guilty of speaking on Gracechurch Street." He stopped and waited. The courtroom was silent. The crowd did not understand and the judges were expecting more.

After a time Howell asked impatiently: "Is that all?"

"That is all I have in my commission."

"You had as good say nothing." Starling tried to force the condemning words: "Was it not an unlawful assembly? You mean he was speaking to a tumult of people there."

Veer was unruffled: "My Lord, that is all I had in my commission."

The ploy which the jurors had adopted was to return a special verdict of "guilty," having been directed to do so, but applied to a harmless act. They had hoped that this would satisfy the directive while making it impossible for the court to declare Penn guilty of any real offense in a general verdict, since to speak on the street was no crime. But the court refused to go along.

Alderman Robinson screamed: "You are scandalous fellows, insolent loggerheads to abuse this court."

Bloodworth whimpered: "You will be carted about the city. We have told you what the law is. You do not obey it."

"We will take great occasion against you," threatened the mayor.

"Cut out their tongues for speaking thus to the court," which was no idle threat because such atrocities were often committed against offenders. Our observer then recounts how the judges "continued to vilify them with most opprobrious language."

"The law of England will not allow you to part 'til you have given in your verdict," Howell stated menacingly.

Bushell, as the strongest man on the jury, spoke for them all: "We have given in our verdict and can give no other."

"Gentlemen," Howell rebuked, "you have not given your verdict and you had as good say nothing. Therefore, go and consider it once more that we may make an end of this troublesome business."

Bushell consulted with Veer and then asked: "We desire that we may have pen, ink, and paper."

Howell instructed the clerk to supply these items, and Starling ordered a longer recess while the court had their dinners. He threatened the jurors that if they did not return with a "proper verdict" they would continue to be confined to "starve until we get it."

One of the jurors called out: "We too are starved," to which Starling responded: "That is the penalty you have brought upon yourselves and you must take the responsibility for it. When we have your proper verdict you shall dine."

Bushell protested: "We have given in our true verdict."

"It is no verdict you have brought. Bailiffs, take the jurors up."

It may have been an hour and a half before the court reassembled. We are left to imagine how the jurors spent the time, but when they did return we find that their hunger and discomfort had only served to strengthen their resolve in their confrontation with a well-fed court. "Call the roll of the jury," the mayor ordered, and when done: "Are you agreed of your verdict?"

"We are," they shouted.

"Who shall speak for you?"

"Our foreman, Thomas Veer."

"What say you? Look upon the prisoners. Is William Penn guilty in manner and form as he stands or not guilty?"

Veer rose and handed a paper to the clerk. "Here is our verdict," and the clerk read in a monotone their formalized response: "We, the jurors hereafter named, do find William Penn guilty of speaking or preaching to an assembly met together in Gracechurch Street, the 14th day of August last, 1670. And that William Mead is not guilty of the said indictment." He then read the names of all the jurors who had signed: "Thomas Veer, foreman; Edward Bushell, John Hammond, Henry Henley, John Brightman, Charles Milson, Gregory Walklet, Henry Michel, John Bailey, William Plumstead, Thomas Damask, William Leaver."

The gallery burst into cheers and roars so wild that none could hear the calls for silence from the crier, nor the mayor banging with his gavel. Our reporter tells us that the judges "resented the verdict at so high a rate that they exceeded the bounds of all reason and civility."

"What?" screamed Starling, "will you be led by such a silly fellow as Bushell? An impudent, canting fellow! I warrant you you shall no more come upon juries in haste." And turning on Veer: "You're a foreman indeed. I thought you had understood your place better."

"Gentlemen," Howell addressed the jurors imperiously. "You shall not be dismissed until we have a verdict the court can accept; and by the laws of England you are to be locked up without meat, drink, fire and tobacco. You shall not think thus to abuse the court. We will have a verdict by the help of God, or you will starve for it."

Penn, as surprised as any at the resistance of his jurors, had witnessed more than enough abuse. He sprang to their defense: "My jury, who are my judges, ought not to be thus menaced. Their verdict should be free and not compelled. The bench ought to wait upon them, but not forestall them. I desire that justice may be done me, and that the arbitrary resolves of the bench may not be the measure of my jury's verdict."

Howell, after so many humiliations by Penn, dared not take him on directly. He appealed to the mayor. "Stop that prating fellow's mouth or have him put out of court."

Starling tried to coerce the jury: "Gentlemen, you have heard that Mr. Penn preached; that he gathered thereby a tumult of people; that Mr. Mead was there and abetted him, and that they not only disobeyed the martial power but the civil also. The evidence is clear and shows their guilt."

Penn would not be silenced. "It's a great mistake. We did not make a tumult but they that interrupted us. The jury cannot be so ignorant as to think that we met there with a design to disturb the peace since, first, we were by force of arms kept out of our lawful house, and met as near it in the street as their soldiers would give us leave. Secondly, our worship was no new thing, but what is customary with us. It's very well known that we are a peaceable people, and cannot offer violence to any man."

"A peaceable innocent people indeed," Howell spat, "that when the king has seized the meetinghouse into his hands, as by law he might, they would come and break open the doors; and there congregate expressly against the king's commands. And therefore there was a necessity of soldiers to keep the king's possessions. They violently overpowering the constable and his watchmen, he endeavoring only to dissipate this unlawful assembly, as is sworn by Reed the constable."

"This is all a bunch of stuff," Penn answered, "and the agreement of twelve men is a verdict in law, and such a one being given by the jury, I require the clerk of the peace to record it, as he will answer to his peril. And if the jury bring in another verdict contrary to this, I affirm they are perjured men in law." What Penn meant was that if the jurors, under such heavy pressure, impeached their own verdict after it had been lawfully delivered, they would be committing perjury.

Alderman Browne added his intelligence: "Mr. Penn, you abuse this court, for it is the court and not the prisoners who are by law judges of what is a verdict in law and what is not a verdict in law."

"The jury are perjured men," from the whimpering Bloodworth, "to bring in a verdict contrary to law."

Starling continued to press: "Is not this evidence clear to the jury that you would go against it and disgrace this court?"

The defense of the jury now fell upon Edward Bushell as its strongest member. Our on-the-spot chronicler has failed us at this point by not having recorded a colloquy that must have developed between Bushell and Starling to build to a highly dramatic climax. It is quite plausible to imagine it might have gone something like this: Bushell, responding to the mayor, rising to address him, says: "No, My Lord, we desire to bring honor to the court."

"You call it honor when you do violate your oaths and the evidence?"

"We call it honor because we violate neither our oaths nor the evidence."

"How, then, do you say you do not violate your oaths?"

"Our oaths, which we take at each session, are that we will 'well and truly try' and 'true deliverance make' according to our evidence, and this is what we most conscientiously are doing."

"You do violate the evidence."

"We do not violate the evidence, but we 'truly try' according to our evidence as we see it, and we deliver the verdicts according to our best judgments."

"You do violate the express order of this court, which is to disgrace it." The mayor was unable to appreciate that the harder he pushed his proud adversary, the more firm became that adversary's resolve.

"The court has no power in Magna Charta to dictate the jury's verdict."

"This court has any power it chooses, and to disobey it is to bring disgrace upon the court as well as upon yourselves."

"We do follow our consciences, which is to bring honor to this court, and we can do no other. If this be not honor, then we charge the court has no honor."

"Your insolence is beyond durance. It is the direct order of this court that you bring in 'guilty' against both prisoners."

"No, My Lord, this the jury will never do," and, as we reach the recorded climax: "We will not betray the liberties of this country. We know our rights in Magna Charta."

"These rights will starve you."

"So be it, My Lord, but on this point we will not equivocate. We will never yield our rights as Englishmen!"

The court was stunned; Sir Samuel paralyzed; the justices muted. But the gallery rejoiced, shouting: "Hear, hear," and Penn sprang to his feet: "Yes, you are Englishmen. Mind your privileges. Do not give away your rights."

"Nor will we ever do it," echoed the jubilant jurymen. For some moments the gallery could not be quieted, shouting back encouragements to bolster the harassed and failing jurors. It was now fifteen or sixteen hours since they had come to court that morning.

Starling hammered his gavel for silence and ordered the bailiffs into the crowd to quiet them; when they did quiet down, it was more out of respect for the jurors so that they could be released from their ordeal. Sir Samuel warned that the court would not tolerate further outbursts or the courtroom would be cleared. Then he addressed the jury: "This court cannot accept your verdict, and you must remain together until you have brought in a verdict the court can accept."

An angry roar rose from the gallery: "The jury has brought in a true verdict."

The mayor pounded again. "Silence, silence or the courtroom will be cleared. Tomorrow is Sunday and the court does not meet on Sunday. However in respect for the health of the jurors who will remain together until an acceptable verdict is brought in, we will call the court to meet at seven o'clock tomorrow, which otherwise we would not do. The bailiffs will take you up to the jury room and there will post two sentries outside the door to keep the jury all night without meat, drink, tobacco, fire, candle nor any other accommodation."

The crowd had again become unruly; one bailiff discharged a musket into the ceiling to quiet them.

"I have warned you, and if you cause another disturbance you will all be charged."

One juror, pale and trembling, pleaded: "Your Honor, I am ill and indisposed. I fear I am running a fever and if locked up all night will become grievously ill."

Starling replied: "You are as strong as any of them. Starve with them and hold your principles."

"We can hold no longer," said another juror. "It's all right for them, for they have brought strong water bottles in their pockets designedly and would starve us while they eat."

"You are as guilty as they," Howell replied derisively. "You must be content with your hard fate which you have only brought upon yourselves and have only yourselves to blame for it. Let your patience overcome it, if you can, for the court is resolved to have a verdict and that before you can be dismissed."

"It's no verdict you have brought," the mayor added.

Seeing the futility of further pleading, Bushell made one urgent request: the comfort of a chamber pot; but Starling, undoubtedly in dread of royal censure, screamed: "You shall have no accommodation whatsoever. That is the fate you have chosen for yourselves."

He was now anxious to be done with it. He ordered the bailiffs to "take the jurors up," and the judges quickly left the courtroom. As the jurors were being herded and shoved by the bailiffs, the crowd shouted encouragements: "Hold to your rights. . . . Do not give up your rights as Englishmen!"

We must turn again to our imaginations as to how the jurors suffered through that hellish night. However, the trial record does inform us that by morning "the jury room was badly fouled," which undoubtedly attracted flies and stinging insects to plague them further. Their sole relief was the inspiriting support of their fellows surrounding the Old Bailey. Some of them managed to devise ingenious means of getting food and water into the jury room.

When morning came, church bells all over the city rang loudly as the court assembled; the Old Bailey was crowded long before seven. The more militant had brought crude weapons to menace the court: daggers, centerbits, kitchen knives, crowbars, hammers, or whatever.

There is no description of how the jurors looked as they entered the courtroom, but they must have been disheveled and dirty. By contrast the judges were dressed in their fanciest Sunday fripperies. The crier commanded silence "upon pain of imprisonment" and called the roll. "Are you agreed upon your verdict?" he asked routinely.

"We are," the jurors shouted in unison.

"Who shall speak for you?"

"Our foreman, Thomas Veer."

"What say you? Look upon the prisoners at the bar. Is William Penn guilty of the matter whereof he stands indicted in manner and form or not guilty?"

Veer, ignoring his physical agonies, must have stood proudly when he called out: "William Penn is guilty of speaking on Gracechurch Street." He said nothing else. The courtroom broke into a storm while the judges sat incredulous.

The mayor tried to extract four damning words from them: "To an unlawful assembly. You mean to an unlawful assembly."

Veer stood his ground. "No, My Lord. We give no other verdict than what we gave last night. We have no other verdict to give."

The uproar continued until the bailiffs stopped by firing their muskets. Starling wheeled upon Bushell: "You are a factious fellow. I'll take a course with you."

Bloodworth, who strikes us as a whimpering fop, droned again: "I knew Mr. Bushell would not yield." To which Bushell responded: "Sir Thomas, I have done according to my conscience as every juror here has done."

Starling broke in: "That conscience of yours would cut my throat."

"No, My Lord, it never shall," but the incensed mayor did not hear him. "But rather than you shall cut my throat I will in defense of myself cut yours as soon as I can."

"He has inspired the jury," Howell wailed. "He has the spirit of divination methinks I feel in him. I will have a positive verdict or you will starve for it."

Penn could never have anticipated that even this court would laden a jury so heavily, and even less that he could have been so fortunate as to have drawn twelve men with the stamina to withstand the burden. He sprang to their defense.

"I desire to ask the recorder one question. Do you allow of the verdict given last night of William Mead?"

Howell wheeled upon him, forgetting who was master in such a confrontation. "It cannot be a verdict because you were indicted for conspiracy, and one being found guilty and not the other . . ." He broke off, realizing he was falling into a trap the jurors had set for the court. "No, it cannot be a verdict."

Penn: "If 'not guilty' be not a verdict, then you make of the jury and Magna Charta a mere nose of wax."

"How," asked Mead, "is 'not guilty' no verdict?"

"No, it's no verdict," responded the recorder inanely.

"I confirm," contended Penn, "that the consent of a jury is a verdict in law, and if William Mead be not guilty it consequently follows that I am clear, since you have indicted us for conspiracy and I could not possibly conspire alone."

"Cease your prating," shouted the mayor. "You are a factious fellow and speak without the court's permission," and turning upon the jurors, "And you, sirs, I warned you yesterday not to violate the good name and honor of this court, and yet you heed not and continue to do so. If you have not suffered enough for your pertinaciousness you will bring more suffering upon yourselves. Return again to the jury room and consider once more your verdict."

He ordered the bailiffs to take them up, and they were gone scarcely a quarter hour before they returned with the verdict unchanged: "William Penn is guilty of speaking on Gracechurch Street." Howell again flew into a mindless rage from "resenting the verdict at so high a rate." He ran back and forth, throwing his arms about. "What is this to the purpose? I say, I will have a verdict." And to Bushell: "Mr. Bushell, you are a factious fellow. I will set a mark upon you and while I have anything to do in the city I will have my eye upon you."

The mayor ranted: "Have you no more wit than to be led by such a pitiful fellow as Bushell? Were I of the jury rather than he would starve me I would slit his nose for him."

Penn continued his defense of the jurors: "It is intolerable that my jury should be thus menaced. Is this according to the fundamental laws? Are they not my proper judges by the Great Charter of England? What hope is there of ever having justice done when juries are threatened and their verdicts rejected? I am concerned to speak and grieved to see such arbitrary proceedings. Did not Robinson of the Tower render one of them worse than a felon? And do you condemn them as factious fellows they who answer not your ends? Unhappy are those juries who are threatened to be fined and starved and ruined if they give not in verdicts contrary to their consciences."

"My Lord," Howell pleaded with the mayor. "You must take a course with that same fellow."

And the mayor: "Stop his mouth, jailer. Bring fetters and stake him to the ground."

"Do your pleasure. I matter not your fetters."

"This is the fourth time the jury has brought in this insignificant verdict that William Penn was guilty of speaking in Gracechurch Street. And how this answers the question I do not know. Let the world judge whether this be a verdict or not."

The recorder became even more malicious: "'Til now I never understood the reason of the policy and prudence of the Spaniards in suffering the Inquisition among them. And certainly it will never be well with us 'til something like unto the Spanish Inquisition be in England." One improvement that a "Catholic"-sponsored Inquisition would have made in England would have been to do away with the likes of anti-Catholics such as Thomas Howell and the judges! He called out: "Return the jury to their quarters to consider a proper verdict."

Above all else the court knew that with all its power to inflict immense tortures upon the jurors, it was totally powerless to condemn Penn and Mead on its own. It had to yield to the superiority of the jury.

A physically weakened but still stoical Veer protested: "We have agreed upon our verdict. We have given it. We will give no other!" and the jurors echoed him: "We are agreed . . . we are agreed!" which served only to increase the recorder's violence. Continuing his mad pacing back and forth in the pit, he shouted: "I protest, I protest. I will sit here no longer to hear these things."

The gallery taunted him: "The world does judge this to be a verdict . . . the jury has given in a true verdict. . . . You are mad, all madmen there behind the bench!"

Starling tried to cool down the ranting recorder. "Stay, stay. Come back, come back." And he again lectured the jury: "Gentlemen, we shall not be at this trade always with you. You will find at the next sessions of Parliament there will be a law made that those that will not conform shall not have the protection of the law." He directed the clerk: "Mr. Lee, draw up another verdict that they may bring it in special."

The clerk was thrown off balance: "My Lord, I cannot tell how to do it."

Bushell came to the rescue: "We ought not to be returned, having all agreed and set our hands to the verdict."

"Your verdict is nothing," the recorder parroted. "You play upon the court. I say you shall go together and bring in another verdict or you will starve for it and I will have you carted about the city as were prisoners in Edward the Third's time."

Veer was near collapse. He gasped again: "We have given in . . . our verdict . . . and all . . . agreed . . . and if we give . . . in another . . . it will be a force . . . to save our . . . lives." The cheers of the crowd strengthened him.

The mayor, probably with the specter of Charles over his shoulder, would not relent. He ordered the bailiffs to "take the jury up," but the jurors would not move. The bailiff appealed: "My Lord, they will not go up."

Starling reviled them: "You are like to be starved indeed. You have had roast beef, capons, wine and strong drink sent up to you, as has been proved, during the time you were considering the verdict." He signaled Sheriff John Smith who went to the jury box and addressed them respectfully: "Come, gentlemen, you must go up. You see I am commanded."

The jurors yielded, and returned to the jury room. As they were leaving the recorder ranted again: "Mind you, if you bring not a proper verdict this time we will not carry on longer this day but lock you up to starve until tomorrow."

The gallery continued shouting encouragements to "Hold to your rights as Englishmen."

The court kept the jury imprisoned for more than an hour, expecting a break in ranks and complete demoralization; they were dismayed to find that the jurors had only grown stronger in their resolve. The verdict was the same. The mayor's revenge was to order the bailiffs to drag the jurors physically back upstairs again and to adjourn the court, though it was only early afternoon, until the next day at seven o'clock, Monday, September 5.

We are again left to conjecture as to how the jurors endured that afternoon and miserable second night on the floor of the jury room, which had now become a full-fledged latrine. The guard must have been increased to prevent relief of any kind from being passed through, and the only comfort they received was from the continued shouts of support from the crowds milling around the court house. The record tells us only that several were "in high fever" and looked as if they could not last another day.

It was the practice of courts in those days to provide the judges with baskets of sweet-smelling herbs to crush against nostrils too tender for the foul odors jurors and prisoners often brought in. On that third morning, however, the herbs were ineffective against the stench of feces, urine, sweat, and perhaps vomit. The jurors were spectral in appearance. The gallery was filled, with more crowds surrounding the Old Bailey. Many persons were armed, ready to attack the judges.

The opening routine was dragged out, as the clerk droned: "Are you agreed of your verdict?" The jurors responded surprisingly strongly: "We are."

"Who shall speak for you?"

"Our foreman, Thomas Veer."

"Look upon the prisoners at the bar. What say you? Is William Penn guilty of the matter whereof he stands indicted in manner and form, or not guilty?"

Veer held out a paper in his hand. "Here is our verdict in writing and our hands are subscribed." The clerk took the paper and would have read it but Howell stopped him. "The court orders you to deliver a positive verdict and not for it to be read. You must face the court and take full responsibility for your verdict from your own mouths."

Veer pointed a bony finger at the paper. "That is our verdict. We have subscribed to it."

The clerk set the paper down on his desk and asked again: "How say you? Is William Penn guilty or not guilty?"

"You, sir, have read in writing already . . . our verdict in writing . . . and our hands are subscribed." Veer was rapidly fading.

The mayor interrupted: "We will hear the verdict from your own mouths that you may take full responsibility."

"If you will not accept our verdict in writing, I desire it back again." He reached for the paper but the clerk would not give it to him.

The mayor ranted: "That paper was no verdict and there shall be no advantage taken against you by it. Give answer to the clerk."

The clerk fretted: "Will you not answer? Is William Penn guilty or not guilty?"

Veer mustered enough of his failing strength to stand proudly. His response that morning was not the special verdict the court had heard so exasperatingly often. That Monday morning, September 5, he spoke only two words, enunciating them loudly and distinctly, with emphasis on the first: "Not guilty!"

The gallery gasped at the jurors' tenacity; the judges were stunned into silence. The clerk droned on mechanically: "How say you? Is Mead guilty of the matter whereof he stands indicted in manner and form or not guilty?"

Again Veer pronounced the two critical words: "Not guilty!"

This clerical robot, this routinized mentality pressed forward as programmed, unvarying the traditional court routine. "Then hearken to your verdicts. You say William Penn is not guilty in manner and form as he stands indicted; you say William Mead is not guilty in manner and form as he stands indicted, and so say you all?"

The twelve jurors shouted in unison: "We do!"

Starling fumed and pounded his gavel. "Poll the jury. Let each juror answer to his name and take full responsibility for his own verdict."

The clerk instructed: "Gentlemen, you will rise and answer to the roll as your name is called. As regards William Penn. Thomas Veer?"

Veer rose once more and shouted: "Not guilty."

"Edward Bushell?"

"Not guilty." The clerk droned through the roll, each juror responding. Then he asked for the individual verdicts regarding William Mead, and again each juror responded: "Not guilty!" Not one of the twelve wavered.

At the end of the roll the gallery burst into cheers, stamping, whistling, shouting glories to the jurors, while Starling pounded his desk demanding silence.

When the crowd quieted, Howell marched before the jurors: "I am sorry, gentlemen. You have followed your own judgments and willful opinions rather than the good and wholesome advice we have given you. God keep my life out of your hands."

The jurors had apparently reasoned that the compromise "guilty" verdict to comply with court directive was not going to work. So they resolved this time to exercise their superior power by moving all the way to a general verdict. This the court was unable to override. The verdicts had to be accepted. The jury had used its ultimate power to nullify the Conventicle Act. To declare it inoperative as if it had never been adopted by Parliament. To wipe it completely off the books.

Penn now addressed the court: "I demand my liberty, being freed by the jury."

But Starling had one more weapon: "No. You are in for your fines."

"Fines? For what?"

"For contempt of court. For wearing your hats. By the laws of England this court has power to fine for contempt." Penn had forgotten the incident which seemed so long ago.

"I ask if it be according to the fundamental laws of England that any Englishman should be fined or amerced but by the judgment of his peers since it expressly contradicts the fourteenth and twenty-ninth chapters of the Great Charter of England which says: 'No free man ought to be amerced but by the oath of good and lawful men of the vicinage.'"

Penn's references were incorrect and the quotation inexact, but he had carried the spirit of the law. Penn was not concerned about accuracy because the judges were not very familiar with the Great Charter either. The only judicial response was more ranting by Howell: "Take him away, take him away. Take him out of the court."

Penn responded: "I can never urge the fundamental laws of England but you cry 'Take him away, take him away,' but it's no wonder since the Spanish Inquisition has so great a place in the recorder's heart. God Almighty who is just will judge you of all these things."

In the meantime the jurors, all in great want, needed immediate release to waiting, anxious relatives. Bushell rose to ask Starling to let them go, but the recorder broke into another paroxysm: "No, you are not excused. For your misbehavior and going against your evidence and the law you are fined forty marks and imprisonment until paid."

The mayor seconded the order: "You must take full responsibility for your verdicts. You have brought this upon yourselves. You will be held until the fines are paid." (It is difficult to assess how steep was a fine of forty marks, but in terms of purchasing power it could have been equivalent to roughly half a year's wages for a working man.)

Again our chronicler has failed to record the colloquy between jurors and the court other than to tell us that "there were many passages that could not be taken which passed between the jury and the court." He continued: "The manner of the court's behavior toward the prisoners and the jury, with their many extravagant expressions, must not altogether slip our observation. Their carriage to the jury outdoes all precedents; they entertained them more like a pack of felons than a jury of honest men, as being fitter to be try'd themselves than to acquit others. In short, no jury for many ages received so many instances of displeasure and affront, because they preferred not the humor of the court before the quiet of their own consciences, even to be esteemed as perjured, though they had really been so had they not done what they did."

Not three years earlier Lord Chief Justice Keeling of King's Bench had been censured by Parliament for imposing "restraints upon Juries" as "Innovations in the Tryal of men for the Lives and Liberties; and that he hath used an Arbitrary and Illegal power, which is of dangerous consequences to the Lives and Liberties of the people of England, and tends to the introducing of an Arbitrary Government.

"That in place of Judicature, the Lord Chief Justice hath undervalued, vilified, and contemned Magna Charta, the great Preservers of our Lives, Freedom, and Property." Parliament then recommended that Keeling "be brought to Trial."

But apparently no heed was taken by the Starling court of the censure. He ordered the jurors to be imprisoned in Newgate, together with Penn and Mead, until they paid their fines.

In short course the fines for eight were paid, probably with the help of friends, and they were released. Although Bushell had become wealthy enough through his "business of sugars" to have been able to pay for all twelve, he refused to pay even his own. Three jurors stood with him on principle, refusing help from others. These four were held in Newgate for an indefinite stay. We should remember their names: Edward Bushell, John Bailey, John Hammond, and Charles Milson. Had they paid their fines—or Bushell for them—the effect of their glorious conquest over king, court, and Parliament might have been short-lived. But having resisted beyond their call of duty, it has become permanent.

Penn and Mead also refused to pay, but were rescued by an unidentified benefactor, presumed to be Penn's father. In respect for his sire, Penn accepted the support, which he otherwise might not have done, so he could spend with him the last eleven days of the elder Penn's life.

Newgate Prison, razed by the British about 1906 in a fit of retroactive guilt, had long had a reputation of being "hell above ground," except that it was not entirely above ground. There were subterranean passages reserved for prisoners who could not pay the jail fees or who otherwise fell into jailer disfavor. From the outside, Newgate was an architectural gem. Much money had been spent on its redecoration and reconstruction after the fire of 1666. Its classical grace and beauty did not have to be disturbed by the sometimes disconcerting feature of windows. This permitted architects to create a sheer wall of rusticated blocks of masonry to the cornice, relieved by deep-shadowed niches. This plan also prevented the interior drafts of cross-ventilation.

The principal façade was adorned with three ranges of Tuscan pilasters with their entablatures. Between the columns were four niches containing figures representing Liberty, Justice, Mercy, and Truth. The first was a female wearing a cap bearing the inscription "Liberator," and at her feet lay a cat, alluding to Sir Richard Whittington, an early fifteenth-century Lord Mayor and benefactor of the prison, of "Dick Whittington and his Cat" fame. Among his lasting benefactions was running water, which he had provided by diverting a small stream passing under the prison to be accessible to the inmates.

The history of this prison was as ancient as the Roman Londinium, when there was erected on this spot an entrance to the city known as the New Gate, to distinguish it from the older Ludgate, Billingsgate, and Cripplegate. No traveler could pass through the gate without shuddering at the thought of what occurred on the other side of the walls.

Into this imposing castle the four jurors now descended with Penn and Mead. They confronted a massive iron gate about twelve feet high and six feet wide mounted with spikes. The door was about a foot thick, locked with heavy double bolts which Charles Dickens would later describe as having been made for the express purpose of letting people in but never out again. The inscription "Abandon all hope ye who enter here" was composed for such a setting as this.

None of the four jurors ever kept a diary of his life in that hell, so again we must rely on the general tales of the tortures and villainies inmates suffered at the hands of tyrannical jailers. But that they were willing to submit for the sake of conscience requires from us a remembrance and respect too long denied them. They even had to pay jail fees and bribes for basic sustenance.

Just before he was taken away, Bushell had requested his supporters to send for an old and well-respected friend, a former Chief Justice of King's Bench, the aging Sir Richard Newdigate, to take appropriate legal action for their release. But Newdigate had retired to one of his two estates outside London, and it would take two or three days to reach him; nonetheless Bushell would have no other.

It was now when having been the son of a strict Puritan schoolmaster would prove almost worth childhood poverty. Having been taught about the guarantee of rights in Magna Charta as well as the Petition of Right, which Charles II's grandfather, James I, had been forced to submit to more than four decades earlier, Bushell composed his own petition to the judges for redress and release. The resulting petition, directed "TO THE CENTRAL CRIMINAL COURT," is his only writing still extant. It is confined to a single page, and copies were distributed throughout the city by his supporters.

It read: "Sirs; we are freemen of England, and therefore are not to be used as slaves or vassals by the Lords, which they have already done and would further do. We are also men of peace and quietness and desire not to molest any person, if we be not forced thereunto. Therefore we desire you, as you tender our good and your own, take this for an answer: that we cannot, without turning traitor to our liberty, dance attendance to their lordships' bar, being bound in conscience, duty to God, ourselves, thine and our country, to oppose their encroachments to the death, which, by the strength of God, we are resolved to do.

"Sirs, you may or may not cause to be exercised upon us some force or violence to pull and drag men out of our chambers, which we are resolved to maintain as long as we can before we will be compelled to go before them; and therefore we desire you, in a friendly way, to be wise and considerate before you do that which, it may be, you can never undo.

"Sir, we are your true and fair-conditioned prisoners, if you will be so to us." Bailey, Hammond, and Milson also signed.

To get the document delivered, they had to bribe the jailers, and about an hour later, as we might expect, it was returned "rejected" with instructions that if they paid the fines they would be released.

Undaunted, the four jurors tried again, and again the same results: "Rejected . . . imprisonment until paid." Since it was now too late for another try that day, the jurors suffered through their first night, relieved only in that they slept in hammocks instead of on the floor, and were furnished with, however unpalatable, some kind of sustenance. They probably also welcomed the relative luxury of Dick Whittington's cold water stream.

The trial record tells us that the jurors continued to submit petitions, perhaps with some changes in wording, most of the day, and while they had undoubtedly given up hope of a positive result, at least it kept them occupied. When Sir Richard Newdigate did arrive to consult them, the character of the appeal changed.

Sir Richard, at that time less than two weeks short of his sixty-eighth birthday, had long disliked Starling, and probably delighted in the opportunity to confront a bumbleheaded adversary. He also enjoyed a special advantage. His family had been members of the peerage since the days of King John, 450 years before, and was closely identified with libertarian causes and the defense of what were later to be called the first three (of six) "Great Charters of Liberty," necessary forerunners of our own Constitution: Magna Charta, the two Statutes of Westminster, and the Petition of Right. The first statute, adopted in 1275, declared that common right was to be done to all, without distinguishing between rich and poor; and the second that elections were to be free and unmenaced. As a young man, Newdigate had helped rid England of the false justice meted out for a century and a half, until the 1640s, by the secret hearings of Star Chamber. He had several times dared the censure of the first Charles by refusing to prosecute Irish nationalists and others who incurred royal displeasure.

He had been equally fearless under the tyranny of the interregnum. When offered a judgeship, he at first declined in protest over Oliver Cromwell's desertion of principle to become a usurper of power. However, Cromwell wheeled upon him to threaten: "If you gentlemen of the long robe will not execute my law, my red coats shall."

Dreading the consequences of military justice, Sir Richard accepted a commission on King's Bench, but he resisted subservience. During the trial of the Yorkshire insurgents for an unsuccessful revolt to restore the monarchy, he directed the jury to acquit because a statute defining high treason as levying war against the king was of doubtful legality when applied against a "Protector." Cromwell removed him "for not observing the Protector's pleasure in all his commands."

But Cromwell needed him more than he needed Cromwell, and sometime before the middle of 1657 he was back on the bench in a desperate move by Cromwell to stave off the collapse of the crumbling

Commonwealth. In January 1660, a younger Cromwell, Richard, inheriting power from his father, elevated him to Chief Justice of King's Bench. His tenure was short. He resigned on April 25 upon restoration of the monarchy, but he had time to grant habeas corpus to Sir Richard Pye, held prisoner for several months without indictment or trial on "suspicion" of treason. Judge Newdigate granted the appeal because "it is the birthright of every subject to be tryed according to the law of the land."

Sir Richard could afford the luxury of principle. Between his Newdigate heritage and inheritances from ancestral marriages, he had acquired so much wealth and property that profligate monarchs turned to him for rescue from their debts. His gain from loans was derived less from the good interest rates as from creating a dependency which virtually secured him immunity from royal wrath. He did not have to pay the price of destitution to maintain principle.

Although it was still nine years before the Habeas Corpus Act, he took the unusual step of filing an appeal not with King's Bench, where it properly belonged, being a criminal matter, but in the older Court of Common Pleas. Keeling, despite his censure, still sat in King's Bench, while a more ethical justice, Sir John Vaughn, was chief of this oldest court in the English government. (The Habeas Corpus Act of 1679 was the fifth of the "Great Charters" and prevented illegal detention of prisoners by requiring them to be present in court. The fourth was in the process of being created by Bushell and Newdigate, to be known as Bushell's Case.)

Newdigate believed completely in the righteousness of the jurors' position and that the Starling court had acted corruptly. His view was that no despot could wield total power without controlling the courts, and as long as there was one part of the judicial system, "as long as juries do operate with independence, the liberties of this nation are secure."

"The boorish fierceness of this Mayor of London is the more barbarous when you consider his eager prosecution of the king's party under Cromwell, as if now he could never give too great testimony of his loyalty to the new royal power."

Newdigate's tactic would be to appeal for what he called a "writ of *Habeas Corpus ad Subjiciendum*," which he defined as a legal term directing the persons detaining a prisoner to produce the body of the prisoner. Sir John Vaughn would be more inclined to grant it than Keeling. He was to argue that fining the jurors was an attaint, which is "despotic because it shuts off all dissent and renders all legal processes a farce." Packaged into a single action in an attaint are accusation, indictment, trial, conviction, and punishment without opportunity for defense.

Further, he would argue, the trial court had no power to say what the facts were since that was a function belonging exclusively to the jury. If jurors were to be punished for any reason, the court would have to follow the mandate of Magna Charta by providing jury trials for them.

Again the lack of a chronicler leaves us to conjecture how the imprisoned jurors spent the next several weeks while Newdigate prepared and presented his appeal. Also missing is a transcript of the hearing before Vaughn in Common Pleas, although there are incomplete sketches of arguments presented by Newdigate and several associates. In one of these, while Newdigate was presenting his reasons why Vaughn should establish the precedent of accepting a habeas corpus appeal, he was interrupted by Justice Richard Raynsford, sitting on Vaughn's right, who questioned him: "Sir Richard, are we to understand that you are requesting this court to hear a plea for habeas corpus?"

"That is correct, Your Honor."

"Why this is ridiculous. This court has never heard such a plea, which is an instance in criminal law, and I for one know nothing of such a writ."

Preventing Newdigate from responding, Justice Timothy Littleton on Vaughn's left sneered: "It is not the business of this court to review such procedures, nor that of attainder, and I add my voice to that of my honorable colleague. We know nothing here of either writ."

Vaughn surveyed Raynsford sitting righteously upright, and then studied the imperious Littleton. Then, raising his hands and gazing toward heaven, he pontificated: "Good God! What sin have I committed that I should sit upon this bench between two judges who boast in open court of their ignorance of the canon law?" He bowed his head in feigned humility.

Sir Samuel Starling was represented by Sir William Scroggs. Sufficiently unprincipled as a favorite drinking buddy of Charles to be elevated to King's Bench eight years later, Scroggs would argue that an attaint upon a jury on a verdict of acquittal was proper, where the grand and petit juries did disagree. Which is the same as rendering jury trials useless: the fact of indictment by a grand jury would preclude anything but conviction by the trial jury—or else!

Charles had commiserated with Scroggs: "How ill the people have used you, but they have used me worse, and I am resolved we stand and fall together."

Scroggs would argue that it was "an outrageous thing to make twelve jurymen, eleven of whom it's possible can neither read nor write, to be sole judges of both law and fact." He would also criticize Vaughn for even considering a criminal writ as being the "improper court to hear an appeal of the crown." But Sir John had risen so high and felt sufficiently secure to allow his independent spirit to resist intimidation.

Unlike other documents, the extreme length of the Vaughn decision, which was laboriously delivered on November 9, is published in full in Vaughn's own papers. Although length and tedium were almost required operating procedure, the content, when shorn of verbosity, is pivotal and controls (or should) every jury trial since.

One of the excuses for length was that since Common Pleas was preparing to set a precedent revolutionary for the time, Vaughn had to build substantiation for apparently usurping the presumed exclusive function of the rival King's Bench. In doing so he advanced the adoption of the Habeas Corpus Act of 1679.

He also had to escape royal censure. He rationalized usurpation, arguing that there could be no plea more common, next to life, than a plea for liberty. (The practice of paying judges by the case may, or then again may not, have been an influencing factor, as well as the opportunity of getting one up on his rivals in King's Bench, especially the despised Keeling.)

Vaughn's background differed from Newdigate's. Although born of a family ancient in name, his forebears were untitled and without wealth or landed estates. In his youth he was ambitious and avaricious, determined to achieve wealth and greatness, even at the price of an active legal practice in Star Chamber from the middle 1620s until about 1641. He had been elected to the House of Commons in 1640, but when Star Chamber was abolished and the civil war broke out, he faced a dilemma. If he remained in the Commons he would be censured should the king's party prevail at a later time; if he resigned while Commons held power, he would be censured by the Roundheads of Oliver Cromwell. He attempted neutrality. He retired to his family home in Cardigan, rationalizing that "it is the duty of an honest man to decline, as far as in him lay, accepting jurisdictions that derive their authority from any power but their lawful prince."

Commons retaliated by terming Vaughn "malignant" and "secluded" him from the House. However, he had by this time acquired an upgraded conscience without risking stomach or limb. Throughout the Commonwealth he would take no fee from any person, nor could he be prevailed upon to appear in court, though often pressed. He limited his legal practice to free advice.

Upon restoration of the throne, Charles rewarded him. Vaughn returned to his profitable legal practice in London, and the restored king knighted him and elevated him to Serjeant-at-Law, and in 1667 to Lord Chief Justice of Common Pleas. During the entire decade he had built a new reputation as champion of popular causes and a legislator "of great reason and eloquence." Newdigate appraised him as a "man of excellent judgment and learning, but passionate and opinionated."

The decision which Vaughn delivered that chilly Monday morning in Westminster is recorded under the prosaic title of "Bushell's Case," but is ranked by historians such as the *Encyclopaedia Britannica* on a level with Magna Charta, the Statutes of Westminster, the Petition of Right, preceding, and the Habeas Corpus Act and the English Declaration of Rights, following, as one of the six necessary precursors of our Declaration and Constitution. It is the only one of the six which originated spontaneously, without planning, from the people, or rather twelve of them randomly tapped by fate to represent all.

Eleven of the twelve judges concurred in what Vaughn called: "The clearest position that I ever saw considered, either for authority or reason of law" that no court can punish by fine or imprisonment a jury "for not finding according to their evidence and his direction" because the judge cannot know the evidence nor the fact as seen by the jury. "Without a fact agreed, it is impossible for a judge or any other to know the law relating to that fact, or to direct concerning it. Hence it follows that the judge can never direct what the law is in any matter controverted without first knowing the fact; and then it follows that without previous knowledge of the fact, the jury cannot go against his direction in law, for the judge could not direct, the jury alone knowing the fact."

The "court has no power to superimpose its opinion over that of the jury," he declared. "If the jury had felt the evidence to be full and manifest, the jury would have convicted; but since the jury has evidently judged the evidence not to be full and manifest, then the evidence thereby was not full and manifest, and the charge that the jury violated either law or evidence is without substantiation.

"To what end, then, must hundreds be of the jury whom the law supposes to have nearer knowledge of the fact? To what end are they challenged so scrupulously? To what end must they undergo the heavy punishment of the villainous judgment if after all this they implicitly must give a verdict by the dictates and authority of another man? A man cannot be another's eye, nor hear by another's ear; no more can a man conclude or infer the thing to be resolved by another's understanding or reasoning. It is thus absurd that a jury should be fined by a judge for going against their evidence when he knows but part of it."

Vaughn's acknowledgment of jury superiority and discretion to nullify written law or action distasteful to the jurors formed only half of his precedent-setting decision. He now had to build a firm foundation for invading the precincts presumed to be reserved exclusively for the rival King's Bench. Without this he risked challenge, should he issue a writ of habeas corpus. To build his foundation required citing precedents, many ancient, so numerous as to weary readers and bewilder listeners. He droned on for more than an hour, maybe two, possibly hoping to lose the attentiveness of his detractors, for the minds of all except the most pedantic scholars had drifted elsewhere. But inevitably he did arrive at the point where he could deliver his second great pronouncement: Every person has a right to appeal to Common Pleas and Exchequer, not only to King's Bench, for the ancient protection of habeas corpus "if it appears the imprisonment is against the law."

"The Court of King's Bench cannot pretend to be the only court to discharge prisoners upon habeas corpus, unless in case of privilege, for the Chancery may do it without question. A habeas corpus may be had in the Court of Common Pleas or Exchequer; and if it appears that his imprisonment be just and lawful, he shall be remanded to the jailer; but if it shall appear to the court that he was imprisoned against the law of the land, they ought, by force of this statute, to deliver him." He probably paused before delivering his everlasting proclamation for liberty.

"The judgment of this court is that commitment of the prisoners is judicially declared to be illegal, and consequently whatever depends upon it; as the fine and commitment do, are outlawed and reversed. The four prisoners are to be discharged at once on habeas corpus, and no attaint is to lie against them." England's first established, therefore highest-ranking court, the Court of Common Pleas, had formally endorsed the superior judicial authority that the jurors had asserted as belonging inherently to themselves.

Vaughn had concluded. He rapped his gavel to indicate adjournment, and the judges exited. His order must have produced a tremendous outburst of joy. The jurors were immediately released to blend back into the larger population. Nothing further is recorded of their lives, except that in 1674 Bushell sued Starling and Howell for damages for false imprisonment. The new Chief Justice of King's Bench, Sir Matthew Hale, denied him relief. While it was true, Hale reasoned, that Starling and Howell had erred by imprisoning the jurors, there could be no action against them because "the matter was done in the course of justice." Bushell should have demanded his own trial by jury.

Presumably Bushell spent the remainder of his life tending to his sugar business, dying at the then ripe age of seventy-three in 1694. He had lived long enough to have witnessed the influence of his jury upon another freedom of religion case, the Trial of the Seven Bishops in 1688, and the resultant downfall of a king and the establishment of the Declaration of Rights. The twelve Penn/Mead jurors are commemorated permanently on a brass plaque in front of the Old Bailey, the only instance of a memorial to a jury. Winston Churchill might have amended his Battle of Britain testimonial to include these twelve: "Never in the field of human conflict was so much owed by so many to so few."

Led by Edward Bushell, these twelve men, having no "First Amendment" to invoke, wrote it for themselves: "Congress shall make no law respecting the establishment of religion, or prohibiting the free exercise thereof." They continued: "or abridging freedom of speech . . . or the right of the people peaceably to assemble."

They also composed, albeit unconsciously, two sections of what was to become Article I, Section 9 of the Constitution: "The privilege of the writ of habeas corpus shall not be suspended," and "No bill of attainder . . . shall be passed." They demonstrated the validity of what would become a part of Article III, Section 2: "The trial of all crimes . . . shall be by jury"; and the Sixth and Seventh Amendments: "In all criminal prosecutions, the accused shall enjoy the right to a speedy and public trial, by an impartial jury . . ." and "In suits at common law . . . the right of trial by jury shall be preserved. . . ."

Eight provisions of our Constitution written because liberty lay in the hearts of these twelve men.

Let us remember the twelve: Foreman Thomas Veer, Edward Bushell, John Bailey, John Hammond, Charles Milson, John Brightman, William Leaver, Henry Henley, William Plumstead, Gregory Walklet, Henry Michel, and Thomas Damask!

The completeness with which these jurymen put the government to rout is shown by the fact that the Conventicle Act was virtually dead following the verdict. Although freedom of religion is challenged in every generation, no other action was ever again taken in the name of this legislation. Whether this would have been true had the four jurors yielded and paid their fines we can never know for sure. We do know, however, that by prolonging their ordeal by nine agonizing weeks they ensured permanence and proved, as we shall see many times in this book, that twelve honest citizens, overcoming fears of acting in good conscience, become "the grand bulwark of every citizen's liberties."[1]

NOTE

1. This chapter has been adapted from my book *The Ordeal of Edward Bushell,* a fictionalized account of the Penn trial (Sacramento: Lexicon Publishers, 1988). General sources used are listed in the bibliography to this chapter at the end of this volume.

2

"IT IS MY ROYAL WILL AND PLEASURE . . . !"

*T*he first time the English people heard King James II proclaim his
"Declaration of Indulgence for Liberty of Conscience," it rang
out like a harbinger of universal peace and religious harmony. (That is
if they didn't listen too closely!) In the century and a half since Henry
VIII had rebelled against the pope's objections to his divorce from
Catherine of Aragon in the 1530s, there was still no agreement as to
the one true and correct method for worshiping God. Differences between Catholic and Protestant forms of piety threatened to split the nation, and opposing interpretations within Protestantism actually did. In
a desire to create unity, the government established the official (and
therefore correct) form, and compelled "all our loyal and loving subjects" to adhere to the rites decreed by the Church of England. (Allowance was made for the Jews, a peculiar people tolerated only because of their special talents for trade and commerce in a time of in-
tense competition for foreign markets.)

Despite the benignity of the commandment, dissidence flourished
and could not be put down no matter how severely those who refused
to conform were punished. Memories were still fresh of the nearly
decade-long savage and devastating internal conflict that did not end
until the first Charles was beheaded by the forces of Oliver Cromwell
in 1649.

The new Cromwell-led government, known as a "Commonwealth," would establish a different true and correct form: Puritanism. However, this government was structured on insecure succession in contrast with a centuries-old monarchy which, except for Mary Stuart, required its monarchs to be Anglican. Moreover, papism remained an ever threatening presence. After a troubled eleven years the official answer was again Anglicanism, and Charles II, following the restoration of the monarchy, proclaimed it so. He got laws through Parliament and suppressed dissidents. Although civil war did not recur, large numbers of his subjects were mightily discontented and refused to go along.

Charles himself contributed to the unrest. It was an open secret that despite his official embrace of Anglicanism in order to remain king, his deepest sentiments were Catholic, which served only to encourage Catholicism. Almost his last act before expiring in 1685 was to convert and confess to his priests that it would take "more days" to catalogue his sins of a lifetime than he had "hours" remaining.

His brother, James II, was more aggressive. He desired to be a Catholic openly, which impelled him to conceive his "Declaration of Indulgence for Liberty of Conscience." On April 4, 1687, James proclaimed that "conscience ought not to be constrained, nor people forced in matters of mere religion." Catholics and dissidents alike were to be permitted to worship howsoever they chose without interference or restraint.

James expressed disapproval "upon the conduct of the last four reigns" (of brother, father, grandfather James I, and great-great-grand aunt Elizabeth) in regard to their "frequent and pressing endeavours . . . to reduce these kingdoms to an exact conformity in religion" because "it is visible the success has not answered the design." In contrast, James's goal would be to encourage his "loving subjects [to] live at ease and quiet."

He summoned the leading bishops to meet with him two weeks later to indicate their assent by signing the declaration, but only two agreed. James was stunned by the rebuff, but did not press the issue. He might have considered what had happened to his brother. Fifteen years earlier Charles had attempted to introduce a milder declaration which had been met by such strong resistance that he quickly canceled it and tore off the seal with his own hand so that it could never be used as a precedent.

James, however, was not so easily quieted. After a year he dared a second challenge with little change in wording. His new declaration, dated April 27, 1688, read:

There is nothing now that we so earnestly desire, as to establish our government on such a foundation as may make our subjects happy, and unite them to us by inclination as well as duty, which we think can be done by no means so effectually, as by granting to them the free exercise of their religion for the time to come, and add to that the perfect enjoyment of their property.

It was to be James's "royal will and pleasure" that all his English subjects would henceforth be permitted unlimited "leave to meet and serve God after their own way and manner . . . in private houses, or places purposely hired or built for that use" except for the caution "that nothing be preached or taught amongst them which may any ways tend to alienate the hearts of our people from us. . . ."

The declaration continued in benign form: "From henceforth the execution of . . . all manner of penal laws in manners ecclesiastical," such as not attending church, attending another church or other failure to conform, were to be "immediately suspended." James also pledged to "protect and maintain our archbishops, bishops and clergy," and commanded that "no disturbance of any kind be made or given under them, under pain of our displeasure." Imprisonment and torture over dissension or conscience would be forbidden.

This time James did not require the bishops to sign the document; instead he ordered every congregation leader in his kingdom to read it from his pulpit, in London on the last two Sundays in May (20th and 27th), and everywhere else on the first two Sundays in June (3rd and 10th).

What more could an obedient subject (or loyal clergyman) expect?

Well there was one little thing: that the people were to be "indulged" for their liberty troubled a few picayunish minds. And then there was the question of "royal will and pleasure," and that phrase about "giving leave" or "permitting" the king's subjects certain liberties. If the people would submit to allowing James on this occasion to "indulge" them through "permitting" liberty of conscience, would this not imply that on another occasion a fickle "royal will and pleasure" would be unrestrained in condemning those liberties and restoring "all manner of penal laws" or even making punishments more severe for not conforming with whatever form the new royal will and pleasure would assume? Was freedom of worship dependent upon royal permission, or was there not a higher source?

This was not all. Since it was presumably Parliament's job to make

even odious laws, how could the king assume power unto himself to
suspend those laws? Would this not entitle him to suspend any act of
Parliament, popular or unpopular, leading, step by step, to the elimi-
nation of Parliament entirely, letting him rule by royal edict?

Some of the establishment bishops objected for narrower self-interests: first, the declaration violated the laws of the realm and challenged the authority of the Church of England, and, second, it was an
affront to their dignity and profession. But something else was disturbing. The proclamation declared that the king did "heartily wish . . .
that the people of our dominions were members of the Catholic church.
. . ." Could this herald sometime later another declaration when the
king's "hearty wish" would metamorphize into "royal will and pleasure," making it treasonous to oppose? What would be the fate of the
Anglican nobility then (and the emoluments attached thereto)?

As it was, to resist so much as a "hearty wish" could mean risking
one's parsonage and earnings, and being pronounced incapable of
holding any office of spiritual preferment. The clergy could protect itself only by unifying, but with only two weeks to act, there was not
enough time to sound out the sentiments of leaders outside London, let
alone organize. Therefore, the clergy vacillated.

Many Presbyterian and Independent teachers were intimidated,
and seemed prepared to submit, but they were restrained by congrega-
tions threatening to walk out on them and not pay them if they did. The
weakest were treated with contempt. The zeal of the people, particularly the Puritans, was so great that the prelates were pushed to act in
some way. At a meeting in London the sentiment at first was to yield
until the Vicar of Saint Giles, Doctor Edward Fowler, spoke: "I must
be plain. The question is so simple that argument can throw no new
light on it and can only beget heat. Let every man say 'yes' or 'no,' but
I cannot consent to be bound by the vote of the majority. I shall be
sorry to cause a breach of unity, but this Declaration I cannot in conscience read."

The vicar's courageous defiance shamed four other clergymen into
supporting him, and under their influence the majority swung to
Fowler's side. A resolution not to read the declaration was drawn up,
and eighty-five signed it. Horsemen carried the message to towns outside London. The Archbishop of Canterbury, William Sancroft, strug-
gled with conscience and then assumed the lead. He wrote out a petition in his own hand, and although described as "cumbrous and inele-

gant" in wording, the sentiments were principled. The Church would not forsake its loyalty, he apologized, but James was constitutionally incompetent to dispense with statutes on ecclesiastical matters. His Declaration was illegal, which the petitioners could not "in prudence, honor or conscience" be parties to "publishing in the house of God, and during the time of divine service."

The archbishop and six other bishops signed. It was Friday, May 18, two days before the first mandated reading; they had to get the paper to the king without delay. Six of the bishops crossed the river to Whitehall without Sancroft, who had been forbidden upon an earlier offense to attend the court. When James heard the bishops were coming, he thought they wanted to present a "humble request" suggesting minor face-saving modifications, which he would magnanimously grant. Anticipating servility put the king in very good humor; he directed that they be admitted.

The bishops knelt before him; the king told them to rise and took the paper from Bishop Lloyd of St. Asaph, who shielded his own transgression behind that of his superior: "This is My Lord Canterbury's hand." The document began with an awkwardly worded apology:

> Humbly sheweth, that the great adverseness (the clergy) find in themselves to the distributing and publishing in all their churches your majesty's late declaration for liberty of conscience proceedeth neither from any want of duty and obedience to your majesty . . . but among many other considerations from this especially, because that declaration is founded upon such a dispensing power as hath been often declared illegal in parliament . . . that your petitioners cannot in prudence, honour or conscience, so far make themselves parties to it even in God's house. . . .

James was not amused. Confronting resistance changed his mood. "This is a great surprise to me," he pouted. "I did not expect this from your church, especially from some of you. This is a standard of rebellion!"

That was a serious charge; several bishops trembled and passionately professed their loyalty, only to increase the king's petulance: "I tell you, this is a standard of rebellion!"

Bishop Trelawney of Bristol fell to his knees and whimpered: "Rebellion! For God's sake, sir, do not say so hard a thing of us. No Trelawney can be a rebel. Remember how I served Your Majesty when

Monmouth was in the west." (The bishop's reference was to a rebellion in 1685 against James's assumption of the throne after the death
of brother Charles II by Charles's son, the Duke of Monmouth, who
was declared ineligible because he was not the son of the queen but of
a mistress.)

"We put down the last rebellion," pleaded another. "We rebel?"
whined a third. "We are ready to die at Your Majesty's feet."

But Bishop Ken of Bath and Wells was bolder. He remained de-
fiant. "I hope you will grant to us that liberty of conscience which you
grant to all mankind."

James ranted. "This is rebellion. I will have my Declaration published," to which Ken replied: "We have two duties to perform, our duty
to God and our duty to Your Majesty. We honor you but we fear God."

This did not assuage the royal bantling. "I will be obeyed. My
Declaration shall be published. You are trumpeters of sedition." In
foot-stamping mood, he directed the bishops to "go to your dioceses
and see that I am obeyed. I will keep this paper. I will not part with it.
I will remember you that have signed it. God has given me the dispensing power and I will maintain it."

"God's will be done," echoed Ken, and the bishops retired.

Somehow, a copy of this petition (even without the benefactions
of Mr. Xerox, born two and a half centuries too late) turned up and was
reproduced by a printer who hastily printed thousands more and sold
them at a penny apiece as fast as he could turn them out. He boasted
that he cleared a thousand pounds that day. In any event, he sold
enough that in spite of the unpopularity of some of the prelates, all
were now exalted as heroes, as no word had escaped about those who
had whined. Such universal support emboldened the resolve of even
the weakest of the seven.

Out of the approximately one hundred parish churches in London,
on Sunday the 20th, the declaration was read in only four; and in each
of these the congregants walked out. The Dean of Westminster trembled so violently, his hands shook; the abbey was deserted before he
had finished.

Would there be a repeat performance the second week? On Sunday
the 27th, hundreds of thousands of people packed all the churches to
find out. Again the declaration was snubbed, even by some of the four
who had read it the previous Sunday. James had put himself in an un-
tenable position: he could either advance at great peril to his throne, or

yield in humiliation. He was also advised that if he did not punish the bishops he would be disgraced. But what to do and how to do it? The king considered and discarded several stratagems.

Two years earlier, in 1686, James had established his Commission for Ecclesiastical Causes, the purpose being "to visit and correct all offences, to inquire of any misdemeanors against the ecclesiastical laws, and to punish the offenders by suspension, deprivation, and excommunication." But the commission's hidden agenda was to subordinate the established church and nation to Rome. The commission was composed of seven of the king's chosen sycophants, whom he presumptively authorized to suspend parliamentary laws and exercise the dispensing power. He would, if he could, render Parliament a nullity and remove from the mandated punishments anyone who had infringed upon a law of that body. His goal was royal absolutism.

In its short life, the commission made synonyms of "heartily wish" and "royal will and pleasure" by dispatching to the Tower of London too many who had transgressed no further in matters of religion than not obliging what he "heartily wish[ed]."

In the bishops' case, there were conflicting interests that could embarrass the king, one being that his principal advisor, Lord Chancellor George Jeffrey Jeffreys, was chief of the commission. So James decided to dodge the grand jury by filing criminal informations against all seven, including Sancroft, and charge them with seditious libel. But he could not escape the hazard of this procedure which necessarily called for a trial in the Court of King's Bench which, by Article 39 of Magna Charta, mandated submission to "the lawful Judgment of [the bishops'] peers. . . ." In short, a jury!

Jeffreys assured the king he need not be distressed about this; that this risk could be easily gotten around. The four judges who sat in King's Bench were so well attached to the comfort their high positions brought them, they would not risk loss by royal censure. Chief Justice Robert Wright had been termed "a beast" even by Jeffreys because of his excesses in the series of "Bloody Assizes" following the Monmouth rebellion three years before. Hundreds were arbitrarily condemned and slaughtered; whereas Jeffreys himself, who had presided at the assize hearings, was characterized by his biographers as "the very worst judge that ever disgraced Westminster Hall."

Judge Richard Allibone would not even have to be instructed that the bishops' petition was "a libel tending to sedition"; Thomas Powell vacillated, but would go along; and although Richard Holloway believed the petition was not a libel, for him to hold to that belief would mean almost certain dismissal and loss of earnings. What good, facing such dire consequences, to withstand the other three? A quartet of this character could be counted on to pressure any jury to return seven convictions.

The first step was to prepare the charges. James summoned the bishops to appear before him but delayed until June 8 to allow another Sunday to pass. The delay did not help. Of the hundreds of parishes outside London, the ministers in only seven or eight would read the declaration, and, as on the previous Sundays, parishioners walked out.

The bishops, now guided by "the ablest lawyers," were called into Council chambers. Lord Chancellor Jeffreys showed the paper to Sancroft in the presence of the king, and asked: "Is this the paper which Your Grace wrote, and which the six bishops present delivered to His Majesty?"

Sancroft studied the paper and replied: "Sir, I stand here a culprit. I never was so before. Once I little thought that I ever should be so. Least of all could I think that I should be charged with any offense against my King; but since I am so unhappy as to be in this situation, Your Majesty will not be offended if I avail myself of my lawful right to decline saying anything which may criminate me."

"This is mere chicanery," James retorted. "I hope Your Grace will not do so ill a thing as to deny your own hand."

"Sir," interceded the more scholarly Bishop Lloyd to anticipate our Fifth Amendment a century and three years in the future, "all divines agree that a person situated as we are may refuse to answer such a question."

The king, as befits a tyrant, ranted, but Sancroft stood firm: "I am not bound to accuse myself." High rank notwithstanding, the archbishop was, nonetheless, vassal to the king. Accordingly he felt obliged to say that if James commanded him to answer he would have to "in the confidence that a just and generous prince will not suffer what I say in obedience to his orders to be brought in evidence against me."

"I will not give you any such command," the king hedged. "If you choose to deny your own hands, I have nothing more to say to you." The seven were dismissed to an antechamber; but since James did have more to say, they were brought back, dismissed, and brought back again several times until James reversed himself and commanded them to answer. The seven then acknowledged their hands, and the king asked them to explain why they had declared the dispensing power illegal.

The archbishop responded: "The words are so plain that we cannot make them plainer."

"What want of prudence or honor is there in obeying the king?"

"What is against conscience is against prudence and honor too, especially in persons of our character."

"Why is it against your conscience?"

"Because our consciences oblige us, as far as we are able, to preserve our laws and religion according to the reformation."

"Is the dispensing power then against law?"

"We refer ourselves to the petition."

"How could the distributing and reading the declaration make you parties to it?"

"We refer ourselves to the petition whether the common and reasonable construction of mankind would make it so."

Having run out of patience, the king directed Jeffreys to prepare criminal informations* and warrants of arrest for imprisonment in the Tower of London. He ordered a barge to be brought to convey them down the river to the Tower.

Word of the bishops' appearance before the Council had spread all over London, and crowds of people filled Whitehall and neighboring streets. When the bishops were brought out under guard, the people cheered enthusiastically; thousands fell on their knees before them, or swam to the barge to ask for blessings. The barge passed between lines of boats from which people shouted "God bless Your Lordships."

Alarmed, the king ordered the Tower guard to be doubled, but the sentinels posted at Traitors' Gate asked instead for blessings from the distinguished prisoners. That day, Friday, June 8, became known as "Black Friday." On Saturday the chaplain of the Tower received a directive to read the declaration at services in the prison the next day. Critics described this as "a mean and childish personal insult" to the confined bishops, and the chaplain refused to comply. The king struck back by dismissing him and shutting down the chapel.

The bishops were held in the Tower for one week, but their imprisonment turned almost into a festival. They were honored by their

---

*An "information" is used as a written accusation, usually arbitrary, prepared by a public prosecutor to dispense with the safeguard of indictment by a grand jury.

guards who supplied every comfort, and asked them for their blessings. They were visited by many of the highest-ranking nobles of England. So much admiration enheartened the bishops, who were "modest in receiving the applauses and blessings of the whole nation." On Friday the 15th, they were brought under guard before King's Bench, passing through cheering throngs, more in the nature of a victorious processional than a line of accused criminals.

When the bishops arrived at court, Attorney General Sir Thomas Powis exhibited the "information" and moved that the defendants enter pleas. Powis, rated as "of the third rank in his profession," was joined in the prosecution by the universally disliked solicitor general Sir William Williams. The reason for the poor quality of the government's law officers was that they were required to perform odious and disgraceful services, which discouraged abler advocates.

The defense enjoyed a professional edge, consisting of highly skilled counsel, Sir Robert Sawyer, Heneage Finch, Henry Pollexfen and Sir Francis Pemberton, who objected that since the bishops had been unlawfully committed, they were therefore not regularly before the court and could not be compelled to plead. Correct legal procedures had not been followed. An extensive "points of law" debate over correct procedures ensued, until the solicitor general, in frustration, accused the bishops of entering "frivolous" pleas. He attacked his principal adversary: "How many times have you been accused of playing tricks, Sir Robert Sawyer?"

"Not so many times as you, Mr. Solicitor."

"I don't ask it as if I questioned it, for I assure you, I don't doubt it of your part at all."

Preventing Sawyer from a second riposte, Wright broke in: "Pray, gentlemen, don't fall out with one another at the bar. We have had time enough spent already."

And time enough it was for three of the judges, except Holloway, who, having grown weary, halted argument by voting to support the Crown and ordering the bishops to plead. Accordingly they were forced to plead "not guilty" and were directed to trial two weeks later, on June 29. They were released from the Tower on their own recognizance without bail. As they proceeded to their homes, they were again acclaimed. Encouraging messages were received from all over the country, even from Scotland.

But popularity could not protect the bishops from conviction. That was the province of the twelve men who would form the jury. Thus the object now of the king and the lord chancellor was to pack the panel. This job fell to Sir Samuel Astry, clerk of the Crown who accomplished his knavery with considerable skill. He drew the initial candidates from the freeholders' book containing the names of relatively upper-class owners of property susceptible to liens.

Astry winnowed out the doubtfuls and presented forty-eight names to the court, among them "several servants of the King and Roman Catholics." Defense counsel was given the Hobson's choice of striking twelve of the most extreme partisans. Powis removed another twelve. Crown lawyers then conducted penetrating inquiries into the sentiments of the remainder, until they were satisfied they had secured a suitably stacked panel. During the process, Powis mouthed the same hypocrisies used by lawyers from earliest days, and ever since: "We desire nothing more but a fair jury!"

In contrast to the great responsibilities thrust upon them, jurors are too often treated ignominiously, not even identified by names. However, in this case we have the twelve names, of whom two stand out: Sir Roger Langley, a knight from an old family, was placed in the most influential position of foreman. The second, handpicked by James, was Michael Arnold, brewer to the palace. Arnold described his predicament. If he did not vote to convict: "I am sure to be half-ruined for I shall brew no more for the King; and if I say 'guilty' I shall brew no more for anybody else."

There was also a second knight, Sir William Hill, and the other nine, all "esquires with substantial estates" vulnerable to royal displeasure, were Roger Jennings; Thomas Harriot; Jeoffrey Nightingale; William Withers; William Avery; Nicholas Grice; Thomas Digs; Richard Shoreditch; and one who was to prove pivotal, the large and burly "built-like-a-bear" William Austin.

A critical hardship imposed on these twelve was that they would not be fed for the duration of the trial, would not be permitted so much as a cup of water, nor access to a chamber pot from start, through arguments, debate, and their own deliberations until they had delivered their verdicts, no matter how many hours or even days—all the while confined to their dismal jury room.

That Friday, the 29th, was a hot day. The court assembled in a crowded Westminster Hall at nine in the morning. Thirty-five temporal peers of the realm were to keep watch over court and crown lawyers.

The stratagem was to stretch out the trial until evening, when the exhausted, distressed jurors would agree to almost anything to obtain relief. The clerk read to the jury the charge that the bishops had "conspired and consulted among themselves to diminish the king's power and prerogative, [and did] write a false, scandalous, malicious and seditious libel under pretense of a petition," all done in the County of Middlesex.

Powis launched his attack by declaring that the bishops were being prosecuted not on any point of religion, but for affronting the king and censuring him, which no man had a right to do. Nor did any man have a right to criticize a judge nor "say of the great men of the nation that they do act unreasonably . . . least of all to say any such thing of the King." Other ways had been provided to seek redress of grievances, Powis maintained, although he did not say what they were.

"You, gentlemen of the jury, are judges of the fact; if we prove that fact, you are to find them guilty."

To do this, the prosecution had first to prove the bishops had actually written and signed the petition. Since they all persisted in invoking the right not to be witnesses against themselves, the Crown had to seek support from other witnesses. Sir Thomas Exton was first to have his loyalty tested. He was shown the incriminating paper by Solicitor Williams: "Sir Thomas, I would ask you one question: Do you know the handwriting of My Lord Archbishop of Canterbury?"

Exton dodged: "I'll give your lordship what account I can."

Williams was annoyed. "Pray, sir, answer my question. Do you know his handwriting?"

"I never saw him write five times in my life."

"But I ask you upon your oath, do you believe this to be his handwriting?"

Exton was sly: "I do believe this may be of his handwriting."

"Do you believe all the body of it to be of his handwriting or only part of it?"

"I must believe it to be so, for I have seen some of his handwriting and this is very like it."

"What say you to the name? Do you believe it to be his handwriting?"

"Yes, yes, I do." This was a frustrating response since "believing" was not proving.

A second witness, his name lost, was more frustrating. "I did not see him write it. I cannot tell whether it is or no."

Chief Justice Wright broke in. "Did you ever see his name?"

"Yes, but it was a great while ago. I was better acquainted with his handwriting heretofore."

"Pray, sir, answer me. Do you believe it to be his handwriting or do you not?"

"I believe it may, sir."

Sawyer for the defense inquired: "Why do you believe it?"

"I have no other reason to believe, but because I have seen something like it."

Judge Powell: "How long ago is it since you saw him write?"

"I have not seen him write, so as to take notice of it for some years."

The next witness gave the prosecution no greater satisfaction: the handwriting "is like it, that's all I can say. I have seen His Lordship write, but I never stood by him so near as to see him make his letters."

Sir Thomas Pinfield confounded the prosecution even more. He did "believe it, but upon any other score I cannot tell what to say. I have been in his chamber several times when he has been writing, but I had more manners than to look upon what he writ."

Powis and Williams would not give up. They brought into court the Misters Clavell and Chetwood; James and Powell; and finally the Clerk of the Privy Council, Mr. Blathwayte. The prosecution derived little satisfaction from the first four, but Blathwayte was different. He had been present when the king had interviewed the bishops, and under interrogation he swore that he had heard the confessions of the accused prelates before the king. This, finally, was the damaging testimony the Crown had been seeking. But it annoyed Judge Holloway.

"Why," he asked Powis, "when you had such evidence, did you not produce it at first without all this waste of time?"

Holloway's question was answered during a searching cross-examination led by Sawyer and Finch. Blathwayte equivocated, shuffled, pretended not to understand, and implored the protection of the court to avoid revealing a dishonesty that would negate his critical testimony, and answer Holloway's question. The bishops had answered under command of the king, and under promise that their confessions would not be used against them. Pemberton for the defense responded: "I will deal plainly with the court. If the bishops owned this paper under a promise from His Majesty that their confessions should not be used against them, I hope that no unfair advantage will be taken of them."

Thus, although the handwriting had been proved, what was not proved was whether the bishops had done the writing—a fine bit of legal maneuvering. How influential such minutiae would be on the jurors could not, as of that time, be known. Wright was forced to admit, "Owning their hands does not amount to publication." To prove publication meant proving first that the petition had been written by the bishops; second, that they owned the paper which lay on the desk of the Privy Council; and third, that it was the same paper which had been delivered to the king. Also that all this was done within the County of Middlesex.

Without the bishops' confessions, proving all this would be difficult, and no confession could be forced. Another string of witnesses was summoned, including Samuel Pepys, Secretary of the Admiralty, but none could recall anything said about delivery. At every rebuff to Crown lawyers, the audience roared in approval.

Solicitor Williams, growing desperate, kept putting leading questions to the succession of witnesses until the defense protested that they had never seen so much "twisting" and "wiredrawing." It was too extreme even for Wright, who warned Williams he had gone beyond the rules.

Nor was Powis able to extract an answer to the question of writing in the County of Middlesex, because Sancroft had never once left the palace at Lambeth from the time when the Order in Council appeared until after the petition was in the king's hands. The whole case for the prosecution had thus clearly broken down, and the audience gleefully expected a speedy acquittal. The jurors asked to see the petition, and it was shown to them. Nonetheless, there was no evidence which even the most corrupt and shameless judge could use against the bishops.

Wright then asked if defense counsel had anything to say, and Finch responded: "My Lord, in short we say that hitherto they have totally failed, for they have not proved any fact done by us in Middlesex, nor have they proved any publication at all." To which Sawyer added: "They have given no evidence of anything."

The Chief Justice was forced to agree. He had no choice but to declare as much, and thus, however reluctantly, to direct the jury to acquit:

Gentlemen of the Jury, here is an information against my lords the bishops. I think I need not trouble myself to open all of it because I see you are men of understanding, men of great diligence, and have

taken notes yourselves, some of you. Therefore I shall say only
something of the proof that is required in this case and the manner
of the proof that has been given in this case, and then tell you my
opinion in point of law. . . .

At this point, Finch, violating court protocol and good manners,
broke in: "I humbly beg Your Lordship's favor."

The interruption astounded the court. "What say you, Mr. Finch?"

"I ask your pardon for breaking in when you are directing the jury. I
know I should not do it, but I hope you will not be angry with me for it."

"If I thought you did any service to your client I should willingly
hearken to you."

"That which I humbly offer Your Lordship is only to remember
Your Lordship where we were." Finch continued: "I only speak it, My
Lord, because if it be evidence, we have other matters to offer in an-
swer to that evidence and in our defense."

Other matters? The crowd gasped; associate defense counsel, unprepared, was stunned. What insipidness was this to suggest "other
matters" at the point of victory?

The Chief Justice was astounded: "If you have more to offer, why
did you conclude here and let me begin to direct the jury? But since
you say you have other to offer, we will hear it."

Pemberton jumped up: "My Lord, we submit to Your Lordship's
direction."

"No, no, you do not," Wright responded. "You have further matter
to offer."

Pollexfen desperately tried to undo the harm that Finch had done:
"My Lord, we shall rest it here."

But the moving hand had writ and Wright would not change its
course. "No, no. I will hear Mr. Finch," and with a touch of sarcasm:
"The bishops shall not say of me I would not hear their counsel. I have
been gently told of being counsel against them, and they shall never
say that I would not hear their counsel for them."

By this time the blood of both defense and the crowd was boiling
at fever point. In less than two minutes Finch had fallen from hero to
villain: "My lord," Pollexfen made one more passionate plea, stumbling over his words: "We beseech Your Lordship, go on with your directions, for all that Mr. Finch said was only that this was not sufficient evidence."

Wright, as surprised as any, was eager to seize this unexpected chance to escape his dilemma: "No, brother, he says you have a great deal more to offer, and I will not refuse to hear him. Such a learned man as he shall not be refused to be heard by me, I will assure you. Why don't you go on, Mr. Finch?"

Finch appeared to want to reverse himself with an apology, perhaps pressed by his co-counsel: "My Lord, I beg your pardon for interrupting you, but all that I was going to say would have amounted to no more than this: that there being no evidence against us, we must of course be acquitted."

Judge Holloway responded: "My Lord did intend to have said as much as that, I dare say."

Solicitor Williams rushed to take advantage of this opening: "I am very glad these gentlemen have given us this occasion because we shall now be able to clear this point. There is a fatality in some causes, my lord, and so there is in this. We must beg your patience for a very little while for we have been notified that a person of very great quality is coming that will make it appear that My Lords the Bishops made their addresses to him to be induced that they might deliver the paper to the king." He asked for a recess to give this "great quality person" time to arrive. The crowd groaned. Finch had snatched defeat from the jaws of victory!

Wright obliged, and the court recessed for half an hour, when all the principals, except the jurors, were able to relieve themselves. However, the "person of great quality" had still not arrived, and the defense pleaded again: "Pray, My Lord, give us your favor to dismiss us and the jury," but Wright would not.

The prosecution took the cue: "Put the case that a man writes a libel in one county and it is found in another. Is he not answerable unless he can show something that he may satisfy the jury how it came there?"

Wright, under scrutiny by the earls and barons before whom he would have to stand at the bar in the next Parliament, made frequent side glances in their direction. He could not appear biased for the king. "No, look you, Mr. Attorney, you must look to your information, and then you will find the case that you put does not come up to it. It is the writing, composing and publishing and causing to be published, and all this is laid in Middlesex. Now you have proved none of these things to be done in the county."

"They did in Middlesex confess it was theirs."

"Ay, but the owning of their hands is not a publication in Middlesex, and so I should have told the jury."

Powis tried once more: "But, My Lord, does it not put the proof upon them to prove how it came out of their hands into the king's hands?"

"No, the proof lies on your part."

When the witness of mystery had still not arrived, Pemberton pleaded again for dismissal, but Wright held firm: "I cannot dismiss you. It is your own fault." The hostility against Finch was almost visible.

"My Lord, there is no one come, nor I believe will come," to which Williams answered: "Yes, he will come presently. We have had a messenger from him."

Pemberton suggested: "My Lord, this is very unusual to stay thus for evidence," for nearly an hour had passed.

Wright did not mind agreeing. "It is so, but I'm sure you ought to not have any favor. Mr. Solicitor, are you sure you will have the witness that you speak of?"

Williams: "Yes, My Lord, he will be here presently."

The courier who had sent for the witness was called to the stand. It was to be Mr. Sunderland, who carried the title of "Lord President," and the irony was that Sunderland would already have been there except he had received word that Wright had begun directing the jury, which meant his testimony would have come too late to be admitted. When the courier informed Sunderland of Finch's interruption, he started out again, and Wright decided that the court "must stay till the evidence for the king comes."

That Sunderland had not been present in the first place confirmed the assessment of Powis as "of the third rank in his profession." Sunderland's testimony would be so critical to the prosecution that nothing short of sloppy preparation had kept him away. All the while the jury was denied so much as a cup of water or chamber pot. It may have been close to two hours before Sunderland arrived. When he did, it was with great ceremony: the "Lord President" was carried in a sedan chair through the hall. Not a hat was doffed as he passed, and there were many catcalls such as "popish dog." Sunderland was pale and trembling. He dared not look at anyone, keeping his eyes to the ground; when he was sworn in and questioned, he responded in a faltering voice.

Powis began the fatal interview: "Did the bishops make their application to Your Lordship to speak to the king?"

The "Lord President" supplied the missing link: "My Lord Bishop of St. Asaph and My Lord Bishop of Chichester came to my office and told me they came in the names of My Lord the Archbishop of Canterbury and four others . . . with a petition which they desired to deliver personally to His Majesty, and they did come to me to know which was the best way of doing it, and whether the king would give them leave to do it or not. They would have had me read their petition but I refused it and said I thought it did not at all belong to me, but I would let the king know their desire and bring them answer immediately . . . which I did. . . . This is what I know of the matter."

"About what time was this?"

"I believe there could not be much time between my coming from the king and their fetching their brethren and going to the king."

Williams was satisfied. He addressed the judges directly: "Then I think now, my lord, the matter is very plain."

Judge Allibone asked: "Did they acquaint Your Lordship that their business was to deliver a petition to the king?"

"Yes, they did. . . . The very same day and I think the same hour, for it could not be much longer."

The Chief Justice was relieved, his dilemma resolved: "Now it is upon you truly. It will be presumed to be the same, unless that you prove that you delivered another." He turned to Sawyer and, with the tone of victory in his voice, asked: "Will you ask My Lord President any questions, you that are for the defendants?"

Sawyer wished to reserve himself for later argument. For the moment he resigned himself to: "No, My Lord."

The momentarily victorious solicitor-general Williams gloated. He asked Sunderland to "turn yourself a little this way and for the sake of the jury deliver the evidence you have given over again that they may hear it." Sunderland obliged.

The proof had now been supplied, and Wright said as much: "Truly I must needs tell you there was a great presumption before, but there is a greater now, and I think I will leave it with some effect to the jury. Now this, with the king's producing the paper and their owning it at the council is such a proof to me as I think will be evidence to the jury of the publication."

However, Williams was enjoying only the first laugh. The second was yet to come, as the matter had not yet been conceded. Finch, the apparent renegade, was now ready to spring the "other matters" that were the causes of his near-fatal interruption. These matters would show a well thought-out, calculated method to his apparent madness. They involved legal questions of the king's power to suspend the laws of Parliament and dispense with punishments. Not less significant was whether the monarch had the power to abrogate the right of the people to petition for redress of grievances. This right was presumed to have been officially acknowledged by James's father, the first Charles, who had signed the Petition of Right under great pressure some sixty years earlier. This petition was forced in 1628, like Magna Charta, upon the reigning monarch to guarantee to the people the right to sue the king for redress.

By introducing this legal issue, Finch had once again altered the whole character of the trial, but this time to the bishops' advantage. For if the bishops had won acquittals on doubt of publication, the victory on fact alone would have been equivocal and indecisive. The king would not have been stopped from invoking these extreme powers, and eventually the battle would have to be refought. By making way for Sunderland's testimony, Finch had actually performed a great service not only for his clients but for the entire nation, which his colleagues and the people quickly realized. The key, however, to the success of Finch's maneuver would rest with how the jurors interpreted this evidence, and this could still not be known.

The several members of the defense counsel spoke in turn, telling the jury that if the king did have power to suspend parliamentary laws, "then pray my lord, where are we? All the laws of the Reformation are suspended, and the laws of Christianity itself."

Therefore, although publication in Middlesex was at length proven, far from being a crime, it was a legitimate petition against illegitimate assumption of powers. And having been "published" as a matter of right, the paper could not be malicious or seditious; it could not be a libel; it did not seek to diminish the king's power since he did not have these powers, in spite of James's hearty wish that they were "grants from God." Some three tedious hours were consumed in argument, and when they were over it appeared as though the weight of evidence lay with the defense. But, of course, this could not be known for certain until the jurors had acted. The disadvantage from the defense view was, first, that most of the jurors were vulnerable to property liens from a vindictive monarch, that they were by this time in extreme physical distress, and that the defense was asking them to transgress beyond the fact to determining lawful limitations on royal power.

Powis proved his inadequacy again with a short and feeble response undeserving of commentary. Solicitor Williams was more aggressive; he delivered a lengthy, acrimonious address to distract attention from the law, but was interrupted frequently by clamors and hisses from the audience. He declared that the Great Petition did not recognize a right of any subject or body of subjects to petition the king except the Houses of Parliament. Therefore, the only consideration for the jury was the fact of publication.

At length Wright had to confront the dilemma. His language showed that despite the awe in which he stood of the government, he was also in awe of the audience, so strongly vocal and passionate as they were. His dilemma stemmed the presumption that law is exclusively the province of judges, while juries are restricted to fact. He knew the king did not have suspending and dispensing powers constitutionally, but to declare this would probably cost him his fine job. Therefore, Wright evaded "instruction," which was tantamount to advising the jurors that they could act on the law.

Two of the other judges were equally intimidated. Holloway dodged, and Allibone played safe and stood for the Crown. Powell took the boldest course: he suggested that the king's declaration was a nullity because such royal prerogatives would end Parliaments and invest all legislative authority in the king. Nonetheless, like Wright, he sidestepped, leaving the ultimate decision "to God and to your [the jury's] consciences."

Wright, in his final address to the jury, slithered out of every major issue: "The dispensing power is out of the case." (He lied to escape acknowledging openly that he had already turned law decisions over to the jury.) "The only question, gentlemen is a question of fact, whether there be a certain proof of publication and whether it be a libel." But publication had been conceded, and a libel, by Wright's definition, was "anything that shall disturb the government or make mischief and stir up the people," which is certainly what did happen. "I do take it to be a libel," he said, coming as close as he dared to directing the jury to override the Petition of Right.

The trial had begun at nine in the morning and it was now nearly midnight. For all those fourteen or fifteen hours the jury had been kept confined. Wright decided to bend the rules and be magnanimous with them. He allowed wine to be brought to abate their thirst after so hot a summer day. Water would have satisfied their needs better. But that was all. The jurors were then locked up without further comfort in a crudely furnished jury room with hardly anything more than benches and a table. The judges, attorneys, and all other principals retired to their homes, except the solicitor. He felt a need to sit up all night with a body of servants on the stairs leading to the jury room to watch the officers who watched the jury. Despite being obedient servants of the king, the officers were under suspicion. The government feared that their sentiments, like those of the Tower guards, were with the bishops and that they might attempt to influence the verdict by bringing food to sympathetic jurors so that they could starve out the others.

Neither candle nor pipe was permitted; at least a fire was not urgently needed, although London summer nights are often chilly. At four in the morning Williams granted a small concession. He allowed basins of water to be passed through so that the jurors could wash themselves. But the jurors, raging with thirst, lapped up all the water and remained unwashed. Although trial records avoid mentioning delicate details, it is unlikely that the jurors would have been able to restrain urgent bodily functions beyond so many unrelieved courtroom hours. Like many before them, they probably sought relief in corners of the jury room, which now required them to submit to the misery of stench and flies and possible courtroom censure. They could do no other than transform the room into a latrine.

Hardly a soul in London over the age of six slept that night. Great crowds of people roamed the neighboring streets awaiting the verdict. Periodically messengers would come from Whitehall to spread anxious rumors, but all that could be known for certain was that "voices in high altercation were repeatedly heard from within the jury room." Whatever the subject of the "high altercations," it did not escape the room. This would be the longest night in the history of England!

Unfortunately no chronicler recorded the minute-by-minute agonies in that room of mystery, but from post-verdict interviews and individual confessions we can learn something of the battles being waged between conscience and fear of royal reprisals. There were well-known precedents of jurors being fined heavily and imprisoned for months, having all their property confiscated for bringing in "wrong" verdicts; their houses burned and their families turned out.

An entire jury in Queen Mary's time was committed to prison

when the court was "dissatisfied with the verdict" of conscience in favor of one Sir Nicholas Throckmorton for speaking the wrong things about the bloody queen. Nine were released upon scraping up fines of 500 pounds apiece, possibly over half a million dollars in today's money. The final three, being the principal "abettors of faction" and unable to raise four times that figure, were held from April 17 to December 21, 1554, upon payment of 60 pounds. The trial records give us only their last names and we can offer them now, four and a half centuries later, no greater solace for our debt to them in the defense of liberty than reverence: foreman Whetston, and jurors Lucar and Kightly. Their sufferings notwithstanding, the decision of their jury and every other conscience-struck, law-making jury held, proving the power honest jurymen have over tyranny.

These three stalwarts never regretted their conscience-driven verdicts, particularly after seeing that the severity of the abuses against them had so intimidated a second jury considering identical charges against Throckmorton's brother John that they succumbed. The hapless brother was beheaded, whereas Nicholas survived, thanks to Whetston, Lucar, Kightly, and their jury. The fearsome trials in Star Chamber had been abolished less than half a century before, leaving the specter of resumption to intimidate this jury. What price conscience!

How much our jurors knew of this history we can never be sure, but since they were all members of the educated class, undoubtedly several of them knew enough. And none was too young to recall the trial of William Penn eighteen years earlier, recounted in the first chapter of this book. Four jurors were imprisoned for nine weeks for bringing in acquittals "against law and evidence."

Relatively early during their confinement, nine of the jurors, considering the fates of the bishops, put aside fears in favor of conscience. Three, including the unhappy brewery master Michael Arnold, supported convictions. We do not know who the other two were, except foreman Langley, on whom the prosecution had especially depended, was probably not one of them. Nor can we tell what factors influenced these nine, nor how early in the trial they had made up their minds. However, I suspect that their innate sense of right and wrong was more influential than either extended legal haranguing or fears of royal reprisals.

By six o'clock two of the dissenters had overcome bleary, sleep-deprived brains to rate conscience above fear, but Arnold remained unconvinced. At which point Thomas Austin, a country gentleman of great estate, came forward to work on him. Austin had paid close attention to the entire proceedings and had taken full notes, but Arnold declined to hear him. He said he was not used to reasoning and debating; it was not fear of loss of business, he maintained, but his conscience told him not to acquit. He did not explain.

Since argument and reason would be naught, Austin offered a proposition. "If you come to that," he is reported as saying, "look at me. I am the largest and the strongest of the twelve here, and before I find such a petition as this a libel, here I will stay till I am no bigger than a tobacco pipe!"

This was no idle challenge, especially for Arnold, of much smaller physique. Being alone now, aching as badly as any other, the only barrier to the relief of all twelve, he knew which half of his business he would have to let go. He studied the determined faces of his fellows, wrestled with conscience, and after a time yielded. Those on the outside knew nothing except that the loud arguing had stopped, which caused the rumor that the jury had come to a decision. But what they had decided no one outside that room knew.

For almost four hours longer—four interminable hours—the starved, exhausted jury was held. Perhaps during this period they were able to sleep on the hard floor, and overcome what must have been the constant buzzing and stinging of insects, parched throats, the agony of empty stomachs, throbbing heads, and miscellaneous other pains and discomforts.

At ten o'clock on Saturday, June 30, 1688, the court reassembled, but it took a longer time than usual to get started because of the overflow crowd. When the jurors did appear in the box, the stillness was oppressive. The traditional ritual of "oyezes" and "hear ye's" to open the formal court session seemed unnecessarily drawn out. Finally it was time for Sir Samuel Astry to pose the momentous question: "Do you find the defendants, or any of them, guilty of the misdemeanor whereof they are impeached, or not guilty?"

The Earth paused in its rotation. All breathing stopped. Foreman Sir Roger Langley, the king's chosen, stood up and shouted: "NOT GUILTY!" At those words a prominent nobleman up front sprang to his feet and waved his hat, which was a signal to those further away who may not have heard. The galleries raised a shout. Hearing this, the thousands who had crowded the great hall responded with a still greater shout, which reportedly caused the old oaken roof of the court-house to crack.

In another moment the crowds on the streets outside sent up a third hurrah, which was heard as far as Temple Bar. The shouting spread to boats which covered the river Thames, with answering cheers. A peal of gunpowder was discharged and then a second and third, to tele-graph in a few moments the glad tidings to Savoy, the Friars, and London Bridge.

In seconds the news was sweeping through streets, squares, mar-ketplaces, and coffee houses, which broke forth in universal acclama-tion. Thousands gave way to weeping for joy, belying the English stereotype for reserve and not revealing emotions. Horsemen spurred their steeds to carry the intelligence all over the nation.

The solicitor general was a poor loser. Vindictively shouting above the din, he demanded that the four judges commit the revelers for having "violated the dignity of the court." One was seized, but the judges reconsidered. It was futile to punish a single individual for an "offense" committed by hundreds of thousands. The judges dismissed the reveler with a face-saving reprimand.

The court gave up trying to conduct other business. Solicitor Williams got into his coach amid a tempest of hisses and curses. One of the prelates who had attempted to read the declaration had com-mitted the folly of appearing at Westminster to hear the verdicts. Rec-ognized by his sacerdotal garb and corpulent figure, he was hooted from the hall. "Take care," shouted one man, "of the wolf in sheep's clothing," and from another: "Make room for the man with the Pope in his belly."

The acquitted bishops, wildly acclaimed, fled to the nearest chapel to seek quieter refuge from the thousands seeking their blessings. The bells of all the parishes rang loudly.

The stoical jurors were mobbed. Thousands of persons, undeterred by the soil that must have covered their bodies, shook their hands. There were shouts of "God bless you" and "God prosper our families." "You have done like honest, good-natured gentlemen," or "You have saved us all today."

Noblemen passing by in carriages flung handfuls of money at the jurors whose friends scooped it up for them. Glorious as the acclama-tions were, the jurors probably would have settled for chamber pots to go around, warm baths, cool water, dinners—and soft, downy beds.

Powis in defeat fled to Sunderland, who happened to be conversing with the papal nuncio. "Never," he is reported to have said, "within man's memory have there been shouts and tears of joy as today."

Sunderland immediately sent a courier to the king, who was visiting a camp at Hounslow Heath; James was in Lord Feversham's tent. Upon hearing the news, James became agitated and exclaimed in French: "So much the worse for them," but what he meant by that was not clear.

He set out for London. The soldiers in the camp, silent while he was there, sent up loud shouts of joy as soon as the king was gone, but not so far away that he could not hear. He sent to find out what the shouting was about and his courier returned answering: "Nothing, My Lord. The soldiers are glad that the bishops are acquitted."

"Do you call that nothing?" James upbraided the message bearer as if he were to blame. Then repeated: "So much the worse for them."

Because Finch had the stamina to stand it out, the king's humiliation was total. Happily for the country, he had allowed the fact of publication of the bishops' paper to be fully established. The jurors would have acquitted before, but that their unanimous action came afterward made the verdict pivotal by proclaiming the Declaration of Indulgence to be illegal, something which three judges had dared not rule upon. Although but "subjects" of the king, the jurors had exercised the power of sovereignty by outlawing his usurpation of parliamentary functions. They had demonstrated as Whetston and many other jurors had done before them, that verdicts according to conscience are the chief bulwarks against tyranny. Finch and the jurors, together with the bishops, had become the great heroes of the hour.

Six months after the momentous verdict, James was forced to yield his throne and flee to the Continent in what became known as the Glorious Revolution. He never returned again to England as monarch. His nephew and daughter, Prince William and Princess Mary of Orange, both Protestants, would reign under a "constitutional monarchy" only after agreeing to sign the Declaration of Rights, which not only guaranteed freedom of religion but strengthened the guarantee of Magna Charta to trials by jury and put freedom of the press under the protection of juries.

The whole day and night following Sir Roger Langley's shout of "not guilty" and several days afterward were spent in revelry. Rockets were fired, bonfires blazed, the pope was burned in effigy. But the king was downcast and gloomy. For some days no one could speak to him about almost anything as mortification hardened his heart. He dedicated his energies to revenge; what he had meant by his repeated exclamation: "So much the worse for them" soon became clear. The king blamed himself not for having prosecuted the bishops, but for having allowed the prosecution to go before a jury where established principles of law could be questioned.

Instead of accepting defeat, he pushed even further. A fortnight after the trial James issued an order commanding all chancellors of dioceses and all archdeacons to report within five weeks to the High Commission and give the name of every vicar, rector, and curate who had refused to read his declaration. The king expected that terror would strike the offenders when they learned they were to be cited and brought before courts. The number was close to ten thousand, and every one of them might reasonably expect to be discharged from all spiritual functions and declared incapable of holding any other preferment. Then, having been reduced to beggary, they would be charged with court costs.

James awarded the obsequious Williams with a baronetcy, which only increased the hatred of the people against both the king and the solicitor general. He dismissed Judges Holloway and Powell. The fate of Wright hung in the balance, but the king allowed him to stay for want of a better (or perhaps worse) "beast" to sit in his place. Allibone escaped censure, having the good fortune to die.

At the end of the five weeks, James was dismayed to learn that not more than one of the chancellors and archdeacons had informed against their colleagues. The High Commission met but could take no action; the chief result was that James had further alienated the people. He alienated them still more by importing troops from Ireland to put down the growing rebellion against him, only to discover an invasion from Holland led, upon invitation, by his daughter and nephew.

Twenty days before the verdict, on June 10, another significant event had occurred. The queen was reported to have given birth to a "Catholic" prince, but the circumstances were suspicious. There were rumors that she could not be pregnant, and that a baby had been rushed in to her confinement in a warming pan. Although never conclusively proven either way, the suspicious rumor has never died. The birth aroused fear of a new line of Catholic monarchs, which may have contributed to the rebellion.

Perhaps it is too simplistic to attribute so complex a historical force as the Glorious Revolution to a jury verdict—but then perhaps not. Many astute historians regard as the catalyst the birth of the prince, except that it happened three weeks before the great outcry, followed by James's rash action against ten thousand clergymen. And how certain could anyone be about what path the newborn prince would follow? Catholic though he was, James already had two daughters, both of whom accepted Anglicanism. It might help us in evaluating to compare the bishops' trial with a series of confrontations between absolute monarchy and juries, as is the subject of the next chapter. There is an important difference: the jurors were not knights and men of relatively high station. They came from the lowest elements of society, the illiterate Russian peasantry, yet they held in thrall no less than the autocratic czar of Russia.

3

WHAT IT TAKES TO BE A GOOD CZAR

*P*ity the poor monarch confronted by twelve free-thinking citizens who have come together as a jury!

As we have seen in the preceding chapter, James II of England, despite his autocratic trappings, despite the groveling of the pompously titled, was so completely undone by a dozen of his "loving subjects" that he could never recover from their censure of him. But his fate was mild when compared with that of another monarch almost two centuries later. Or, depending on your viewpoint, maybe this later tyrant was luckier since he did not have to endure years of humiliation and disgrace in exile. For him, censure ended in an instantaneous flash.

Alexander II wanted to be a good czar, a kindly czar loved by his people. He really and truly did. Growing up, he had observed that under the regimes of his father (Nicholas I), uncle (Alexander I), and the czars before them, corruption had been so deeply embedded in every aspect of their administrations and national life as to offend his youthful sense of justice.

I can add nothing to the stories of oppression that held more than three-quarters of the Russian people in slavery for most of the centuries of czarism, and in subjugation to the Tartars before that; nor can I attempt to detail the atrocities which the people suffered, which were summed up by the nineteenth-century Russian poet Nikolay Nekrasov, who posed for himself the sardonic question: "Who can live happily in Russia?" and then supplied the answer: "Nobody!"

But the young prince who was to become the second Alexander was possessed of an uncharacteristic spirit of humanity. Some of his relative softness may have been inherited through a gene that crept into his makeup surreptitiously from his maternal grandfather, Frederick William III of Germany, who, although a bit dull-witted, was said to have had "a good heart." Alexander was also influenced by his tutor, the amiable humanitarian poet, Vasily Andreyevich Zhukovski, who instilled in his pupil the understanding that freedom depended upon a well-administered judicial system. Thus we find the rare phenomenon of a royal heir desiring freedom for his people, although they remained his subjects.

Alexander desired it so ardently that, immediately upon the death of his father in 1855, under whom the worst atrocities were recorded, he began by freeing the serfs. Since this was almost a decade before the American emancipation, he had no Western model to draw from; he had to create his own. Moreover, his was probably a more gigantic task than the freeing of American slaves, there being in Russia so many more serf-slaves whose living conditions were worse, and who were of various classes and races. Because the lives of the serfs improved considerably as soon as Alexander had acted, we should not, perhaps, fault him for regarding their freedom as a gift arising from his benevolence, rather than their inherent right as human beings, and as an endowment by a far superior donor.

It would probably also be picayunish to criticize Alexander when he voluntarily yielded some of his autocracy in other ways, just because he wished to hang on to a little bit of it. For example, he "allowed" his subjects freedom of the press, although drawing the line when it came to making harsh criticism of himself and his government. The result was the flourishing of newspapers and magazines on a scale never before known in his vast domains. And very vocal they were, too!

What Alexander regarded as his greatest gift to his people came in 1864, when he was able to act on the most basic of Zhukovski's teachings. He instituted his "program for judicial reform," the "justice" system in Russia being so hopelessly corrupt. Alexander's principal philosophy was incorporated in Section 573 of his new Code of Criminal Procedure. Every precaution was to be taken to protect against the possibility of an unjust accusation; therefore, the primary objective of the prosecutor in any criminal trial was not to convict but to seek the truth. The actual wording mandated that the prosecutor "should aim not towards conviction, but exclusively toward the disclosure of truth, regardless of whether it shows the guilt or innocence of the defendant." Although "the prosecutor appears before the court as an accuser" and has the responsibility to expose all the grounds and reasons for the accusation, "he must support the accusation . . . not for the sake of bringing about a conviction of the defendant at any price," but must "give the defense an opportunity to interpret [the testimony] from its standpoint and even to eliminate [the charges] completely if they can be rebutted." The prosecutor must actually cooperate with the defense by summoning all witnesses whose testimony may serve to disclose the truth without regard to whether their testimony supports or refutes the accusation. "The conviction of an innocent person," Alexander's law declared, was even "more contrary [to the attainment of justice] than the acquittal of a guilty person."

This philosophy was revolutionary for a country which for centuries had been throwing people to slaughter or exiling them to Siberia on the flimsiest of charges, without trials, in wholesale lots. The most amazing part of Alexander's judicial reform was that the prosecutor's presentation should be given not to an entrenched venal judiciary but to panels of citizen jurors, drawn from every rank and level of the populace. Except for a short period of modified republicanism a few hundred years before in Novgorod, trials by jury were totally foreign to Russian thinking. Looking to the West and studying the success of this method of administering justice, especially in England and the United States, this "Czar of Freedom" sensed that the jury would be the ultimate force to bring freedom to his people. And thus it was in that fateful year of 1864 that Russians began to enjoy the greatest of Alexander's gifts to them.

The jury, according to the assessment of close observers of Russian life during the czarist period, "was the highest mark of confidence which the imperial government could GIVE [sic] the nation, thus spontaneously to invite it to take a direct share in the repression of crime."[1] However, more than half the people who would be jurors were illiterate, having just emerged from centuries of abject subjugation. Alexander was attacked by members of his court as "imprudent" at best, even "insane." His detractors objected on the ground that the peasant class was unable to consider questions demanding "logical thinking." One of his leading critics, Count Bludov, endorsed the idea of a jury system, but it was not for Russia—at least not yet: "It is not easy to imagine the functioning of such a court when the majority of our people are not only deprived of juridical knowledge, but lack the most elementary education."

The State Council responded to this criticism by stating that the complaint was "unconvincing." People are developed and perfected by good institutions, the council argued, and in this respect a well-organized court is more important than any other institution because it teaches the people about justice and lawfulness. Almost Jeffersonian in its thinking, the council declared that the answer to an uneducated citizenry is not to deprive them but to educate them.

Another critic, at least initially, was law professor V. D. Spasovich, who, in 1861, found the people who would serve on juries to be "simple morally . . . unable to understand the criminal nature of most crimes . . . primitive politically," and so fearful of the court as to run away from it and have no respect for the law. Thirty years later, however, after having observed the Russian jury in practice, Spasovich changed his assessment. "I'm glad more than anyone else that I was wrong, and that the daring experiment was carried out and was crowned with success."

Alexander also had a distinguished, now aged, adviser. He was Nicholas Turguenief, who had been exiled by his uncle Alexander in the 1840s, and who had been biding his time since by drawing up plans which seemed to belong to an infinitely remote future. The jury, Turguenief believed, was born in barbaric ages among half-savage tribes, and was one of the few institutions adaptable to all stages of civilization, capable of suiting infant nations as well as long-established, sophisticated cultures. The surface backwardness of newly liberated serfs would be no handicap, he believed, and he was enthusiastic about the new czar's eagerness to update judicial reform from a remote future to now.

Alexander went beyond even Turguenief. Where the latter would limit juries to members of the same or "higher class" than the defendant, Alexander decreed that there would be no distinction between noblemen, tradesmen, and peasants; they could all serve together on the same jury. The mingling of different classes would be the best means of overthrowing antiquated barriers erected by old prejudices, and raise the moral level of the jury. This "democratization" would impart to the nation a broader, loftier spirit by placing the jury above both caste interests and caste prejudices. It became common for a former lord to sit with his own former serf on the same panel. Conscientiousness, not status or degree of education, should be the chief qualification for jury service, and Alexander somehow sensed that this characteristic could be found in all levels of society—at least in men. That women were not counted in—well, it was 1864. And we must not overlook the fact that these fine ideals were the sentiments of the holder of absolute power (the nature of which tends to intoxication) who drew the line at challenges to his absolutism.

Nor was literacy a qualification. Men who had never held a pen in their hands, who could barely spell their own names, sat together with the best educated, even on forgery cases. The only qualification was a requirement that the foreman of the jury, selected by the jurors themselves, had to be literate. One unfortunate circumstance was that Alexander made no provision for jurors to be paid during their service, which created near-desperation for peasants wrenched from the labor that kept them alive. Some were compelled to beg from door to door, or even steal during court recess. Others were forced to sell their votes, which of course compromised high ideals. In many cases, local provincial assemblies aided destitute jurymen by providing good accommodations for them, and even paying them. In spite of these handicaps, jurors performed remarkably conscientiously, returning often with amazing verdicts.

Looking at bland statistics alone, we learn that the relation of convictions by juries to all cases tried was around 60 percent compared with 73 to 75 percent for nonjury trials over a sample period of about a dozen years.[2] However, these figures do not reflect the full extent of the greater leniency of Russian juries. For example, there is the case where the charge was "stealing horses." The jurors, confronted by the obvious guilt of the accused which called for a too severe punishment, returned one of those amazing verdicts of guilty of "stealing rabbits." The lesser offense carried a very light sentence. This verdict would be tabulated, of course, among the convictions.

Some verdicts at first glance may appear nonsensical, in respect to the reasoning applied for acquitting the guilty, but juror leniency may be attributed in part to reaction against the excessive rigor of so many centuries of injustice. When the previously disenfranchised found at long last that their voices counted, they quickly took advantage of the situation. Their natural inclination was kindliness and sensitivity toward the human tendency to transgress. Jurors were especially lenient when the crime resulted from desperation created by poverty. The Russian peasant had seen so much persecution of innocence that he found it hard to believe that the guilty were really guilty. The jurors were merely putting into action the philosophy of Alexander's Section 573 that it is better to acquit the guilty than convict one innocent. (Which is also presumed to be the American philosophy.)

Russian juries went even further. Where a confession of guilt in the United States implies waiver of a jury trial, in Russia at this time the jury would nonetheless hear the case and could, on the basis of conscience, acquit, the defendant's confession notwithstanding. Alexander's law actually said as much. Samuel Kucherov reports that "The judicial institutions of Alexander II . . . have conferred to the jurors the right to pronounce verdicts (accusatory or exculpatory) without being hindered by evidence, according to conscience only."[3]

In a case of arson reported by Maurice Baring,[4] the evidence of guilt was very clear. The penalty upon conviction was six years' imprisonment, and the defendant, a peasant, was the chief support of his wife and children. The jurors asked themselves why his family should be forced to suffer for his transgressions. Finding no justification, they sent him back home to work.

Another jury of "merchants and peasants" brought in a verdict of "not guilty, with extenuating circumstances." The trial occurred during Holy Week, when jurors usually forgave everybody. Other juries might acquit swindlers when they interpreted the offenses as no more than good jokes or harmless tricks; or where obvious thieves had repented, or their families were dependent on their labor.

Juror leniency loosened the rigidity of the law and adapted it to public sentiment. One series of trials dealt with "crimes against religion." In 1877 the court of assizes of Odessa was trying a group of peasants known as "Stundists," who emphasized brotherly love and the necessity of manual labor, and who rejected the clergy and the sacraments of the official church. These "Stundists" were indicted for "apostasy from the Orthodox faith," to which the accused confessed. Nevertheless, the jury refused to convict, as if to tell the government that every person had a right to worship according to his own conscience. By nullifying the written law, they replaced it with a higher, natural law.

This case was followed in 1880 by another religious trial in St. Petersburg, which, although occurring after his death, kept up the Alexandrian tradition. Again the defendant was technically "guilty": A Jewish boy had been taken from his parents at age eleven, brought up as a reluctant soldier, baptized against his will, and after more than thirty years of conscription (a usual method of forcing Jews into the Russian army) had escaped, returned to his faith, and married. He rejected the baptismal name of Alexis Antonof and took back his birth name of Moses Eisemberg. He was therefore prosecuted for the twofold offense of falsifying an official document and abjuring the Russian Orthodox faith. The Russian jury, on which probably sat not a single Jew, did not hesitate to acquit him.

There were many freedom of religion trials before juries, some resulting in convictions and some in acquittals. The spotty record may be due in part to the fact that the Russian practice was to accept majority verdicts, and the historical record is clear: nonunanimity always means a higher conviction rate. Most historians, no matter how meticulous they might be in other areas of research, tend to disregard juries, treating them as footnotes to other events, even though jurors, being responsible for the verdicts, play the central roles. Thus when the record tells us that a Russian jury convicted or acquitted, they leave open the tantalizing question whether the verdict was split or unanimous. Was the verdict seven to five? ten to two? Without this and other details, we cannot know how many split convictions would not have been convictions. Nonetheless, the overall assessment was an improvement over an almost universal venal judiciary.

Another significant trial occurred in 1913. Whereas the prosecution of this case was one of the darkest spots on the administration of Russian justice, the response of the jury is one of the brightest.

The case arose from the perpetuation of a medieval prejudice, long before discarded in Western Europe, that Jews used Christian blood for certain rituals. Originating in the first centuries of the Christian era, this madness was the cause of innumerable persecutions, tortures, and executions. The pogroms were particularly vicious if a Christian child had been murdered. And this was the reason for the victimization of a thirty-nine-year-old Jewish father of five.[5]

On March 12, 1911, a thirteen-year-old boy, Andrei Yushchinsky of Kiev, left home for school but never arrived there. After a search of eight days, on March 20, his body was discovered in a cavern. It was covered with seventeen wounds, and had been drained of most of its blood. Since no traces of blood were found in the cavern, the examiner presumed the boy had been murdered elsewhere and brought to the cavern after the blood was drained.

At first, suspicion centered on members of the boy's own family. Andrei's deceased father had left him a considerable amount of money which, it was believed, was coveted by his mother, stepfather, and uncle. The three were arrested, but the examiners could find no evidence to support the charges, so they were released.

Continued investigation produced several other legitimate suspects, but chief prosecutor Chaplinsky ignored them, and chose Mendel Beilis because he was a Jew, to be his victim. Beilis's only connection to the case was that he was a janitor in a Jewish-owned brick factory on a plot of land adjacent to the cavern. Chaplinsky ordered investigator V. I. Fenenko to arrest Beilis, but Fenenko refused because of lack of evidence. Chaplinsky then gave him a written directive, which meant Fenenko had to obey or resign. Since resignation would mean the appointment of a Chaplinsky toady, Fenenko thought the wiser course was to make the arrest himself, which he did on August 3. In reporting the arrest he said that "the proofs against Beilis are ridiculous and absurd. I am convinced that he will be released within a few days."

What had actually happened was that Andrei at first had played hooky, going to a friend's house. There was a complex tie-in between the mother of his friend, and "a gang of dangerous criminals" who would meet at the mother's apartment. Andrei, apparently, had learned too much of what went on, and thus it seems likely that he was killed by associates of his friend's mother. Strangely also, his friend and friend's sister died suspiciously in early August of "dysentery." Although the friend's mother was tried and convicted on charges of fraud and resale of stolen goods in February of 1913, and although she accused a former lover who had beaten her of the boy's murder, Chaplinsky was determined to persecute an innocent Jew.

Beilis was indicted on January 20, 1912, after five months in prison, and he was scheduled for trial on May 17. In the meantime stories and photographs of the real criminals were published in the press of Kiev and St. Petersburg, arousing sympathy. Nonetheless Beilis was kept in jail for continued investigations, and the trial was postponed for another year. He was reindicted in the spring of 1913, charged with having "killed Yushchinky with premeditation . . . moved by motives of religious fanaticism, for ritual purposes."

Beilis's trial began on September 25, 1913, more than two years after his arrest, and continued for almost five weeks, until October 28. Despite the prosecution's most venal efforts, the evidence against Beilis was weak. Fortunately, a strong defense team consisting of five barristers had come to his aid. The Jewish community also offered support. The key, of course, was the jury. We have no details about these jurors other than that there were "seven peasants" and five "small officials" on the panel. None of the twelve is reported as being Jewish.

The defense team appreciated the pivotal role of the jurors, and appealed directly to them:

> Everything will be forgotten, everything will be forgiven but this verdict. This verdict will not be forgotten; this verdict will remain as a sentence passed by a jury on a man whom it has been tried to picture as your enemy. You are told that Jews are your enemies, that they laugh at you, that they do not consider you as human beings. Should you sentence Beilis in spite of the absence of evidence, should you sentence him for our sins, and should some people cheer at the sentence you pass, they will be sorry afterward and your verdict will remain a mournful page in the history of our justice.

The jurors were reminded that if they convicted Beilis, they would be sending him to "twenty years of forced labor" after having already spent two and a half years in prison. In closing, the chief defense counsel, N. P. Karabchevsky, told the jury:

> If till now there was a pure and holy institution which did not yield to any outside influences, it was our court, the court with jury, which we venerated, of which we are proud, and which we protected as something sacred. Gentlemen of the jury, I beseech you, keep it as such also by your verdict. May God help you.

Two questions were now posed to the jurymen. The first was whether Andrei had been killed "in such manner as to inflict upon him great suffering and to drain his body of blood." The second question was: "if the event described in the first question did occur, is Mendel Beilis guilty of having killed Andrei Yushchinsky on March 12, 1911, acting with premeditation and stimulated by religious fanaticism in agreement with other persons who remained undiscovered?"

The trial record does not state how long the jury deliberated, but it apparently was not very long. The record states only that they returned with the answers to the two questions. To the first the jury answered yes, but to the second the response was no. Beilis was acquitted. Whether this jury was unanimous was not regarded as significant enough by historians writing about the trial to record. It is a good guess that the apparent swiftness with which the verdict was reached would indicate insufficient disagreement to warrant a discussion that would delay them.

There is an important characteristic in all of these cases whether during or after Alexander's lifetime: not one of them was a direct challenge to czarist autocracy. None involved the government or could be called "political." As generous as Alexander was with his "gifts" of freedom, he would remain an autocrat. If he allowed "political crimes" to go to juries, who could know but that some of them might question his style of despotism, benevolent as it might have been? His ministers had divided opinions. Whereas the State Council refused to refer "political crimes" to juries, the State Chancellery would recommend that to use the jury in these cases "is a real guarantee of equity for the accused."[6]

The chancellery argued that to deny the right to a jury was to commit an injustice, "because in these cases the state, which prosecutes the crime, is at the same time the legal entity offended or harmed by the crime." No matter how impartial or independent were the judges appointed by the state, their decisions could never enjoy the confidence of society. Convictions by jury would have a moral power that would increase the influence of law on society.

The czar prevailed—most, but not quite all the time. In December 1876, a street demonstration broke out in the center of fashionable St. Petersburg in front of the Cathedral of Our Lady of Kazan. There was to be a double memorial service to honor not only several persons who had died in prison after being convicted in juryless trials but also Russian volunteers in a war against the Turks. The demonstrators were mostly very young men and girls, many in their teens. The leaders were two sixteen-year-olds, a boy, Potapov, and Felicia Sheftel.

Political demonstrations, as expressions of free speech, were new phenomena in Russia. The police would try to control them not directly by dispersing the crowd, but by spreading malicious, false rumors among illiterate townsfolk, inciting them to attack. When they did attack the demonstrators, the police would move in. In the demonstration before the cathedral, the police arrested thirty-two bystanders.

The czar's government, assuming that its humanitarian front would forestall revolutionary activity, was enraged. It rushed twenty-two of the demonstrators into almost immediate trials before defending lawyers had had a chance to become fully acquainted with the accusations. The victims were "tried" en masse without jury by a special court dealing with crimes against the state. Not surprisingly, all were convicted and given excessively harsh sentences for offenses no greater than exercising Alexandrian-style "freedom of speech." Potapov was exiled for five years, and Sheftel for six years and eight months.[7] Among the convicted was young Arkhip Bogolyubov, who had been only a bystander and had taken no part in the demonstration.

Mass trials were the standard. In 1877 there were two known as the Trial of the Fifty and the Trial of the 193, respectively. Both before special courts and both without juries. In each case the "crimes" were peaceful protests against government policies. The first was organized by the South-Russian Workers' Union, and was a protest against harsh working conditions, particularly for children enslaved for seventeen-hour workdays.

The one saving feature of the trial was that it was public and, therefore, many details were reported in the press. This provided a forum of which the demonstrators took full advantage by delivering long addresses to the court. Their lengthy "final words" maddened the judges who ordered them silent, but they would not be stopped. Predictably, the special court convicted, imprisoned, and exiled all fifty, but they had captured the sympathy of the people.

The government retaliated by excluding the public entirely and limiting press coverage for the trial of the 193. That trial lasted five months, with the defense growing bolder each day. Surprisingly at first, ninety of the defendants were acquitted, but eighty were rearrested by the secret police and sent into exile by "administrative directive." The remainder were convicted and received harsh sentences.

But in 1878 the defense, in what was unquestionably a "political trial," managed to obtain a trial by jury for a single defendant, twenty-eight-year-old Vera Zasulich. The fact that a jury was allowed was due to the exceptional judge who presided at the trial, Anatoly Fyodorovich Koni, who invoked certain special circumstances forcing the government to consent to a jury. Koni reported on the trial at great length in Russian. There are several English translations.[8]

Vera Zasulich was a true heroine of freedom. Born in 1849 to an upper-class family in St. Petersburg (her father having been an army officer), she had a deep sense of conscience. She had been imprisoned for several years in the early seventies for political protest, but instead of being dissuaded, she became more deeply involved. On February 6, 1878, Zasulich was one of several visitors to the offices of General Trepov, governor of St. Petersburg and a favorite of Alexander. She had come ostensibly to ask for a "certificate of conduct" to become a private tutor. While Trepov was writing, she took out an English Bulldog pistol from under her shawl, and in front of several witnesses, shot him. She did not kill Trepov, as this was not her intention, but struck him in the pelvis. Then she dropped her gun and waited, expecting to be killed or at least shot herself. Instead she was seized and beaten. She told friends later: "What surprised me was that I did not feel the slightest pain."

The shooting commanded international attention. The news was telegraphed to the *New York Times,* which carried the story the next day: "The prefect was dangerously wounded by the shots; the ball has not been extracted. The emperor and Prince Cortashakoff have visited him. The city is greatly excited. The woman, who was immediately arrested, preserves complete silence in regard to her motives." Despite her act of terrorism, Zasulich was not reviled by the public because Trepov was so unsavory a character and so unscrupulous that he was universally hated.

But it was not his unpopularity which motivated Zasulich. General Trepov controlled all the prisons and prisoners in St. Petersburg. One day in July 1877, he crossed the yard of a prison where several inmates were out on their walk. One of them was Arkhip Bogolyubov, who had been arrested at the demonstration in St. Petersburg. He was now awaiting an appeal on his sentencing (without jury) to fifteen years' hard labor in the Siberian mines. Trepov, irritable as usual, complained that Bogolyubov had failed to take off his cap when he passed. Without giving the prisoner a chance to respond, he roared to the guards: "Have him flogged." Although several years before, the "humanitarian" emperor had outlawed the flogging of prisoners, the practice did continue. The guards obeyed. While some of them held the hapless prisoner down on the whipping block, another cracked the lash. The sound of the slow, steady strokes on his naked body, heard throughout the prison, caused a riot.

The flogging was so brutal as to reduce this young innocent to a physical wreck. He became deranged, was sent to a mental hospital, and died soon afterward. Despite widespread indignation at the whippings, even in the salons of the czarina, Trepov was not censured. He was not even reprimanded. When Vera Zasulich read about it in a St. Petersburg newspaper, she was so outraged that she decided, since no one else had done anything, to deliver the reprimand in her own fashion. She cared nothing about danger to herself. She expected to be arrested, and although she would appeal for a jury, she held little hope of getting one. Trial by a military court would almost certainly mean conviction, execution, or sentencing to Siberia.

The Minister of Justice, Count Pahlen, desired speedy conviction behind closed doors. Since Zasulich's was a "political offense," this Russian form of the English "Star Chamber" would be the proper way to handle it.

However, the government feared violence. The people, from peasant to high government officer, were hostile against the mass trials of 1876 and 1877 and the severity of the sentences. There was also universal sympathy for Vera Zasulich, so that Pahlen did not dare attempt another secret trial. He rationalized that if a court could induce a properly stacked jury to convict her—and this would not be hard to do—public resentment would fall upon the jurors and take pressure off the government. He told the czar that a jury conviction would "teach a sobering lesson to the insane, small coterie of revolutionaries [who were Zasulich admirers] that the Russian people bow before the Czar and revere him."[9]

But this "small coterie" expanded quickly to cover most of the populace. Zasulich was referred to endearingly as "Verochka," or "Little Vera," or alternately "Brave Vera." Thus the government relented and granted her a jury trial. The reasons for this are described in some detail by Margaret Maxwell in *Narodniki Women*: Pahlen

> was aware of the silent resentment against the Ministry of Justice boiling beneath the smooth surface of St. Petersburg society. From the lowly man on the street to high officials in the government came whispering about the ministry's mishandling of punitive actions against hundreds of young people picked up for "political offenses"

that were peaceful in nature. Rumors were circulating, and some hard evidence had come to light of inhuman treatment by the police, the army and the jailers of these men and women, almost all of them sons and daughters of Russia's landowning and office-holding class. There was also criticism of the secret trials and the long sentences to hard labor in Siberia. Even women, in the recent trial of the 193, had been sentenced to five or more years in the mines of Kata.

Comment in St. Petersburg society and officialdom on such matters rarely got beyond the walls of private homes and a few liberal clubs, but in the tsarist autocracy, that such discussion took place at all was considered dangerous. Even more frightening, a girl had dared to shoot a government official and, to the amazement of all officials of the autocracy—and the Tsar himself—had become an instant heroine. All over Russia, but especially in St. Petersburg, people at first whispered, then began to shout, "Brave Vera" to show their approval of her attack on an old officer whose flagrantly corrupt practices, maladministration, and cruelty had earned him the hatred of the people while he had gone unreprimanded by the Tsar whose favorite he remained.

The autocracy was caught in a dilemma. For its higher purpose of absolute rule, quick, severe punishment of Zasulich was required; but to avoid what threatened to become open criticism of yet another secret trial, the Ministry of Justice decided to give her a public jury trial.[10]

The people hoped for, but still did not expect, justice from the kind of jury that would be carefully picked for Zasulich's trial. They planned a huge demonstration to follow the verdict, expecting bloody confrontation with the police.

The trial was scheduled for April 12, 1878. Several days before that, Count Pahlen invited Judge Koni, who would preside, to his office. When they were both seated comfortably in armchairs and as a servant poured tea, Pahlen began: "You know the czar is very much interested in this case. He even went to the House of Preliminary Detention to look at the prisoner. Trepov is, as I'm sure you know, a great favorite of his."

Koni listened apprehensively as the minister arrived at his point: "It is possible, is it not, dear Anatoly Fyodorovich, that as presiding judge you can guarantee a guilty verdict?"

Koni was astounded. After a painful pause he replied: "No. Never.

I cannot." Pahlen was taken aback. The Russian aristocracy usually accepted the czar's slightest wish as law, but Koni was too honest. "When a case is tried before a jury," Koni replied, "the decision on guilt or innocence is made by the jury." He told Pahlen that if the government wanted a fixed verdict, the case should be tried before a court-martial or a senate judicial committee.

"Too late, too late," Pahlen moaned, as the trial was already well publicized. The minister "clasped head to his hands and repeated over and over, 'What's to be done? What's to be done?' " The czar also pressured Koni with the suggestive "hint" that he hoped Koni would "continue to serve successfully." Pahlen, as quoted in Koni's diary,[11] added another imperative that Koni deliberately commit technical violations of the law so that if the jury should acquit, the verdict could be overturned on appeal. He "requested" Koni to formulate his jury "instructions" in such a way as to give no alternative but conviction.

What was done was that the trial began on the day scheduled in the main Criminal Court in St. Petersburg. It became a major social event, attracting women of fashion and generals in full-dress uniform whom Margaret Maxwell describes as having "more orders on their chests than hairs on their heads." There were "silk-hatted men wearing heavy, black, fitted great-coats with beaver collars," and officers of the General Staff. The crowds were so large that admission was restricted to holders of tickets.

Shortly after ten o'clock the uniformed court officials filed in, followed by members of the jury formally, if not formidably, attired "in frock coats and white ties." As to how the twelve men in the jury box were selected, Bergman reveals only that defense attorney, P. A. Alexandrov, "accepted as jurors mostly petty bureaucrats potentially sympathetic to Zasulich but, at the same time, not likely to respond favorably to any indictment of autocracy itself."[12] Maxwell describes the panel as consisting of "distinguished-looking state counselors of various ranks," including one "titled landowner, a principal of a religious school, an artist and a student."[13] Thus a relatively homogenous group, conservative in appearance.

The black-robed, stern-faced jurists then entered, led by Koni. The jurists sat at a long table facing the audience, and behind them, acting like censors, were many of the highest officials in the czar's government, including Chancellor Prince Alexander M. Gorchakov, several secretaries of state, and Field Marshall Count Barantzev in full-dress uniform. Places were reserved for several leading foreign journalists such as Sir Donald MacKenzie Wallace and the novelist Fyodor Dostoevsky. Dostoevsky, who had himself been sentenced to death by a czarist (no jury) court, had had his sentence revoked at the last moment and replaced by a term of imprisonment at hard labor. He would later use this trial as a model for the trial of Dimitrii in *The Brothers Karamazov.*

Although Koni confessed privately to believing that Zasulich should be convicted but given a light sentence, he did not express this feeling to the jury. He opened by explaining that the jurors should evaluate all the evidence impartially, and render a verdict based only on what they heard in the courtroom. He told them they had "a great responsibility before society and before the accused, whose fate lies solely in your hands."

A secretary read the formal criminal indictment accusing Zasulich of attempting to murder Trepov and planning his assassination. Asked to plead, Zasulich acknowledged that she had indeed shot Trepov, but that this was irrelevant to whether she killed him or merely wounded him. Several witnesses, including two of Trepov's aides, then testified in turn that she had shot the governor after he had complied with her request for a certificate. They agreed that after one shot she dropped the pistol, made no attempt to retrieve it for a second shot, and did not resist arrest. There was no testimony about the severe beating she had received during the interrogation following her arrest, and the need to restrain one guard from attempting to gouge out her eyes.

After their testimony, Koni addressed Zasulich: "You have been accused of a premeditated attempt to murder Governor-General Trepov. These witnesses have testified that you came to his residence posing as a petitioner, carrying a revolver, and that with the weapon you seriously injured him. Are you guilty of this crime?"

Zasulich replied calmly: "I admit that I fired one shot at him."

"Would you tell us why you committed this act? Was it your intent to kill Governor-General Trepov?"

"It was indifferent to me whether I killed or merely wounded Trepov. My motive was to punish the one who ordered a prisoner named Bogolyubov whipped with birch branches in the St. Petersburg House of Preliminary Detention. If he had not done that, I would not have shot him."

"How did you know about the whipping?"

"I read the St. Petersburg newspaper. I came across a small item about the beating of a prisoner on the order of Trepov because that prisoner had failed to take off his cap."

"Did you know the prisoner?"

"He is completely unknown to me."

Zasulich testified that she had expected a great public outcry over the flogging, but was disillusioned to find nothing but "indifference." Only a highly dramatic act such as an assassination could rouse the Russian people.

"I didn't find, I couldn't find any other means to direct attention to this event," she said. "I didn't see any other means. . . . It is terrible to raise one's hand against one's fellow man, but I decided this was what I had to do."[14] She testified that she hoped her example would preclude further atrocities, and that she was not so much seeking revenge as trying to elevate the moral consciousness of the nation.

The prosecutor, K. I. Kessel, presented to the jury several arguments which may appear cogent and logical under an honest judicial system, but tend to irony against the background of the mass trials immediately preceding. No matter how reprehensible Trepov's action might have been, he told the jury, Zasulich's response was a crime because she had taken upon herself the roles of court, judge, prosecutor, jury, and even executioner in carrying out the sentence.

"I do not think for one minute that you will disagree that every public figure, whoever he may be, has a right to a legal trial and not a trial by Zasulich . . . however they acted," he argued self-righteously. "Did she have the right to impose justice herself? I do not believe, gentlemen of the jury, that you can excuse such conduct. Vera Zasulich is guilty of murder. It is the inviolability of human life I defend in calling for a guilty verdict."

The spectators stared at him in glacial silence. The jurors sat stone-faced. Vera bowed her head, understanding the legal rationale of Kessel's presentation.

Zasulich's own lawyer, Alexandrov, then brought in three prisoners who had been in the detention prison the previous July when the Bogolyubov whipping took place. The prosecution objected to their testifying, but Alexandrov declared it was essential for the jury to have the full picture of the graphic sadism of the whipping in order to feel Zasulich's emotional reaction.

Maxwell adds:

Two wan, pale men and a young woman appeared. They had been brought in directly from one of Russia's grimmest prisons, the Peter Paul Fortress. They told in thin voices, trembling with tears and indignation, their stories of Trepov's cruelty.[15]

When Koni asked Zasulich if she had a statement to make, she spoke at length. She had heard that Bogolyubov had received not just the usual twenty-five lashes, but had been whipped until half-dead.

> I happen to know well the horror imprisonment can inspire—not to mention what happens to those who have been whipped, maltreated, placed in dungeons. I also know well the hardness of the heart, the barbarity of those who inflict such tortures not as punishment, but as viciousness, as an outpouring of personal vengeance. It seems to me such things should not pass unnoticed by the public.
>
> I searched for but could not find any other means [to alert the public]. Even now I do not see any other means. So I resolved at the price of my own life to show society and to those in authority that no one can be sure of doing whatever he likes with impunity; that no one can be allowed to carry his contempt for human dignity to such lengths.

Zasulich became so choked with emotion she could hardly continue. She had expressed herself so effectively as to cause one highborn lady in the audience to weep: "I felt I was guilty." A foreign journalist seconded this emotion: "I felt it was not she who was being judged, but me, all of us—society."

Koni continued to ask several more questions of Zasulich, and then turned the case over to Kessel for his summation. Kessel rose slowly to his feet and began to speak in a voice so low-pitched it was hard to hear him. Maxwell describes Kessel as being so nervous that he had to take repeated sips of water and looking as if he were about to faint. He went over the case purely on criminal grounds, reviewing the evidence and the confession to show that she had committed an act of premeditated attempted murder; that it did not succeed was due to accident and not to any precautions taken by her.

> What Trepov did or did not do is not the question at issue here. Everyone has his or her own sentiments, sympathies, antipathies. But when these sentiments are transformed into acts that violate the

law, with the intent to kill, justice demands punishment. Did she have the right to impose justice herself? Could she act as prosecutor, defender and judge? I do not believe, gentlemen of the jury, that you can excuse such conduct. If any official is guilty, he in answerable to the courts, has the right to the justice of the law, and cannot be exposed to the summary justice of an individual outside the law.

Vera Zasulich is guilty of murder!

Alexandrov then began his rebuttal, starting off quietly, his voice building in resonance and strength. He acknowledged that, in legal terms, what Zasulich had done was a crime.

Who dreams of denying that to take justice into your own hands is a crime? This is an incontestable verity. But justice is not ordinarily served by examining only the crime itself. It is necessary to consider and weigh the motives.

He described his client's own years in prison: how she had been arrested on suspicion only, confined in Peter Paul Fortress without trial, held in solitary confinement for one year without a shred of evidence against her. He pictured her life of idleness within the grim walls without contact with any members of her family or friends, consoled only by prisoners to the right and left of her confined in the same manner, with whom she could communicate only by tapping on the walls.

After two years Zasulich was released, but within a few days a police officer came to the house where she was staying to rearrest her on a made-up charge. She protested that she was innocent, that no evidence had been found to incriminate her, but it was no use. Once again without trial, let alone a jury, she was back in prison.

One night Zasulich was put in a horse-drawn police carriage and taken three hundred miles west of Moscow to a town called Kresty. Police there told her that while she was not a prisoner, she could not leave the town. She had to report to the police bureau every Saturday. Then she was taken to the door and turned out onto the street, homeless. She had two rubles in her pocket and somehow a box of French chocolates under her arm. She knew nobody.

By good fortune Zasulich met a sympathetic family who took her in and cared for her for a few months. Just as she was becoming comfortable, the police seized her again and sent her to another unfamiliar town under the same conditions and restrictions. She was not allowed to remain there for more than a few more weeks when she was moved for a third time and then a fourth, compelled to live as a wandering exile far from her family. Her harassment continued for more than a year, until one day she just walked away and went to a sister near Moscow. The police did not follow her. She was at last left alone. She was living with her sister helping to care for her children when she read the newspaper item about Bogolyubov.

Alexandrov's oratory moved the audience and jurors to tears. The courtroom burst into applause. How empty and unconvincing seemed Kessel's plea for justice for Trepov in the face of Vera's years of suffering with no opportunity to defend herself anywhere!

Alexandrov then directed attention to Zasulich's warm compassion for Bogolyubov after she had returned to St. Petersburg and learned about his suffering and torture. She searched for someone or some authority who would stand up for the honor of defenseless political prisoners. She had hoped for intercession by the press, but the press remained silent. She hoped for a great public outcry, but public opinion did not venture beyond the seclusion of study rooms, intimate circles, and shocked but hushed private conversations.

Zasulich looked for the possibility that lawyers and judges would speak out, but all were too intimidated to do more than grumble in silence. As the months passed, she found that nothing would ever be done to prevent Trepov, untouched by censure, or any other official from repeating the atrocity. Her conscience would give her no peace. She relived her own years in prison when nobody had come to her aid. Finally she realized that nobody would take any action here either, unless it was she herself. And if she did, her action would have to be bold and highly dramatic. The only hope for redress, the only way to attract public attention would be to sacrifice herself, if it meant her life. Alexandrov quoted Zasulich's sentiments:

> Everyone is silent. A shout is needed. I myself can do that! I have enough breath in my body for a loud shout and force people to listen. When I commit a crime the silenced question about the disgrace of Bogolyubov's punishment will be forced into the open. My crime will provoke a public trial, and Russia, in the person of her people's representatives—the jury—will be compelled to pronounce a ver-

dict, and the verdict will not be on me alone. Europe will be looking on, that Europe which likes to call us a barbarian state in which the knout serves as the main attribute of government.

Since public attention was Vera's chief aim, it did not matter whether she killed Trepov or simply injured him. That is why she did not shoot a second time. What she wanted was her day in court in a public trial where she could speak out about Bogolyubov and prison treatment generally. And in this she was succeeding extremely well, as her present trial and the international attention it was attracting had proven. Alexandrov described her emotions:

> It is not to bargain over this or that extenuation of her guilt that she is here today, gentlemen of the jury. She was and she remains the selfless slave of her idea, in the name of which she raised the bloody hand. She came in order to submit to you all the burden of her aggrieved soul, to open before you the sorrowful page of her life, to relate honestly all that she has endured, thought, and felt, all that moved her to commit a crime, and she has exposed her aim and what she expected from it.

He told the jury that this was the first time a jury in Russia was being asked to judge a woman who had committed a crime for principle. But it was not the first time "in the court of the people's conscience" where a jury was asked to pass sentence on a woman accused of attempted murder as a result of oppressive suffering and physical abuse. Alexandrov was introducing to the jury their ultimate power of "jury nullification"—their power to review the law or laws related to the case, and to reject or "nullify" those they determined to be bad law. Any lawyer daring to suggest such a power to the jury risks severe judicial censure. Alexandrov continued:

> Women have appeared here who have avenged their seducers by killing them. These women left this place acquitted. Their verdicts were just, an echo of divine justice, which takes into consideration not only the external side of an action, but its inner meaning as well. These women fought for and avenged themselves. But for the first time there appears a woman who had no personal interest in her crime, who linked her crime with the fight for an idea, for the sake of a man who was for her no more than a companion of distress.

Alexandrov concluded his passionate presentation by emphasizing the strategic role of the jury:

> If for the general welfare, if for the sake of public safety she must be punished, then let your chastising justice take place. She may go out of here judged guilty, but she will not go out disgraced, and her wish will remain that there be no future repetition of the causes that will evoke acts like hers.

Zasulich's defender had struck a sympathetic chord; the audience broke into a thunderous applause. Literally "there was not a dry eye in the house." When the room had quieted down, Judge Koni turned to the defendant: "To you belongs the last word. What do you have to say?" She replied: "I have nothing to say."

Koni then began his "instructions" to the jury. Again, taking care not to reveal his sentiments, he reviewed the evidence. What the jury had to decide, he said, was whether Vera had intended to murder Trepov. He defined for the jurors the legal definitions of "premeditation," "revenge," and "culpability."

He edged the jurors toward conviction by "instructing" that Zasulich's "agitation" was irrelevant to premeditation; that since she had had time to reflect before committing the crime, the shooting should be considered as premeditated. However, he softened this interpretation by suggesting that motives and character could properly be taken into consideration. He concluded by reminding the jurors that his words were meant "only as advice" and that, in the end, "only the voice of your conscience" should determine the verdict. In effect, by advising the jurors to be guided by conscience, Koni was giving judicial endorsement to Alexandrov's muted suggestion of the power to nullify.

Koni handed the foreman a paper on which he had written three questions for the jurors to answer: (1) Is Vera Zasulich guilty of shooting General Trepov with a large-caliber gun? (2) In firing this shot, was she guilty of an attempt to kill him? and (3) If she did intend to kill him, did she with premeditation take all measures to achieve her aim? And, if he did not die, was it due to circumstances and not her will?

The judge sent the twelve jurymen into the jury room with a parting caveat: "Gentlemen of the jury, in reaching your decision, examine coldly the arguments of the accusation and the defense."

When the jurors were led away by bailiffs, Koni called a recess, but the audience refused to leave their seats. Despite Alexandrov's brilliant oratory, virtually every spectator, including Koni, knew that conviction was inevitable. Koni went into his chambers and gazed out the window. He was astounded at the size of the crowds gathered on Liteiny Prospekt and Shpalernaya Street. Many were young people wearing wide hats, high boots and plaid shawls, and all were in a high emotional state. Police ringing the crowd were on the alert against demonstrations that would break out upon a verdict of guilty.

It was now seven o'clock in the evening. Court had been in session since 10:00 A.M. without a meal break or any relief for the jurors. After only ten minutes, the jury foreman rang a bell to signify they had reached a verdict. Koni walked back into the courtroom. The jurymen followed, staying close together to seek each other's support against public reaction to the great pronouncement they would were about to make. The jurors were expressionless, white-faced, apprehensive. The foreman, his hand trembling, handed the judge the sheet of paper he had given them. Koni read it to himself and, poker-faced, handed the paper back to the foreman and asked him to read it aloud.

This routine served only to intensify the anxiety in the courtroom. There was a deathly silence. Every spectator held his breath; hearts stopped beating. Only Vera was emotionless, her eyes riveted on a distant point in the ceiling.

The foreman, holding the paper, read hesitantly the first question: "Is Vera Zasulich guilty of shooting General Trepov with a large-caliber gun?" He paused. "No. Not Guil————!" He got no further. The room burst into ear-splitting applause, pandemonium. According to one observer in the courtroom:

> It is impossible for one who was not present to imagine the outburst of sounds that drowned out the foreman's voice and the movement like an electric shock shot through the entire room. The cries of unrestrained joy, hysterical sobbing, desperate applause, the tread of feet, cries of "Bravo! Hurrah! Good girl! Vera! Verochka! Verochka!" merged in one roar both moan and howl. Many crossed themselves; upper, more democratic sections for the public people embraced; even in the places reserved for the judges there was enthusiastic applause.[16]

The foreman never did get to answer the other two questions. Among those applauding were many high officials, including the foreign minister, Prince Gorchakov. Dostoevsky remarked that "punishment of this girl would have been inappropriate and superfluous."

The great joy in the courtroom was shared by the dignified high officials of the government who clapped and "hallooed" without restraint, the most enthusiastic of all being the Chancellor Prince Gorchakov. Red-faced, bemedaled Field Marshall Barantzev was yelling and clapping excitedly. But Koni was apprehensive. Did they not realize the full impact of this verdict? Could they not understand the meaning of these jurors of low rank turning the trial into an indictment of the entire czarist government itself?

Heedless, these high-ranking spectators hoisted Alexandrov on their shoulders and carried him out of the building. Above the din Koni tried to tell Zasulich she was free to go, but she was already being carried out.

The enthusiasm spread to the crowds on the streets outside who broke into high-spirited tumult; Koni, fearing that restraint would increase the boisterousness of the demonstrations, ordered the bailiffs not to interfere; but the officers were taking part in the wild rejoicing themselves, and probably would not have restrained the crowd anyway. But Vera Zasulich was disappointed. She had so conditioned herself to a guilty verdict that she was stunned. Later she said she was numb. She had expected to have lost her freedom permanently, and now that the jury had given it back to her she knew not how to handle it.

Her supporters knew. They hoisted her on their shoulders so all could see and cheer her. They marched through the streets to cries of "Long live Zasulich . . . Verushka" and others. She was borne to a carriage surrounded by sympathizers when police rushed up. They said they wanted to transfer her to another carriage, but her followers were suspicious. They did not know at the time, although they suspected, that their great "czar of freedom," fearing the possibility of an independent-minded jury, had prepared an order in advance for Zasulich's rearrest in the event she was acquitted. Count Pahlen and his underlings were standing by to execute it.

Alexander had reserved for himself a proceeding known as "by administrative decree," which meant seizure without warrant. It permitted arrests despite jury acquittals, turning the police into a kind of court of last resort with power to break any verdict or sentence.[17] However, Zasulich's friends closed in around her. Three rifle shots rang out, and two people fell injured, one slightly, the second fatally. The third bullet hit a gendarme. It was discovered later that all three shots were fired from a pistol carried by the man who had been killed, a medical student. The supposition was that the student, fearing the police were about to seize Vera, took out his pistol to protect her, and thought that his first shot had killed another supporter. Struck with remorse, he turned the gun on himself. The student was immediately revered as a revolutionary martyr.

The heroine of the anti-czarist movement was whisked away to prevent rearrest, and kept in hiding. After several weeks she was taken to Switzerland, where she lived for some years. She returned to the Soviet Union decades later as a heroine of the revolution of 1917.

As for the jurors, they were forgotten as soon as they had completed their extraordinarily courageous action. The possibility of czarist retaliation against them was very real. Yet, judging by their swift action, they had not concerned themselves with it. And no one seemed to have thought to question them. Apparently there was no disagreement between the jurors, for they barely had time to take but one vote, and that unanimous. The crowd and historians alike disregarded their bravery and resistance to intimidation. They had stood on principle and conscience; and by doing so they frustrated one of the world's most powerful tyrants, even threatening to topple him, as the jury had done to James II two centuries earlier. In only ten principled minutes! These twelve true heroes faded into obscurity. Their names are not recorded for us to honor.

But they had done their damage to prove again the awesome power a jury holds. While one spectator told Koni: "This is the happiest day of my life," Koni replied: "It might yet turn out to be a fatal day."[18]

And he was right on two counts. First, Koni was blamed by the czar and his ministers as a "culprit" for "permitting" the acquittal. Some said he should have knocked over his inkwell to blot out the jury's written answer. Koni and two other judges were ordered to appear before the senate, where they were severely reprimanded without a chance to defend themselves. It was suggested that Koni be put on trial himself—but under what charge?

Koni was forced to resign his chair at the law school, and Alexander pressured him to resign his judgeship. However, by one of the czar's own laws, Alexander could not remove him. In an 1864 outburst of benignity, he had made judges immune from czarist retaliation, and Koni remained on the bench for three more years, despite the czar's hostility and malicious intrigues against him. Many high officials who had initially rejoiced at the verdict became so fearful of royal vengeance, that to cover themselves they ostracized Koni. A lesser man might have broken, but Koni persevered. As time dimmed the memory, he eventually became procurator, senator, and a member of the state council.

The second fatality resulting from the verdict was due to the jurors' courage which, if not fatal to them, was nearly fatal to the institution. Because this grand bulwark of all liberty had been so flimsily based on the czar's "pleasure" and not, as in England or the United States, inherently or at least constitutionally grounded, Alexander needed to do no more than take back his "gift." This he did almost immediately—but he had to compromise. The jury as a whole had become so strongly entrenched in only a decade and a half, that he dared not go further than restrict its use from "political crimes" and "crimes of the press." He did not dare prohibit juries for such "minor" offenses as murder, rape, arson, and even offenses against the state religion— that is, crimes that were not challenges against czarist autocracy. Throughout the reigns of the last two czars, Alexander III and Nicholas II (Alexander's son and grandson, respectively), juries continued to operate, not being completely abolished until the revolution of 1917.

But Alexander II did not escape unscathed. Trial by jury had become so cherished by the people that resentment ran very high. On March 13, 1881, after several unsuccessful attempts on his life, he was blown to bits by a bomb thrown at his carriage. The assassins and their defenders tried to gain a jury trial, but the new czar, more autocratic than his father, would not permit it. They were thus tried militarily, and (need I add) convicted and put to death.

We can only conjecture the fate of Alexander III and all of czarism had the assassins been tried by a jury of independent spirit.

Indeed, Leroy-Beaulieu observed in his classic study that if the reform laws of 1864 had been strictly enforced, "autocracy would no longer be whole and sound."[19]

NOTES

1. Anatole LeRoy-Beaulieu, *Empire of the Tsars and the Russians* (New York: G. P. Putnam's Sons, 1903), p. 349.

2. Samuel Kucherov, *Courts, Lawyers and Trials under the Last Three Tsars* (New York: Frederick A. Praeger, 1953), p. 81.

3. Ibid., p. 65.

4. Maurice Baring, *Mainsprings of Russia* (Edinburgh: Thomas Nelson and Sons, 1914), pp. 282 ff.

5. LeRoy-Beaulieu, *Empire of the Tsars and the Russians,* pp. 341ff.

6. Kucherov, *The Last Three Tsars,* p. 64.

7. Vera Broido, *Apostles into Terrorists* (New York: The Viking Press, 1977), pp. 127ff.

8. Margaret Maxwell draws a detailed picture of this trial in her book *Narodniki Women* (New York: Pergamon Press, 1990), especially chapter 1: "Vera Zasulich: The Victory of Conscience over Force." "Narodniki" refers to "Russian women who sacrificed themselves to the dream of freedom." See also Jay Bergman, *Vera Zasulich* (Stanford, Calif.: Stanford University Press, 1983). Details in these two works are corroborated by Broido, *Apostles into Terrorists,* and elsewhere.

9. Bergman, *Vera Zasulich,* p. 40.

10. Maxwell, *Narodniki Women,* pp. 8–9.

11. In Bergman, *Vera Zasulich,* p. 41.

12. Ibid., p. 43.

13. Maxwell, *Narodniki Women,* p. 6.

14. Bergman, *Vera Zasulich,* p. 46.

15. Maxwell, *Narodniki Women,* p. 10.

16. Bergman, *Vera Zasulich,* p. 50.

17. LeRoy-Beaulieu, *Empire of the Tsars and the Russians,* p. 367.

18. Broido, *Apostles into Terrorists,* p. 151.

19. LeRoy-Beaulieu, *Empire of the Tsars and the Russians,* p. 366.

Part 2

THE JURY RESPONDS TO PUBLIC HYSTERIA

4

PRACTITIONERS OF THE DETESTABLE ARTS

*N*ineteen practitioners of the "detestable arts called witchcraft and sorceries" were strung up on Gallows Hill in Salem, Massachusetts, during the mad, mad summer of 1692—fourteen women and five men. One woman was hanged in June, five at one time on July 19, one in August, and twelve in September, plus Giles Corey, pressed under heavy weights because he refused to submit to trial. And then no more. All but Corey—"only" nineteen—had been sent to their deaths by trial juries.

We might expect prejudice from judges or boards of inquisitors or the likes of Cotton or Increase Mather; but how could jurors, presumably the grand defenders of liberty, condemn victims of hysteria on the basis of what we, of superior wisdom, know was insupportable, insubstantial evidence?

Standing as we do today at the very apex of civilization, operating entirely by logic, sanity, and rational thought, we righteously sneer at the narrow-thinking of forebears of three centuries ago. We are appalled, shocked, astounded, sickened by people cowering before apparitions, specters, ghosts, and devils directed against a few nice old ladies. Two or three of them might have been a little daft but harmless; several were not so old, five were men; there was even a four-year-old girl who had to be carried into the court for her hearing (she escaped conviction and hanging, but her mother did not) and one dog!

When we appraise historical events, to be fair to our ancestors we must reject the wisdom that accompanies hindsight and sophistication. We must make assessments in the context of the time and the social forces then in existence. I have used the term "only" advisedly. It is not that the slaughtering of nineteen persons is to be passed over lightly. Our obligation is to view what happened in the framework of the time, confident that our twenty-third-century descendants, rather than sneer at us, will judge our transgressions (if they can find any) by twentieth-century standards.

Belief in supernatural evil in one form or another is as ancient as human society. For most of the two centuries preceding Salem, witches were hunted, tried, burned, or hanged throughout Europe. The highest-ranking persons preached against the evil, and it was proscribed in England by the monarchs Henry VII and VIII, Elizabeth I, James I and II, and many others. The opening of *Macbeth* is a witch scene, and elsewhere in his historical plays, Shakespeare brings in ghosts and apparitions.

The Puritan religion, dominant in Salem at the time, was enamored of the Old Testament, which contains in Exodus 18:22 the ominous injunction: "Thou shalt not suffer a witch to live," without defining what a witch was. Apprehension about witches was a general character of the sixteenth and seventeenth centuries. As Chadwick Hansen observes in this regard, the least educated "shared the feelings and beliefs of the best hearts and wisest heads. . . ."[1]

Witchcraft, according to Hansen, can be explained through "psychogenic rather than occult means"; the mental images become very real, capable of "producing hysterical symptoms as a result of the victim's fear, and sometimes, when fear was succeeded by a profound sense of hopelessness, even producing death."[2]

"The behavior of the afflicted persons was not fraudulent but pathological. They were hysterics . . . not merely overly excited [but] mentally ill." The public excitement was caused by "popular fear." Given the nature of paranoia, perhaps it was inevitable that people would be persecuted. Witchcraft has a "genuine power in a society that believes in it," Hansen concludes.[3] Whatever may be the proper explanation, it is outside the realm of this study to analyze the psychology of witchcraft as much as to observe the response of jurors. As is characteristic of juries, they were ahead of their time. This becomes clear by comparing the action of juries with the concurrent Spanish and Portuguese inquisitions.

By 1692, the inquisitions were an even two centuries old, originated by the same Queen Isabella who had financed Columbus not so much, perhaps, by selling her jewels as by plundering the Jews in her kingdom. This holocaust, which dispatched millions, was likewise based largely on superstition, and would continue for more than a century. In Salem there were "only" nineteen convictions in a period of less than four months, with a reprise and no convictions in 1693. Why the difference? The prosecutions on the Iberian peninsula were held before single, rapacious inquisitors or boards of inquisition. Jury trials were as remote and unknown as the distant Betelgeuse. The Salem trials were all by juries.

The Salem madness began early in 1692, when several girls developed convulsive episodes "so grotesque and violent that they could not be acting, as a well person could not screw her body into." The Reverend Deodat Lawson observed that the violence was "preternatural, being much beyond the ordinary force of the same persons when they are in their right minds." The girls were tormented by hallucinations; they saw specters, felt themselves pinched and bitten, and often there were actual marks on their skin.[4]

That two of the girls, Elizabeth Parris and Abigail Williams, were a daughter and a niece of the distinguished Reverend Samuel Parris made the panic seem plausible. A third girl was the overwrought Mercy Lewis, who was "hurt, tortured, afflicted, wasted and tormented." After several doctors examined them, Dr. William Griggs pronounced that "the evil hand is upon them." And so the witch-hunt began.

The prime characteristic of a witch-hunt, especially if the hunted are innocent, is to suppress or ignore all evidence contrary to its objective. All that was necessary to accuse was to point the finger, and over the next few months not only did the girls point at several, but the number of afflicted became epidemic and pointing became indiscriminate. Everybody wanted to get into the act, until the only defense against becoming an accused was to be an accuser. By the end of May, the crude prisons not only in Salem but Ipswich, Boston, and Cambridge were crowded.

To protest innocence only aggravated one's situation; high standing in the community was no protection. Captain John Alden, the seventy-year-old namesake son of him whom Priscilla admonished to speak for himself, was victimized despite decades of maritime service.

He was charged and imprisoned in Boston, but managed to escape trial until the fever had passed.[5]

Bridget Bishop, however, was not so fortunate. She became the first victim brought to trial before a special court created for the purpose. The court was unquestionably illegal. It had been set up in May by the just-arrived royal governor of the colony, Sir William Phipps, who was a firm believer in witchcraft. Since the jails were full, and there was no provision for trials, Phipps felt impelled to take action of some kind. As governor, he had no power to create a judicial commission, but he did it anyway. He appointed eight justices, headed by sixty-one-year-old William Stoughton. Upham assesses this court: "In a free republican government, the executive department ought never to attempt to dispose of difficult matters of vital importance without the joint deliberations and responsibility of the representatives of the people."[6]

"Goodwife" Bishop was a relatively easy first mark. Widowed, remarried, and elderly, she had a reputation for cantankerousness. She had a violent temper, was on poor terms with her neighbors, and long had a reputation of "witchlike" behavior.[7] About the only accouterment she did not possess was a broom. She had been indicted on April 19, forced to suffer the indignity of examination in the nude by "a jury of women" who found a "preternatural tet" upon her body. That the "tet" had disappeared upon reexamination a few hours later only increased suspicion. Bishop tried to explain the reason for this, but was harassed, and became confused and disconcerted from the intensity of prejudice against her. She contradicted her testimony.

She was brought to trial on June 2 before a jury this time consisting of twelve men. Who the jurors were or how they were chosen is not in the record, except we know that only members of the official Puritan church were permitted to serve. The jury base was kept so narrow deliberately to ensure unsympathetic panels. Both Cotton Mather and his father, Increase, testified against her.

Several witnesses alleged that Bishop had "hexed and tormented" them, using "spectral" evidence, wild in imagination. For example, Deliverance Hobbs testified that "the shape of the prisoner [Bishop] whipped me with iron rods . . . was now tormenting me. . . ." Witness John Cook complained that some "five or six years ago I was assaulted in my chamber by the shape of this prisoner [who] very much hurt me with a blow on the side of the head."

Samuel Gray was assaulted by the Bishop specter "about fourteen years ago," although he did not know her then; "but when I saw her after this I knew by her countenance and apparel that it was the apparition of this Bishop." That there was no Bridget Bishop at that time, she then being Bridget Oliver, escaped judicial logic. John Bly accused her specter of afflicting his sow "with strange fits, knocking her head against the fence." Whenever Bishop tried to refute a charge, her accusers writhed from new assaults by her specter, which they alone could see. Yet after recovering from their spasms, they remained "hale and hearty, robust and lusty." Against these incongruities Judge Stoughton "instructed the jury" that they were "not to mind," but were to consider only "whether the said afflicted did not suffer from the accused such afflictions as naturally tended to their being pined and consumed, wasted, etc. This is a pining and consuming in the sense of the law."[8]

What defense can be offered against one's out-of-control, misbehaving, misanthropic specter?

Thus entrapped by hers, the luckless "Goodwife" was provided with no defense counsel, nor given meaningful opportunity to speak in her own behalf. Even if she could have spoken it would have helped her little, considering her state of confusion, and that after weeks of prison abuse and poor sanitation, she appeared unwashed, eerily ghostlike. Open and shut! Can we fault this first jury for accepting "spectral evidence" and pronouncing her guilty? Although she maintained innocence to the end, she was hustled off eight days later to inaugurate the macabre rites which gave Gallows Hill its chilling epithet.

After Bishop had been dispatched, the members of the court suffered a pang of conscience and took a recess. Someone pointed out that there was no law in the colony against witchcraft, let alone as a capital offense. There had been a statute of James I which either was or was not in force. A bit of research dug up an old colony law with little meaning, but good enough for the rabid authorities. Nevertheless, "witches" were still being accused, examined, and stashed into already overcrowded cells.

The real cause for delaying further trials was carefully kept from the public: the judges were in disagreement about procedure and the interpretation of spectral evidence. At least one, probably Nathan Saltonstall, observed that had spectral evidence been excluded from Bishop's trial, she would have been convicted of no greater offense than "wearing scarlet, countenancing 'shuffleboard,' and getting herself talked about. . . ."⁹ In any event, Saltonstall resigned because he was "very much dissatisfied with the proceedings."¹⁰

With Saltonstall gone, the seven remaining judges were then able to resolve their outcroppings of conscience and reconvened on June 28. Between that date and the 30th, five women were brought before juries which were drawn, as Bishop's had been, from members of the official church. The pattern for each trial was similar. First there was the "Warrant for Jurors: To the Sheriff of the County of Essex: You are Required In their Majesties Name to Impanel and return—Forty good and lawful men of the freeholders and other Freemen of your Bailiwick duly qualified to Serve on the Jury of Tryals of life and death, at the next Session of their Majesties Special Court of Oyer and Terminer, in Salem," followed by the respective dates and signed by presiding judge William Stoughton.¹¹

Details of how each group of forty was reduced to twelve were not preserved, nor how many jurors may have served on more than one case. Second, the indictments were read. For example, the charge against Sarah Good was that she

> on the Second day of May in the fourth year of the Reigne of our Sovereigne Lord and Lady William and Mary . . . and Divers other Days and times as well as before and after, certaine Detestable arts called Witchcrafts and Sorceries, Wickedly and feloniously hath used, Practiced and Exorcised . . . upon and against one Sarah Vibber, by which said wicked Arts, the said Sarah Vibber . . . was and is Tortured Afflicted, Pined, Consumed, wasted and Tormented. . . .¹²

As with Bridget Bishop, a parade of accusers appeared before each jury in turn, conjuring up apparitions and specters. Each defendant, for the most part appearing wasted and tormented herself after many weeks' imprisonment, might then be examined by the judges assuming the roles of prosecutors. A portion of Sarah Good's drawn-out (and tedious) inquisition can stand for all:

"Why doe you hurt these children?"

"I doe not hurt them, I scorn it."

"Who do you imploy then to doe it?"

"I imploy no body."

"What creature do you imploy then?"

"No creature but I am falsely accused."

"Have you made no contract with the devil?"

"No."[13]

The accusing children were directed to look upon Sarah, and they said that she was one of the persons who tormented them; then they threw themselves to the floor, writhing and screaming.

"Sarah Good do you not see now what you have done? Why doe you not tell the truth; why doe you thus torment these poor children?"

"I do not torment them."

"Who do you imploy then?" and the questioning went around again. No defendant ever was provided with counsel or assistance, and in this manner they were condemned by the respective juries—Sarah Good, Sarah Wildes, Elizabeth How, and Susanna Martin, all between June 28 and 30.

One of the witnesses against Goodwife Good was her own four-year-old daughter Dorcas, who alternately was charged as a witch herself. Dorcas, however, escaped trial and execution.

Sarah Good fought back with vigor to the end. She charged the court with making her a victim, having herself been "oppressed, outraged, trampled upon, and about to be murdered." Brought to Gallows Hill on July 19 for a mass hanging, she cursed her persecutors: "I am no more a witch than you are a wizard, and if you take away my life, God will give you blood to drink!"

Her prophecy came true. Her chief persecutor died several years later of internal hemorrhaging, bleeding profusely at the mouth.[14]

But the fifth trial in this series (there are discrepancies as to the order in which they were held) was of a vastly different character and the most significant of all nineteen. That Rebecca Nurse, then seventy-one, was charged at all must be because her accusers' hysteria was overpowering and the judges bloodthirsty. She was matriarch of a large and prominent family who owned substantial farm land. At the time of her trial she had eight children and several grandchildren. She was a member of the church, considered "intelligent, pious, devout and a veritable 'mother in Israel' " with a reputation for gentleness.[15]

A smoldering resentment over the ownership of the Nurse farm may have provoked an accusation as vague as a "vehement suspicion of having committed sundry acts of witchcraft" against Mrs. Ann Putnam, her daughter, and Abigail Williams. A warrant was issued on March 23; Mrs. Nurse was examined the next day when the younger

Ann and Abigail cried out that she had hurt them. Nurse responded that she had "never afflicted no child, never in my life," which did nothing to influence her rabid examiners, in view of the children writhing on the floor. She was jailed and indicted on four counts. To defend her, thirty-nine lifelong friends submitted to the court a testimonial to her innocence, but Stoughton and his judicial confederates ignored it. Two days before her trial, Mrs. Nurse was subjected to the indignity of being stripped by a covey of women who inspected every crevice of her body for telltale witchcraft marks. Because of her age, Nurse's skin was naturally wrinkled, which all but one of this misnamed "jury" interpreted as marks of the devil.

Goodwife Nurse pleaded with the court to understand that her disfigurements were due to natural causes, but the examiners succumbed to pre-adolescent hysterics. Mary Walcott and Abigail charged her, or her apparition, with having committed several murders. The child Mercy Lewis was sent for and, upon entering the room, was struck dumb and fell into a trance. Upon recovery she swore that she had seen the specter of Goody Nurse holding the head of a sick man.

There followed a string of depositions from accusers much in the vein of earlier trials. The elder Ann Putnam testified that the apparition of Rebecca Nurse told her she had killed her next-door neighbor, Benjamin Houlton, and several others. Houlton's widow, Sarah, then testified that Goody Nurse had "railed at him and scolded a great while" because several Houlton pigs had come through a broken portion of a fence separating their properties and was damaging the Nurse farm. That her "railing" at having her property destroyed may have been a natural reaction was not considered by the judges.

A few days afterward, Benjamin "was taken with a strange fit, struck blind and stricken down two or three times." After a few weeks of suffering "he was again most violently seized upon with violent fits, til the next night [when] he departed this life by a cruel death."[16]

The jurors, after receiving biased instructions from Stoughton, were given the case and sent out. However, they did not come back quite as soon as had earlier juries. When they did return and Stoughton asked for their verdict, the foreman, Thomas Fisk, stood up and astounded the crowded courtroom by saying: "Not guilty."

Immediately all the accusers present "cried out with renewed vigor and were taken in the most violent fits, rolling and tumbling about, creating a scene of the wildest confusion."[17] The judges panicked. They feared that an acquittal at this point, when there had been so few convictions and only a single hanging, would make prosecutions more difficult. If there were to be a second acquittal, the trials most certainly would come to an end. Some persons expected the judges to put Nurse in jeopardy again with another indictment, but the chief justice found a better escape. During the trial, Deliverance Hobbs, who had been pressured into confessing she was a "witch," had been brought in to testify against Nurse. When Nurse saw Hobbs, Nurse asked: "What, do you bring her? She is one of us."

Stoughton reminded the jurors of this, and told them they had not carefully considered that by linking the confessed witch Hobbs with herself, Nurse was in effect making a confession. All the while the pining, consuming, screaming, and the "hideous outcry" continued, causing the jurors likewise to panic. Subjected to such heavy censure, the intimidated jurors begged to be allowed to reconsider, and the judges were only too eager to let them defy unvarying, ancient precedent.

After many minutes the jurors returned, troubled. They wanted to ask Rebecca a question. What did she mean by "She is one of us"? Rebecca did not reply. They asked her again, they waited, but she remained silent. Then the jury retired and returned a third time. Fisk rose to impeach the verdict and pronounce her "guilty." He explained later that the jury interpreted her silence as confession.

Rebecca's relatives crowded around her to ask her why she did not answer? and Rebecca asked them in turn: "Answer what?" This gentle woman was hard of hearing and had not heard the jurors' question. When the question was explained to her she said that what she meant was that Hobbs was, like she, one of the accused. Her supporters told this to Stoughton, but he snubbed them. Rebecca made a statement:

> I intended no otherwise than as they were prisoners with us, and therefore did then, and yet do judge them not legal evidence against their fellow prisoners; and I being something hard of hearing and full of grief, none informing me how the court took up my words, and therefore had not opportunity to declare what I intended when I said they were of our company.

Stoughton would not tolerate the impeachment of an impeachment. But the jurors were conscience stricken. Fisk declared a few days later that they had been pushed and humiliated when the court "objected to the verdict" and "manifested dissatisfaction." He confessed that "several of the jury declared themselves desirous to go out again and thereupon the court gave them leave."[18]

Stoughton then sentenced Nurse to be hanged, but Governor Phipps granted a reprieve. Immediately the clamoring of the afflicted began again, and so Phipps recalled the reprieve. On July 19, together with the four other women convicted at this time, she was hanged. It is clear that if the jury had understood its full powers and had not been intimidated, Rebecca Nurse would have been acquitted and the trials might have ended after only a single hanging.

The Rebecca Nurse story does not end there. For four years the jurors, the intact panel having served on more than one case, were burdened by conscience. In 1696 they tried to relieve themselves by writing an apology to the families of witches they had condemned: "We whose names are underwritten," their unique document began,

> being in the year 1692 called to serve as jurors in court at Salem on trial of many accused of witchcraft confess that we ourselves were not capable to understand nor able to withstand the mysterious delusions of the Powers of Darkness and Prince of the Air, but were, for want of knowledge in ourselves and better information from others, prevailed with to take up with such evidence against the accused as on further consideration and better information we justly fear was insufficient for touching the lives of any, whereby we fear we have been instrumental with others, though ignorantly and unwittingly, to bring upon ourselves and this People of the Lord the guilt of innocent blood. . . .
>
> We do therefore hereby signify to all in general (and to the surviving sufferers in especial) our deep sense of and sorrow for our errors in acting on such evidence to the condemning of any person, and do hereby declare that we justly fear we were sadly deluded and mistaken, for which we are much disquieted and distressed in our minds, and do therefore humbly beg forgiveness, first of God for Christ's sake for this our error, and pray that God would not impute the guilt of it to ourselves nor others.
>
> We do heartily ask forgiveness of you all, whom we have justly offended, and do declare according to our present minds, we would none of us do such things again. . . .[19]

All twelve jurors signed the apology.

Awkward and archaic phrasing notwithstanding, this statement eloquently depicts the overriding importance of an independent jury, unmanipulated by outside forces, in possession of the full evidence, and being knowledgeable about their power to act in good conscience. Of the Nurse trial, Upham has written:

> The case of Rebecca Nurse proves that a verdict could not have been obtained against a person of her character . . . had not the most extraordinary efforts been made by the prosecuting officer, sided by the whole influence of the Court and Provincial authorities. The odium of the proceedings at the trials and at the executions cannot fairly be laid upon Salem or the people of the vicinity.

The court held three more sittings, one in August and on September 9 and 17; four and eight persons, respectively, were tried. In each case the verdict of "guilty" was pronounced by a jury drawn only from the official church. However, the judges, to prevent any further juror strikes for independence, took firmer control. They themselves became the prosecutors, presuming guilt. They put leading and ensnaring questions to the defendants, browbeating them with obvious hostility. The thoroughly befuddled prisoners were denied defense counsel and left to defend themselves entirely by their own inadequate devices.

Hysterical people, noisy and clamorous, were incited to surround and besiege the courtroom. The juries were overawed and intimidated. Any sign of wavering and the judges rebuked them. When an accused offered as defense the argument that a specter appearing in her shape was the devil's deception which she could not control, Stoughton instructed the jurors that the devil could not assume the shape of an innocent person; he established this as a rule of court, binding upon the juries. He directed the juries to follow the law as he dictated it, and the juries, through fear, intimidation, and ignorance of their ultimate supremacy over the court, succumbed to Stoughton's terrorizing behavior. The series of judge-dictated convictions continued another thirteen times.

The twelve jurors who were to write their apology in 1696 probably served together, well subdued, on several of them.

When Giles Corey was charged with wizardry, he refused to enter a plea because he did not wish to make himself a party to the proceedings and subject himself to "a blind, maddened and utterly perverted tribunal." By standing resolute he prevented the court from trying him.

In retaliation, the judges forced Corey to suffer "peine forte et dure," which was to strip him naked, except for a piece of cloth out of respect for decorum and propriety; laying him on his back on a stone floor in a low-ceilinged, darkened cell; and placing a weight of iron on his chest, though not enough to crush him, where he was kept for two days while the weights were increased. He was given only standing water and moldy bread until he died. Corey was eighty-one years old. His resistance saved his property for his heirs, as the marshals and sheriffs would seize the movables of convicted persons under a system of asset forfeiture. They could not seize property of the unconvicted. Corey's last words were for "more weight . . . more weight" on his chest.

The prisoners condemned in the September trials were hanged all together on the 22nd. The court then adjourned temporarily, expecting to resume on a monthly basis. However, public opinion began to swing against them, and some of the accusing girls struck too high, even against the wife of the governor, Sir William Phipps, and the wife of the minister of the First Church of Beverly.

The special court was disbanded. But about 150 accused, at least fifty-two of whom had been indicted by the Grand Jury, were still being held in prisons under the cruelest conditions. Three are known to have died, but probably others did as well. A new tribunal was formed as the Superior Court of Judicature, which was hardly more than a name change because the same William Stoughton was chief justice, and of his four associates, three had sat on the special court.

For three and a half months no action was taken against the prisoners, who were all the while held without relief. On January 3, 1693, the reconstituted court came together for its first session. Rebecca Jacobs, who had been held since the previous May 18, was first to be brought before a "jury of tryals," who were read her indictment alleging that she had practiced "detestable arts called Witchcraft and Sorceries, Wickedly, Mallitiously and feloneously" and performed other "wicked acts." Several of Jacobs's "victims" testified against her, including Elizabeth Hobert and Elizabeth Howard. The jurors took in the heavily adverse testimony, much of it repetitive; they were then "instructed" by Stoughton, and retired to deliberate. These jurors wrote out their verdict, which has been recorded for posterity, and when they returned their foreman, Edward Flint, stood up and read it: "That they do not find Rebekah [*sic*] Jacobs Guilty of the felony by Witchcraft she hath been indicted."[20]

Stoughton became "enraged and filled with passionate anger," but unlike the previous June was restrained from pressuring the jury to reconsider. This Rebecca was discharged, to demonstrate the jury's power over the most arbitrary court. She was, however, forced to pay "jail fees" to cover her months of imprisonment.

Margaret Jacobs (no kin) came next before the same "jury of tryals," but the indictment against her was more savage. Her victims, the same benighted Elizabeth Howard and Mary Walcott, were "Tortured afflicted consumed wasted pined and Tormented." Nonetheless, the panel again voted to acquit. Foreman Flint read their decision, that the jurors "Gave in their Verdict viz't They find that Margaret Jacobs the Prisoner at the Barr is not guilty of the felony by Witchcraft, whereof Shee hath been indicted."[21] Despite her acquittal, Margaret, too, was held until she had paid jail fees.

The court would not let the Flint jurors sit for the next trial, so Sarah Buckley faced a different panel. It didn't help. This jury made the same decision. The foreman, James Freind, wrote in less formal terms: "The said Sarah Buckley is not guilty of the felony by witchcraft. . . ."[22] Foreman Freind also delivered an acquittal in the next trial for Mary Witheridge. On January 5 the Edward Flint jurors returned to free Job Tookey. The same day Nathaniel Howard was foreman of a third jury which let Hannah Tyler go free; and on the 6th, Foreman Richard Gross happily read the seventh verdict freeing Candy, described as "a Negroe Servant." The enraged judges could exact revenge in only one way. They forced every acquitted defendant to pay jail fees before releasing them, thus placing a great burden upon their families.

There are three reasons for the difference between the responses of the juries meeting in 1693 and those of the previous year: first, judicial conscience prompted the jury base to be expanded to include the entire community, not just the Puritan church. This allowed unindoctrinated persons and provided diversification. Second, spectral evidence was no longer admissible; any pining, wasting, consuming, and afflicting had to be caused by the witch herself, not her (in some cases his) apparition. Thus Stoughton lost some of his ability to dominate the panels. Third, public hysteria was waning.

Stoughton did control the reorganized court, although it was not considered illegal as the special court had been. Backed by the Mathers and Governor Phipps, he pressed for further prosecutions. Forty-five more trials were held through May of that year, and the juries pronounced "not guilty" in forty-two of them. Not one jury would convict; three defendants "confessed," but were later given reprieves.

Stoughton was furious with the juries. He raved: "We were in a way to have cleared the land of these witches. Who it was that obstructed the execution of justice, or hindered these good proceedings we had made, I know not, but merely the Kingdom of Satan is advanced." In April he resigned and went to Boston; Thomas Danforth succeeded him as chief justice.

Danforth was no better. In the trial of Lydia Dustin, seventy and a widow for twenty-one years, he was prevented from allowing spectral evidence, but the accusers talked of strange accidents and illnesses befalling them. When the jury acquitted, Danforth railed: "Woman, woman, repent, there are shrewd things come in against you." Neither Lydia nor her family could pay the jail fees, and Danforth held her in a cold cell for six more weeks, until she died. "Danforth's act was equivalent to a death warrant made against a woman who had just been found innocent in trial by jury."[23]

By mid-May, despite Danforth, the jurors' message finally got through to Governor Phipps. Against the judge's wishes, the governor issued a proclamation discharging the one hundred or so prisoners remaining. The trials were over. Nevertheless, there remained jail fees, covering board for the entire time of their imprisonment, the jailers, and various court fees. Those prisoners were lucky if the results were merely impoverishment of their families.

Some prisoners had no family remaining. Consider the acquitted Margaret Jacobs, held from May 18, 1692, until January 3, 1693. Her grandfather had been convicted and executed, and all his assets forfeited, seized by the marshal and sheriff. Her father had fled to escape trial and was "in exile beyond the seas." Her mother had been imprisoned; the younger children, left without care, were dispersed, thrown upon the charity of neighbors; her house, left open, was deserted and raided. She had not a shilling left.

Jacobs was taken back to jail until a stranger named Gammon, hearing about her, was touched with compassion. He raised money for her release, and it was years before she could repay him. How many others were held in prison and for how long we shall never know. Unfortunately no provision was made to appeal to juries to determine the lawfulness of jail fees.

That the trials were submitted to juries was because of the foresight of the original settlers of the colony seventy years earlier. These *Mayflower* voyagers had had such great faith in juries as the final defense of citizens against oppressive government, that they chose in 1623 as their very first law of any description that all trials, civil or criminal, would be by "twelve honest men." Massachusetts has never been without juries since. Thus, how much we may condemn juries convicting nineteen, we must compare this against trials before the likes of Stoughton, Danforth, or the Mathers without juries or panels of judges. Or the historically overlapping Iberian inquisitions extending, juryless, for three and a quarter centuries. Picture Spanish and Portuguese history had those trials been submitted to juries. Would we now condemn whatever number of benighted panels for convicting, say, fifty over a year, never knowing, as we know, from what far worse travails they would have rescued their fellow citizens?

Salem was not the only town hit by witchcraft fever, but it is the only one we hear about. Epidemics budded in Andover and Boston, Massachusetts, and in Fairfield County, Connecticut, but never bloomed. In Fairfield, Mercy Disborough was brought before a Special Court of Assistants and a trial jury in September 1692. As in Salem, the judges "were very zealous" to convict her, and almost did. Eleven jurors went along, but one resisted. That one was enough to save her.

The court adjourned to seek advice from the Connecticut General Court which would meet in October. The local clergy urged moderation, suggesting that the accusations were based "upon very slender and uncertain grounds." The Special Court met again on October 28 not only to retry Disborough but also Goodwife Clawson. The jury acquitted Clawson outright. Disborough faced the same jurymen she had in her first trial except one, who had gone to New York. Whether the missing juror was the acquitting juror or another is not known; in any case, the jury again hung eleven to one. Since unanimity was required, Disborough was released and granted immunity from further prosecution on grounds that it was improper to have tried her before, in effect, the same convicting jurors as previously.

That ended the trials in Connecticut.

Andover escaped without trials. The local justice of the peace, Dudley Bradstreet, had issued warrants for some thirty or forty accused, then rebelled against the witch-hunts and would issue no more. Whereupon the accusers turned upon him, and he fled. Emboldened, the accusers struck at persons of such high rank that they lost their credibility, and the persecutions collapsed.

After his failure in Salem, Stoughton moved to Boston to try a case, but the jury acquitted, thus ending the hysteria in a single stroke.

There was one more episode in 1696—not a witchcraft trial as such, but related in that the charges were based on "cutting and sarcastic remarks" made against the authorities who had prosecuted the trials. Salem merchant Thomas Maule, a dedicated and outspoken Quaker, had been resisting for almost thirty years the Puritan prejudice against Quakers. He had vigorously condemned the trials from the start, climaxing his censure of them with the publication in 1695 of his book *Truth Set Forth*. In it he identified the victims of his sarcasm as the "persecuting priests and rulers in general, and in particular those responsible for the trials."[24]

The authorities were so enraged by Maule's accusations that they had him arrested, searched his house, and seized and destroyed whatever books and papers they could find. Brought to Boston for an inquisition before the governor and council, Maule refused to respond to any of their questions. He demanded his right to trial by jury in his own county, as established by the law of 1623. The Boston court submitted by dismissing Maule, and returned him to his home county, Salem, but placed him under heavy bail. In Salem he appeared before the Supreme Court of Judicature and a jury on September 17, 1696. The chief justice was once again Thomas Danforth; one of the associate justices, Samuel Sewall, had been also been on the bench for the witchcraft trials. As to the jury, other than that the foreman was a man named John Turner, we have no information about who they were or how selected, least of all their religious affiliations, which would not necessarily have a bearing on how the jurors would respond. Undoubtedly some were Puritans. It is unlikely that any was a Quaker. But the trial record does reveal something of the characters of both Maule and Turner.

The prosecuting attorney, Anthony Checkley, had represented the government in several of the witchcraft trials. The indictment read to the jury identified Maule's book as *Truth Held Forth and Maintained,* and alleged that it "contained divers slanders against the churches and government of this province," and that Maule had told the court during his preliminary hearing that "there was as great mistakes in the scriptures as in his book."

Although Maule did have as defense counsel a Dr. Benjamin Bullivant, who told the court that the charge regarding the scriptures was too general and under any condition not punishable, Maule was fully qualified to handle his own defense. And what an outspoken defense it was! He began by insulting the three-man court, charging that as they were

> invested with magisterial power, I respect you; but wherein you assume to yourselves the power of the Bishops' Court, as in this case, I no more value you than I do Jack Straw. If you would approve yourselves wise men, you ought to amend the many rents you have already made by the mismanagement of the trust committed to your charge.

Still, this was not enough for him. Maule challenged his judicial adversaries (for they had already shown hostility and would show more) that if they were "resolved to make a rod for me, see that it be light for the more care of your own that is to come, for it is said by Him that cannot lie: 'the same measure that men make, the same shall be made to them again.' "

Checkley's role as prosecutor became superfluous. Danforth took over his role completely. When it came time to "instruct" the jury, he ignored Maule's admonitions and dictated:

> Having taken a solemn oath to do the thing that is right in the sight of God as near as you can; you ought to well consider the horrid wickedness of Thomas Maule's setting forth the book now before you, in which there is contained a great deal of blasphemous matter against the churches and government of this province . . . this work of Thomas Maule wholly tends to overthrow all good in church and commonwealth, which God has planted amongst His people in this province . . . perform your duty relative to the same as God shall enable you.

But Maule was not to be silent, and he had the last say before the jury retired.

Jurymen, look well to the work which you are now about to do. . . .
No part of the king's law have I broken. The book is no evidence in
law against me, further than you are satisfied that I have written anything contrary to sound doctrine and inconsistent with the holy scriptures. If you favor any of the unjust charges of the judges against me,
and say there is such matter in the book as they charge me with, you
must go to the printer for satisfaction, for I am ignorant of any such
matter in the book. My hand is only to my copy . . . and my name in
the printed book does not in law prove the same to be Thomas
Maule, any more than the specter evidence is in law sufficient to
prove a person accused by such evidence to be a witch.

The jurors then withdrew, and the record reports only that they
"soon returned." Danforth asked for the verdict, and Foreman Turner
replied clearly: "We find the defendant not guilty according to indictment." The three judges became petulant. Chief Justice Danforth again
transgressed judicial bounds by asking Turner how they could return
such a verdict with the book before them.

Turner was straightforward in his reply: "The book was not sufficient evidence, for Thomas Maule's name was placed there by the
printer. And the matter contained in it was not cognizable by us. A
case like this required the wisdom and learning of a jury of divines."
Whether or not these jurors actually felt inadequate, they had not
shirked their responsibility. They had held to the dictates of their consciences.

Danforth attacked the jurors a second time: "Thomas Maule may
escape the hands of men, but he has not escaped the hand of God, who
will find out all his evils and blasphemies against His church and
people; and has reserved him for further judgement."

Maule replied to this blasphemy against the basis for trials by jury,
and thereby stated the chief argument for their support:

I am in no way guilty of your charge, but have great cause to praise
God for my deliverance by the jury who are made instruments of
freeing me out of the hands of them who have manifested their up-
righteous words against the people of God and the king's subjects as
their fathers did before them.

"Take him away, take him away," responded the annoyed Danforth, but Maule was already out of his reach.

Thus did a jury once again demonstrate the validity of William Blackstone's assessment (as well as that of our nation's founders) that the jury is "the grand bulwark of the people's liberties."

NOTES

1. Chadwick Hansen, *Witchcraft in Salem* (New York: Braziller, 1969), p. xiii.

2. Ibid., p. x.

3. Ibid., p. xvi.

4. Ibid., pp. 21ff.

5. Charles Upham, *Salem Witchcraft* (Williamstown, Mass.: Corner House Publishers, 1867).

6. Ibid., p. 252.

7. *American State Trials,* 1: 514ff.

8. Bernard Rosenthal, *Salem Story* (Cambridge, Mass.: Cambridge University Press, 1993), p. 69.

9. Marion L. Starkey, *The Devil in Massachusetts* (New York: Dolphin Books, 1961), p. 156.

10. Winfield S. Nevins, *Witchcraft in Salem Village in 1692* (Salem, Mass.: North Shore Publishing Co., 1852), p. 72.

11. *Records of Salem Witchcraft Copied from the Original Documents* (Roxbury, Mass.: W. Eliot Woodward, 1864), 1: 10.

12. Ibid., p. 11.

13. Taken from *Records,* 1: 17ff.

14. Upham, *Salem Witchcraft,* pp. 269–70 and passim.

15. Nevins, *Witchcraft in Salem Village in 1692,* pp. 113ff.

16. Upham, *Salem Witchcraft,* pp. 281ff.

17. Nevins, *Witchcraft in Salem Village in 1692,* pp. 124–25. This description is corroborated by other sources previously cited.

18. Ibid., pp. 127–28.

19. *A Casebook of Witchcraft,* William Woods, ed. (New York: G. P. Putnam's Sons, 1974), pp. 214–15.

20. *The Salem Witchcraft Papers,* Paul Boyer and Steven Nissenbaum, eds. (New York: da Capo Press, 1977), p. 905.

21. Ibid., p. 906.

22. Ibid., p. 907.

23. Enders A. Robinson, *Salem Witchcraft and Hawthorne's* House of the Seven Gables (Bowie, Md.: Heritage Books, Inc., 1992), p. 201.

24. *The Trial of Thomas Maule for Slander and Blasphemy, Massachusetts, 1696, American State Trials,* 5: 85.

Part 3

JURORS RALLY IN DEFENSE OF FREEDOM OF SPEECH

5

"THE GREATER THE TRUTH, THE GREATER THE LIBEL":
THE TRIAL OF JOHN PETER ZENGER, AUGUST 4, 1735, NEW YORK CITY

*A*ndrew Hamilton was one of the most brilliant, high-principled advocates in colonial America. On August 4, 1735, while defending publisher John Peter Zenger for "publishing a libel," he "stated Zenger's cause so eloquently that the jury returned a verdict of not guilty."

That is how the *Encyclopaedia Britannica* explains a jury's decision to nullify repressive legislation against freedom of expression and the press. Zenger had published not just one but an extended series of disparaging and defamatory accusations against the priggish royal governor of New York colony, Sir William Cosby. Cosby struck back by having him charged criminally, and labeling the accusations "libels" to cover the fact that Zenger was writing the truth.

Historian Leonard W. Levy, in his *Emergence of a Free Press,* attributes the verdict to the fact that the jury was "responding to the magnificent forensics of a great lawyer engaged in a popular cause,"[1] And Livingston Rutherfurd, editing in 1904 the original papers of the trial written in 1736 by Zenger himself, reports that popular enthusiasm over the verdict prompted "above forty of the Citizens [to] entertain Mr. Hamilton at the Black Horse Tavern that day at dinner to express their acknowledgment of his generosity on this occasion." Hamilton was "saluted with great guns of several ships in the harbor, as a publick testimony of the glorious defense he made in the cause of liberty in this Province."[2]

No doubt about it! Hamilton's forensics were magnificent and he did make an eloquent appeal to the jurors, urging them to follow precedents set some two generations earlier by juries which had nullified tyrannical laws in the trials of William Penn and the seven bishops (see chapters 1 and 2). Hamilton invoked the jury decisions in both trials to enlighten Zenger's jury.

As well merited as the universal praise for Hamilton might be, these three accountings of the case mistake the true agents of victory. It was not Hamilton who delivered the verdict. The verdict was the unanimous, almost instantaneous resolve of twelve citizens, each driven independently by conscience and a love of liberty. And in the end it was the verdict, not eloquence, that mattered. These twelve unknowns recklessly challenged royal censure; they did what no other division of government dared or was able to do, what few others dared even to speak out on. Driven by conscience, they successfully bound down king and autocratic governor to First Amendment principles not to be formally expressed for another fifty-six years. They brought down the most powerful authority in the land by dictating their law that no agency of government could abridge the freedom of the press. They declared null and void the official law limiting publication to a single state-controlled newspaper. They overrode long-enduring official policy that not only was truth no defense against a libel, but "the greater the truth the greater the libel."

By directing attention most heavily to Hamilton, the historians reflect a subtle, albeit unintentional, disrespect for jury trials generally, overlooking the fact that the sole responsibility for verdicts rests with jurors.

Based upon my own studies of jury trials and the behavior of jurors throughout history—regardless of century or geography—and what little information we can garner about the jurors in the Zenger case, and the sentiment of the community, I contend that these twelve would have acquitted the publisher had Hamilton been less eloquent, or had a less competent advocate stood for Zenger; even if his defense had remained with the inexperienced counsel chief justice James De-Lancey had appointed for Zenger; and even if he and second justice Frederick Philipse had not been distracted long enough to permit an exchange of letters and another day and night for Hamilton to take the coastal journey from distant Philadelphia to the place of trial in New York City. At worst the jurors would have divided so heavily in

Zenger's favor that it would have had the effect of acquittal. The jurors' consciences would not have let them do otherwise.

The casual sloughing off by historians of twelve citizens in their exalted roles as jurors is to degrade them to the status of push-button automatons reacting to prearranged stimuli. These men were three-dimensional figures who thought for themselves, who distinguished right from wrong, and could respond to conscience regardless of rank. Not considering this, the "above forty" citizens, as soon as the verdict was delivered, discarded as inconsequential those who had delivered it. By their oversight, they second-classed the jury's role as decision makers, although praising the jury as an institution.

Belated as we might be, let us honor now the twelve who wrote that government shall make no law abridging the freedom of the press so many years before it was officially codified as part of our First Amendment. Their names have been preserved. The foreman who courageously defied a court that pressured them to do otherwise was Thomas Hunt, a "mariner"; juror Harmanus Rutgers, a brewer, had actually served on the first grand jury which had refused to indict Zenger in January 1734. Seven of the twelve were of Dutch ancestry, likely to be out of sympathy with the rival English governor: Egbert van Borsom, a vintner; John Goelet, an artisan; Benjamin Hildreth, a tailor; Andries Marschalk, a baker; Abraham Keteltas, a merchant; Hercules Wendover, a blacksmith; Edward Man, a carpenter; Samuel Weaver, a currier; Stanley Holmes, a tradesman; and John Bell, a clerk.[3] They were a relatively homogenous group as all had to own property just to be summoned, and thus were established in trades and professions; undoubtedly all were white men. They were "notable only for their obscurity," although what they did is remembered and celebrated to this day. They were to be branded by a pair of angered judges as "perjured men."

However, in 1953, these men were honored. A Zenger Memorial Fund was supported by 450 newspapers who donated $45,000 to establish a memorial in the Federal Hall, Wall and Nassau streets, at the site where the trial was held. Although the chief honorees were Zenger and Hamilton, the jurors were not forgotten. A plaque lists the names given above.

The twelve had been picked randomly. Before Hamilton had arrived, court-appointed counsel John Chambers had asked for a "struck jury." The proper method of "striking a jury" was for the clerk of the court to draw forty-eight names at random from the freeholders register. Of these, each side would reject twelve peremptorily. The remaining twenty-four would be examined until twelve of them had been challenged.

But this clerk was sly. He compiled a list consisting of Cosby partisans: former magistrates displaced in the previous elections; tradesmen dealing with Cosby; office holders serving at Cosby's pleasure; and his baker, tailor, shoemaker, candlemaker, and joiner.[4] Some of these were not freeholders at all. Chambers, although a government man, had the integrity to challenge the entire *venire*.

The next day another panel of forty-eight was struck, but the sheriff had altered the order of their names so that the most desirable jurors, from his view, would appear first.[5] It was the job of the sheriff, an appointee of the governor, to summon the jury candidates, which meant controlling the basic panel. When Chambers complained about the sheriff's "trick," DeLancey ordered that the names be ranged as they were struck. There was then no further objection, and the jury was finally sworn.[6] James Alexander, together with William Smith, had been Zenger's original attorneys and were too skilled, in DeLancey's eyes, to be permitted to serve. So DeLancey, overstepping authority, arbitrarily disbarred them. This necessitated first the appointment of Chambers and then the call for Hamilton.

The case arose over a question of politics. Before Cosby had arrived, in August 1732, as the king's chosen governor of New York, there had been a temporary vacancy due to the death of his predecessor. In the interim, a New York merchant, Rip Van Dam, had assumed the executive powers by virtue of being senior member of the provisional council. Cosby believed that Van Dam should have set aside half his salary for the incoming governor, but Van Dam did not agree. Cosby, backed by the authority of an instruction from the Privy Council, demanded half almost immediately upon arriving. Van Dam refused him unless he received certain favors in return.

Cosby turned to the courts for relief, but which court? To bring a common law action in the Supreme Court of New York would mean going before a jury likely to be unsympathetic to a governor who had made himself unpopular from the moment he landed. The details of how Cosby escaped a jury and got his appeal before a Court of Exchequer are not part of our story, except to note that the chief justice of the Supreme Court, Lewis Morris, attacked the legality of such a court. His associates, DeLancey and Philipse, disagreed, so Cosby dismissed Morris and elevated DeLancey to chief judge.

But Morris wielded considerable power in the colony. There was at the time a single newspaper called the New York *Gazette,* published since 1725 by William Bradford under the supervision of the government. The Morris faction decided to inaugurate its own paper critical of the governor. They selected Zenger, a printer, to set up competition in the form of the New York *Weekly Journal.* As a boy in Maryland, Zenger had been apprenticed to the older Bradford from 1711 until 1719. He and Bradford moved separately to New York, and for a short time in 1725 were partners.

The first issue of the *Journal* was dated November 5, 1733, "containing the Freshest Advices, Foreign and Domestick." One piece of fresh advice was that "Our Governor who came here but last year has long ago given more Distaste to the People than I verily believe any Governor that ever this Province had during his whole government."[7] Most of the articles in the *Journal* were written by James Alexander, who had represented Van Dam and was now to be co-counsel with William Smith for Zenger. The *Journal* boldly proclaimed that it was "designed to be continued Weekly and chiefly to expose him [Cosby] and those ridiculous flatteries with which Mr. Harison [an associate of Bradford] loads our other Newspaper which our Governor claims and has the privilege of suffering nothing to be in but what he and Mr. Harison approve of."

The idea of censoring the press was born even before newspapers came into existence. In 1697 a directive was sent to the then governor of New York colony that "For as much as great inconveniences may arise by the liberty of printing within the province of New York, you are to provide all necessary orders that no person keep any press for printing, nor that any book, pamphlet or other matter whatsoever be printed without your especial leave and consent first obtained."[8]

How much force this directive had in the 1730s is uncertain, but censorship was secured largely by the law of libel, usually qualified as "seditious libel." It was the chief device used by government to silence its attackers. "Libel" is currently defined in *Black's Law Dictionary,* fifth edition, as "a maliciously written or printed publication which tends to blacken a person's reputation or expose him to public hatred, contempt or ridicule, or to injure him in his business or profession." The key word here is "malicious."

But *Black*'s drops that word in an extended definition "Accusation in writing or printing against the character of a person . . . to degrade him in the estimation of the community, to induce an evil opinion of him . . . to make him an object of reproach . . . to dishonor or discredit him," etc.

Bouvier's Law Dictionary (1870) uses "malicious" in one definition of "libel," but in another refers only to "that which is written or printed and published, calculated to injure the character of another by bringing him into ridicule, hatred or contempt," or "a malicious defamation, expressed either in printing or writing. . . . It differs from "slander," which is spoken or oral.

The libel becomes "seditious" when, according to *Black's,* the written communication has "the intent to incite the people to change the government otherwise than by lawful means, or to advocate the overthrow of the government by force or violence."

What is missing from these definitions is the word "false." Is it a libel if printing something nasty about a person is the truth? For example, when Cosby deprived Van Dam of his right to trial by jury, the *Weekly Journal* published the following criticism in issue No. 5: "Deservedly therefore is this Tryal by Juries, ranked amongst the choicest of our fundamental Laws, which whosoever shall go about openly to suppress, or craftily to undermine, does ipso facto, ATTACK THE GOVERNMENT, AND BRING IN AN ARBITRARY POWER, AND IS AN ENEMY AND TRAYTOR TO HIS COUNTRY."[9]

The second and third issues of the *Journal* were critical of Cosby's attempt to suppress criticism:

> For if such an overgrown criminal, or an impudent monster in iniquity, cannot immediately be come at by ordinary justice, let him yet receive the lash of satire, let the glaring truths of his ill administration, if possible, awaken his conscience, and if he has no conscience, rouse his fear by showing him his deserts, sting him with shame, and render his actions odious to all honest minds.[10]

Derogations such as these, and many stronger, appeared in every issue of the *Weekly Journal*; although Zenger as printer was held accountable by Cosby, most articles were written by James Alexander or other associates. Zenger, of German birth, did not speak English well. The paper even published sham advertisements in which the governor was attacked in a metaphor:

A Large Spaniel, of about Five Foot Five Inches High, has lately stray'd from his Kennel with his Mouth full of fulsom Panegericks and in his Ramble dropt them in the NEW YORK GAZETTE; when a Puppy he was marked thus F (inverted) (lying sideward), and a Cross in his Forehead, but the Mark being worn out, he has taken upon him in a heathenish Manner to abuse Mankind, by imposing a great many gross Falsehoods upon them. . . .

As strong as these condemnations were, they were hardly derogatory enough, in the opinion of a contemporary observer who would become a New York governor three decades later when he was in his seventies. Cadwallader Colden, who wrote a history of the colony, described several "flagrant instances of tyranny and robbery" in which Cosby had been involved at an earlier time when he was governor of Minorca. Cosby had "acted as if he thought no measures unlawful or dishonorable that could serve to make his fortune, and as if government were only given him to make money by any means that his absolute and despotic power could give him."[11]

The *Journal*'s commentaries, while true, were so clearly designed to "blacken [Cosby's] reputation or expose him to public hatred, contempt or ridicule, or to injure him in his business or profession" as to be libelous, even if true by Colden's assessment; and they appeared so regularly as to be describable as "malicious." Further, they were certainly designed to stir up the people against the government. To repeat, the philosophy then was that the greater the truth the greater the libel, which meant that all the elements of seditious libel were present. By printing them, Alexander, with Zenger as front man, was asking for trouble. Could he fault Cosby for bringing charges?

It became the responsibility of the new chief justice, DeLancey, and his one associate, Philipse, to do the work. Both were young men with little legal skill and greater venality than integrity, but were deemed qualified for office by reason of partisanship with the government.

On January 15, 1734, DeLancey addressed the grand jury, whose members are not identified, except for Harmanus Rutgers, who later served on the trial jury:

You must have observed, that of late there have been served Papers printed, with a Design and a Tendency to alienate the Affections of His Majesty's Subjects of this Province from the Persons whom His

Majesty has thought it fitting to set over them; and in particular . . .
to vilify his Administration. . . . I know most of you Personally, and
I make no doubt but that you will discharge your Duty.[12]

He presented the jury with six folio pages of allegations, but despite
the length and the personal association between the jurors and De-
Lancey, they surprised him by refusing to discharge the duty he had
prescribed.

With an indictment denied, Cosby's opposition was emboldened
to defame further. Morris published a pamphlet critical of his suc-
cessor: *Some Observations on the Charge delivered to the Grand Jury
by the Honorable James DeLancey.* Cosby was in a quandary. He had
been forced to drop the case against Van Dam because of rising indignation among the people abetted by the *Journal,* and now Zenger (or
rather Alexander) was attacking his party even more severely, as if it
had been given special license to do so. Sedition surely! Attempts to
defend the governor by the *Gazette* did not silence criticism. Frustrated, but with a new grand jury, DeLancey tried again. On October
15 he lectured the grand jurors on libel law:

I shall conclude with reading a Paragraph or two out of the same
Book concerning Libels; they are arrived to that Height that they call
loudly for your Animadversion; it is high Time to put a Stop to them;
for at the rate Things are now carried on, when all Order and Government is endeavored to be trampled on; Reflections are cast upon
Persons of all Degrees, must not these Things end in Sedition if not
timely prevented? Lenity you have seen will not avail, it becomes
you then to enquire after the Offenders, that we may in a due Course
of Law be enabled to punish them. If you, Gentlemen, do not inter-
pose, consider whether ill Consequences that may arise from any
Disturbances of the publick Peace, may not in part, lye at your
Door?[13]

We might question the proper role of this "judge," presumably
nonpartisan, acting as prosecutor. His threat did not move the jurors
who refused again to do their DeLancey-prescribed duty. No indictment. Five of the nineteen members had been in the first grand jury,
and are believed to have influenced the other fourteen.

Growing desperate, the Cosby government tried the futile gesture
of ordering token copies of four of the most offensive issues to be

burned "by the Hands of the common Hangman or Whipper." He also offered a reward of fifty pounds for the conviction of the author of the articles. But the aldermen of the city protested. Obedience to the order to burn would be "an opening a Door for arbitrary Commands, which, when once opened, they know not what Dangerous Consequences may attend it."

> Wherefore this Court conceives itself bound in Duty, (for the Preservation of the Rights of this Corporation, and as much as they can, the Liberty of the Press . . . and several Grand Juries, have refused to meddle with the Papers) to protest against the ORDER aforesaid and to forbid all the members of this Corporation, to pay any Obedience to it, until it be shown to this Court, that the same is Authorized by some known Law, which they neither know nor believe that it is.

The only way any of the papers got burned was when the sheriff "delivered them into the Hand of his own Negroe, and ordered him to put them into the Fire, which he did."

Trying to get around the grand jury, the council issued a warrant for Zenger's arrest "for printing and publishing several Seditious Libels . . . as having in them many Things, tending to raise Factions and Tumults . . . with Contempt of His Majesty's Government. . . ." The warrant, however, was illegal since the council did not have power to issue such process, and the "warrant" was no more than the expression of the opinion of some of the council members. It was supported by no evidence, and had not provided Zenger an opportunity to defend himself.

Illegal or not, muscle prevailed and Zenger was jailed. For several days he was denied pen, ink and paper, causing him to miss one issue of his *Journal*. The following week, the issuance of a "Habias Corpus" [*sic*] enabled him to write an "Apoligy" [*sic*], having been granted "the Liberty of Speaking through the Hole of the Door, to my Wife and Servants by which I doubt not yo'l think me sufficiently Excused for not sending my last weeks Journal. . . ."

The vindictive DeLancey, who had issued the habeas corpus, set Zenger's bail at eight hundred pounds to discourage publication so that "I could not ask any to become my Bail for me." Zenger estimated his total worth at forty pounds exclusive of personal belongings. However, publication of the *Weekly Journal* was continued on a regular basis by his wife and associates, who received their instructions through the hole in the door. There were at the time scarcely one thousand men in New York with the qualifications for jury duty, so the *Journal* articles were carefully written to ensure that they would all be fully informed as to the real questions at issue, and of their rights and duties in cases of libel.

In the meantime, Zenger was kept in jail to await a third grand jury hearing on Tuesday, January 28, 1735; but, like the first two, this panel refused to indict. Zenger wrote that the jurors, "having found nothing against me, I expected to have been discharged from my Imprisonment. But my Hopes proved vain; for the Attorney General then charged me by *Information* for Printing and publishing *false, scandalous, malicious, and seditious* [*sic*]" (italics in original).

These descriptive adjectives apply more precisely to an "information" than to the charges within it, for it is truly a malicious device to get around recalcitrant grand juries. An "Information" is defined by *Black's* as "an accusation in the nature of an indictment, from which it differs only in being presented by a competent public officer on his oath of office instead of a grand jury on their oath" or by "a public prosecutor." The form is the same as an indictment, "except that it is filed at the mere discretion of the proper law officer . . . without the intervention of a grand jury."[14] And, malice notwithstanding, an "information" is still used today under certain conditions in many states, which would seem to render null and void the Fifth Amendment caveat that "No person shall be held to answer for a capital, or otherwise infamous crime, unless on a presentment or indictment of a Grand Jury. . . ."

By such deviousness they caught him, and Zenger now had to stand before a fourth jury, not "grand" this time but, without indictment on the "information," a "petit jury" for actual trial. As I stated in the foreword, these two terms are French and are not to be misinterpreted respectively as "exalted" and "petty," that is, insignificant. The terms relate merely to the size: "grand" being French for "large" and "petit" for small—nineteen persons compared with twelve.

James Alexander and William Smith, representing Zenger before DeLancey and Philipse, objected to indictment by information; whereupon DeLancey delivered a foot-stamping address to Smith:

That they would neither hear nor allow the Exceptions; *for you thought to have gained a great Deal of Applause and Popularity by opposing this Court, as you did the Court of Exchequer; but you have brought it to that Point, That either, We must go from the Bench or you from the Barr: Therefore We exclude you and Mr. Alexander from the Barr.*[15] (Italics in original)

This may be the only instance in history of disbarment under such prejudicial circumstances. Although Alexander and Smith presented good legal argument for remaining as counsel, neither DeLancey nor Philipse would hear it. They carried their complaint to the assembly of the province: "We would humbly ask, whether any Thing can be more Arbitrary, than these Gentlemen's pretending to make the Notification of their *Displeasure* to be the Rule of our Conduct?" (italics in original)

The two lawyers accused DeLancey of prejudice when he "vented his displeasure" against Zenger upon meeting him by accident on the street the week before his arrest; when he ordered copies of the newspaper burned, and when he set bail at eight hundred pounds.

We had heard the Chief Justice declare, in the fullest court we had ever seen in that Place, *That if a Jury found Zenger Not Guilty, they would be perjured* . . . even this before any Information in Form was lodged against him.[16]

The skill with which Alexander and Smith argued against their disbarment worked against them because it was that very skill which the two autocrats on the bench feared. There were no other attorneys in the province vigorous, bold, and knowledgeable enough to defend Zenger, and by disbarring them, the venal court would enjoy an advantage. Nonetheless, it should still be noted that however autocratic the court, both it and the government knew they would have to submit to the superior power of a decision by everyday jurymen drawn from the citizenry.

The court then assigned John Chambers to represent Zenger because Chambers had been one of the signers of an address complimenting Cosby's administration; but Chambers, by his handling of the struck jury incident (see above), proved to have more integrity than the two judges had anticipated. Trial was set for August 4. Lewis Morris Jr. offered to send for Andrew Hamilton in Philadelphia, and volunteered to contribute part of the expense. Hamilton is reported as being either fifty-nine or seventy-nine at the time, but more likely he was seventy-nine. He presented himself as more elderly to play upon the sympathy of the jurors.[17] He was in fact suffering from gout and other physical infirmities. Nevertheless, he possessed an "unclouded and vigorous intellect" with a "reputation of being the best advocate in North America."[18]

Colden found that the "silencing" of Alexander and Smith proved a boon for the defense because neither of them would "durst have taken the freedom [Hamilton] did nor would they've been so much minded by the jury and auditors because he was look'd upon as a more indifferent person and had gain'd an esteem of many years standing for his skill in the law."[19]

Zenger's trial was held in the City Hall—"the finest building in the city"—built in 1700 at the corner of Nassau and Wall streets. Long before court opened on August 4, the little room was crowded beyond capacity. Virtually all were Zenger supporters. If the jury convicted, it would mean that the people would be powerless to resist any hardship the governor might impose; if the jury acquitted, on the other hand, it would be a decided check upon tyranny, which would affect all of the other twelve English colonies.

Hamilton's coming had been kept secret from the court, who were confident that Chambers, young and inexperienced, would be no match for the more experienced prosecuting attorney general, Richard Bradley. (Of course, they were putting too much faith in legal argument and too little in jury integrity.) So when Hamilton did appear on opening date, DeLancey and Philipse were dismayed. Both Alexander and Smith, who had already briefed Hamilton, sat close to him. The court might have disbarred Hamilton also, except that his reputation was so great that they dared not take such arbitrary action.

Attorney General Bradley opened by reading the Information:[20]

> May it please Your Honours, and you, Gentlemen of the Jury; the Information now before the Court . . . is an Information for printing and publishing a false, scandalous and seditious libel, in which His Excellency . . . is greatly and unjustly scandalized, as a person that had no regard to law nor justice. . . . This of libelling is what has always been discouraged as a thing that tends to create differences among men, ill blood among the people, and oftentimes bloodshed between the party libelling and the party libelled. There can be no doubt but you Gentlemen of the Jury will have the same ill opinion of such practices, as the judges have always shown upon such occasions.

Bradley proceeded to make certain that anybody who had not heard the accusations against Cosby would certainly hear them now. He gave them widespread publicity in the crowded courtroom by reading the charges from selected editions of the *Journal,* thereby extending the defamation he was trying to conceal. "To this Information the defendant has pleaded not guilty, and we are ready to prove it."

Hamilton then made his introduction. He astounded the court with an admission. Because it was

> the right of every free-born subject to make, when the matters so published can be supported with truth . . . I cannot think it proper for me (without doing violence to my own principles) to deny the publication of the complaint . . . and therefore I'll save Mr. Attorney the trouble of examining his witnesses to that point; and I do (for my Client) confess, that he both printed and published the two news papers set forth in the Information, and I hope in so doing he has committed no crime.

Several witnesses had been summoned to prove the fact of publication (including Zenger's two sons), and were now dismissed because the fact they were to attest to had been stipulated, "and there was silence in the court for some time." DeLancey broke it by asking Bradley to continue.

> As Mr. Hamilton has confessed the printing and publishing these libels, I think the jury must find a verdict for the king; for supposing they were true, the law says that they are not less libelous for that; nay indeed the Law says, their being true is an aggravation of the crime.

To which Hamilton gave a bold response: "Not so neither, Mr. Attorney. . . . You will have something more to do, before you make my client a libeller, for the words themselves must be libelous, that is false, scandalous and seditious, or else we are not guilty."

Hamilton began his defense by criticizing the too grandiose ego of "a Governor of a Colony in America" for "immediately imagining himself to be vested with all the prerogatives belonging to the sacred Person of his Prince" and finding it "yet more astonishing to see that a people can be so wild as to allow of, and acknowledge those prerogatives and exemptions, even to their own destruction."

He posed a series of rhetorical questions: "Is it so hard a matter to distinguish between the majesty of our sovereign, and the power of a governor of the plantations? Is this not making very free with our prince, to apply that regard, obedience and allegiance to a subject which is due only to our sovereign?"

Bradley countered by asking what this had to do with "actions in trespass" as the case before the court was "whether Mr. Zenger is guilty of libelling His Excellency . . . and indeed the whole administration of the Government." He attempted to close out all grounds for defense by arguing that "Mr. Hamilton has confessed the printing and publishing, and I think nothing is plainer, than that the words in the Information are scandalous, and tend to sedition, and to disquiet the minds of the people of this province. And if such papers are not libels, I think it may be said, there can be no such thing as a libel."

Hamilton answered: "May it please Your Honour; I cannot agree with Mr. Attorney for tho' I freely acknowledge that there are such things as libels, yet I must insist at the same time that what my client is charged with is not Libel; and as I observed just now that Mr. Attorney in defining a libel, made use of the words scandalous, seditious, and tend to disquiet the people; but (whether with design or not I will not say) he omitted the word false."

"I think I did not omit the word false; but it has been said already, that it may be a Libel notwithstanding it may be true."

"In this I must still differ with Mr. Attorney for I depend upon it. We are to be tried upon this Information now before the court and jury, and to which we have pleaded not guilty, and by it we are charged with printing and publishing a certain false, malicious, seditious and scandalous libel. This word false must have some meaning, or else how came it there? I hope Mr. Attorney will not say he put it there by chance, and I am of the opinion his Information would not be good without it. No, the falsehood makes the scandal, and both make the libel. And to show the court that I am in good earnest, I will agree that if he can prove the facts charged upon us to be false, I'll own them to be scandalous, seditious and a libel. So the work seems now to be pretty much shortened, and Mr. Attorney has now only to prove the words false in order to make us guilty," which, of course, is exactly what the government could not permit.

"We have nothing to prove," Bradley responded. "You have confessed the printing and publishing; but if it was necessary (as I insist it is not) how can we prove a negative?"

Hamilton answered: "We will save Mr. Attorney the trouble of proving a negative, and take the *onus probandi* upon ourselves and prove those very papers that are called libels to be true."

DeLancey squelched this: "You cannot be admitted, Mr. Hamilton, to give truth of a libel in evidence. A libel is not to be justified, for it is nevertheless a libel that it is true."

Hamilton shot back: "I am sorry the Court has so soon resolved upon that piece of law. I expected first to have been heard to that point. I have not in all my reading met with an authority that says we cannot be admitted to give the truth in evidence upon an indictment for a libel."

"The law is clear," the chief justice said, "that you cannot justify a libel."

But Hamilton was not to give in so easily. Whether it was a libel or not depended upon whether the words could be justified "as it is in the case upon and indictment to murder, or an assault and battery. There the prisoner cannot justify but pleads Not Guilty. Yet it will not be denied that he may, and always is admitted, to give the truth of the fact, or any other matter in evidence which goes to his acquittal."

"I pray show that you can give the truth of a libel in evidence," DeLancey charged him.

Hamilton was ready: "Information for libels is a child if not born yet nursed up and brought to full maturity in the court of Star Chamber."

DeLancey showed himself not much of a scholar: "Mr. Hamilton, you'll find yourself mistaken, for in Coke's *Institutes* you'll find Information for libels long before the Court of Star Chamber."

Hamilton demonstrated he was the better scholar: the case Chief Justice Coke referred to, he replied, was not "upon Information, and I have good grounds to say it was upon indictment . . . and I think there cannot be a greater, or at least plainer authority for us than the judgment in the case of John de Northampton, by which judgment it appears the libelous words were utterly false, and there the falsehood was the crime and is the ground for judgment. And is not that what we contend for? Do not we insist that the falsehood makes the scandal, and both make the libel? Besides, is it not against common sense that a man should be punished in the same degree for a true libel (if any such thing can be) as for a false one? I know it is said that the truth makes a libel the more provoking, and therefore the offense is the greater, and consequently the judgment should be heavier. This is a monstrous and ridiculous doctrine . . . that truth makes a worse libel than falsehood."

Hamilton then proposed "to show what in my opinion will be sufficient to induce the court to allow us to prove the truth of the words, which in the Information are called libellous." He cited several earlier cases, one of which was the trial of the seven bishops in 1688, wherein Justice Thomas Powell defined libel as necessarily being "false and malicious," and since "there was no falsehood nor malice in what the [defendant] bishops wrote, it was no libel." Apparently the jury not only agreed but set the standard, for they acquitted all seven bishops.

That opinion "to this day has never been contradicted," Hamilton said, and thus "might be of sufficient authority to entitle us to the liberty of proving the truth of the papers." Hamilton also invoked the case of Sir Samuel Barnardiston, in which the defendant "insisted on the want of proof . . . notwithstanding he stood before one of the greatest monsters that ever presided in an English court [Judge George Jeffrey Jeffries]." He also quoted an earlier chief justice who challenged the accused to "make it appear [his writings] are true. Have you any witnesses? . . . If you take upon you to write such things as you are charged with, it lies upon you to prove them true, at your peril."

But DeLancey apparently feared that if he failed to win a conviction in this case, he would be severely censured by His Gracious Lord King George II. He continued to push: "Mr. Hamilton, the court have delivered their opinions, and we expect you will use us with good manners; you are not permitted to argue against the opinion of the court."

Sensing that there was no point trying to reason with unreason, Hamilton appealed directly to the jurors:

> It is to you we must now appeal for witness to the truth of the facts we have offered, and are denied the liberty to prove, and let it not seem strange that I apply myself to you in this manner. I am warranted so to do both by law and reason. The last supposed you to be summoned out of the neighborhood where the fact is alleged to be committed; and the reason of your being taken out of the neighborhood is because you are supposed to have the best knowledge of the fact that is to be tried. And were you to find a verdict against my client, you must take upon you to say the papers referred to in the In-

formation, and which we acknowledge we printed and published, are false, scandalous and seditious; but of this I can have no apprehension. You are citizens of New York; you are really what the law supposes you to be, honest and lawful men; and, according to my brief, the facts which we offer to prove were not committed in a corner; they are notoriously known to be true; and therefore in your justice lies our safety. And as we are denied the liberty of giving evidence to prove the truth of what we published, I will beg leave to lay it down as a standing rule in such cases, *that the suppressing of evidence ought always to be taken for the strongest evidence*; and I hope it will have that weight with you. (Italics added)

Hamilton then asked if "Mr. Attorney" would "favor us with some standard definition of a libel."

Bradley attempted one: "The books, I think, have given a very full definition of a libel; they say it is in a strict sense taken for a malicious defamation, expressed in printing or writing, and tending either to blacken the memory of one who is dead, or the reputation of one who is alive, and to expose him to publick hatred, contempt or ridicule."

"Ay, Mr. Attorney; but by what certain standard rule have the books laid down, by which we can certainly know, whether the words or the signs are malicious? especially those of the ironical sort of words? And what rule have you to know when I write ironically? I think it would be very hard when I say such a man is a very worthy honest gentleman and of fine understanding that therefore I meant he was a knave or a fool."

"I think the books are very full, that such a scandal as is expressed in a scoffing and ironical manner. I think nothing can be plainer or more full than these words."

"I agree the words are very plain and I shall not scruple to allow that they are really libelous; but here still occurs the uncertainty which makes the difficulty to know what words are scandalous and what not; for you say they may be scandalous, true or false. Besides how shall we know whether the words were spoke in a scoffing and ironical manner or seriously? Or how can you know whether the man did not think as he wrote? For by your rule, if he did it, it is no irony and consequently no libel."

This banter between Bradley and Hamilton continued a while longer until DeLancey, seeing that Hamilton was getting the better of it, intervened by suggesting that the jury limit itself to considering only the stipulated fact issue of publication: "Mr. Hamilton, the jury may find that Zenger printed and published those papers and leave it to the court to judge whether they are libelous. You know this is very common. . . . *It is in the nature of a special verdict, where the jury leave the matter of law to the court.*"

With exceeding restraint and good manners, Hamilton disposed of this last gesture of the chief judge: "I know, may it please Your Honor, the jury may do so; but I do likewise know they may do otherwise. I know they have the right beyond all dispute to determine both the law and the fact, and where they do not doubt of the law, they ought to do so. This of leaving it to the judgment of the court whether the words are libelous or not in effect renders juries useless (to say no worse) in many cases."

DeLancey and Philipse deserve credit at least for not silencing Hamilton, who continued at considerable length to appeal to the jurors over the heads of the judges. He asked them once again what would be the point of a constitution giving the people opportunities to have wrongs redressed, only to be prevented from speaking out when they realize that a chief magistrate abuses the power with which he has been entrusted. "Of what use is this mighty privilege if every man that suffers must be silent? And if a man must be taken up as a libeler for telling his sufferings to his neighbor?"

"I differ very widely from Mr. Attorney when he would insinuate that the just complaints of a number of men who suffer under a bad administration is libeling that administration. I have reason to think that those in the administration have in this prosecution something more in view, and that the people believe they have a good deal more at stake than I apprehended, and therefore it is become my duty to be both plain and particular in this cause."

Except for an occasional archaic phrase, Hamilton could be appearing before a late-twentieth-century American jury. But instead of arguing against a "true libel," a charge rendered obsolete by the Zenger jury supported by both our Constitution and the English "Fox's Libel Act" of 1791, he would be speaking against the hypocrisy which would deny the people their right of redress of grievances in order to shield authority against public criticism. Today that deceit is called "sovereign immunity" which likewise would sanctify government and make it holy.

Have you not a legislature? Have you not a House of Representatives to whom you may complain? And to this I answer, we have, but what then? Is an assembly to be troubled with every injury done by a governor? Or are they to hear of nothing but what those in the administration will please to tell them? Or what sort of tryal must a man have? And how is he to be remedied? . . . I pray what redress is to be expected for an honest man who makes his complaint against a governor to an assembly who may properly be said to be made by the same governor against whom the complaint is made?

No, it is natural, it is a privilege, I will go farther, it is a right which all freemen claim and are entitled to complain when they are hurt. They have a right publickly to remonstrate the abuses of power in the strongest terms, to put their neighbors upon their guard, against the craft or open violence of men in authority, and to assert with courage the sense they have of the blessings of liberty, the value they put upon it, and their resolution at all hazards to preserve it as one of the greatest blessings heaven can bestow.

When a governor departs from the duty enjoined him by his sovereign and acts as if he were less accountable than the royal hand that gave him all that power and honor, this sets people upon examining and enquiring into this power authority and duty of such a magistrate and to compare those with his conduct.

This is precisely the same argument against "sovereign immunity."

Hamilton capped his presentation by telling the jury: "Upon these occasions it may be justly said that under plausible pretences of preventing sedition and other enormities, the people of England were cheated or awed into delivering up their ancient and sacred right of Tryals by Grand and Petty Juries."[21]

There are two types of men: "Men of honor and conscience when they see the liberty of their country is in danger, either by concurrence or silence . . . they freely make a sacrifice of any preferment or favor rather than be accessible to destroying the liberties of their country and entailing slavery upon their posterity." And "another set of men, of whom I have no hopes, who lay aside all other considerations and are ready to join with power in any shape, and with any man or sort of men by whose means or interest they may be assisted to gratify their malice and envy against whom they have been pleased to hate.

"The right of complaining or remonstrating is natural, and the restraint upon this natural right is the law only, and that those restraints can only extend to what is false."

At this point—and frequently during his presentation—"the numerous auditors" in attendance in the court room applauded, "and the approbation they gave it by their countenances made the court think proper to pass it over without notice."[22]

In concluding, Hamilton ignored DeLancey and Philipse completely, saying to the jurors: "Gentlemen, the danger is great in proportion to the mischief which may happen through our too great credulity. As the verdict (whatever it is) will be yours, you ought to refer no part of your duty to the discretion of other persons. If you shall be of opinion that there is no falsehood in Mr. Zenger's papers, you will, nay you ought to say so because you don't know whether others (I mean the court) may be of that opinion. It is your right to do so and there is much depending upon your resolution as well as upon your integrity.

"Power may justly be compared to a great river; while kept within its due bounds it is both beautiful and useful, but when it overflows its banks it is then too impetuous to be stemmed. It bears down all before it and brings destruction and desolation wherever it comes. If, then, this is the nature of power, let us at least do our duty, and like wise men who value freedom use our outmost care to support liberty—the only bulwark against lawless power."[23]

DeLancey then issued his "instructions." Knowing that he could not, of course, tell the jurors they had no power to act on the law, he tried to influence them. But realizing he was no match for Hamilton, he virtually capitulated, and delivered a short discourse:

> Gentlemen of the jury. The great pains Mr. Hamilton has taken to show how little regard juries are to pay to the opinion of the judges, and his insisting so much upon the conduct of some judges in trials of this kind is done, no doubt, with a design that you should take but very little notice of what I might say upon this occasion. I shall therefore only observe to you that as the facts or words in the Information are confessed: The only thing that can come in question before you is whether the words as set forth in the Information make a libel. And that is a matter of law, no doubt, and which you may leave to the court. But I shall trouble you no further with anything more of my own, but read to you the words of a learned and upright judge in a case of like nature.

He then quoted the jury instructions once given by Chief Justice Holt: "To say that corrupt officers are appointed to administer affairs is certainly a reflection on the government. If people should not be called to account for possessing the people with an ill opinion of the government, no government can subsist, for it is very necessary for all governments that the people should have a good opinion of it."

He concluded by advising that the only function of the jury was "to consider whether the words I have read to you do not tend to beget an ill opinion of the administration of government."[24]

The jury then withdrew, but was not out long. "In a small time returned, and being asked by the clerk whether they were agreed of their verdict, and whether John Peter Zenger was guilty of printing and publishing libels, they answered by Thomas Hunt, their foreman, Not Guilty, upon which the numerous audience expressed their joy in three loud Huzzas, and scarcely one person except the officers of the court were observed not to join in this noisy exclamation!"[25]

Resisting court pressure, the jurors had taken the law into their own hands and nullified it, believing, perhaps, that if it were necessary to the success of a government for the people to have a good opinion of it, the responsibility lay with the government to behave responsibly. That they came to their decision so quickly indicates no dissension in the jury room. It was a "one vote" verdict. This would indicate a probable disposition to acquit whoever might have been Zenger's advocate.

The jurors had agreed with Hamilton's defense that open criticism of government was proper. Today's judicially endorsed doctrine of "sovereign immunity" prevents that open criticism in exactly the same way as libel by stifling the vital redress against government excess, presumed to have been guaranteed by the First Amendment. Harvard professor Stanley Nider Katz analyzed the root of Hamilton's defense of Zenger as being the right of citizens to criticize their rulers. The law of seditious libel, as is the judicially imposed doctrine of sovereign immunity, was drawn up to shield the king and his ministers.

The proper function of government, as the twelve Zenger jurors determined by their verdict, was, and is, to protect each person's liberty; the rulers should serve as guardians of liberty, not offenders against it. The people are not obliged to support a government working against their interests. Freedom to criticize will prevent the commission of social evil "by making a governor sensible that it is in his interest to be just to those under his care."[26]

In a free society, the jury prohibits the neglect of laws, ensuring that popular rights will not be abused in the courts. Free speech and jury trial are thus the bastions of individual liberty in America, the bulwarks against lawless power.[27]

Colden, who was on the spot at the time of the trial and later became both a lieutenant governor and, at seventy-four in 1762, governor of the colony, added a postscript to the jury verdict. There certainly

> can be no fault or crime for exposing the publick faults or crimes of publick officers in a republick where the people are the supreme judges.
>
> What can be more astonishing in a free country than for judges in the seat of justice executing the most sacred trust that is delegated by mankind who in the execution of their offices ought to be [free] of all motives either from pleasure or displeasure, favor or fear who cannot suffer the least mixture of these to sway their judgments or influence their determinations without violation of their oath and sacred trust [or] to make either their pleasure or displeasure the rule of their conduct? For if a commission issue to try my life or take away my estate not according to the law of the land but by discretion or will of my judges and I may not except to that commission and show it to be unlawful, what security can I have of a tryal by a jury and the law of the land?

Rutherfurd observed that the only restraints upon the right to freedom of discussion were those imposed by the law of libel. This law was enforceable only by general judgments of courts founded on special verdicts of juries. "For though the law of the country entitled a defendant to a trial by jury, yet as the judges were allowed to pass upon both the facts and the law, the result was a practical denial of the right of trial."

The jury in Zenger's trial first established in North America the principle that in prosecutions for libel the jury were the judges of both the law and facts, a principle incorporated in 1791 in Fox's Libel Act. The liberty of the press was secure from assault, and the people became equipped with the most powerful weapon for successfully combatting arbitrary power—the right of freely criticizing the conduct of public men. The result of the trial was to imbue the people with a new spirit, and henceforth they were united in the struggle against government oppression.

Gouverner Morris at the time of the signing of the Declaration of Independence said: "The trial of Zenger was the germ of American freedom, the morning star of that liberty which subsequently revolutionized America."

New York Times publisher Arthur Hays Sulzberger, in his dedication of the Zenger Memorial plaque on April 23, 1953, stated that "The fundamental premise of a democratic government is that ultimate control will be exercised by sound public opinion operating through the ballot and the many other channels of expression available in a free society."

Although Sulzberger did not specifically say it, chief among these "other channels" is trial by jury as manifested by the jury's "ultimate control" in the Zenger case (and others in this book). Thus, applying his reasoning to the jury as well as to the press, Sulzberger advised:

> To safeguard their sacred liberties, the people must not only have the final voice, but they must also have the full, unimpeded information on which sane appraisal and wholesome judgment can be based.
>
> A partially informed public—or, worse yet, a misinformed public—is an easy prey to tyranny and dictatorship. The history of our times spells this sad moral all too clearly.[28]

The people's "final voice" is expressed through the jury—a jury not partially informed, per current court practice, but having "full, unimpeded information."

NOTES

1. Leonard W. Levy, *Emergence of a Free Press* (New York: Oxford University Press, 1985), p. 130.

2. Livingston Rutherfurd, *John Peter Zenger, His Press, His Trial* (Gloucester, Mass.: Peter Smith, 1963), p. 126.

3. James Alexander, *A Brief Narrative of the Case and Trial of John Peter Zenger*, reprint edition edited by Stanley Nider Katz (Cambridge, Mass.: The Belknap Press, 1963), p. 210, n. 56; *New York Times*, April 24, 1953, p. 19.

4. Rutherfurd, *John Peter Zenger, His Press, His Trial*, p. 56.

5. *The Letters and Papers of Cadwallader Colden, 1749–1755* (New York: New York Historical Society, 1937), p. 326.

6. Alexander, *A Brief Narrative of the Case and Trial of John Peter Zenger*, p. 11.

7. Rutherfurd, *John Peter Zenger, His Press, His Trial,* p. 28.

8. Ibid., p. 29.

9. Ibid., p. 31.

10. Alexander, *A Brief Narrative of the Case and Trial of John Peter Zenger,* p. 11.

11. *The Letters and Papers of Cadwallader Colden,* p. 283.

12. Rutherfurd, *John Peter Zenger, His Press, His Trial,* pp. 33–34.

13. Ibid., p. 39.

14. 4 Blackstone Comm. 58.

15. *The Letters and Papers of Cadwallader Colden,* p. 325.

16. Rutherfurd, *John Peter Zenger, His Press, His Trial,* pp. 52–53.

17. Alexander, *A Brief Narrative of the Case and Trial of John Peter Zenger,* p. 210, n. 61.

18. Rutherfurd, *John Peter Zenger, His Press, His Trial,* p. 58.

19. *The Letters and Papers of Cadwallader Colden,* p. 339.

20. The quotations that follow and details of the trial are taken from sources already cited, including Rutherfurd, *John Peter Zenger, His Press, His Trial,* p. 56; *The Letters and Papers of Cadwallader Colden*; and Alexander, *A Brief Narrative of the Case and Trial of John Peter Zenger,* as well as T. B. Howell, *The Trial of John Peter Zenger,* in *Complete State Trials* (1813), 17: 675 ff., and *The Trial of John Peter Zenger for Libel, New York City, 1735,* vol. 16.

21. *The Letters and Papers of Cadwallader Colden,* p. 336.

22. Ibid., p. 337.

23. Ibid.; Rutherfurd, *John Peter Zenger, His Press, His Trial,* pp. 121–22; Alexander, *A Brief Narrative of the Case and Trial of John Peter Zenger,* p. 98.

24. Alexander, *A Brief Narrative of the Case and Trial of John Peter Zenger,* pp. 99–100.

25. Ibid., p. 100; *The Letters and Papers of Cadwallader Colden,* p. 339; Rutherfurd, *John Peter Zenger, His Press, His Trial.*

26. Alexander, *A Brief Narrative of the Case and Trial of John Peter Zenger,* pp. 23–24.

27. Ibid., p. 25.

28. *New York Times,* April 24, 1953, p. 19.

6

ALIEN AND SEDITION ACTS TRIALS, 1798 TO 1800

*U*ntil the American revolutionary movement had solidified the new government and established George Washington as president, the great patriot party, the Federalists, had always been on the outside. At long last, in 1789, they were *in,* and they remained the *in* power through both Washington's and John Adams's administrations. By 1798, after nine years, they were getting so used to it that, in keeping with the character of almost every revolution before theirs, staying "in" had replaced in priority a declaration of high ideals. Whatever the cost, the "outs" had to be kept out. The most troublesome "outs" were Republican blasphemers of the "ins." They were especially obstreperous about President Adams, taking him on in speech and through their press. All the while, immigrants were illegally flooding American shores, among them nonconforming Irishmen.

Extreme steps had to be taken in time to secure the election of 1800. The Federalist-dominated Congress knew what to do: silence the Republican opponents and keep out the immigrants.

They would do this with two laws, the Alien and Sedition Acts, one declaring that defamatory remarks about the government were "seditious libels," and the other limiting immigrant rights. It is difficult to accept the fact that so many declarers of independence only two decades earlier could rationalize such a 180-degree turn, unless we are able to view the history of revolutions through the eyes of Catherine

Drinker Bowen and appreciate the sagacity of her observation that every successful revolution adopts the tactics of the tyranny overthrown. The Federalist "ins" had begun to operate under the delusion that resistance to them was "faction" and not in conformance with the Constitution. As for aliens, they had no business opposing anything.

The "in" party refused to accept criticism as honest political dissent and the expression of minority opinion. To be on the other side was, by definition, to threaten the stability of government; the people had to be protected against dangerous ideas. Now, wasn't that the policy of the British royalists the revolutionaries had so recently fought against as outsiders?

But, of course, dissent could not be silenced, and never can be, however "seditious" and whatever the punishment. Speakers and writers of it would be charged, indicted, and brought to trial; their trials would be before "juries." As it turned out, however, these "juries," in every instance except one and a half, convicted almost summarily, sending their victims to prisons and often imposing heavy fines.

Looking back two centuries, we might question how we can rate the jury as so grand a defender of liberty when it has so dismal and consistent a record of failure in these cases. In every trial of a dozen or so except one, and half of another, the jurors did not nullify; they "follow[ed] the law as I dictate it to you." They were specifically instructed by judges that they had no power to nullify. The law was read to them— but not the whole law. They were given the Federalist version of "seditious libel," but what was not read to them was a provision in the Sedition Act which spelled out that the jurors most certainly had the right to veto the act itself if they didn't like it. Any attempt by the defense to read to the jurors that part of the act was judicially squelched. But this was not the only reason for the series of less than heroic verdicts.

British historian Lord Acton coined in 1887 a phrase which is usually misquoted by elision. The way he said it was: "Power *tends to* corrupt, and absolute power corrupts absolutely."

One hundred and five years before that, British jurist Sir William Jones expressed the same concept in different words: "Power should always be distrusted in whatever hands it is placed." And Henry Brooks Adams might have been commenting about his great-grandfather's presidency when he recorded in his *Education of Henry Adams* that "A friend in power is a friend lost."

Even Adams himself, who in earlier decades had been proclaimed justly as one of the greatest champions of liberty, is supposed to have mused when power came to him in 1797 that perhaps he, too, had been corrupted by it. And perhaps he had, or allowed himself to be by so many of the ministers surrounding him, including his wife, Abigail.

The Constitution nominally divides government into three divisions to prevent concentration of power, but actually there are four—three comprise the government itself; the fourth operates outside the government and has supervision over it. Outside supervision is essential because government holds the power which tends to corrupt it. Policy making is given exclusively to the legislature; implementing policy is the responsibility of the executive. Judicial power was intended to be limited to the single function of measuring policy against the Constitution, but not to evaluate or censure it. Each division was to be restrained from encroaching upon the province of another. However, encroachment, being temptation, was and remains a constant danger, as demonstrated by the judiciary which has, without constitutional authority, made itself into an unlawful, dominant legislature.

The fourth division stands outside the government to cry "stop!" whenever it goes too far. This division is composed of the whole body of citizens who, as "the governed," retain veto over their governors who "derive their just powers from the *consent of the governed.*" Since the "whole body" cannot act in unison, it acts in representative units. The most effectual units for expressing consent and supervision are, without question, trials by jury. Through their verdicts as members of jury panels, the governed express their consent, or exercise their veto. The effect is direct and immediate. When their power to express consent is seized or denied, as in the Alien and Sedition Acts trials, the government dominates and becomes tyrannical. If the people are frustrated beyond their ability to endure, when the evil is longer sufferable, they are impelled to turn to militant action. It is far less disruptive to society to respect the consent of the governed through the legal process established in the courtroom, which, although consistently breached, is constitutionally mandated. Our educational system fails to inform the people of their ultimate sovereignty, and thus we tend to allow ourselves to be subdued by government *servants.*

Thirty-three years before he signed the repressive legislation, a youthful John Adams, twenty-nine, wrote that the power of the people to vote for legislative representatives together with trials by jury comprised "wholly the liberty and security of the people."

> They have no other fortification against wanton, cruel power; no other indemnification against being ridden like horses, fleeced like sheep, worked like cattle, and fed and clothed like swine and hounds; no other defense against fines, imprisonments, whipping posts, gibbets, bastinadoes and racks. . . . A man can be subjected to no laws which he does not make himself, or consent to. . . . What a satisfaction is it to reflect that he can lie under the imputation of no guilt, be subjected to no punishment, lose none of his property . . . but by the judgment of his peers, his equals, his neighbors, men who have no end to serve by punishing him.[1]

How necessary it is to establish and enforce restraints was made evident almost as soon as they had been established. Only eleven years after the Constitution was written, and less than seven after the Bill of Rights, the safeguards would be invoked to protect the nation from the transgressions of many of the very founders who wrote the safeguards in. During Adams's second year in office, a notable band surrounding him attempted to knock down the barriers against tyranny they themselves had set up. For a short period they succeeded, but these same men had embedded the safeguards so securely that they held against the attacks, and their own challenges against them collapsed within three years.

When John Adams signed the Alien Act on July 6, 1798, he was nominally invested with power to order

> all such aliens as he should judge dangerous to the peace and safety of the United States, or should have any reasonable grounds to suspect were concerned in any treasonable or secret machinations against the government thereof to depart out of the territory of the United States within such time as should be expressed in such order.[2]

An open-ended invitation to absolutism! No checks! no balances! Clearly antithetical to a declaration that all people are endowed by their Creator with certain *unalienable* rights! And in another eight days, this one-time champion of the right of every person not to lose his property "but by the judgment of his peers, his equals, his neighbors," would sign the Sedition Act, which described sedition as almost any oral or published statement unfavorable to the president, Congress, or government in general. The heart of this act was that if any person should write, print, utter, or publish, or shall cause or procure to be written, printed, uttered or published, or shall knowingly assist or aid . . . any false, scandalous and malicious writing or writings against the government of the United States, or either House of the Congress of the United States, or the President . . . with intent to defame the said government . . . or to bring either of them into contempt or disrepute; or to excite against them . . . the hatred of the good people of the United States or to stir up sedition within the United States . . . excite any unlawful combinations . . . opposing or resisting any law . . . or any act of the President . . . done in pursuance of such law . . . or to resist, oppose, or defeat any such law or act . . . then such person, being thereof convicted . . . shall be guilty of misprision of treason. . . .[3]

Two palliatives softened the sting. The first was that the Sedition Act would expire absolutely on the third day of March 1801, coincident with the end of the first, and as it turned out only, term of the Adams presidency. The second was more significant: any person prosecuted under the act would be able

to give in evidence, the truth of the matter contained in the publication charged as a libel. And the *jury who shall try the cause, shall have a right to determine the law and the fact,* under the direction of the court, as in other cases.[4] (Italics added)

Didn't this last conform to the philosophy expressed by John Adams back in 1766? Wasn't this no more than his endorsement of jury review of the law?[5]

Two years earlier, Chief Justice John Jay wrote in *Georgia* v. *Brailsford* (3 Dallas 4, 1796) for a majority of the United States Supreme Court that the jury had a right "to determine the law as well as the fact in controversy." This caveat would several times be either prominently evaded or invoked during the three years that the two acts were in force.

Conspicuously omitted from "protection" was the vice-president. This would seem almost prescient. Adams, Congress, and the government were controlled by the Federalist party; the vice-president was a rival Republican. Indeed, he was no other than Thomas Jefferson, who, with full Republican support, resisted both acts. The Senate had passed the bills 18 to 10, and the House with a squeaky majority of two and four votes respectively for each.[6] If their intent was to secure Federalist power, the bills were defeatist. Adams, who had won his presidency over Jefferson by a slim three votes in the electoral college in 1796, would, largely as a consequence, lose in 1800 by a larger margin. (He came in third, after Aaron Burr.) The Federalists' nine years of contagious contact with power (since the Washington presidency began in 1789) had apparently infected them. Even Washington himself, who, as president, resisted attempts to enthrone him as an American king, may have been corrupted when he endorsed the two acts and the prosecutions under them in August 1799, less than four months before his death on December 15.

Attempting to sidetrack this legislation, Jefferson authored and Madison became involved in what have come to be known as the Kentucky and Virginia resolutions. These were protests against both acts, declared by the respective state legislatures (Kentucky had become the fifteenth state in 1792) to violate the Constitution and to thus be unenforceable. Invoking the Tenth Amendment that "The powers not delegated to the United States . . . are reserved to the states respectively or to the people," the resolutions declared generally that the acts were "altogether void and of no force."[7] Both houses in Kentucky adopted the resolutions with only a single dissenting vote, to exercise the nullification power of a sovereign state over what the state decrees is an unconstitutional action by the federal government.[8]

There were approximately a dozen indictments and trials under the two acts; but before them, there were four indictments that did not reach trial stage. The first indictment was against Philadelphian Benjamin Franklin Bache, namesake of an illustrious grandfather and publisher of the money-losing newspaper *Aurora.* Bache had been needling the Adams administration so frequently that the agents of censorship were too impatient to wait until Adams had signed the bill. Two weeks before the effective date, on June 27, 1798, Bache was arrested on a warrant issued by judge Richard Peters.

At first this proved a boon to the *Aurora*'s circulation. Bache welcomed, indeed was almost eager to face, trial which was set for late 1798. He was secure in feeling that any jury would declare the law unconstitutional by acquitting him. Tragically, that was the summer of a devastating yellow fever epidemic in Philadelphia, and in September Bache fell victim to it. History and we lose because his probably would have been a crucial trial. The *Aurora* nonetheless continued to flourish under the guidance of Bache's widow, aided by William Duane, a very vocal Irishman, whom we shall hear more about later.

The second indictment was against a native Irishman, John Daly Burk, publisher of the *New York Time Piece*. He was doubly vulnerable because the Irish were selected targets of the Alien Act. Burk was arrested in July 1798, and was urged to deport himself rather than face a risky trial. He fled no further than Virginia, where he hid under an assumed name and escaped trial.

The third was Thomas Adams (no presidential kin), publisher of the Boston *Republican Independent Chronicle*. His warrant was signed by a judge of the Supreme Court, William Paterson, who was distinguished for having been a representative from New Jersey to the Constitutional Convention, and a signer, which would seem to indicate support for the unalienability of individual rights, such as free expression. This Adams was as scrappy and eager to contest charges as Bache had been, but history lost out again. Adams fell too seriously ill to stand trial.

One reason why indictments were coming so early, thick, and fast was that Secretary of State Timothy Pickering, in the face of his own proud revolutionary record opposing British oppression, did a volte-face by assuming the nonconstitutionally delegated function each day of scrutinizing all the Republican papers just to look for trouble. Exulting in his paranoia three days after the president had signed the Sedition Act, Pickering enjoyed being offended by a small upstate New York newspaper, the *Mount Pleasant Register*. He pounced upon publisher William Durrell.

Durrell was arrested, held on $4,000 bail (contrary to the Eighth Amendment's prohibition against excessive bail), and released when supporters put up the money. Despite their help, he could not carry the financial burden of trial. Fearful that he might unwittingly offend Secretary Pickering's pickiness further and be multiply charged, Durrell suspended publication. He succeeded in delaying trial for one year, but was reduced to poverty.

The first offender actually to go to trial was Vermont newspaper publisher Matthew Lyon. When charged with libeling Adams and other members of the government, he was a member of the government himself, having been a Republican congressman for two years and now running for a second term. His offenses had occurred before the Sedition Act had become effective on July 14, 1798, but the government found excuse enough for not treating this as *ex post facto* since publication came after that date.

Lyon was an ideal target; not only did the Federalists want to defeat him in that year's elections, but he was Irish-born, although he had lived mostly in Vermont since before the Revolution. Two judges presided at his trial, acting more like prosecutors than impartial arbiters. Little wonder. The senior judge was the same William Paterson who had ordered the arrest of Thomas Adams; the second was Samuel Hitchcock, reported in *American State Trials* as having been a member of the Vermont delegation to ratify the Constitution.[9] (Vermont had become the fourteenth state in 1791.) Hitchcock's prejudice against Lyon was strident, since he had been defeated by Lyon in the runoff election for congressman in 1796.[10]

The first count against Lyon was a letter he had written in response to an earlier letter in a Federalist newspaper in Vermont attacking him for not supporting the president. Lyon replied that he could not support "the Executive" because he saw "every consideration of the public welfare swallowed up in a continual grasp for power, in an unbounded thirst for ridiculous pomp, foolish adulation, or selfish avarice," and that "men of merit [were] daily turned out of office for no other cause but independence of sentiment," to be replaced by "men of meanness."

There were two other counts involving the revolutionary government of France in which Lyon denounced Adams for sending a message to Congress advocating preparedness for war. Lyon did not want war.

His trial began on Monday, October 9, 1798. So confident was Lyon of the unconstitutionality of the Sedition Act that he continued to publish freely while conducting his campaign for reelection. He sought no quarter from his political enemies. When he appeared for trial, he discovered that the Federalist marshal Jabez Fitch had produced a jury *venire* of only fourteen candidates, all members of the Federalist party. Twelve of these had opposed Lyon in the previous election, and were described as zealous partisans for presidential infallibility."[11]

Lyon has told us how his jury was stacked: "So ignorant was I of law proceedings, that I expected to object off the inveterate part of the jury without giving particular reason. . . . I was, therefore, unprepared." It did not occur to him that he could have challenged the entire *venire*.[12]

He relates that when "the Attorney for the United States" was asked if he had any objections to the jury, he said he objected to a Mr. Board. The sheriff had had a conversation with Board the previous Saturday when Board expressed the opinion that Lyon should not be condemned. Judge Paterson ordered him off. Lyon lamented that this juror "was the only man that knew me well enough to judge my intentions."

"I objected to two of the jury on account of their violent opposition to me," Lyon has recorded. "I called on some persons present to see if they could recollect any virulence made use of by those two." One of these "was shown to have been the author of an article in a newspaper, inveighing politically and personally against the defendant."[13]

Lyon continues: "The Judge observed that a difference in political opinion could be reason against a juryman" and he ordered this one off, reducing the panel to twelve.[14] Lyon had wished to challenge up to six more, understanding that the law permitted him that many challenges, but Paterson forbade him.

Unable to secure professional legal representation, Lyon conducted his defense himself. He readily admitted authorship and publication, relying for his defense upon proving the truth of his accusations or, more effectively, the unconstitutionality of the law. He called no witnesses and presented a brief and weak defense because of a lack of courtroom skills.

Although the prosecutor addressed the jury at length, his services were hardly needed. Paterson assumed the prosecutor's function in his closing "instructions" to the jury. He set the tone for future trials by not only refusing to cite but actually denying the critical caveat regarding jury nullification: "You have nothing whatever to do with the constitutionality of the sedition law," he lied. "Congress has said that the author and publisher of seditious libels is to be punished; and until this law is declared null and void by a tribunal competent for the purpose, its validity cannot be disputed."

But even this deception was not enough. Paterson continued:

Great would be the abuses were the constitutionality of every statute to be submitted to a jury, in each case where the statute is to be applied. The only question you are to determine is, that which the record submits to you. Did Mr. Lyon publish the writing given in the indictment? Did he do so seditiously?

The balance of Paterson's charge was weighted against Lyon so heavily that if "nullification" was involved, it was Paterson who was nullifying true law, a power not given to judges by the Constitution—patriot Paterson, founder Paterson, signer of the Constitution guaranteeing freedom of expression! Unquestionably his was judicial encroachment upon the province of the legislature and of the jury.

Paterson misled the jurors by "instructing" them that Lyon's defense was merely an appeal to their feelings, calculated to excite pity; but mercy had no place in their deliberations. He "directed" the jurors to "follow the law" as he explained it, and that the law was constitutional.[15] He did not inform the jurors about the nullification clause in the Sedition Act, and it was still a month before the Kentucky Resolution.

It was now about seven o'clock in the evening, and the jurors were sent out to deliberate. There is no mention in trial records as to whether they had been fed during the day. The English practice was to starve jurors until they had delivered the verdict. The Lyon jurors returned in one hour, but they had not nullified. They took the law as it had been dictated to them. Paterson vindictively sentenced Lyon to four months in prison and fined him one thousand dollars plus the costs of prosecution.[16]

If the Lyon trial is counted as a success for the Federalist tyranny, it certainly cannot be counted as a "jury trial," whatever the historical record shows. The twelve men in this jury box were no more a "jury" than a manikin in a store window is a person. The form is not the substance. If you are not deceived by the second, you cannot let yourself be deceived by the first.

Imprisonment stunned Lyon as its purpose was pure persecution; but as far as his campaign for reelection was concerned, it boomeranged. Even though he was suffering an unusually arduous, cruel term (or maybe because he was), he was reelected by almost double the number of votes over his Federalist opponent. The Federalist press fumed.

Lyon later moved to Kentucky and served several terms in Congress as a representative from that state until his death in 1822. Eighteen years later, Congress ordered his fine refunded with interest to his heirs.[17]

The next effort by the Federalists to silence opposition was to turn back to the influential *Aurora* in what was, until 1800, the nation's capital, Philadelphia. William Duane, who had taken over editorship following the death of Bache, continued shooting barbed arrows dipped in acid at the administration. He had also taken over the Widow

Bache. Duane was looked upon by the Federalists as a double target, prosecutable under both acts as opposition editor and Irish "alien."

However, this was not entirely correct. The Federalists would classify him as an immigrant who "arrived" in this country only two years before. Except it was not an "arrival" but a return after twenty-two years' absence. Duane had been born in 1760 in colonial New York, and his widowed mother brought him to her native Ireland when he was fourteen. He came back to the United States in 1796.

Secretary Pickering decided to harass Duane in December 1798. The editor was a sympathizer with the Irish rebellion against England, and had written that "the United Irishmen stand precisely in the same odious circumstances with relation to England that John Adams stood twenty years ago—they consider George III an intolerable tyrant now and he did then."[18] Pickering chose to interpret this as a libel against Adams, and denounced Duane as a United Irishman himself.

On Friday, February 7, 1799, a proposal was introduced into Congress to repeal the Alien Act, and hearings were scheduled for the following Monday, the 10th. A group of citizens and Irish-born "aliens" voted to present a petition to Congress urging repeal of the act. Seeking support for it, and because time was short, Duane and three recent immigrants from Ireland circulated petitions for signatures by visiting St. Mary's Catholic Church on Sunday and posting a number of small signs requesting "Natives of Ireland who worship at this church . . . to remain in the yard after divine service until they have affixed their signatures to a memorial for the repeal of the Alien bill."

Some of the Federalist church members, objecting to the postings, ripped the signs down. One member reported to the priest that "a seditious meeting" was being planned after the service. A large number of people gathered, and many signed. Someone shouted "Turn him out," and one of the three immigrants with Duane, a Dr. James Reynolds, was pushed. Reynolds drew out a gun to defend himself, aiming it at his attacker, James Gallagher, who knocked him down, disarmed and kicked him. Although there was no basis for accusing Duane, he and the other three men were charged with "being evilly disposed persons" who maliciously wanted to stir up a riot and "subvert the government of the United States."

Duane protested the indictment in part on the ground that to seek signatures was no more than to exercise a citizen's inherent right to petition for redress of grievances. Prosecutor Joseph Hopkinson, a prominent Federalist lawyer from Philadelphia, countered by arguing that the First Amendment guarantee did not apply to aliens who "have no right whatever to petition, or to interfere in any respect with the government of this country, as the right of voting in elections is confined to our citizens . . . if aliens do not like the laws of this country, God knows there are ways and wishes enough for them to go back again."

This Hopkinson had demonstrated a kind of double standard. Only the year before he had written the militantly patriotic song "Hail Columbia" which served as the unofficial national anthem until replaced by "The Star Spangled Banner." Hopkinson also contended that America's greatest evils arose from the "Introduction of this foreign leaven amongst us," which had "fermented the whole mass of the community" and "divided and rent" the country into contending political parties.[19]

Duane and his three associates were brought to trial in Philadelphia on February 21, only a dozen days after posting the petitions. Wharton in his *State Trials* does list the names of the twelve jurors, but reports nothing more about them than that "The names of the jury were then called over, and they were severally impanelled."[20]

The court began by asking the four defendants if they wanted to be tried separately by two different juries on separate charges, or all four together. The first charge against them was the same for all: maliciously and willfully stirring up a riot and assault on a holy day.[21] The second charge was against Reynolds alone for attempted murder. Although it would complicate the trial, the defendants chose to be tried together before a single jury, having confidence that the jurors would be capable of distinguishing between the two charges, and of separating the three other defendants from the second charge against Reynolds only.

Andrew (alternately Alexander) Dallas, who was to have been defense counsel for Benjamin Bache, now became Duane's chief counsel. The presiding judge was John D. Coxe with three assistant judges, one of whom, Jonathan B. Smith, had been a delegate to the Continental Congress and had signed the Articles of Confederation.

The accusers objected that the defendants had selected the hour of "divine worship" on church property to distribute petitions. Pastor Rev. Leonard Neale testified that posting the notices was "an insult to me and the board of trustees[, being] without my positive consent." The defense replied that since the hearings were to be held the next day, there was no time to wait. As to the charge of attempted murder, the defense argued that Reynolds was the true victim, having been threatened and attacked, and that he had drawn his gun only in self-defense.

Judge Coxe was not as fierce a prosecution's partisan as Paterson had been at Lyon's trial. He would allow the jury wider discretion; he suggested that "there is evidence of actual violence; now whether that violence has arisen out of the time and place chosen to collect subscriptions is a matter for consideration. Suppose the paper legitimate in all its parts but if it is carried in an illegitimate manner and a riot and trespass ensue, it matters very little what the contents of the paper may be."[22]

Although he did not cite the nullification clause directly, Coxe did suggest that the jurors had the right to determine how to apply the law: "If you should be of an opinion that the defendants came here with a view of doing an unlawful act, though one of them only might have committed the act, then there can be no kind of doubt that you can pronounce the whole of them guilty upon common law principles." But if their meeting was lawful and only one of them committed an unlawful act, "then only he would be guilty and the rest innocent."

He continued:

> It is now our duty . . . to compare the evidence with the law. . . . If you should be of the opinion that [the church] have this right to exclude any stranger [from what] is not common property . . . then certainly it was unlawful for the defendants to come and put up notices on that church, and particularly as they received the warning by the clerk pulling down the notices.

In further contrast with Lyon's judges, Coxe did not dictate the law. Coxe was also restrained with respect to Reynolds:

> There can be no doubt but he did present a pistol at J. Gallagher, but whether with intent to murder or not, you may judge by the circumstances. I do not doubt but you will dispassionately weigh the circumstances with due attention, and give that verdict which the various facts related to you dictate.[23]

The trial had taken the whole day; it was now about 9:30 on a dark, cold February night. The jury needed only half an hour to reach a verdict, which they inserted and sealed in a letter, but the court would not receive the letter that night. The trial record does not tell us whether the jurors were released or locked up, and if the latter, under what conditions. Nor do we know if the jury was fed or starved during the day.

As to the letter, was it deposited with the court or did the jurors keep it overnight? Wharton and *American State Trials* report only that the verdict "was delivered to the court the next morning." In whatever way it was handled, when the letter was opened it revealed that the twelve had agreed unanimously and very quickly to override both laws. They acquitted the four defendants on all counts.

These verdicts, reflecting jury independence, threatened the entire Federalist program, particularly coming so early in the prosecutions. The Federalists struck back insanely. First, they attacked Duane with greater ferocity (to libel him?), but Duane would not retreat. They would have indicted him again for further libeling President Adams by bringing him before United States Supreme Court Justice Bushrod Washington, nephew of George Washington; but Duane presented a letter from Adams admitting the truth of his allegations, so the attempt was frustrated. Blocked in this endeavor by the very safeguards against double jeopardy which they themselves had written, and fearing the likelihood of a second jury acquittal, his enemies attempted to try him before the Federalist-dominated United States Senate, despite the absence of any lawful authority for such a method of trial.

Ignoring this, the Senate, in March of 1800, acted on its own, and found "him guilty of seditious utterances." Duane responded by declaring that he would respect only the lawful and constitutional action of the Senate, as he also owed duties to be faithful to the Constitution and to public rights involved in the case. "No terror—no force—no menace—no fear" could make him betray the rights which the Senate had put at stake.[24] He continued to publish.

The third victim was the older brother of Thomas Adams, Abijah Adams. If the rapacious Federalists could not silence the *Republican Independent Chronicle* because Thomas was too critically ill to stand trial, they would try another angle. But Abijah was only the book-keeper and had nothing to do with printing or publishing the paper. The prosecutor stretched the definition of "publishing" to cover the handing out of papers to customers, and to the extent Abijah did this, he was engaged in "publishing." The brother was accordingly charged and brought before a jury on March 1, 1799. Chief Justice of the Massachusetts Supreme Court, Francis Dana, presiding, said nothing to the jury about their right to judge the law, but did declare that the English common law was the birthright of every American. The jurors (about whom we have no information) provided a perplexing half victory: not guilty of printing a libel, but guilty of publishing. Dana intervened by directing a verdict of guilty as charged. He sentenced Abijah to thirty days in the county jail and court costs, plus a surety bond that he would not commit a similar offense for one year.

Adams served the sentence "with resignation and fortitude." From his sick bed, Thomas proclaimed the *Chronicle* would continue publishing in the "cause of freedom." However, his illness became worse, and only a week after Abijah's release, he was forced to sell the paper to his young Republican printer, Ebenezer Rhoades. A week after that, Thomas died.

On September 21, 1799, Holt was brought before Oliver Ellsworth, a prominent figure at the Constitutional Convention only twelve years before. Ellsworth, now a Supreme Court justice, set trial for the following April. Bushrod Washington, who had been a member of the Virginia convention which had made that state the tenth to ratify the Constitution, was selected to preside at Holt's trial. Washington was a recent Adams designee to the high court.

Despite so honorable a background, this Washington stooped in his charge to the jurors to demonstrate extreme prejudice against Holt. He virtually convicted Holt himself by striking down defense arguments, which, of course, should be a function exclusively reserved for the jury uninfluenced by a judge. Washington told the jurors that Holt's publication was "libellous beyond even the possibility of a doubt" and declared the law constitutional. Without compunction, he passed over the vital nullifying clause.[25] (We might wonder how Uncle George reacted to his nephew's forsaking the principles of liberty.) These jurors, whose names we do not know, "retired overnight and returned a verdict of guilty" the next day.

When the Federalists decided to go after the Republican *Argus* in New York City, they did not choose as victim the editor but journeyman David Frothingham on the ground that almost anybody involved in printing and publishing was equally liable. Frothingham's trial started on November 21, 1799, before a jury which was cautioned by the judge that his was "a prosecution under the common law of our country, by which we and our ancestors had been governed from the earliest times; that according to that law, he who published a writing or printing, or even a picture tending to expose a man to hatred, contempt or ridicule, was guilty of the offence charged against the defendant." Frothingham's alleged libel was against "the name and reputation of General [Alexander] Hamilton," in an attempt "to cause it to be believed that [Hamilton] was opposed to the Republican Government of the United States."[26] Presiding Judge Radcliffe told the jury that there "could be no doubt" that Frothingham's attack was libelous.

The defendant was prohibited from introducing evidence proving the truth of his accusations because he was being tried, strangely, under a doctrine of libel derived from colonial days. Smith explains that "under this doctrine, the truth of the libel was no justification" as long as the statements exposed a man to "hatred, contempt or ridicule."[27] I am perplexed that Frothingham should have be so prosecuted sixty-three years after the John Peter Zenger jury had put down that philosophy, and six years since the passage in 1792 of Fox's Libel Act in England.

Judge Radcliffe, sitting with two other partisan Federalist judges, refused to permit the defense to introduce evidence to the jury to prove Frothingham's innocence and lack of malice by showing that the article in question was copied from another paper.[28] In his final charge to the jurors, Radcliffe virtually seized from them any discretion to acquit by announcing that it was the unanimous decision of the court that the matter was libelous. Although the stacked panel, handpicked by a Federalist sheriff, could nonetheless have made an independent decision, they were cowed by court pressure and did their judicially imposed duty.[29] But the jurors recommended clemency since Frothingham was the sole support of his wife and children. The vicious Radcliffe ignored the jury's recommendation, declaring that if the defendant had a wife and children, "he ought to have thought of them before he violated the laws of this country." Radcliffe excused his vituperation by declaring that the Sedition Act had nothing to do with liberty of the press, only with "licentiousness."

Two or three other editors were accused and indicted during the first half of 1800, but they were troubled by the rigid control over juries and decided to take the easier course of pleading guilty and dispensing with the ordeal of a rigged trial. The presidential election was so near at hand.

As these elections drew near, the Federalists stepped up the rate of prosecutions, hoping to ensure victory by disgracing the opposition with a series of quick convictions. They may have succeeded in the latter, but this did not contribute to victory. When Anthony Haswell was brought to trial in May 1800, his accusers in effect revived the jingoism that "only a witch defends a witch." Haswell was, like Matthew Lyon, a Vermont publisher and younger admirer. When Lyon was jailed, Haswell came to his defense by publishing in his *Vermont Gazette* an attack against the "political persecution" which had convicted him:

> Your representative [Matthew Lyon] is holden by the oppressive hand of usurped power in a loathsome prison, deprived almost of the right of reason, and suffering all the indignities which can be heaped upon him by a hard-hearted savage, who has, to the disgrace of Federalism, been elevated to a station where he can satiate his barbarity on the misery of his victims.[30]

His reference was to Jabez Fitch, the marshal who had assembled Lyon's jury, and who was now his jailer. Haswell had established a lottery to raise money to pay Lyon's fine of $1100. As a defender of a "libeler," the Federalists accused him also of libel.

This was not Haswell's only "offense." When deputies came to arrest him, he wrote that they were "as silent as the midnight police officers of the French Bastile [*sic*], the secret messengers for the Spanish Inquisition or the Mutes of the Turkish bowstring for strangling."[31]

Haswell was brought before the senior justice of the United States Supreme Court, William Cushing, where he was charged with a "false malicious wicked and seditious libel" against the government. His accusation read that he did "with force and arms wickedly, knowingly and maliciously, write, print, utter and publish . . . a certain scandalous and seditious writing or libel." Here is a kind of reluctant testimonial that by its character, the pen becomes "arms" of greater might than the sword.

Although neither Wharton nor *American State Trials* provides any information as to who composed the jury or how it was selected, we may presume that since Jabez Fitch was involved, Haswell's "jury" was stacked in the same way Lyon's was. Also, the presiding judges were the same persecuting pair of William Paterson and Samuel Hitchcock. In charging the jurors, Paterson practically ordered them to convict. He passed over the jury nullification clause.

Paterson, more prosecutor than judge, told this jury that Lyon was "a seditious libeller of your government, a convict justly suffering the penalty of a mild law, that spares the lives of those who had aimed at the subversion of all lawful authority," thus implying that only a seditious libeler would defend a seditious libeler. He asked the jury to consider Haswell's statement an "oppressive hand of usurped power," and said that if Lyon was in a "loathsome dungeon" [*sic*], it was because that place was proper "to correct a turpitude darker than its deepest gloom."

This judge now twisted the Constitution's defense of freedom to dissent into implied treason. It was up to the jury, he continued, "to preserve the Constitution from the malicious attacks of unprincipled sedition,"[32] which was to call resistance to Federalist policies "faction." Opposition to the administration was opposition to the Constitution, meaning that the party of Jefferson and Madison was not lawfully begotten.[33]

Added to this, Paterson directed that "If the jury, therefore, believe, beyond reasonable doubt, that the intent was defamatory and the publication was made, they must convict."[34] Operating under such conditions, and chosen as it had been, this "jury" could not have had the character of independence, which is essential to the nature of a true jury. After a brief deliberation, they followed orders. Haswell was condemned to two months in prison, and fined two hundred dollars and court costs.

In spite of this, Haswell still won. He did not have to suffer much of an ordeal because he served most of his time in his home town jail in Bennington under the watchful eyes of townfolk sympathizers. He continued to publish his paper, writing about his jail treatment, but underwent severe financial hardship. When Haswell appealed to John Adams for remission of a fine he could not pay, Adams ignored him.

In consideration of Haswell's being imprisoned, the town of Bennington postponed its "Independence Day" festivities in 1800 for five days until he was released on July 9. When the gates swung open for him he was given a hero's welcome by two thousand supporters. A band played "Yankee Doodle," and there was a parade through town. He was hailed as a martyr, and the Federalists lost that year's elections largely as a result. Haswell continued to publish the *Gazette* until his death in 1816. In 1844 Congress ordered that his fine be refunded to his heirs, together with over forty years' interest.

Ironically, at the same time as the government was persecuting the Republican press, the Federalist press was criticizing the Republicans in or out of government with no fear of being charged. Thus their *Hartford Courant* fired shrill invectives at rival Connecticut Republican editor Charles Holt of the *New London Bee,* but it was Holt, daring to answer, who got indicted.

William Durrell, who had ceased publication of his *Mount Pleasant Register* in 1799, was brought before Judge Washington when he came to trial in April 1800. Without hearing any defense testimony, Washington read his "charge to the jury," which essentially was a directive to convict; the pro-Federalist stacked jury obeyed him.[35]

When Jedediah Peck got the Federalist finger pointed at him, he was not in the newspaper business. Actually he had been for a time a Federalist judge of the Court of Common Pleas of New York State. He was twice disloyal to the party by supporting resolutions declaring the Alien and Sedition laws unconstitutional. His reward was to lose his judgeship. So he joined the party of Jefferson, and was elected to the General Assembly of New York from Otsego. He was indicted for having written a petition to Congress to repeal the acts.

One midnight shortly thereafter, several desperados entered Peck's home, manacled him, and dragged him to prison. Peck had been scheduled for an April 1800 trial, the same month of the new elections. But after his abduction and imprisonment, the Federalists feared that he had become a martyr to sympathize with, and that prosecution would go against them. They postponed his trial; his abductors released him, but he had already won sufficient sympathy to be re-elected. He never was brought to trial.[36]

Ann Greenleaf, the only woman to be indicted, had continued to publish the *New York Journal and Patriotic Register* and the *Argus* following the death of her husband also in the yellow fever epidemic. Mr. Greenleaf had already been accused of "audacious calumnies against the government." She had been scheduled for trial in April 1800, before Bushrod Washington. However, she decided to cease publication in March and Secretary Pickering recommended that John Adams drop the charges. The president suggested *nolle prosequi,* indicating unwillingness to press suit. Ann Greenleaf escaped trial.

When Thomas Cooper was brought to trial in Philadelphia on April 19, 1800, he raised the issue of selecting juries by Federalist sheriffs. However, he did not so much contest or challenge the method as complain after the fact. Cooper was accused of defaming President Adams in his new *Sunbury and Northumberland Gazette,* but, he alleged, it was "nothing which truth will not justify."[37] The records tell us only that a jury was "selected," but not how, and jurors were "sworn," but not identified. Not until after this was a *fait accompli* did Cooper question the procedure:

> Directly or indirectly, the public if not the private character of the President of the United States is involved in the present trial. Who nominates the judges who are to preside? the juries who are to judge of the evidence? the marshall who has the summoning of the jury?— the President! Suppose a case of arbitration concerning the property of any one of you, where the adverse party should claim the right of nominating the persons whose legal opinions are to decide the law of the question, and of the very man who shall have the appointment of the arbitrators—what would you say to such a trial? and yet in fact such is mine, and such is the trial of every man who has the misfortune to be indicted under this law.[37]

With the jurors already sworn, Cooper expressed confidence in them, addressing them as follows:

> Although I have a right to presume something of a political bias against my opinions, from the court who try me, to you who sit there as jurymen, I am still satisfied you will feel that you have some character to support and some character to lose; and whatever your opinions may be on the subjects alluded to in the indictment, you will reverence as you ought the sacred obligation of the oath you have taken.

The prosecutor, William Rawle, had already advised the jurors that they, "as citizens, must determine whether from the publications of this kind, the prosperity of the country was not endangered; and whether it was not their duty, when a case of this nature was laid before them and the law was applicable, to bring in such a verdict as the law and evidence would warrant; and show that these kinds of attacks on the government of the country were not to be suffered with impunity."

Presiding at this trial was a four-year member of the United States Supreme Court, Samuel Chase, who, when he was thirty-five, had joined the Second Continental Congress to help write the Declaration of Independence and then signed it. He had also been a member of the Maryland convention which had ratified the Constitution. Additionally he had endorsed the policy of jury nullification. But now, in his sixties, he had put all that behind him. By 1800 as an in-power Federalist, he had become affected by the contagion.

From the beginning of the trial, Chase used prosecutorial talk, not that of a supervising judge. He challenged Cooper, who had just told the jury he had published nothing but the truth, that: "If you undertake to publish without having proper evidence before you to justify your assertions, you do it at your own risk." He suggested that Cooper "could not offer the evidence [regarding Adams] you mention."[38]

He demonstrated extreme prejudice throughout the trial, and was unrestrained when he delivered his "Charge to the Jury":

> When men are found rash enough to commit an offense such as the traverser is charged with, it becomes the duty of the government to take care that they should not pass with impunity. It is my duty to state to you the law on which this indictment is preferred, and the substance of the accusation and defense.

As the several judges before him had done, when it came to reading the Sedition Act to the jury, Chase elided all references to the power of the jury to determine the constitutionality of the act. Instead he held over them the fear of destruction of the "republican government" by "luxury, or the licentiousness of the press." Chase would not leave even the determination of the fact to the jurors. He delivered dictatorially his interpretation, leaving the jurors no alternative but to convict. He may have suggested to the jury that "It is your business to consider the intent" of publication of "a false, scandalous and malicious libel upon the president," but he proceeded to direct the jurors that what Cooper had published was "false, scandalous and malicious."

Cooper's "crime" had been to charge Adams with having advocated "saddling" the nation "with the expense of a permanent navy and the existence of a standing army." He had also accused the president of having reduced the country's credit "so low as to borrow money at eight per cent in time of peace." This was a very high rate at that time.

"This is a gross attack upon the president," Chase would dictate the verdict to the jurors. "Can you believe it?"

"The other part of the publication is much more offensive." Chase continued, "where the traverser charges the President with having influenced the judiciary department. . . . Upon the purity and independence of the judges depend the existence of your government and the preservation of your liberties. They should be under no influence—they are only accountable to God and their own consciences."

The publication, Chase said, "is the boldest attempt I have known to poison the minds of the people . . . there is no subject which the people of America feel more alarm about than the establishment of a standing army. Once persuade them that the government is attempting to promote such a measure, and you destroy their confidence in the government." Chase accused Cooper of not having proved that the president had advocated a standing army.

Finally Chase instructed that Cooper had to prove every charge "to the marrow. If he asserts three things and proved but one or two, he fails, for he must prove the whole of his assertions to be true." And this, Chase had determined, Cooper had not done.

With directives such as these, there was little space for jury discretion, particularly when it had been stacked by a Federalist marshal. This non-jury acceded to the demands of the Federalist judge.

Several months later, the *Gazette of the United States* revealed how well stacked the jury was. On October 13 and 15 the paper identified three members of the indicting grand jury as candidates for offices on the Federalist ticket; and one member of the trial jury, even as he was serving, as a Federalist candidate for the Philadelphia common council.[39]

Chase fined Cooper four hundred dollars and ordered him imprisoned for six months, but imprisonment did not silence him. Cooper accused Chase of "improper conduct," saying that Chase had no right to argue the case against him, to correct the weaknesses of prosecutor Rawle, or to let the jury perceive his bias.[40]

Forty years afterward, in 1840, Congress ordered the fine repaid with interest. And just in time. It was the year of Cooper's death at age eighty-one.

Chase operated under a double standard—one for himself and another for the jurors. He was open and unabashed about expressing hostility against defendants, with no compunction to recuse himself. But he would not tolerate bias in the jurors. That is, he would not tolerate a bias favorable to the defendants. After he had victimized Cooper,

Chase "presided" over the most celebrated, the most significant, and also the final trial in the series during the first week of June 1800 in Richmond, Virginia. "Presided," in his case, is not quite the verb to use. "Prosecuted" is more appropriate, and his quarry was James Thompson Callender, "of whom," according to *American State Trials,* "nothing good is known."[41] But we are not so much interested in Callender's personality or character as in his trial. At least he was not Irish, but an émigré from Scotland, and was not an editor but a pamphleteer. But he must have done something good to get himself charged largely on the basis of his pamphlet titled *The Prospect Before Us,* wherein his principle target was Adams. His specific invectives and vituperations, acidic as they were, are not as important to our discussion as is the trial.

He managed to acquire an outstanding defense team of three brilliant young lawyers so dedicated to the cause of liberty of the press that they served without fee. (He didn't have the money anyway.) They were Philip Nicholas and George Hay, both of whom later became judges themselves, and William Wirt, who was to be attorney general of the United States during the administration of President James Monroe.

Chase's prejudice was so obvious from the opening of the trial on June 2, it is a wonder that the three did not try to force him to withdraw. They did, however, challenge the method of jury selection, the only time this was done.

When the jurors were assembled and Chase ordered them impaneled, Nicholas interrupted with a challenge to the array. Chase thundered, but Nicholas persisted: "I believe there is testimony in court to prove that one of the jurors returned by the marshal has expressed his sentiments hostile to the traverser. It is like a case stated in the books, where a verdict was set aside because a juryman had previously said that the man accused ought to be hanged, and in that case, on the second trial, every juryman was called to say whether he had formed any opinion on the subject or not."[42]

The challenge was justified. This panel, like all the rest, had been picked by Federalist marshals, in this case David Randolph, who, according to John Heath, a member of the bar of the Richmond circuit, had been instructed by Chase to strike "any of those creatures or people called democrats."[43] Chase later denied having said this.

An argument ensued between Chase and Nicholas as to the method of challenging juror prejudice. Nicholas maintained that finding a partial juror was ground for challenging the array based on the partiality of the sheriff. Since the clerk of the Circuit Court, William Marshall, did swear that every talesman was opposed to Callender "in political sentiments," Nicholas believed this to be sufficient ground for fearing bias in all of them.

But Chase wanted to protect his position. He had already been unrestrained in condemning Callender, a supporter of Jefferson, for his writings. Callender had assisted William Duane in editing the *Philadelphia Aurora* before fleeing to Virginia to escape prosecution and to write for the *Richmond Examiner.* The Virginia legislature had declared the Alien and Sedition Acts unconstitutional, making Callender feel safer there—for two years anyway. He published *The Prospect Before Us* from there in 1799. Chase had labeled this "seditious" and "utterly depraved."

While Chase professed to be a "great friend" of liberty of the press, he saw a difference between "liberty" and "licentiousness." "Licentiousness," he said, was "an abusive press" which would destroy any government, especially a republican government, by "corrupting public opinion and undermining the morals of the people." Judging by his behavior in the Cooper and Callender trials, his definition of "liberty of the press" appears to have meant freedom of Federalist editors to criticize Jeffersonian republicanism, while "licentiousness" meant Republican criticism of Federalism. Ben Franklin had expressed a different view:

> If by the liberty of the press were understood merely the liberty of discussing the propriety of public measures and political opinions, let us have as much of it as you please.

Chase declared that "if a jury of honest men" could be found in Richmond, Callender would be punished, and he made it his crusade to find his kind of "honest men."

Thus he went to Richmond for the specific purpose of prosecuting (i.e., as presiding judge) Callender in trial. Now that he was there, he could not allow the defense team to defeat his primary purpose. He directed Nicholas either to "bring in proof if you can that any juror has delivered his opinion upon that case heretofore; or you may examine the juror himself. . . . You may do either but not both."

Nicholas decided to examine the jurors individually, but Chase stymied his examination. When the defense sought permission to ask jurors if they had formed and delivered an opinion on *The Prospect Before Us,* Chase declared the question improper. The only question he would allow was "Have you ever formed and delivered an opinion upon the charges contained in the indictment?" But the jurors had not as yet seen the indictment, so of course they would all answer no. Then defense counsel George Hay asked that the indictment be read to each juror in turn, because perhaps when they had heard and understood the charges they would answer that they had both formed and delivered opinions upon them.

But Chase felt he had already indulged the defense as far as he would allow, and would go no further. This frustrated the team by preventing a successful challenge of any juror. Even when a talesman named Bassett voluntarily confessed that he had read *The Prospect Before Us* and had formed a negative opinion, Chase refused to let him be excused. The result was, according to the *Aurora,* "a jury conveniently packed."

Chase continued to express his bias throughout the trial. He placed the burden of proof upon the defendant under presumption of guilt, declaring that every person who published an alleged libel ought always to have on hand the documents to prove the truth of his assertions. Hay had tried to argue that the writings in question were expressions of opinion not covered by the law, but Chase declared them to be facts falsely stated, and declared it "sufficiently obvious" that he had published them with "bad intentions."

He allowed prosecuting counsel to introduce at least nine witnesses to testify against Callender, and to permit a lengthy argument before the jury, but he rebuffed defense requests for witnesses to justify Callender's accusations against the president. Chase told Nicholas that "Juries are only to hear legal evidence, and the courts are the only judges of what is or is not legal evidence." "Illegal evidence once heard may make an undue impression, and therefore ought not to be heard at all by the jury."[44]

"My country has made me a judge, and you must be governed now by my opinion, though I may be mistaken," Chase declared pompously. He refused to allow defense witnesses to testify and frequently interrupted the defense attorneys. When Nicholas suggested that it might be proper to prove one part of a specific charge by one witness and another part by other evidence, Chase told him his recommendation was "irregular and subversive of every principle of law . . . calculated to deceive the people but very incorrect." He would demean defense counsel by addressing them as "young gentlemen," which they were, but in a manner to degrade their erudition, which was, in their youth, considerable. Nicholas was twenty-seven, Wirt was twenty-eight, and Hay their contemporary.

The climax of Chase's duplicity came when the defense tried to bring before the jury the third clause of the law recognizing the right of the jury to determine constitutionality. William Wirt introduced the subject:

> Permit me, gentlemen of the jury, to pass on to the law under which we are indicted. You will find that a material part of your inquiry will relate to the powers of a jury over the subject committed to them, whether they have the right to determine the law as well as the fact. In Virginia an act of the assembly has adopted the common law of England [and] . . . by an act of Congress the rules of proceedings in the Federal courts in the several states are directed to conform to the rules of the states. . . . By the common law of England, juries possess the power of considering and deciding the law as well as the fact, in every case which may come before them. I have no doubt I shall receive the correction of the court if I am wrong in these positions. If, then, a jury in a court of the state would have a right to decide the law and the fact, so have you. The Federal Constitution is the supreme law of the land; and a right to consider the law is a right to consider the Constitution. If the law of Congress under which we are indicted be an infraction of the Constitution, it has not the force of law, and if you were to find the traverser guilty under such an act you would violate your oaths.[45]

This was getting to be too much for Chase. He interrupted and angrily ordered Wirt to "Take your seat, sir, if you please. If I understand you rightly you offer an argument to the petit jury to convince them that the statute of Congress . . . is contrary to the Constitution of the United States, and therefore void. Now I tell you this is irregular and inadmissable; it is not competent to the jury to decide on this point; but if you will address yourselves, gentlemen, to the court they will with pleasure hear any reason you may offer to show that the jury have the right contended for. . . . I have deliberately considered the subject and I am ready to explain my reasons for concluding that the petit jury have not the right to decide the constitutionality of a law, and that such a power would be extremely dangerous."

The "young gentleman" Wirt would not be squelched. "I will state to the court in a few words the reasons which have induced me to ascribe this right to the jury. They are sworn to give their verdict according to the evidence, and the law is evidence; if the jury have no right to consider the law, how is it possible for them to render a general verdict?"

To this Chase retorted that "No man will deny your law—we all know that juries have the right to decide the law and the Constitution is the supreme law of the land."

Wirt responded: "Since, then, the jury have a right to consider the law and since the constitution is the supreme law, the conclusion is certainly syllogistic that the jury have a right to consider the Constitution."

But Chase would put him down. "A *non sequitur,* sir."[46]

Nicholas came to Wirt's defense: "I am so much under the influence of duty that, though I am in the same situation with the gentleman who preceded me, and though the court seem[s] to be impressed with the opinion that the jury have no right to determine the constitutionality of an act of Congress, yet, arduous as the task may be, I shall offer a few observations to show that they have this right."

Nicholas then gave an extensive opinion on the jury's ultimate right, which Chase apparently allowed, knowing that he had the final say:

First it seems to be admitted on all hands that when the legislature exercise a power not given them by the Constitution, the judiciary will disregard their acts. The second point that the jury have a right to decide the law and the fact appears to me equally clear. In the exercise of the power determining the law and the fact, a jury cannot be controlled by the court. The court have a right to instruct the jury, but the jury have a right to act as they think right; and if they find contrary to the directions of the court and to the law of the case, the court may set aside the verdict and grant a new trial.

If this jury believed that the Sedition Act is not the law of the land, they cannot find the defendant guilty. The Constitution secures to every man a fair and impartial trial by jury . . . and to preserve this sacred right unimpaired, it should never be interfered with.[47]

George Hay, the eldest (but not by much) of the "young gentlemen," who would become a United States district attorney and district judge himself, and the son-in-law of future president James Monroe, offered further support. In what is almost a direct quote from Chief Justice John Jay in the four-year-old case of *Georgia* v. *Brailsford* (1796) he told Chase: "It is a universal principle of law that questions of law belong to the court, and that the decision of facts belongs to the jury; but a jury have the right to determine both law and fact in all cases."

Chase tried to interrupt, but Hay continued: "If ever a precedent is established that the court can control the jury so as to prevent them from finding a general verdict, their important right, without which every other right is of no value, will be impaired if not absolutely destroyed."

Chase did interrupt this time to ask Hay if he meant to extend this proposition to civil as well as criminal cases, and said that if he did the law was clearly otherwise. Hay replied that he believed the proposition to be universally true, and Chase interrupted him again. Whereupon Hay refused to continue.

This left an opportunity for Chase to deliver a lengthy address to the jury denying their right to determine constitutionality of the Sedition or any law, regardless of the provision in the act to the contrary. Chase cited the nullification clause, but by convoluted reasoning, nullified it. He lectured the jury first that: "It is one thing to decide what the law is on the facts proved, and another and very different thing to determine that the statute produced is no law."

> Was it ever intended by the framers of the Constitution, or by the people of America, that it should ever be submitted to the examination of a jury, to decide what restrictions are expressly or impliedly imposed by it on the national legislature? I cannot possibly believe that Congress intended by the statute to grant a right to a petit jury to declare a statute void. The man who maintains this position must have a most contemptible opinion of the understanding of that body; but I believe the defect lies with himself.[48]

He continued with a longer, misleading, bitter discourse from which the following are excerpts:

> If any one can be so weak in intellect as to entertain this opinion of Congress, he must give up the exercise of the power when he is in-

formed that Congress had no authority to vest it in any body whatsoever because by the Constitution this right is expressly granted to
the judicial power . . . by a perpetual statute. . . . It never was pretended before this time that a petit jury in England or any part of the
United States ever exercised such power. . . . If this power be once
admitted, petit jurors will be superior to the national legislature and
all its laws will be subject to their control. . . . The evident consequences of this right in juries will be that a law of Congress will be
in operation in one state and not in another . . . the right now claimed
has a direct tendency to dissolve the Union . . . the power of deciding the constitutionality of any law . . . is one of the greatest and
most important powers the people could grant.

But of course this is precisely what "consent of the governed"
means: power invested in the sovereign people, implemented through
the jury. Nevertheless Chase, owing to the authority of his black robe,
had the advantage, particularly before a "jury" well stacked with Federalists, and pretty well preconditioned.

Chase did not stop with dictating the law; he also directed the panelists on the fact, to leave them no discretion at all. Callender never
had a chance. Why this "jury" needed two hours to bring in what was
in effect a directed verdict is not explained.

The date was June 3, 1800. Chase sentenced Callender to a fine of
two hundred dollars and imprisonment for nine months, until March 3,
1801, coincident with the expiring of the law. But he failed to silence
Callender, who from prison called Chase "the most detestable and de-
tested rascal in the state of Maryland." He also wrote *The Prospect Before Us II.*

This was the last trial; the principle lesson, never to be learned by
politicians under the contagion of power (at least through the end of
the twentieth century), is that suppression is self-defeating. The Federalists gained nothing; rather, the attempt at censorship had the reverse effect of extending criticism. It also was political suicide, and
the end of the Federalist party. One of Jefferson's first acts as president
was to release all the prisoners.

It proved also that for liberty to survive the jury must be independent. Controlled panels are instruments of tyranny. In this series of
trials, the "juries" were no more than machines that registered the will
of the judges, and thus were not true trial juries—with the two notable
exceptions: the William Duane and half of Abijah Adams trials.

Why was the Duane trial different? We can only surmise that in this early case the jury selectors were less diligent. Trial records tell us nothing about how the panel was formed, only that "the jury was then called over and severally impaneled," listing their names. After Duane's acquittal, the Federalists supervised selection more rigidly.

POSTSCRIPT

As a result of his conduct in presiding over the Cooper and Callender trials, as well as others carrying different charges, Samuel Chase was impeached by the House of Representatives on November 30, 1804, "for high crimes and misdemeanors." The first article of impeachment charged that he "did in his judicial capacity, conduct himself in a manner highly arbitrary, oppressive, and unjust, viz. . . . .: In debarring the prisoner from his constitutional privilege of addressing the jury [through his counsel] on the law, as well as on the fact . . . and at the same time endeavoring to wrest from the jury their indisputable right to hear argument, and determine upon the question of the law. . . ."[49]

The case referenced in this charge was not a Sedition Act trial, although, based on his expressions of prejudice, Chase's offenses were much the same. Several of the succeeding articles dealt with his handling of the Callender trial.

Chase was tried by the Senate beginning on January 2, 1805, and continuing for two months. On March 1 the Senate acquitted him on all charges. In the assessment of historians who have studied his trial, he escaped because while he was a bad judge and his conduct was "unfair, biased, partial and oppressive," bad behavior was not an impeachable offense.[50] Chase was saved probably because he had signed the Declaration of Independence, and one or more members of Congress could not bring themselves to punish anyone who had had the courage to confront the wrath of the government of George III, no matter how much he had changed in later years.

NOTES

1. *Boston Gazette,* January 1766, in *John Adams, A Biography in His Own Words,* James B. Peabody, ed. (*Newsweek,* 1973), pp. 93–95.

2. Francis Wharton, *State Trials of the United States during the Administration of Washington and Adams* (Philadelphia: Carey and Hart, 1845), p. 22.

3. Manning J. Dauer, "Draft of Sedition Act," from *The Adams Federalists* (Baltimore: Johns Hopkins University Press, 1968), pp. 343–49.

4. Ibid., p. 348.

5. John Proffatt, *A Treatise on Trial by Jury, Including Questions of Law and Fact* (San Francisco: Sumner Whitney and Co., 1877), p. 376.

6. Wharton, *State Trials,* p. 22.

7. E. D. Warfield, *The Kentucky Resolutions of 1798* (New York: G. P. Putnam's Sons, 1894).

8. *Encyclopaedia Britannica,* 13: 333–34.

9. *American State Trials* 6:689.

10. Aleine Austin, *Matthew Lyon* (University Park: Pennsylvania State University Press, 1981), p. 111.

11. Ibid., pp. 108–18.

12. Tom W. Campbell, *Two Fighters and Two Fines* (Little Rock, Ark.: Pioneer Publishing Co., 1941), p. 65.

13. Austin, *Matthew Lyon,* pp. 108–18.

14. Campbell, *Two Fighters and Two Fines,* p. 65.

15. Ibid., p. 67.

16. *American State Trials,* 6:687–94; Wharton, *State Trials,* pp. 333–44.

17. Austin, *Matthew Lyon*; also, James Morton Smith, *Freedom's Fetters* (Ithaca, N.Y.: Cornell University Press, 1956), pp. 221–46.

18. Smith, *Freedom's Fetters,* p. 278.

19. Ibid., p. 281.

20. *American State Trials* 347; 7:676ff.

21. Ibid., p. 363.

22. Wharton, *State Trials,* p. 358; *American State Trials,* 7:689–90.

23. Wharton, *State Trials,* pp. 366–68; *American State Trials,* 7:738–41.

24. Smith, *Freedom's Fetters,* pp. 298–301.

25. Ibid., pp. 373–81; John C. Miller, *Crisis in Freedom* (Boston: Little, Brown and Co., 1951), pp. 126–30.

26. Smith, *Freedom's Fetters,* p. 406.

27. Ibid.

28. Ibid., p. 408.

29. Wharton, *State Trials,* pp. 649–51; Smith, *Freedom's Fetters,* pp. 410–12.

30. Wharton, *State Trials,* pp. 684–85; *American State Trials,* 7:695–96.

31. Smith, *Freedom's Fetters,* p. 362.

32. Ibid., pp. 369–70.

33. Miller, *Crisis in Freedom,* p. 11.

34. Smith, *Freedom's Fetters,* pp. 369–70.

35. Ibid., pp. 387–88.

36. Ibid., pp. 392–97.

37. *American State Trials,* 10:787.

38. Ibid., p. 792.

39. Smith, *Freedom's Fetters,* p. 332n.

40. Ibid., p. 332n.

41. The trial is reported in *American State Trials,* 10:813n; Wharton, *State Trials,* pp. 688–72, with collaborative information by Smith, *Freedom's Fetters,* pp. 334ff., and Miller, *Crisis in Freedom,* pp. 210ff.

42. Wharton, *State Trials,* pp. 695–96.

43. Smith, *Freedom's Fetters,* p. 348.

44. *American State Trials,* 10:857.

45. Ibid., pp. 861–63.

46. Ibid.; Wharton, *State Trials,* pp. 709–10.

47. *American State Trials,* 10:863–65.

48. Ibid., p. 869.

49. *The Trial of Samuel Chase* (New York: Da Capo Press, 1970), 1:5.

50. Irving Brant, *Impeachment, Trials and Errors* (New York: Alfred A. Knopf, 1972), p. 82, and William H. Rehnquist, *Grand Inquests* (New York: William Morrow and Co., 1992).

Part 4

JURIES AS EARLY ABOLITIONISTS AND DEFENDERS OF MINORITY RIGHTS

LAWS DO NOT MAKE PEOPLE FREE, PEOPLE MAKE LAWS FREE;

OR, WHO NEEDS A PROCLAMATION OF EMANCIPATION ANYWAY?

*B*y the mid-nineteenth century the pro-slavers had become alarmed. The American Anti-Slavery Society was spreading its influence, and as new states were being added, the imbalance between "slave" and "free" was swinging against them. Then there was the conviction of Edward Prigg in 1841 by a Pennsylvania jury for having seized a fugitive slave and two children in that state and returning them to Maryland. The U.S. Supreme Court agreed unanimously the following year to reverse the jury's conviction. However, when each of the nine justices delivered his own opinion to justify his position, the various opinions were so equivocal on the whole that they actually aided and abetted abolitionists in the Middle Atlantic states. Stubborn pro-slavery forces had fought extension of jury rights within their respective jurisdictions, although trials by jury had endured since early colonial days as inviolate and absolute in all other cases. New York and Vermont passed laws guaranteeing jury rights to fugitives, a right long before recognized in Massachusetts. And before the 1840s were over, Pennsylvania and Connecticut had followed suit.

All these things had so effectually vitiated the national Fugitive Slave Act of 1793 that slave holders pressured Congress to strengthen the act, and Congress obliged in 1850. Like the earlier act, the new Fugitive Slave Law pretended to require the return of runaways to their "masters," but in addition it denied appeals by slaves or their protectors to juries.

The fierceness with which pro-slavery forces opposed using juries in runaway slave cases, in contrast with the fervor of abolitionists who made appeals to juries central to their cause, suggests that juries exercised a strong influence over public policy, which was not in the slavers' favor. This influence was all the more forceful, considering the fact that the panels were composed exclusively of white males, probably most of them property owners.

These phenomena also suggest an interesting theory regarding the Civil War, that had the resolution of slavery been left to juries, the nation, insofar as slavery was a contributing factor, might have escaped war entirely. Slavery would have ended by jury verdicts, as it had ended in the previous century in Massachusetts, as this chapter relates. Freedom for slaves achieved without a president to proclaim it or a Thirteenth Amendment to guarantee it!

While it may be difficult or impossible to prove this theory, historical research offers considerable support for its validity and plausibility. First, to speak about juries generally, this book demonstrates that when the jury is unshackled and fully informed, when jurors are guided by conscience and act independently of outside influences, they almost always prove to be the ultimate guardians of the people's liberties. Where the jury fails, it is usually because the panel is not free to act on conscience. Failures occur when evidence is withheld so that the jury is not fully informed, or where it succumbs to judicial pressure or is otherwise misguided, or yields to fear or intimidation.

Specific support for the theory is provided by the story in Massachusetts, and further, by the surprisingly large number of jury trials in the Southern states when all-white jurymen brought in verdicts antithetical to the slavers' narrow interests. Given a few years or perhaps a decade or so, this trend might have resulted in total abolition as gently and as surely as it was achieved in Massachusetts in seventeen years without war.

We applaud Lincoln's Emancipation Proclamation of January 1, 1863, but we forget the trauma it caused on both sides: white slaveowners counting their wealth in human property, no matter how abhorrent it sounds to us; going to bed rich, waking up poor, often destitute. Their property was taken from them, seized without "due process of law."

On the other side, no matter how benign the intent of abolitionists, the slaves were abruptly deprived of food, shelter, and care, and had new responsibilities thrust upon them without preparation. How would they handle the vicissitudes of freedom (for independence is more difficult than being totally in someone else's charge)? Had it been purposely planned so, there could hardly have been a situation more ripe for conflict.

We tend to think of the pre-Civil War period as the time of a "Free North" and "Slave South," but this is imprecise. In the beginning, slavery existed throughout all the colonies, and indeed it was in Massachusetts that the mid-eighteenth-century contemporaries of Kunta Kinte, if not Alex Haley's ancestor himself, who had been brought to Maryland, were beaten until they broke. A census in New Jersey counted seven hundred slaves as late as 1845, and Connecticut held on to this "peculiar institution" until 1848—a mere thirteen years before the outbreak of the Civil War.

Only in New Hampshire, Rhode Island, and especially Massachusetts was slavery a "relatively minor" issue—minor unless you happened to be one of the 158 listed in the New Hampshire census of 1790. John Adams was a troubled observer at the time. As vice-president in 1795 he reminisced about pre-Revolutionary experiences in a letter to the Reverend Jeremy Belknap of Boston, founder of the Massachusetts Historical Society. "I never knew a Jury by a Verdict to determine a Negro to be a Slave," he wrote. "They always found them free."

This was not quite precise. Adams may have skewed his recollections to satisfy the sensibilities of Dr. Belknap, who was one of the earliest and most steadfast abolitionists. Some thirty years earlier the youthful attorney Adams had become "Concerned in several Causes in which Negroes sued for their Freedom before the Revolution." His legal papers document seven or eight cases, depending upon how you count them, in which he was sometimes an observer, sometimes a participant. In all but one of these the jurors had determined that the black appellants before them were not slaves. Only one jury returned the slave to his master, but here there may have been extenuating circumstances.

In another half-dozen cases or so, the proportion was about the same—all but one resulting in freeing the slave, and that one case being equivocal. While there may have been some cases earlier, the first of the Adams cases is identified as *"Jenny Slew, Spinster, versus John Whipple, Jr., Gentleman"* of Ipswich in 1765.

Whipple, according to the complaint, had "on the 29th day of January, A.D. 1762 at Ipswich aforesaid with force and arms took her the said Jenny, held and kept her in servitude as a slave in his service, and has restrained her of her liberty from that time to the fifth of March last [1765] without any lawfull right & authority to do so and did her other injuries against the peace & to the damage of said Jenny Slew as she saith in the sum of twenty-five pounds." Jenny reasoned that since she was the product of a black father and a white mother, she had as much right to be free as a slave. But Whipple contested this, saying she had never proved her right to liberty—and besides he had a bill of sale. He hunted her down.

Jenny inadvisedly filed her complaint in the wrong jurisdiction: the panel of judges who comprised the Inferior Court of Common Pleas at Newburyport. These dignified gentlemen, having no precedent to guide them, refused to set one. They evaded the issue by using the spurious ground that there was no such person as "Jenny Slew, Spinster."

Jenny, these judges declared, was a married woman, thus placing themselves in an insoluble dilemma. Slaves were not permitted to marry (their children being ipso facto bastards). Thus while dismissing the case of Jenny as a "spinster," they were tacitly acknowledging her as married, thereby, albeit unconsciously, defining her as a free woman. Paradoxically, they required this little-woman-who-wasn't-there to pay very-much-there court costs, and they shifted resolution to a more exalted forum: trial by jury.

The following year, 1766, Miss or Mrs. Slew, however designated, took the judicial clue and sought a jury trial. It was a hazardous risk. She very likely knew there would be no possibility of any blacks or mulattoes, slave or free, on the panel drawn by the sheriff. All twelve jurors would be white men, several of them very likely not literate or at least not well educated. Probably most would be of the same class as "Gentleman" Whipple and, like him, farmers.

The only encouraging aspect from Jenny's view (although she probably didn't know it) was that the original settlers of the Massachusetts colony had had so much faith in the jury as defender of liberty that they had established it as the first act of organization in 1623, specifying that "the verdict of twelve honest men" should prevail in both civil and criminal cases. And, among other glories, a series of white, mostly illiterate male juries returned verdicts ending the persecution of "witches" seventy-five years before.

There is no record of how excessive panelists were winnowed out, but when they did come together in 1766, "Gentleman" Whipple quite confidently presented to his peers in the box evidence of his purchase and contended that Jenny had never proved a right to liberty. Except for a line in the trial record that: "The case after a full hearing was committed to a jury sworn according to law to try," there are no details other than its outcome: the twelve gentlemen on the jury, after a short period of deliberation, set aside the question of Jenny's married state and brought in a verdict in her favor. Not only did they determine she was free, but they directed Whipple to pay her four pounds in damages and all court costs. From then on she was, by implication, officially Mrs. Slew, possibly the first person held in slavery to be recognized as free by a jury verdict. We draw some of our information from the notes of the thirty-one-year-old John Adams, supplemented by, respectively, records of the Inferior Court and Superior Court of Judicature.

Why should these twelve white gentlemen, whose names we do not know, act against what would seem on the surface to be in their interests by denying to another of their number what he claimed was his right to property, and to do it without dissent and in brief time? But they did, and we can only conjecture and hope to find an answer by studying subsequent slave appeals.

Possibly encouraged by the outcome, in 1768, Amos Newport sued his master, Joseph Billing, for his freedom, again before a jury of twelve white men. Billing produced a bill of sale dated March 15, 1728, as proof of his ownership of Newport. Now, after forty years, the question was put to the jury: Is Newport a slave? His defenders argued that "every man has a right to freedom that no law or Usage can take away." Newport had been "stolen in Affrica," where "they had the Same Right to enslave us."

Despite this reasonable argument, the jury found for Billing, and returned Newport to slavery. Again we can only conjecture why this jury acted in opposition to its predecessor. Were the jurors influenced by his age and length of servitude? did they fear that Newport, at least in his sixties, would become a public charge, as was the fate of many elderly freedmen not able to take care of themselves? We can never know.

Nonetheless, the outcome of the Newport trial did not discourage one "Margaret." She had been held for less than nine months, from August 31, 1767, until May 3, 1768, by William Muzzy, when a deputy sheriff removed her, and she appealed to a jury. It will surprise us to learn that John Adams was the attorney on what is, from our view, the wrong side. He defended Muzzy in the case known as *Margaret* v. *Muzzy,* but apparently did not do it well enough for his client. The jury declared her free.

Muzzy appealed for a second trial in 1770, probably before another jury, since juries were used in almost every species of legal action, although the record here does not specifically state as much. This panel upheld the verdict of the first and Margaret went free. The count now stood three juries to one against slavery.

Next in time is a pair of cases involving "James" (again not dignified with a surname) who sued his master, Richard Lechmere of Cambridge. In the first trial, 1769, James made the same mistake that Mrs. Slew had made four years before—he appealed to the Inferior Court of Worcester without jury, and he was denied.

James tried again, but apparently he had not learned his lesson well. He appealed to the Superior Court of Suffolk, again to a panel of judges without jury. Their decision was a compromise which hedged on the issue of James's right to be free.

In the same year a different kind of case arose in Nantucket. The captain of a whaling vessel, Elisha Folger, engaged among his crew a young slave by the name of "Boston" who belonged to John Swain. At the conclusion of the voyage, Folger paid directly to Boston instead of to Swain his portion of the proceeds, which was tantamount to acknowledging Boston as a free man. Swain sued the captain of the vessel in the Court of Common Pleas in Nantucket before a jury, and this jury returned a verdict in favor of Folger, thus acknowledging Boston's freedom. Again, although we don't know their names or anything about them, we can marvel that these twelve white men, more closely allied to the social class of Swain than Boston, when coming together as a jury, would fly in the face of their apparent narrower self-interests in defense of a broader liberty.

The following year, 1770, slave "Caesar" sued Elkanah Watson of Plymouth. The twist in this case is that Watson had transferred ownership of Caesar to a captain of the French navy, who granted him manumission (release from slavery) in 1758. For whatever reasons, Caesar returned to Plymouth, where Watson seized him and held him for the next twelve years. Possibly encouraged by the earlier trials, Caesar appealed to a jury who found in his favor, although they were a little stingy in the amount of damages—a mere six pence. The count is now five to one, in contrast with three to nothing when judges were the decision makers.

In 1771 a second "Caesar" sued his master, "Taylor." Once again the central issue was whether a slave could marry. Caesar's wife, or paramour as the case might be, was prohibited from testifying in his behalf. A slave cannot marry, dictated the presiding judge. But the suppression of uxorial testimony did not damage Caesar's appeal; the Massachusetts jury did not need it to find in his favor.

Taylor would not accept the decision, so he appealed, as had Muzzy, and this time the record is clear—to a second jury in 1772. Again the wife was not permitted to testify, but it still did not help the complainant. Taylor learned he should have left bad enough alone. Not only did this jury confirm the verdict of the first, but added a double penalty, assessing Taylor five pounds, thirteen shillings and four pence damages, plus court costs of twenty-four pounds, seven shillings and two pence.

Another year, another Caesar, this third Caesar dignified with a surname, Hendrick. This was the last of the Adams recollections. Hendrick had been held by Richard Greenleaf of Newburyport only from January 1 to March 16, 1773; he asked for fifty pounds in damages. The unidentified jurymen gave him only eighteen pounds plus costs, but, more significantly, declared him free.

Although eight juries and ninety-six jurors had taken stands against slavery, with one having voted in its favor, the legality of slavery in the commonwealth remained in doubt. There was no legislation that declared slavery specifically lawful or unlawful; it was excused largely on the ground of "common usage." For whatever reason there appear to be no further appeals for the next eight years, but between 1781 and 1783 there was a series of four trials and two additional actions centering around one Quock Walker, variously known as Quarco, Quack, Quaco, and Quork.

Born into slavery in 1753, Quock as a boy belonged to a farmer named James Caldwell, who, on his death, passed ownership to his widow. Mrs. Caldwell married another farmer, Nathaniel Jennison of Barre in Worcester County. She brought Quock, now a teenager, with her, promising him manumission on his twenty-fifth birthday in 1778. When Quock was twenty-one, Mrs. Jennison died, and her husband assumed ownership. But Jennison's memory proved faulty. He forgot, or otherwise did not honor, the contract his wife had made with Walker.

Unschooled, Walker was not sure what to do; he may not have fully understood what a contract of manumission meant. At any rate, he surrendered to his exploitation by Jennison for the next three years.

In the meantime Massachusetts had adopted its first constitution in 1780 which contained the heroic clause: "All men are born free and equal, & have certain natural, essential, & unalienable rights; among which may be reckoned the right of enjoying and defending their lives and liberties; that of acquiring, possessing, and protecting property; in fine, that of seeking and obtaining their safety and happiness."

Whether or not the clause was intended to abolish slavery, it had no greater effect in this respect than the four-year-old Declaration of Independence: "We hold these truths to be self-evident, that all men are created equal, that they are endowed by their Creator with certain unalienable rights, that among these rights are life, liberty and the pursuit of happiness." Slavery continued in the new state.

But Quock had two friends, John and Seth Caldwell, brothers of his original master. They assured Walker that the contract of manumission establishing his freedom was not only lawful, but that the state constitutional clause applied to Negroes as well as whites. They "aided and abetted" him (by later admission) to assert his rights, and offered him a job and a wage to work as a free man on their farm.

Walker accepted, and left Jennison for the Caldwells. When Jennison discovered where Quock had gone, he enlisted two aides and, while Walker was harrowing a field, the three of them "got the negro down" and "struck him with the handle of a whip," according to testimony in one of the resulting trials. Hearing Walker's cries, the Caldwells rushed to his rescue and, seeing "a young fellow upon the negro, I took him off" and announced to Jennison that Walker had been manumitted. But he had been badly injured, suffering from "wounds in his hands and arms."

There is conflicting evidence as to precisely what happened then, but by some device or other Jennison managed to carry Walker back to his farm and lock him up in an outbuilding for several hours. The Caldwells re-rescued him, and then backed him in filing a civil suit in Barre for damages in the amount of 300 pounds.

The country justice of the peace did not care to be put on the spot, so he referred the case to the Worcester County Court of Common Pleas where the series starting as *Walker* v. *Jennison* became known alternately as the Quock Walker or Worcester cases.

The Caldwells secured the services of the most prominent attorney in the county, thirty-two-year-old Levi Lincoln (later lieutenant governor of the state, and attorney general of the United States). Lincoln assured the Caldwells that Walker had a right to work for whomever he chose. On that basis, *Walker* v. *Jennison* went to trial in June 1781. Except for unembellished references to "the jury," there is no record of who the jurors were or how they might have been selected. We can know only that they were all white men and, as in the earlier trials, likely to be of the same social class as the Caldwells and Jennison.

Jennison refused to join the issue, basing his defense on a bill of sale proving that he was the owner of Quock, and had administered only a disciplinary beating proper to use against runaways. Lincoln countered by declaring Walker was a free Negro, having passed his twenty-fifth birthday in 1778, and charged Jennison with assault and battery.

It did not take these jurymen very long to agree: ". . . that the said Quork is a Freeman and not the proper Negro slave of the defendant." This verdict also had the effect of declaring that the beating was an unlawful assault, and to compensate Walker, the jurors ordered Jennison to pay him fifty pounds.

Jennison angrily struck back with a double action: he filed an appeal in the next session of the Superior Court of Judicature and another against the Caldwells, accusing them of "aiding and abetting" and enticing Walker, as Jennison's property, to their own benefit and profit. He asked for damages of twenty-five pounds. For some reason, Jennison did not press the first suit, which he lost by default. As to the second, despite Lincoln's strong defense, "the jury" found for Jennison, and awarded him the twenty-five pounds. The contradiction in the verdict of the second jury may be explained by the fact that the principal issue was whether the Caldwells had encouraged Walker to leave, and not Walker's status as free man or slave. This the Caldwells not only admitted to but boasted of. In that respect they were "guilty."

To clear up this point, the Caldwells now countered with a third suit known as *Caldwell* v. *Jennison*, also before a jury. Levi Lincoln once more represented the Caldwells. The principal question put before this jury was: "Is Quock Walker a slave or is he free?" Did the Caldwells aid and abet a slave to run away from his rightful master, or did they assist him in asserting his rights as a free man?

Jennison was represented by William Stearns, who opened the de-

bate with a twofold plea in support of Jennison's claim that Walker
was his proper slave: first, that Quock and his parents had been purchased by James Caldwell in 1754 when Quock was an infant, and
ownership had passed to him following his marriage to Mrs. Caldwell.
He produced for the jury the bill of sale and probate papers. Therefore,
Jennison argued, the Caldwells had clearly deprived him of his legal
property and that was the only issue.

Jennison supported this argument by declaring that "custom and
usage have made slavery a respectable institution" which the laws of
Massachusetts recognized. Lincoln told the jury that whatever the law
might be, if it contravened natural law and reason, it must be by that
very character wrong and thus null and void. There was a higher law
of the Creator that all persons are by right free, and the jury had the
right, power, and duty to overturn an unjust law.

Boldly admitting that the Caldwells had indeed aided Walker, Lincoln described their action as a charitable deed because, when the liberty of one man is attacked, it is tantamount to an attack upon the liberties of all men; therefore, it is not only a right but a duty of every citizen to see that the wrong is corrected.

Stearns came back with unrelated arguments comparing the American and European slave systems, and warned of dire economic consequences from abolition. He offered a rather farfetched analogy between the fall of mankind and the fall of Adam from Eden. He also denied that the state constitutional clause could have any effect on the
sanctity of a contract because it would be acting retroactively by de-
priving a rightful owner of property acquired lawfully before ratifica-
tion of the constitution.

Nathaniel Jennison also petitioned the court, using rather curious
reasoning which sounds almost like an argument for the other side:

> That by the Bill of Rights prefixed to the Constitution it is among
> other things declared "that all men are born free and equal" which
> clause . . . has been the subject of much altercation and dispute—
> that the Judges of the Supreme Judicial Council have so construed
> the same as to deprive your Memorial [*sic,* presumably a reference
> to himself] of a great part of his property to which he tho't his title
> good . . . that your memo: having been possessed of ten Negro Ser-
> vants . . . is now informed that by the Determination of the Supreme
> Judicial Council [i.e., the jury], the . . . Bill of Rights is so to be con-

strued as to operate to the total discharge and manumission of all Negro Slaves whatsoever.

Jennison continued with a rambling, pointless "prayer" which expounds a principal problem that slavery creates for itself: "that if the servant is set free, the master may be free too . . . for it is nowhere to be found in Revelation that Christians shall be bond men to the Heathen or Negroes—which is really the unhappy situation of every person that ever owned a Negro Servant—who is at liberty which the master by Law is bound to maintain and support him . . . although he can have no control over him."

Jennison may have felt impelled to present his prayer in this hesitant manner because the presiding judge over the judicial panel hearing the case, Judge Sargent, an anti-slavery activist himself, had, in his charge to an earlier jury, invoked the "free and equal clause" as "the law of the land."

Lincoln easily disposed of both Stearns and Jennison by damning the whole institution of slavery and declaring that the only law to be considered was "natural law and reason": "Is it not a law of nature that all men are equal and free?" he asked the jurors rhetorically.

We are all born in the same manner, have our bones clothed with the same kind of flesh . . . had the same breath of life breathed into us . . . inhabit the same common Globe of earth . . . die in the same manner. The white may have their bodies wrapt in rather finer linen, and his coffin a little more decorated . . . we all sleep in a level in the dust . . . shall all be raised by one common trump. Shall be arraigned at one common bar, shall have one common judge, tried by one common jury, condemned or acquitted by one common law—by the Gospel, the perfect law of liberty.

This cause will then be tried over again, and your verdict will then be tried, gentlemen of the jury. Therefore let me conjure you to give such a verdict now as will stand the test, as will be approved of by your own minds in the last moments of your existence.

Is not the law of nature the law of God? Is not the law of God against slavery? If there is a law of men establishing of it, then there is the great difficulty to determine which law you ought to obey. The worst that can happen to you for disobeying a law of men is the destruction of the body, but for disobeying the law of God your own souls.

Following Lincoln's closing, each judge on the panel delivered his own separate charge to the jury, but none has been preserved. It is assumed that at least one of them, probably Sargent, once again invoked the "free and equal" clause.

These twelve jurors, like their predecessors, did not take long to deliver the verdict. Unconsciously duplicating the sentiment of the first panel they declared: "The said Quork is a free man and not the proper slave of the defendant," which in effect was to declare that Walker had been free since 1781 at least. It necessarily followed that Jennison's attack was assault and battery, but it is unclear how much damages the jurors awarded Walker. Of more lasting importance is the fact that the jurors had assumed the judicial function of "interpreting" the constitutional clause themselves. That this power was inherent in the sovereign people was unquestioned and recognized still eight years before the Tenth Amendment formally pronounced it as follows:

> The powers not delegated to the United States by the Constitution, nor prohibited by it to the States, are reserved to the States respectively, *or to the people.* (Italics added)

Or, in the more succinct wording used by many state constitutions: "All political power is inherent in the people." The government retains only those powers specifically delegated to it by constitutional contract, and nothing else.

The result of this civil verdict now was to impose upon the Commonwealth of Massachusetts the responsibility of reinforcing it. Since Jennison had by admission attacked Walker, and since Walker was, by jury acclamation, a free man, Jennison had committed a criminal assault. If that were true, the Commonwealth had the duty to charge Jennison criminally and bring him to trial. Accordingly, the Commonwealth had him indicted, and in 1783 the case of *Commonwealth* v. *Jennison* was brought before a four-man court, including Sargent, and a fourth jury. This, the sixth and final action in the series, attracted great attention because its outcome would determine the legal position of slavery in Massachusetts. It was also the only criminal trial.

Over the previous two years, several petitions had been presented to the Massachusetts legislature demanding legislation that would outlaw slavery; at least one petition asked that compensation be paid to those who would lose their slave "property" to ease their financial burden. The legislators dodged positive action on all petitions with the excuse that they did not know how to frame a satisfactory measure. Their indecision, combined with the vacillation of judicial panels, left ultimate determination with those who possessed all political power— The People through their best voice in government, Trial by Jury. *Commonwealth* v. *Jennision* became the vehicle to carry it.

The Attorney General, Robert Treat Paine, opened by producing evidence that an assault had actually taken place. This was uncontested, since Jennison himself had confessed to it. Paine then had to prove the attack was made upon a free citizen, not a chattel slave. He produced the contract of manumission drawn up by Mrs. Caldwell granting Walker liberty on his twenty-fifth birthday in 1778, five years before, and evidence that Jennison knew of the contract when he married her.

John Sprague, who had replaced the inadequate Stearns as Jennison's counsel, did not contest these arguments. This change in representation made little difference because Sprague merely reprised Stearns's argument of the original bill of sale and probate records which, if upheld, would have turned the "assault" into proper discipline for a runaway.

Sprague argued that the law recognized slavery through implication because it prescribed procedures to be followed by masters who wished to liberate their slaves. Under any condition there was no legal prohibition against it. Nor did the state constitution of 1780 contain a specific proscription, whatever the clause meant. Therefore, it was wrong to read into it an implication contravening a proper contract. Sprague apparently shunned reference to the equally valid, by his reasoning, contract of manumission.

Chief Justice William Cushing then charged the jury. Like Sargent, his colleague on the bench, Cushing was an anti-slavery advocate, and he almost dictated the jury's verdict. He lectured that the defense

is founded on the assumed proposition that slavery had been by law established in this province: that rights to slaves as property . . . ought not to be divested by any construction of the Constitution by implication; and that slavery in that instrument is not expressly abolished. [It has existed] by usage which took its origins from the practice of some of the European nations . . . but whatever usages formerly prevailed or slid in upon us . . . they can no longer exist. Sentiments more favorable to the natural rights of mankind, and to that innate desire for liberty which heaven, without regard to complexion or shape, has planted in the human breast, have prevailed since the glorious struggle for our rights began. And these sentiments led the framers of our constitution of government . . . to declare that all men are free and equal; and that every subject is entitled to liberty, and to have it guarded by the laws as well as his life and property. . . . Slavery is in my judgement as effectively abolished as it can be by the granting of rights and privileges as wholly incompatible and repugnant to its existence.

The court are therefore fully of the opinion that perpetual servitude can no longer be tolerated in our government, and that liberty can only be forfeited by some criminal conduct or relinquished by personal consent or contract. And it is therefore unnecessary to consider whether the promises of freedom to Quaco [*sic*] on the part of his master and mistress amounted to manumission or not. The defendant must be found guilty as the facts charged are not contraverted.

As vigorously as we might applaud Cushing's sentiments, we must condemn him for expressing them to the jury. We would not hesitate to criticize a pro-slavery chief justice in his place, for the recital in either instance was judicial usurpation of jury independence.

Whether these jurors were influenced by Cushing or the verdicts in the previous cases, or whether they acted separately on conscience alone, we can never know for sure; but whichever, they returned in short time with a guilty verdict against Jennison, although they did not inflict much of a punishment—a fine of forty shillings. However, the jury had added its voice to its predecessors by settling for all time the greater issue that both the official lawmakers and law adjudicators had dodged, that slavery was not a lawful institution. The jury had done this eighty years before the grand action by Abraham Lincoln!

Some observers such as the Reverend Jeremy Belknap, founder of the Massachusetts Historical Society, described the series as dealing "a mortal blow" to slavery in Massachusetts, although it did not bring a total end. There are records of a slave population for perhaps another twenty or more years, but these were "voluntary" slaves. Freedom is difficult. It imposes a burden of responsibility for oneself, and you can't blame anyone else for your deprivations. Thus apathy, lethargy, and the comfort that comes from a master who might be gentle enough to supply all material needs weigh more heavily than confronting the competitive struggle accompanying freedom. Every slave had at least the freedom to determine his status for himself.

Was this the reason why a Ku Klux Klan did not develop in Massachusetts?

No other state recorded experiences as dramatic as these. In neighboring Connecticut only four jury trials are reported by Helen T. Catterall in her *Judicial Cases concerning American Slavery and the Negro*: 1788, 1793 and 1796 and 1809. Although all verdicts were anti-slavery, they may have been too widely separated to have had a direct impact, for slavery was not declared officially outlawed in Connecticut until 1848—after the state had extended jury rights to slaves.

8

A MAN'S HOME, A MAN'S CASTLE:
THE TRIALS OF DR. OSSIAN SWEET AND FAMILY, OCTOBER AND NOVEMBER 1925, AND APRIL AND MAY 1926, DETROIT, MICHIGAN

On March 16, 1926, the Indianapolis City Council, amid "loud cheering, hand-clapping and stamping of feet by more than 800 spectators," as reported in the *New York Times* the next day, adopted an ordinance which restricted the districts in the city where Negroes could buy homes. The ordinance was advanced by the White People's Protective League.

On May 24, 1926, the United States Supreme Court weaseled out of a confrontation with a declaration by a Court of Appeals that the right of white residents of Washington, D.C., "to enter into indentures or agreements against the sale or conveyance of property to persons of Negro blood"[1] did not offend the Constitution of the United States. The evasion was expressed by Associate Justice Edward T. Sanford and supported by a majority of the other justices, William Howard Taft, Oliver Wendell Holmes, Willis Van Devanter, James Clark McReynolds, Louis D. Brandeis, George Sutherland, Pierce Butler, and Harlan Fiske Stone.

The Court did not actually say the restrictive covenant contained no constitutional fault; it merely "dismissed for want of jurisdiction" (thereby backhandedly endorsing) the lower court's decree that "The constitutional right [*sic*]* of a Negro to acquire, own or occupy prop-

---

*This is not a right ratified by the Constitution but an inherent right.

erty does not carry with it constitutional power to compel sale or conveyance to him of any particular private property."[2]

Perhaps it was still too soon for the illustrious nine to have learned of a precedent, only five days old at the time, set by a higher legal authority. (Or perhaps they were too dazzled by the brilliance of their own exalted ranks to defer to the superiority of that authority.) On May 19, 1926, in the Detroit Recorders courtroom a panel of twelve sovereign citizens brought together as a trial jury decreed that not only did a Negro family have the right to buy a home wherever it chose, but that the family and friends were constitutionally protected in the right to defend that home against attack by whatever means, even to the point of killing a suspected attacker.

The jury was doing no more than lending sovereign citizen endorsement to a sixty-six-year-old opinion of the Michigan Supreme Court. In 1860 this honorable body had written: "There are many curious and nice questions concerning the extent of the right of self-defense, where the assailed party is in fault. . . . A man is not, however, obliged to retreat if assaulted in his dwelling, but may use such means as are absolutely necessary to repel the assailant from his house, or to prevent his forcible entry, even to taking his life. . . . Where the assault or breaking is felonious, the homicide becomes justifiable, and not merely excusable."[3]

Not a single black person was needed on the Detroit jury to know that race was no factor in the unequivocal support of the right of self-defense. All twelve were white, middle-class, middle-aged men; several, possibly a majority, may have been actually bigoted in their personal relationships, or at least repelled by the idea of living next door to blacks. Nonetheless, as jurors, they understood that a man's home is his castle. They acted upon a common-law right, anciently enshrined in jurisprudence, that is universal with all mankind. After deliberating for less than four hours following a three-and-a-half-week trial, this jury unanimously agreed to acquit twenty-year-old Henry Sweet, black, of killing thirty-three-year-old Leon Breiner, white, and of injuring twenty-two-year-old Erik Halberg, also white, although Henry had admitted that he had fired a rifle from the second-floor bedroom window of the new home of his older brother, Ossian Sweet, a physician.

This was the second trial. On the day after the previous Thanksgiving, ten different white jurors had been blocked by two others from acquitting nine of eleven accused Sweet family members and friends; in the cases of brothers Ossian and Henry, seven jurors had held for acquittal against five for conviction. In this first trial, the juror described as being "the most hard-boiled looking man on the jury" was heard through the thin walls of the locked jury room shouting to his conscience-troubled colleagues in a high-pitched voice: "I'm younger than any of you fellows and I'll sit here forever before I condemn those niggers."[4]

The deep consciences of the majority jurors in the first trial, sensitive to the serious responsibilities laid upon them, were frustrated by two hopelessly insensitive jurors who held them to a deadlock for some forty-six hours of deliberations over three days. Yet in spite of the heavily one-sided split favoring acquittals, prosecutor Robert M. Toms would not yield to demands from the skillful legal defense team of Clarence Darrow and Arthur Garfield Hays to dismiss the charges. He believed it was to his political advantage to try again to convict.

What caused the problem was nothing more complex than the natural desire of a successful young physician, thirty-year-old Ossian Sweet, to own a home in a clean, quiet residential area for his attractive, educated wife, Gladys, and their baby girl. The trouble was that the "Black Bottom" district (incongruously known as "Paradise Valley") to which whites would consign all blacks, was overcrowded, unclean, noisy, and crime-ridden. There was no place else to buy except in an "exclusive" white neighborhood. In the late summer of 1925, the Sweets settled on a home at 2905 Garland Avenue at the corner of Charlevoix Street, even agreeing to pay an elevated price. Whereas other homes in the neighborhood sold for $15,000, Dr. Sweet agreed to $18,500, with $3,000 down. Before completing the purchase, he had made a point of making himself conspicuous to neighbors by sitting on the front porch with the owner-seller, Mrs. Edward Smith, a white woman who was married to a black man and who had lived there for two years. Mr. Smith, however, was so light skinned he could "pass." Residents of the area could not conceive that a respectable white woman had married a black man.

All this would never have happened if it had not been for Henry Ford. When Ford built his automobile factory in Detroit and offered his workers the incredible salary of five genuine gold dollars a day, he attracted so many thousands of displaced, mostly black, persons from the impoverished South that the black population of 6,000 in 1910 rose to about 80,000 fifteen years later. Black Bottom could not hold so large a number. Black families tried to break out.

Nineteen-twenty-five became the year of revolt. Before Dr. Sweet bought his home, an associate, Dr. A. L. Turner, moved his family into a house on Spokane Street in June 1925, and found it surrounded by 3,000 angry whites. When he called for police protection, the guardians of law and order responded by driving Dr. and Mrs. Turner back to their previous home on Warren Avenue, then arranging for the neighborhood "Improvement Association" to return all his furniture.

Vollington Bristol managed to survive three nights in his home on American Avenue before constant demonstrations made living there too dangerous. Two other attempts to establish homes on Bangor Street and Merrill Street also brought out the bigots. The Fourth of July was celebrated by the burning of a cross in front of the Vincent Park home of a black attorney, with a sign: "No niggers allowed in this vicinity."

To prepare for the Garland invasion, a "Waterworks Improvement Association" was formed principally to "cooperate in the enforcement of existing property restrictions and to originate such other restrictions as would preserve and protect the locality as a respectable community." At an organizing meeting on July 14, the biggest cheer came when a speaker told a crowd of 700 persons that "Where the nigger shows his head, the white must shoot."

But Ossian Sweet was committed. On the day of his move, September 8, he left his baby girl with Mrs. Sweet's mother, and was joined by his two younger brothers, Henry, a pre-law student at Wilberforce Academy, and Otis, a dentist, as well as several friends—eleven in all. They stocked themselves with rifles and ammunition.

Although a crowd had gathered around the house in the early evening and remained all night, there was little violence; but the situation was too tense for much sleep. In the morning, when two men left the house, somebody in the crowd shouted threats. Ossian called for the police, and at least six officers came to guard them and to assure the Sweets there would be adequate protection.

During the day people roamed around the house, and a crowd slowly gathered. Gladys received a phone message telling her of an overheard threat that the Negro family who had moved into the neighborhood would be out by the next evening. Testifying later at the trial, Ossian confessed to "fright" after he returned home about five:

At about eight o'clock something hit the roof of the house. Somebody went to the window and shouted: "People, the people." I ran
out to the kitchen where my wife was and several lights were
burning. I turned them off. I opened the door and saw a mob. I realized I was facing the same mob that had hounded my people through
our entire history. I had my back against the wall. I was filled with a
peculiar fear, the fear of one who knows the history of my race. I
knew what mobs had done to my people before.

Pandemonium broke loose. Every one was running from room
to room. Stones were hitting the house intermittently. A stone came
though a window. Part of the glass hit me.

Ossian had good reason for fright; the crowd around his home was
large enough even if the estimate by police of "several thousand persons," as appeared in the *Chicago Tribune* next day, was inflated. The
newspaper reported that the crowd had "gathered around the house . . .
[and] remained until after midnight when a heavy rainstorm drove
most of the crowd to seek shelter. The police guard around the house
was maintained."

When brother Otis and a friend arrived, someone shouted: "Here's
niggers. Get them, get them." Rocks were thrown, but the men escaped into the house unharmed.

Then there were rifle shots. At about 8:30, Henry, at an upstairs
bedroom window, fired a single warning shot above the crowd. From
the ground there were a number of police shots. Several minutes afterward the police discovered that Leon Breiner, who lived across the
street and was on his front porch smoking a pipe, had been struck and
killed and that Erik Halberg had been injured in the leg. Who had fired
the fatal shot?

The police did not conduct a very thorough examination, but it
was shown later that the bullet had passed completely through
Breiner's body, and that the trajectory indicated a greater likelihood
that the rifle shot had come from ground level rather than a higher el-
evation. The bullet was lost and never found. This made it impossible
to match the bullet with the rifle, and it handicapped attempts to identify the shooter. But it was not sufficient to dissuade police from
faulting the single shot from the upstairs bedroom window. And if it
had come from inside, although only one shot by one person, all
eleven in the house would be under suspicion.

The police, whom the Sweets had called to protect them, moved in on the startled family. Without informing them of Breiner's death, they herded them all into the living room; handcuffed each one of them, including Mrs. Sweet; and, still without giving them the reason why, carted them off to prison.

Prosecutor Toms did no investigating either. Nor was he concerned that Henry was the only one who had fired. He conspired with the police to encompass all eleven within the murky criminal scope of "conspiracy" to commit murder. The worst that Gladys Sweet was guilty of was being in the kitchen preparing a never-to-be-eaten ham dinner. We might conjecture whether baby Sweet, had she not been at her grandmother's, would also have been named a conspirator.

"Conspiracy" is a slippery charge. It is of relatively late development in the history of jurisprudence, a kind of a catch-all generalized charge to cover everybody who happens to be around; it is often used vindictively to conceal the absence of anything meaningful. Sometimes called "the evil genius of the common law" or "the prosecutor's delight," it has grown to become a device to suppress "virtually any activity which the prevailing morality considers threatening."[5]

Both *Black's* and *Bouvier's* law dictionaries agree in their definitions of "conspiracy" as "a confederation of two or more persons to commit by their joint efforts an unlawful or criminal act." Toms distorted this definition to cover the eleven whose conspiring together had extended no further than to assist in settling five of the family, including the two brothers, peaceably into a new home. He brushed off as not conspiracy the rallying cry of 700 whites: "Where the nigger shows his head, the white must shoot" at the organizing meeting of the Waterworks Improvement Association, and echoed by the crowd surrounding 2905 Garland on the night of September 9.

The eleven spent the next night in prison for want of excessive bail of $10,000 each. The politically ambitious thirty-five-year-old judge assigned to the case had a reputation for being "liberal" and fairminded. His ambition carried greater weight than his liberalism when he brushed aside urgent pleas by black attorney Cecil Rowlette, retained by Mrs. Sweet's mother, to dismiss the nebulous charges. It was bold enough for the judge to risk public wrath by reducing bail to a still excessive $5,000 if only for Gladys Sweet, and only on October 2, after three weeks. The others were held at the higher bail.

This judge knew his politics well. He was Frank Murphy, who, a decade and a half later, would win the favor of Franklin Delano Roosevelt to get himself appointed to the United States Supreme Court.

The National Association for the Advancement of Colored People (NAACP) in the persons of assistant secretary Walter H. White and W. E. B Du Bois, editor of *Crisis,* supported the defense. They embarked upon a $50,000 fund-raising campaign, and appealed to Clarence Darrow to fight for them. Darrow hesitated at first. He had just exhausted himself, at age sixty-eight, in the Scopes "monkey trial" in Dayton, Tennessee. But the challenge and cause enticed him. Darrow received the NAACP's invitation while he was in New York from his Chicago offices visiting his good friend and colleague, forty-four-year-old Arthur Garfield Hays. He asked that Hays serve as co-counsel and White and Du Bois agreed. Darrow accepted the "low" fee of $5,000, compared to a compromise of $30,000 after being refused his asking fee of $100,000 the previous year in the Loeb-Leopold murder trial.

Although unsuccessful in convincing Murphy to reduce bail or release his clients on recognizance, Darrow succeeded in getting an early trial date of October 30. He decided against a change of venue because he found Murphy likely to be as amenable to reason as any judge anywhere else. His greater dilemma was that the prospective jurors would be all white, probably of the same caliber as the mob. He pondered waiving a jury to depend on Murphy's good side. Jurors, he believed, were much the same anywhere in the country, but judges were different. Nonetheless, if there was any possibility of acquittals, jury acquittals were more influential than judicial acquittals. He decided to take his chances with a jury.

On October 30 Darrow confronted a *venire* which contained several women (a new phenomenon, albeit all white) and a single black face. All, or certainly most, of the grim visages, as he had expected, reflected bigotry. This combined in him a feeling of hopelessness with hope that underneath the forbidding fronts he would find the buried treasure of a sense of equity.

Although Darrow exploited the juror inquisition process of *voir dire* extensively, he knew that its purpose was to secure not impartial panels but stacked, biased juries. Nonetheless, he participated because it was standard operating procedure in the courts. It took about a week to settle on a panel that was "as good or as bad as any other panel of twelve," as Hays describes in his book, *Let Freedom Ring.*[6]

Darrow and Hays questioned about one hundred prospective jurors (talesmen), including several women, as to their feelings about black neighbors, and Hays reported that "without exception" they recognized the Negro's right of "free residence as well as his right of self-defense." Toms, his prosecutor's instincts honed to convict whatever the evidence, suggested to the talesmen that there were times when a person should not exercise his rights, and ludicrously compared this with the "right" to attend a formal dance in a bathing suit or to snatch a seat in a streetcar from a woman.

The single black man was summoned to the box, but eliminated peremptorily (arbitrarily not subject to challenge) by prosecutor Toms and co-prosecutor Lester S. Moll. Every female candidate was also excused. Hays partially recognized the futility of the inquisitorial process by discovering after the trial that "some of those of whom we had been most fearful were our best friends." Which, if so, makes us wonder why waste a week, spend so much money on juror inquisitions, and invade juror privacy (constitutionally impermissible) if the end result is a panel that is "as good or as bad as any other group of twelve"? Why not simply accept the first group?

Hypocrisy rears its ugly head again in the conduct of trials. We have been deluded for many centuries to believe that the objective of the American adversary system is to seek justice. This is accomplished by allowing each side to argue its respective partisan interpretations of the evidence before a jury made "impartial" by the inquisitorial process used in jury selection. The procedure becomes more complex by the restrictive guides found in "Rules of Evidence" which control what evidence is presented to the jury. By these rules, some evidence may be barred if it does not conform to set standards. The control over what evidence gets in and what is held back lies with the presiding judge, and we generally do not question how often his decision might depend upon judicial whim or prejudice. One judge interprets the rules one way, and another takes a different view. Whoever controls, the jury almost never gets to hear all the evidence—only that which passes through the judicial sieve—but nevertheless is expected to make an evaluation based upon the distortion.

Too often the results are post-verdict juror lamentations that "if we had only known that, we would have decided differently." This was the approach to trial in 1925 and this is the approach to trial three-quarters of a century later.

There are, however, inaccuracies in that approach. The adversary system was never designed to discover truth and justice, but to *win*! It copies the ancient, presumably discredited trial by battle by substituting oratory for sword. The battle is further refined in that the decision is not measured by the amount of blood spilled, but by a panel of reasonably rational observers presumed immune to blood-spilling. To put it another way, the respective combatants will employ whatever tactics they can to deceive, confuse, befuddle so as to sway those observers away from rational thought; it will cast facts, evidence, truth to the wayside. The remarkable and near miraculous result of this procedure is that, as these chapters have been showing, the panel manages— in the face of so many odds against it—to cut through befuddlement and hypocrisy to reveal the buried treasure of equity concealed inside.

When this happens, the advocate for the winning side bedecks him(her)self in the glory, and figuratively paints a skull as symbol of victory on his fuselage. He is proclaimed in the legal press as a model to adulate, and he raises his fee to the next client. The annual Prosecutor-of-the-Year award goes to the D.A. who captures the greatest number of convictions, without considering how many convictions might be of innocent persons.

The possibility that the observers might have independent minds and consciences gets lost. When the jury verdict is fair, it is difficult to apportion the credit due respectively to oratory and to innate juror equity and conscience. But it is not difficult to understand that the attorney oversteems his contribution on the one occasion, and ridicules the mindless "warm bodies" in the box as being at fault for the other.

Which is not to say that a good advocate might not make a difference: that skill might "win" and lack of skill "loses." But he is not necessarily pivotal. It depends more heavily upon how well informed the jurors are as to facts and evidence. When they see the entire picture, they are more apt to return a fair verdict or block a bad one; but when the view is partial or distorted, as it often is by following "rules of evidence," the verdict is likely to be distorted. It is more to the credit of jurors no matter who we are that so many cut through distortion than that others succumb to it with inequitable verdicts.

That the exceptionally skillful Clarence Darrow had great influence on both juries cannot be denied, nor that the outcomes might have been more equivocal with a less qualified champion, but there never would have been convictions even with the poorest advocate.

The buried treasure of juror equity he sought at both trials would have surfaced anyway, and truth and facts exposed. Perhaps the second jury would have deadlocked as did the first. Darrow dug for the treasure by forcing the jurors to face their potential bigotry and by appealing to their sense of fairness. He exposed the deception and trickery of the prosecution. From overheard views expressed by jurors in the jury room, we can be certain that at least several of any given twelve would have put conscience ahead of personal prejudice no matter what. One juror alone is enough. Darrow probably overcame the indecision of waverers and encouraged conscience more effectually than many other defenders, which might have made the difference between a second split vote and unanimity. There is no yardstick to measure by.

Certainly the prosecution was no match for him. Both Toms and Moll acted stupidly and venally. They were, like Murphy, politically ambitious. Their ambition blinded them to the absurdity of trying to show that there was no crowd outside the house by bringing in seventy witnesses—*seventy* no less—to testify to having been there but seeing hardly anybody else.

If only seventy were there, it would be a frightening enough crowd. One witness, a sixteen-year-old boy, replied to Darrow's questioning: "There was a great crowd. . . . No," he stammered, "I won't say a great crowd, a large crowd—well, there were a few people there and the officers kept them moving." Darrow closed the trap: "When you started to answer the question you forgot to say 'a few people,' didn't you?"

"Yes, sir," the confused boy responded. Obviously he had been coached to perjure himself.

Another witness, a neighbor from two blocks away, also slipped when asked by Darrow what had attracted her "to come out to the corner of Garland and Charlevoix."

"Curiosity," she replied.

"Curiosity as to what?"

"The crowd," she began, and then hastily tried to cover up the forbidden word.[7]

Years later, in 1941, when it was safe to confess, Toms and Moll owned up to the fact that they themselves were the principal perjurers. Reminiscing about the trial, Toms replied to a questioner: "There were probably more people around the Sweet house than the people's witnesses testified. At any rate, there were enough to frighten a group of nervous, apprehensive Negroes who anticipated trouble."

Having known this when they were encouraging witnesses to lie, this deceitful pair should have been been brought to trial themselves on conspiracy to commit fraud. But after sixteen years they were beyond censure. By that time they had achieved the prize most dedicated prosecutors with political ambitions will perjure themselves for. Both had become members of the Exalted Brotherhood of the Black Robe. Apparently it was a qualifying factor for judgeship that Toms should hold no compunction about corroborating Moll's opening mendacity of picturing to the jury a group of friendly, peaceful neighbors, albeit an unusually large group, out for a late summer evening stroll. Suddenly the peace and calm were shattered "without provocation [by] a fusillade of shots [which] rang out from the rear, sides, and front of the house."[8] Toms had screamed: "Cold-blooded murder!" and the local newspapers echoed the libel: "Another murder by negroes. They are becoming a menace to the community." (The newspapers would except as not menaces those taking care of white folks' children, cleaning white folks' houses, and working in the Ford factory!)

What the newspapers did not report was that during the previous year the police had killed "40 or 50 colored people" in Detroit. Although the mayor wrote a letter to the police commissioner complaining of "unwarranted killings and mistreatment of negroes," there was no investigation and no prosecution. The newspapers repeatedly generalized about the "lawlessness of negroes."

Only a single shot had been fired from the house as Henry himself admitted to. That the fatal bullet "had gone through Breiner in a straight horizontal line led to the suggestion that the shot was fired by an officer from the yard in the rear of the house."[9] Whether or not it had, the evidence of Henry's guilt, to say nothing of the others, was so inconclusive as to create much more than "reasonable doubt." When the coroner testified, he admitted that the shot could just as well have been fired from the ground as from a second floor.

The prosecution, relentlessly pushing the conspiracy angle, tried to show that they didn't have to prove all those things; the gathering of weapons indicated a plan to commit a crime, rather than being the response of a frightened "group of nervous, apprehensive Negroes who anticipated trouble." The bearing of arms was fully consistent with the legal purpose of self-protection as "a necessary feature of organized society."

After the parade of seventy witnesses in the first trial, Darrow and

Hays were fearful that prejudice within the jury was too deeply ingrained to overcome the equivocal nature of the testimony. How many jurors might have been sympathizers with the "curious" outside 2905 Garland the night of September 9 they could not guess. For a time they doubted the wisdom of passing over the shaky fairness of Judge Murphy. Still, twelve consciences independent of each other are a stronger repository of liberty than a single ambitious judge.

Nonetheless, Darrow and Hays decided not to chance it. They asked for a "directed verdict." This meant taking the case from the jury on the ground that the prosecution had not proved any crime had been committed—not even disturbing the peace—and thus there was nothing for the jury to decide. Acquittal by default!

Sending the jury out of the courtroom so that they would not hear what was going on (another adversarial device for distorting the jurors' view of the trial), the two sides argued before the judge. Hays's position was that the only "conspiracy" the defendants were guilty of was a conspiracy to protect their property, which was lawful and not chargeable.

Toms argued that the killing of Breiner of itself proved a conspiracy, and a conspiracy "lightens the burden of proof to featherweight."[10] "The prosecution does not need to show that the conspirators met and agreed jointly before the crime. The act of any one defendant in a conspiracy in taking a life is the act of all," he told the judge while the jurors were excluded.

Toms offered a compromise: he would drop the charge against Gladys Sweet. He sensed her presence was weakening his case anyway because she was evoking juror sympathy. But Darrow, Hays, and the Sweets saw through this. To except Mrs. Sweet alone would be tantamount to a judicial statement of the possible guilt of those not excepted. Murphy was unwilling to take full responsibility for all of them, and so refused to issue a directed verdict. "I consider it my duty under the evidence submitted to let this case go to the jury."

Returning to open court, the defense began its testimony with an explanation by Hays of the law of self-defense, followed by witnesses who estimated the crowd at "over one thousand"; probably a high estimate, but not as high as the *Chicago Tribune* had reported. One witness had seen rocks and bricks thrown at the house and heard shouts: "Here's a nigger now. Kill him!" A white newspaperman guessed there were more than five hundred there, and also testified that he saw stones thrown at the house.

The defense desired to bring Walter White of the NAACP to the stand to introduce records and reports of lynchings and race riots, but Toms objected to this as being "philosophy not fact." Murphy disagreed with Toms, and "allowed" White to testify. Another judge might have sided with the prosecution, which demonstrates again how judicial whim controls the evidence reaching the jurors—and often the outcome of the trial.

Ossian Sweet, the only defendant to testify, was particularly articulate. Regardless of the fact that it was not he but his brother who had fired the shot, he was regarded as the principal "villain" because of his "rashness and stubbornness" in insisting upon moving into a house "where he was not wanted." Both he and White recounted for the jurors a history of terrorism against black people who often quivered in fear of white mobs. Toms's cross-examinations of both Sweet and White were unable to dispel that image of terror.

When Sweet had concluded, the case of the *People of the State of Michigan* v. *Ossian Sweet et al.* was ready for final argument. Toms spoke first, rehashing his witnesses' testimony which, as he admitted to sixteen years later, had been perjured at his behest; Darrow in response faced the dilemma of having to attack the integrity of the Detroit police while knowing that to do so in a community obsessed with law and order would be risky. The trial was now a month old, and while the local newspapers were strongly hostile at the beginning, by late November they had been softened by Darrow's and Hays's conduct, and Judge Murphy's control of the proceedings. Boldness and candor, Darrow decided, straightforward frankness, would be his best defense.

> It is my conviction that every one of the witnesses for the State perjured himself time and time again in this case. There was not an honest person in the whole bunch. . . .
>
> There isn't an officer in this case who isn't partly guilty of the crime and who hasn't committed perjury to protect himself. And this doesn't necessarily mean they are bad, but they are victims of an instinctive hatred of anything which appears as social equality of the black race, that they are willing to perjure themselves for what they conceive of as their superb nordic race. . . .
>
> That's what I am afraid of, gentlemen. . . . If I thought any of you men had any opinion about the guilt of my clients I wouldn't worry because that might be changed. What I am worried about is

your prejudices. They are harder to change. They come with your mother's milk and stick like the color of skin. . . .

My clients are charged with murder but they are really here because they are black.

Darrow then resumed his attack on the integrity of the police.

I tell you that these policemen were no good. They lied and were evidently in league with this glorious league, this Waterworks Improvement Association. . . . I say that a man who has been on the police force thirty years and who comes here as your assistant commissioner and swears that there was no crowd at the Sweet house is not to be trusted. He lies!

Darrow ended by imploring the jurors to balance their prejudices against their natural sense of fairness. He often would recite poetry in his summations, and for this one he chose a poem with a punch, by Countee Cullen, a popular black poet:

> Once riding in old Baltimore
> Heart full, head full of glee
> I saw a Baltimorean
> Stand gazing there at me.
>
> Now, I was eight and very small
> And he was no whit bigger
> And so I smiled, but he stuck out
> His tongue and called me nigger.
>
> I saw the whole of Baltimore
> From April till December
> Of all the things that I saw there
> That's all that I remember.

The Sweets spent their first night in their first home afraid to go to bed. The next night they spent in jail. Now the State wants them to spend the rest of their lives in the penitentiary. The State claims that there was no mob there that night. Gentlemen, the State has put on enough witnesses who said they were there, to make a mob.

There are persons in the North and South who say a black man is inferior to the white and should be controlled by the whites. There are also those who recognize his rights and say he should enjoy them. To me this case is a cross-section of human history; it involves the future, and the hope of some of us that the future shall be better than the past.

Toms countered in his afterword with as much deceit as he could muster:

> Back of all your sophistry and transparent political philosophy, gentlemen of the defense, back of all your prating of civil rights, back of your psychology and theory of race hatred, lies the stark body of Leon Breiner with a bullet hole in his back. Bury it if you will or if you can, beneath an avalanche of copies of the *Crisis,* or the *Defender* or the *Independent,* or reports of committees and commissions in other cities, still out from under the avalanche peers the mute face of Leon Breiner, its lips silent forever.
>
> All your specious arguments, Mr. Darrow, all your artful ingenuity born of years of experience—all of your social theories, Mr. Hays; all your cleverly conceived psychology can never dethrone justice in this case. Leon Breiner, peacefully chatting with his neighbor at his doorstep, enjoying his God-given and inalienable right to live, is shot through the back from ambush. And you can't make anything out of these facts, gentlemen of the defense, but cold-blooded murder.[11]

The sting of Toms's words was lessened when Judge Murphy delivered a "fair and impartial" charge to the jury, in the estimation of Weinberg, "weighted toward the defendants."[12] Murphy suggested that the conspiracy theory was invalid because only those defendants whose overt acts indicated individual responsibility could be found guilty. This would have limited the possibility of guilt to only Ossian and Henry—Ossian for having directed and controlled the operation; Henry for having fired the shot.

But not even they could be found guilty, Murphy advised, if the jurors believed that the force used by them in defense of the house was reasonable under the circumstances. The NAACP commented favorably on Murphy's charge in *Crisis*: "Seldom in any court has a more impartial, learned or complete charge to a jury been heard," and, quoting the judge: "Dr. Sweet has the same right under the law to purchase and occupy the dwelling house on Garland Avenue as any other man. Under the law, a man's house is his castle. It is his castle whether he is white or black, and no man has the right to assail or invade it. . . ."

It was now the day before Thanksgiving. Hardly had the jury been secluded when rumors started to fly—eleven to one for acquittal, then ten to two for conviction. Angry shouts were heard from inside the jury room. The intensity of the sharp division, and the intransigence of two of the jurors was expressed by another shout: "Two of you had these fellows convicted before you came here," and later: "What's the use of arguing with these fellows?" At midnight the jury asked for clarification of the judge's instructions on self-defense, but there was no apparent progress. At 2:00 A.M. the jury was put to bed for the night.[13]

The jurors did not get Thanksgiving Day off, remaining locked up in the jury room, except the court allowed them a short break for a special turkey dinner. As fine as their dinner might have been, it did not produce harmony. That the jurors had now split into two camps was obvious not only from the length of deliberations, but from shouting inside the jury room, not all of it intelligible. The *New York Times* reported on November 27 that "voices raised in heated debate could be heard from the jury room. Lulls followed in which the strains of popular songs were wafted into the courtroom." Darrow "lolled on a sofa in the judge's office and confessed to being very tired."[14] At midnight the jurors were put to bed for the second night of seclusion.

They were closeted again during the morning of the third day, but by 1:30 in the afternoon they gave up—hopelessly deadlocked. They reported to Murphy the surprising news that ten had stood firmly for acquittal of all defendants except Ossian and Henry. In their case, three acquitting jurors appeared to try appeasement by joining with the minority of two for a reduced charge of manslaughter—thus, on the surface, five to convict on a lesser charge against the seven not willing to appease, according to the *New York Times* of November 28.

Some of the jurors confirmed after the trial that deliberations were prolonged because the ten were trying to shake the bigotry out of the other two. But no appeal, no reasoning, not even the questionable attempt to appease could sway them for forty-six hours. Had it not been for this, the jury would have brought in quick acquittals for all defendants on the first day.

Under such conditions, Darrow expected Toms to drop the charges; but the vindictive prosecutor, feeling it was to his political advantage, insisted upon a retrial. Nor would "liberal" Murphy dismiss the charges, perhaps feeling it was politically too risky. Toms, however, made one concession. Without releasing any defendant from indictment, he would not pursue the conspiracy issue; he would concentrate upon the most vulnerable of the eleven to stand trial alone. That was twenty-year-old law student, Henry Sweet.

All except Gladys Sweet had been in jail for almost three months, and no one had spent a single night in the new house. Gladys, afraid to live there alone, had gone to her mother, Mrs. Mitchell. Darrow asked that the defendants be released, but Toms felt that he was condescending enough to agree to a lowered bail for all except Henry and Ossian. Although Darrow argued reasonably that they would be the least likely to fail to appear, Toms, in true prosecutorial fashion, would use bail as a weapon against due process of law. High enough by today's standard, $5,000 was exceptionally cruel in the face of the Eighth Amendment. The NAACP raised enough support to pay the bail for all in bonds, enabling all defendants to leave. Henry and Ossian joined Gladys and the baby at Mrs. Mitchell's, leaving their Garland Avenue home empty; Henry prepared to face a second jury the following spring.

One night during the winter, the empty house was set on fire but the blaze was quickly extinguished without extensive damage. Thereafter the house was kept under constant police guard.

While awaiting the second trial, the NAACP and others sponsored rallies in several cities to garner support for the Sweets and to raise money. At a rally on January 3, 1926, in New York, Hays declared that the principal issue in the trial was "to preserve the fundamental spirit of the Constitution. Nobody, white or black, deserves his home and liberty unless he is ready to fight for it." Other black families were forced from their homes, but "lacked the courage to fight it out as Dr. Sweet did."

Ossian Sweet spoke at the January 3 rally, attended by 1,500 persons, saying that the outcome of the trial "will determine whether or not mobs shall tell colored people where or where not to live."[15]

Henry's trial began on April 19. Hays was unable to join Darrow, who replaced him with two black lawyers from Detroit, Thomas Chawke and Julian Perry. Again he pondered waiving the jury, but feeling there was a reasonable chance of acquittal, and that acquittal by jury would influence black-white relationships all over the country, he stuck with the jury.

Missing from several reports of the trial is how this second jury was selected, how extensively both Darrow and Toms invaded juror privacy by *voir dire* questioning, and on what basis veniremen were rejected. However the jury was selected, no blacks or women survived the process, and Darrow resigned himself to the inevitability, as before, that some of the talesmen could have been part of the menacing crowd.

Toms demonstrated a singular lack of imagination and integrity; he repeated the inanity of producing a multitude of witnesses each to testify that no one—or hardly anyone—else was there. Searching cross-examination exposed discrepancies in the testimony. Darrow also found three more white witnesses to testify they had seen a crowd of over three hundred and it was hostile. He shunned the question of the fatal bullet being fired from ground level rather than the second floor because if the jurors found the latter, he felt, they would be more likely to disregard other arguments. Therefore, he conceded the possibility that the fatal bullet might have come from either direction.

When Henry testified, he was honest about having shot a rifle, telling the jury he was terrified, feeling that the family was in great danger. The fear justified defensive action.

Darrow made his own observations of the trial witnesses. All the Negroes, he said, were educated men and women "of culture and refinement, many college graduates, and in every way the superiors of the witnesses for the prosecution." The white witnesses were mostly crude and vulgar.

The trial lasted for a little over three weeks. Darrow described his own summation as "one of the strongest and most satisfactory arguments that I ever delivered." Judge Murphy agreed that it was "the greatest experience of my life. . . . Clarence Darrow at his best." He spoke for over eight hours and his full statement has been preserved as a classic. One observer said that "the collars of the jurors wilted. They sat tense in the grip of historic events and tragic happenings which he made real and present again before their very eyes."

Darrow began by countering Moll's argument that "this isn't a race question. This is a murder question," but obviously it was a race question because had the situation been reversed, eleven white defendants would never have even been brought to trial.

I haven't any doubt but that every one of you is prejudiced against colored people. I want you to guard against it. I want you to do all you can to be fair in this case. . . . I think not one man of this jury wants to be prejudiced. It is forced into us almost from our youth, until somehow or other we feel we are superior to these people who have black faces. . . . Take the race hatred away and you have nothing left.

Henry Sweet never knew that such a man as Leon Breiner lived. He didn't shoot at him. Somebody shot out into that crowd and Breiner got it. But who was Breiner anyway? . . . Breiner was a conspirator in as foul a conspiracy as was ever hatched in a community; in a conspiracy to drive from their homes a little family of black people. . . . Mr. Moll says that these colored people had a perfect right to live in their house. He did not say it was an outrage to molest them. . . . Now you know that the mob met there for that purpose. They violated the Constitution and the law; the violated every human feeling and threw justice and mercy and humanity to the winds, and they made a murderous attack upon their neighbor because his face was black. Which is worse, to do that or to lie about it?

Who are the cowards in this case? Cowards, gentlemen! Eleven people with black skins, eleven people whose ancestors did not come to America because they wanted to, but were brought here in slave ships, to toil for nothing for the whites—whose lives have been taken in nearly every state of the Union—they have been victims of riots all over this land of the free. . . . Were they cowards? No, gentlemen, they may have been gunmen, they may have tried to murder, but they are not cowards.

Eleven people knowing what it meant, with the history of the race behind them, with the picture of Detroit in front of them—with the knowledge of shootings and killings and insult and injury without end, eleven of them go into a house, gentlemen, with no police protection, in the face of a mob, and the hatred of a community, and take guns and ammunition and fight for their rights and mine, and for the rights of every being that lives. They went in and faced a mob seeking to tear them to bits. Call them something else beside cowards. The cowardly curs were in the mob gathered there with the backing of the law.

Aren't you glad you are not black? You deserve a lot of credit for it, don't you, because you didn't choose black ancestry? People ought to be killed who choose black ancestry. Imagine yourselves colored gentlemen. Imagine yourselves back in the Sweet house on that fatal night.

White people invited colored people to come to Detroit to work and they always have a corner on the meanest jobs. The city must grow or you couldn't brag about it. The colored people must live somewhere. Everybody is willing to have them live somewhere else.

The very presence of the crowd was a mob. . . . How long are you going to live in that condition with a mob surrounding your house? and the police force standing in front of it? How long should these men have waited? . . . until dozens of stones were thrown against the house? Instead of being here under indictment for murder, they should be honored for the brave stand they made for their rights and ours.

Every man has a right to kill to save his life . . . to defend himself or his family. There isn't any question about it. . . .

I do not believe in the law of hate. I may not be true to my ideals always, but I believe in the law of love, and I believe that you can do nothing with hatred. I would like to see a time when man loves his fellow man, and forget his color and his creed. We will never be civilized until that time comes. . . . The law has made the Negro equal but man has not. And, after all, the last analysis is, what has man done and not what the law has done. . . .

I have watched day after day these black tense faces that have crowded this court. These black faces that now are looking to you twelve whites, feeling that the hopes and fears of a race are in your keeping. This case is about to end, gentlemen. To them it is life. Not one of their color sits on this jury. Their fate is in the hands of twelve whites. Their eyes are fixed on you. Their hearts go out to you, and their hopes hang on your verdict.

This is all. I ask you, on behalf of this defendant, on behalf of these helpless ones who turn to you, and more than that—on behalf of this great state and this great city which must face this problem, and face it fairly—I ask you, in the name of progress and of the human race, to return a verdict of Not Guilty in this case.[16]

This jury needed only about three and a half hours to arrive at a unanimous verdict of not guilty. The relative shortness of their deliberations would indicate near harmony from the outset. No matter what the jurors' individual feelings may have been about blacks, or blacks as neighbors, they were all able to understand the basic right of every human being to defend home and family.

Even yet, Toms would not give up. He refused to dismiss the charges against the other defendants, holding their indictments over them vindictively for more than a year. It was not until July 21, 1927, that he would concede. In his dismissal motion, Toms admitted that the "proofs [*sic*] on behalf of the State as to the defendant Henry Sweet were of greater weight than the proofs against any other defendant." Therefore, "if the jury in the trial of Henry Sweet was not convinced of his guilt . . . a jury trying any of the other defendants . . . would undoubtedly do likewise."

Toms had known this on May 19, 1926, as well as he knew it on July 21, 1927.

The prosecutor expressed another sentiment to explain his motion, which he could not have said a year earlier. Following the jury acquittals, there was "a noticeably improved spirit of tolerance and forbearance" between blacks and whites. The Waterworks Improvement Association did not survive the trial, and several black families had moved, unmolested, into the neighborhood. But it was not the end of racial strife in Detroit.

The Sweets at first did not move back to Garland. They tried to sell but were unsuccessful; in 1928 they returned. The widow of Leon Breiner sued Sweet for $150,000 for wrongful death, but her suit was dismissed without coming to trial. However, the emotional burden on the family had taken its toll. The Sweet's baby daughter died of tuberculosis. The strain of her child's death, following the two trials and now the Breiner suit were too much for Gladys. Since she was ailing herself, this combination may have hastened her early death. Ossian remained in the house, and over the years married twice again, both marriages ending in divorce without children. His medical practice thrived and he became so well known that he twice ran for political office. He survived the primaries each time but lost in two general elections.

Henry did become a lawyer, but died in 1940 at age thirty-five. After Ossian's second divorce in 1944, he moved out of the house, sold it, and lived alone the rest of his life. He became increasingly despondent and reclusive. On March 19, 1960, at age sixty-five, suffering severely from arthritis, he committed suicide by shooting himself in the head.

Brother Otis Sweet continued his dentistry practice until his office was destroyed in the Detroit racial riots of 1967. Now in his seventies he was asked about the trials; Otis replied, "I don't think much about it any more. You forget and forgive."

NOTES

1. *New York Times,* May 25, 1926.

2. *Corrigan et al.* v. *Buckley* 299 F 899, 1924, and 271 US 323, 1926.

3. *Pond* v. *The People,* April 1860 term, pp. 175–76.

4. Arthur Garfield Hays, *City Lawyer: The Autobiography of a Law Practice* (New York: Simon and Schuster, 1942), p. 209.

5. Kenneth G. Weinberg, *"A Man's Home, a Man's Castle"* (New York: McCall Publishing Co., 1971), p. 82.

6. Arthur Garfield Hays, *Let Freedom Ring* (New York: Liveright Publishing Corp., 1937), p. 199–201.

7. Weinberg, *"A Man's Home, a Man's Castle,"* p. 91.

8. Hays, *City Lawyer: The Autobiography of a Law Practice,* p. 202.

9. Ibid., p. 208.

10. Weinberg, *"A Man's Home, a Man's Castle,"* p. 99.

11. Ibid., p. 120.

12. Ibid., pp. 120–21.

13. Hays, pp. 231–32.

14. *New York Times,* November 27, 1925.

15. *New York Times,* January 4, 1926.

16. Richard J. Jensen, *Clarence Darrow: The Creation of an American Myth* (Westport, Conn.: Greenwood Press, 1992), pp. 219–51.

Part 5

JURIES SUPPORT
WOMEN'S SUFFRAGE

"I HAVE DECIDED SHE WAS NOT PROTECTED IN A RIGHT TO VOTE!"

E arly on Friday morning, November 1, 1872, Susan Brownell Anthony marched with fifteen other women, including her three sisters, down to invade the exclusively masculine precincts of a barber shop, doubling that day as the election headquarters for the eighth ward in Rochester, New York. She confronted three startled young men, Beverly Jones, twenty-five, chief; Edwin F. Marsh, thirty-three; and William B. Hall, who composed that day's Election Board of Registry.

Unwarned and unprepared, the three election officers turned for advice to two older supervisors, Silas J. Wagner, a Republican, and Daniel J. Warner, a Democrat, but Wagner had darted out a back entrance. Warner asked Jones if he knew the penalty for refusing to register an eligible voter. But he did not answer the question the women had startled them with just by their appearance: were women eligible voters?

Jones and Marsh were hesitant but wanted to play safe. Hall resisted. The two-to-one majority prevailed, and all sixteen women were registered for the presidential election between Ulysses S. Grant and Horace Greeley the following Tuesday, November 5. The women were doing no more than responding to the urging of the Rochester *Democrat and Chronicle* for citizens to "Register NOW," meaning on Friday or Saturday, with no suggestion that eligibility might be confined only to males.

Saturday's papers carried the story that the sixteen had been registered, which encouraged thirty-five other Rochester women to register in their respective polling places; but at least one paper, the *Union and Advertiser,* denounced the women and demanded that they, as well as any election official accepting their ballots, be prosecuted "to the full extent of the law."

The *Union and Advertiser* cited the pertinent section of an enforcement act implementing the newly passed Fourteenth Amendment: "Any person . . . who shall vote without having a legal right to vote; or do any unlawful act to secure . . . an opportunity to vote for himself or any other person shall be deemed guilty of a crime" punishable by a fine of five hundred dollars and/or imprisonment up to three years.

This warning was so intimidating that on election day no official in any ward except the eighth would accept the women's ballots. At seven o'clock on election morning, the sixteen women, hoping by their early arrival to create less attention, arrived at the polls before the same three young men now constituted as Inspectors of Election. They asked for ballots; they received them, and all the women voted. Most of the ballots were returned to Jones and Marsh, and even Hall accepted some, albeit begrudgingly. The women returned home, ballots were counted, and the story was telegraphed across the nation, appearing in many newspapers over the next two or three days.

On Thanksgiving Day, November 28, Anthony was at home with her family when an imposingly tall, impeccably dressed, and very fidgety gentleman arrived at the door. After a few bland comments about the weather, he began hesitantly: "Miss Anthony . . ." but he was too unsettled to continue.

"Won't you come in and sit down?" she tried to comfort him.

"No, thank you. You see, Miss Anthony," he stammered. "I am here on a most uncomfortable errand." He hesitated again. "The fact is, Miss Anthony . . . I have come to arrest you." He seemed about to collapse. Anthony remained composed, although the possibility of arrest had not occurred to her. Deputy Marshal E. J. Keeney tried to be courteous. "If you will oblige me by coming as soon as possible to the district attorney's office, no escort will be necessary."

Anthony had experienced so many confrontations with officialdom in her fifty-two years that she could ready herself for almost any assault. "Is this the usual manner of serving a warrant?" she asked calmly. Keeney blushed and drew the warrant from his pocket. The warrant alleged that she had violated an act of Congress by voting illegally.

"I prefer to be arrested like anybody else. You may handcuff me as soon as I get my coat and hat." The marshal then served warrants on her three sisters, while other deputies were visiting the other twelve women. But Keeney refused to handcuff her.

For some time Susan B. Anthony had been determined to make a direct challenge against the policy of disenfranchising women by casting a ballot when she had been in Rochester for thirty days before an election, and she would not be mollified by a presidential boast. Earlier that year she had confronted Ulysses S. Grant, who had proclaimed himself "the first president to recognize the right of women to be postmasters," and he had pointed (with pride) to his record of having named five thousand to the positions. He had hesitated, thinking perhaps he should have used the word "postmistresses," but that sounded awkward. At any rate, his "pro-women" position was evident. "I have already done more for women than any other president," he boasted.

Anthony objected to the paternalistic character of that comment but let it pass as unconscious. Women were not to be treated as "adornments" or "property" to supplicate blessings from a "political sovereignty" restricted to "an odious aristocracy of sex." It was humiliating enough to have to "beg" any man of whatever office to do anything "for" women. Anthony waved the banner of her National Woman Suffrage Association (NWSA): "Men—their rights and nothing more. Women—their rights and nothing less." "Principle, not Policy; Justice, not Favors" was her motto.

The Republican national convention was scheduled for June 1872, in Philadelphia, and Grant's nomination for a second term seemed assured. Anthony had been seeking Grant's support for the NWSA's resolution for women's suffrage. She had resented the snub she and her association had already received on Thursday, May 2, from the National Liberal Convention in Cincinnati, where a political coalition had selected newspaper publisher Horace Greeley as their candidate. The men had been stiffly polite and overbearingly gallant, in conformance with current masculine standards of propriety. They had invited women to decorate the platform with their presence, but had permitted them no voice. And the convention ignored the resolution.

Anthony had sought Greeley's support five years earlier, but he had disdained her. "The bullet and the ballot go together, madam. If you vote, are you prepared to fight?"

"Yes, Mr. Greeley, just as you fought in the late [Civil] war—at the point of a goose quill."

She did not endear herself to him any further by observing that by his logic young boys, ages sixteen to twenty-one, should be voting, being of bullet-shooting draft age, but men above sixty, including Greeley himself, should not.

In the five years since, Greeley had not changed his position, observing: "The best women I know do not want to vote."

Anthony had a little more hope for better treatment from the Republicans. Henry Wilson, who would be the vice-presidential nominee, was less equivocal about suffrage than Grant. Nonetheless, she arrived in Philadelphia on Friday, June 7, with a number of colleagues confident of only one thing—that somehow her supporters would dig up enough cash contributions to sustain the delegation of the NWSA.

Again the gallantry, again the flattering phrases to conceal the excuse of "party expediency." Anthony was told that the chief objective of the convention was to ensure full citizenship and voting rights for "the colored male citizen." Further distractions would have to be postponed. Apparently full citizenship and voting rights for the colored female citizen were "distractions." Anthony had toiled many years for the abolition of slavery, and now found the Thirteenth Amendment unsatisfactory. Black as well as white women remained de facto slaves of male relatives.

Anthony had to settle for a "faint" acknowledgment of the "obligations to the loyal women of America for their noble devotion to the cause of freedom" and the hope eventually for "admission to wider fields of usefulness." This campaign plank concluded with the banal pledge: "The honest demands of any class of citizens for equal rights should be treated with respectful consideration." No party had ever said even that much before, and it would be the first presidential campaign where women took a significant part.

In another month the Democrats would convene in Baltimore, and Anthony expected even less. That party would merely endorse Greeley, who, said Anthony "neither desires our help nor believes we are capable of giving any."

Thus the suffragettes favored the Republicans, and Anthony began a speaking tour September 20. She proclaimed there was a more solid base for "Women—their rights and nothing less" than just a slogan. She was convinced "without a particle of doubt" that the Constitution already recognized equal rights because there was no reference in it "which could be construed into a barrier." Specific enumeration of voting eligibility was never necessary; the national Constitution never mentioned gender, until the Fourteenth Amendment, and "anything for human rights is constitutional, and everything against human rights is unconstitutional." This is the essential philosophy of the Ninth and Tenth Amendments, which Anthony apparently did not invoke at that time.

But now there was "enumeration." The Fourteenth Amendment, just four years old, decreed that "All persons born or naturalized in the United States . . . are citizens" and "No state shall make or enforce any law which shall abridge the privileges or immunities of citizens." Women, whether born or naturalized, were, by definition, citizens whose rights were not to be abridged. The Fifteenth Amendment prohibited any state from withholding the right to vote from any citizen "on account of race, color, or previous condition of servitude." The suffragettes had lobbied to include the word "sex," but again "party expediency" had reared its hypocritical head. But even without that inclusion, she argued, the Constitution would not tolerate gender discrimination by the caveat in the Fourteenth Amendment that no state could deny "to any person . . . the equal protection of the laws." This was certainly enumeration enough.

Totally convinced, Anthony now decided to perform a daring act. Importuning and entreating could go just so far; direct action, confrontation at whatever price, was necessary. She would present herself to the Board of Registry on the designated date, and on election day she would vote. She did not require the endorsement of two territories which had already acknowledged women's voting rights, Wyoming in 1869 and Utah in 1870, nor a near miss in the new state of Kansas. Nor would she be the first woman to attempt to vote outside those areas. Marilla M. Ricker of Dover, New Hampshire, had been rebuffed in 1870. She would have sued, except that she was dissuaded from doing so by friends.

On April 3, 1871, Nanette B. Gardner voted in Detroit and got away with it. Later that same month seventy-two women tried to register in the District of Columbia but were denied. They appealed to the district supreme court, whose judges decided that the granting of citizenship did not necessarily confer the right to vote. These Brethren of the Black Robe had apparently chosen to ignore several definitions found in law dictionaries describing "citizen" as necessarily including "the right to vote . . . for public officers" or having "the qualifications which enable him [sic] to vote," or Noah Webster's enduring authority that a citizen is "a person . . . who has the privilege of exercising the elective franchise."

The peerless percipience which composes the United States Supreme Court managed, on appeal, to conjure up grammatical rationalization for substituting a judicially contrived definition of "citizen" which does not necessarily include the franchise over the universal agreement of dictionaries.

There were several other voting attempts frustrated at one level or other, but Mrs. L. D. Mansfield "and three other ladies" registered and managed successfully to vote in Nyack, New York, in 1871. "No evil results followed," editorialized the *New York Times* some days later.

Anthony sought substantiation for her decision from the most prominent lawyers in her home town of Rochester, but evoked no interest until she called upon Henry R. Selden, a former judge of the New York Court of Appeals and of the State Supreme Court. Selden, after reviewing Anthony's argument for women's suffrage, did advise her that the Fourteenth and Fifteenth Amendments, if no other provision of the Constitution, did indeed guarantee voting rights for women as United States citizens even if the New York State Constitution did not touch on the subject as regards state citizens. However, state requirements could not be more restrictive than federal. Selden promised to support Anthony's claim.

Meanwhile, Mrs. Gardner tried to repeat her earlier success in Detroit, and although she was able to register, this time she was denied the ballot. Mrs. Sarah Huntington of Norwalk, Connecticut, had also registered in October 1871, with the local board of selectmen, but the registrar refused to enter her name. When she appealed to a local judge for a writ of peremptory mandamus, or order directing the selectmen to enter her name, he turned her down. Later she received a second rebuff from the Connecticut supreme court. Mrs. Virginia Minor was not even permitted to register in St. Louis, and her husband, Francis, a lawyer, brought a test case before the U.S. Supreme Court. That court once again twisted dictionary definitions by decreeing, in 1874, that neither the Fourteenth nor Fifteenth Amendments "conferred" suffrage on women.

Anthony thanked Judge Selden for his endorsement, but with it or without she had already decided she would proceed, which led to her descent upon the three boggled members of the Eighth Ward Board of Registry on that fateful Friday, November 1. On the day after the election the *New York Times* prophetically described her as having "the bounce to lead to the polls the advance guard of the coming squadron of female voters" as "the prelude to that 'more glorious era' when women everywhere would be permitted to vote."

After their arrest, the sixteen women were brought into the same bleak, dirty courtroom where only a few years earlier runaway slaves had been assembled. But there was no court in session, no one to acknowledge their presence, no gallantry now. The women were held until early evening, when the commissioner of elections arrived to inform them that the district attorney had failed to appear, and that they could go home to return the following morning. The next day Anthony was chosen as the chief subject for inquisition. "Would you have made the same efforts to vote that you did if you had not consulted with Judge Selden?"

"Yes, sir," she replied, ignoring Fifth Amendment protection against being a witness against herself.

"Were you influenced in the matter by his advice at all?"

"No, sir," she answered straightforwardly, although she might have escaped censure if she had turned to the doctrine that to follow professional advice, even if the advice were erroneous, would have absolved her from being charged.

"You went into this matter for the purpose of testing the question?" her interrogator queried.

Fearing nothing, Anthony again challenged the hostile court. "Yes, sir. I had been resolved for three years to vote at the first election when I had been at home for thirty days before."

The hours-long tedium of the previous day proved an advantage. It had given time for the fast-spreading publicity about the arrests to prevent the court from operating in secrecy. The room was overcrowded, mostly with women, forcing the judge to move the inquisition to a larger, cleaner room. One local newspaper prejudged "these law-breakers" inaccurately and patronizingly as "elderly, matronly-looking women with thoughtful faces, just the sort one would like to see in charge of one's sick room; considerate, patient, kindly." Anthony, at fifty-two, was hardly "elderly" and most of the others were younger; all but three of the defendants were married. And most of the women in the courtroom were simply observers, not, by anybody's definition, "law-breakers."

The defendants, who pleaded not guilty, were placed under bail of five hundred dollars each, and ordered to appear before a grand jury the following January 16, not in Rochester, but in Albany, some two hundred miles away. In 1872, five hundred gold dollars was a considerable sum of money, roughly equivalent to $10,000 in today's money. Travel to Albany in heavy midwinter snows by slow train or horse-drawn carriages as well as the cost of lodging in Albany imposed a harsh, prejudicial ordeal.

In January 1873, twenty grand jurors swore that "the said Susan B. Anthony, being then and there a person of the female sex [which] she well knew . . . now or late of Rochester . . . with force of arms, etc., to wit . . . on the 5th day of November, 1872 . . . did knowingly and unlawfully vote," which she also "well knew" was unlawful. The indictment was signed by the prosecuting attorney Richard Crowley. The three election inspectors were also indicted for registering the women and for later accepting their ballots, although William Hall protested (unsuccessfully) that having been against it, he should not be indicted.

Anthony asked Judge Selden to represent her, which he agreed to do without fee, and was joined by John Van Voorhis, a younger Rochester lawyer. A vindictive district judge, Nathan Hall, pretending to fear that Anthony would leave the country (which of course she would not have done), raised her bail to a spitefully high $1,000 as punishment for asking for habeas corpus. She refused to pay, electing prison, but to Judge Selden, a gentlewoman in irons was too much. He pledged the bail. As she was leaving the courtroom, Van Voorhis informed her that by this gallantry she had lost a right to appeal to the United States Supreme Court. Anthony rushed back into the courtroom to ask Selden to withdraw his pledge, but it was too late. The bail had been recorded.

A jury trial was set for June 17 in Rochester. On all previous court reviews, adjudication had been by judges, singly or as a panel. This would be the first involvement with a jury. The government decided to prosecute Anthony alone as representing the sixteen. The three inspectors were ordered to trial on the 18th, over William Hall's continued protests.

Free until then, Anthony took her case directly to the people, the prospective jurors, in Rochester's Monroe County. In these pre-telephone days, the district post offices were the first places to receive news of the outside world, from telegraph reports and newspapers from other cities, and they became natural gathering and social centers for exchange of gossip. There, speakers could almost always find ready-made audiences eager to hear their messages.

Between the indictment and late May, Anthony appeared at all twenty-nine post offices in the county. She and her supporters would erect posters at each location to advertise her appearances. Her message was simple: "I not only committed no crime, but instead simply exercised my citizen's right, guaranteed to me and all United States citizens by the National Constitution, beyond the power of any state to deny."

Reaching far beyond any dependency upon a specific "grant" of voting rights in the Fourteenth and Fifteenth Amendments, Anthony, drawing from the concept of "unalienable rights" in the Declaration of Independence, declared: "We throw to the winds the old slogan that government can give rights." When "people enter into a free government, they do not barter away their natural rights; they simply pledge themselves to protect each other in the enjoyment of them through prescribed judicial and legislative tribunals."

Those "grand documents," the Declaration of Independence and the United States Constitution, do not delegate to government "the power to create or confer rights," but "propose to protect the people in the exercise of their God-given rights." The constitutions of every one of the then thirty-six states "are all alike" in that "not one of them pretends to bestow rights." There is "no shadow of governmental authority over rights, nor exclusion of any class from their full and equal enjoyment," Anthony preached.

It is contrary to the spirit of the Constitution that one-half of the people should be subjugated to the other half through "a hateful oligarchy of sex," she contended. Women were compelled to obey laws written by men for men; to pay taxes without representation. They were brought to trial "without a jury of their peers," imprisoned and often hanged; they were "robbed" in marriages of the custody of their own children and their own persons, and, if they worked, of their own wages. They had no voice in government, no control of their lives.

"We, the people" did not mean "We, the white male citizens" or even "We, the male citizens." It meant "We, the whole people" and it "is downright mockery to talk to women of their enjoyment of the blessings of liberty" when they had so little liberty to enjoy.

The Constitution had avoided using any sexual reference, speaking

only of "the people" or "citizens," until the second clause of the Fourteenth Amendment. Anthony had objected to inserting "male inhabitants" and "male citizens" in the second clause. Up to that point, the
pronoun "he" and the adjective "his" were used only to refer to the
president in a generic sense. She found some solace in the first clause,
reading "No State shall make or enforce any law which shall abridge
the privileges and immunities of citizens of the United States." Statutes
defining crimes and levying taxes applied to both men and women regardless of the pronoun used. Therefore, if women were to be covered
by these statutes, they were also protected by the Constitution.

Anthony noticed that the printed indictment served upon her used
only masculine references, but the clerk of the court had inserted a
caret to the left of "he" to add the letter "s." He had then scratched out
"i" and "s" in "his" to insert "e" and "r."

The city of Rochester had scheduled a municipal election on
March 4, and Anthony again went down to the eighth ward and voted,
but she could induce only two or three other women to vote with her.
The remainder were apparently too intimidated, or perhaps they had
been dissuaded by apprehensive male relatives.

She covered the county so thoroughly that by May the rabid prosecutor Crowley feared he could find no Monroe County jury, though composed entirely of men, to convict her. He carried his complaint to Judge
Hall in Albany, with the request to move the trial to the more remote, and
therefore untainted, town of Canandaigua. Hall willingly complied, and
only twenty-two days before trial he imposed upon the defendants the additional expense and burden of a thirty-mile trip each way.

There is no record of how Anthony, the three inspectors, or their
supporters managed the journey that would have taken two to two and
a half hours by train nor the sixty to seventy-five cents for the fare each
way, equivalent to about twelve or fifteen dollars today. Nor is there
any record of whether she went back and forth or stayed in Canandaigua. In any event, she got in twenty-one appearances speaking on
the subject: "Is it a crime for a United States citizen to vote?" A friend,
Matilda Joslyn Gage, traveled with her for sixteen appearances, their
last being on the evening of June 16. Mrs. Gage titled her discussions
"The United States on Trial, Not Susan B. Anthony."

By 2:30 P.M. on the 17th, according to the next day's *New York
Times,* "a jury was impaneled without difficulty." The government removed one juror by peremptory, or arbitrary, challenge and the de-

fense three. Nothing else was reported anywhere about this jury, a failure to recognize that the supreme power of deciding the constitutional issues of women's eligibility to vote would rest with them. While every other participant in the trial is identified by name, even the twenty members of the indicting grand jury, the trial jurymen are not. The standard procedure in federal courts for selecting the basic *venire* from which the final jury would be chosen usually conformed with the respective state procedures. New York restricted jurors to "male inhabitants" between twenty-one and sixty who owned personal property assessed at $250 or greater (more than $5,000 today), or a "freehold estate" valued at $150 belonging to them or their wives, and used the land assessment rolls to find their names. This, of course, was one of Anthony's chief complaints—that women should be forced to surrender their right to own property upon marriage.

Thus juries were composed of a higher proportion of wealthier, propertied men, presumably more conservative than the population at large. The New York statutes made no reference to race, but it is likely all of the jurors were white. Otherwise, the newspapers of the time would surely have reported it. Up to this point there is record of only one trial in Massachusetts in the early 1860s when blacks were impaneled as jurors.

The courtroom was crowded with many prominent persons attending, including ex-president Millard Fillmore and Judge Hall. Selden asked Hall to sit jointly with presiding judge Ward Hunt, despite his prejudice, because Selden believed he would be more successful with two sitting judges should he wish to appeal on reversible error to a higher court. Hall refused.

It was evident almost from the first "Hear ye, hear ye" of the bailiff that trial judge Hunt, a native and former mayor of Utica, would actually be an ally of Crowley as the member of the prosecution team best positioned to intimidate the jury. The constitutional outrage he was about to commit was all the more scandalous because Hunt was a member of the United States Supreme Court. He had been a local judge before being appointed by Grant six months earlier to repay a political favor to Republican boss Roscoe Conkling, an avowed enemy of woman's suffrage.

Hunt's first prejudicial action was to deny to Anthony her right to be a witness in her own behalf, ruling that her gender, ipso facto, made her "incompetent." But the fact of gender was not so strong as to keep from the jury the hearsay evidence of her own testimony at pretrial hearings. Hunt placed no restriction upon the evidence which assistant U.S. district attorney John E. Pound wished to introduce. Judge Selden objected to allowing Pound to introduce this evidence because it would be to let the jury hear only "the version which the United States office took of her [Anthony's] evidence" without opportunity for rebuttal. If Miss Anthony were given no chance to answer, Pound's version was prejudicial and should be excluded.

Hunt ignored Selden, giving him no direct response. He then delivered a two-word directive to Pound: "Go on!"

Hunt did permit Selden to offer himself as a witness. Selden desired the jury to know that he, with a background of about a dozen years as a judge plus more as a practicing lawyer, supported by scholarly research, had advised Anthony that she had constitutional endorsement to vote, and that he continued to be assured of it. Therefore, when Anthony acted, she was only following in good faith a professional interpretation of constitutional authority. This was her entitlement. To follow professional advice even if erroneous would absolve her of culpability. He testified to a long series of historical precedents from English law which in substance agreed that for an act to be classified as criminal it must be "in the mind," or "committed willfully with a knowledge that it is without right."

"There can be no crime unless culpable intent accompanies the criminal act," Selden argued, quoting from several cases. "Felony is always accompanied with an evil intention, and therefore shall not be imputed to a mere mistake. The essence of an offense is the wrongful intention without which it cannot exist. An innocent mistake, though a wrongful act, cannot constitute a crime."

Therefore, even if her voting were illegal, Miss Anthony could not possibly have done it "knowingly," and it was no offense. Had she posed as a man and assumed a man's name she could be prosecuted. However, she presented herself to the election board not as a woman but as a citizen to deny gender discrimination, and as a citizen she honestly and in good faith believed she had a right to vote and had been so professionally advised.

If she were to be condemned for this, Selden continued, it "would add another most weighty reason to those which I have already advanced, to show that women need the aid of the ballot for their protection."

Selden knew the odds against him. He wanted to present to the jury three propositions which seem ridiculously elemental to us today, benefitting from unerring hindsight. He asked the jury to consider first, if the defendant was legally entitled to vote at the election in question. Second, if not actually entitled but believing she was because of professional advice received, was she not acting in good faith and belief, and could such belief constitute a crime? Third, did the defendant actually vote in good faith and belief?

Putting on a front of fairness, Hunt allowed Selden to try to lead the jury to accept his own propositions. On the first, Selden argued the syllogism that the principles upon which all just governments are founded are that "every citizen has a right to take part upon equal terms with every other citizen." An inherent character of citizenship is the right to vote; and no citizen can be charged with a crime for invoking an inherent right. Therefore, when a citizen votes, he (or she) is expressing the character of citizenship, which is no crime.

Selden demonstrated the syllogism by reading definitions of "citizenship" from several dictionaries, which the court of the District of Columbia had ignored the previous year. Since the government accepted the fact that women were citizens, born or naturalized per the mandates of the Fourteenth Amendment, or by the Constitution itself, it logically followed they had the right to vote. To argue otherwise would mock the Constitution and establish lexical definitions of "citizen" by holding women "in absolute political bondage." Selden likened women's position to slavery because women's rights were not treated as inherent endowments "by their Creator" (as per the Declaration), but were "subject to the will of those who held political power." During senatorial debates on the Fourteenth Amendment, its supporters argued that specific enumeration was not necessary to ensure the protection of "every citizen, black or white, male or female." To treat lack of enumeration now, after the fact, as fatal to the right as universal, would be to break faith with the sanctity of contract between government and citizens.

At the very worst, Selden repeated, if the advice he had given was wrong and Miss Anthony had no right to vote, she nonetheless had acted in good faith and the charge of "knowingly" committing a crime would be by definition void. The fault would be Selden's own for giving poor advice.

"It is incumbent on the prosecution to show affirmatively that she voted knowing she had no right to vote," he told the jury, emphasizing the word "knowing." "The essence of the offense is that it is done with a knowledge that it is without right."

" 'Knowingly' was inserted," Judge Selden said at risk of judicial censure, "to furnish security against the inability of stupid, prejudiced judges or jurors to distinguish between willful wrong and innocent mistake. An innocent mistake is not a crime. An innocent mistake, whether of law or fact, can never constitute a crime."

Hunt tolerated all this because he knew that the prosecution had yet to speak, and that he would have the final say, when he could exploit his absolutism under color of law. Crowley began what he intended to be an address of considerable length to the jury. There was no law permitting women to vote and not knowing this was no excuse. That there was also no law "permitting" men to vote escaped him, as the right to vote is a natural right of citizenship and does not have to be expressed or "enumerated" per the Ninth Amendment. If there was no law for men without men's rights being questioned, there needed to be no separate law for women.

Crowley retorted that the "good faith" defense was "abhorrent" even though he himself had added the word "knowingly" into the indictment. But it was unnecessary for him to deliver his full speech. Judge Hunt, impatient to win a conviction, interrupted to take this chore from him and to lay on the jury the additional pressure of the authority of a black robe. He began his "instructions to the jury" by reading "a brief statement" he had written before he had heard from Selden; before he had heard any evidence; before Selden had presented his defense, arguments, or points of law. In fact he had written the statement before the trial had even begun, thus making a farce of the whole proceeding.

I have given this case such consideration as I have been able to. The defendant is indicted under the act of Congress of 1870 for having voted for Representatives in Congress in November, 1872. Among other things, that Act makes it an offense for any person knowingly to vote for such Representatives without having a right to vote. It is charged that the defendant thus voted, she not having a right to vote because she is a woman. The defendant insists that she has a right to vote; that the provision of the Constitution of this State limiting the right to vote to persons of the male sex is in violation of the Fourteenth Amendment of the Constitution of the United States, and is thus void. The right of voting, or the privilege of voting, is a right or privilege arising under the Constitution of the State and not of the United States. By the Fifteenth Amendment, a State is forbidden "to abridge the right of voting on account of race, color, or previous condition of servitude." [However], the amendment does not contain the word "sex" [and] the Legislature of the State of New York has seen fit to say that the franchise of voting shall be limited to the male sex.

He told the jury that of the two amendments neither "gave" her the right to vote, nor prohibited the State from denying the right. "The principle is the same in the case before us, and in all criminal cases," Hunt began an exaggerated metaphor.

Whoever, without justifiable cause intentionally kills his neighbor, and an intentional killing bears with it evidence of malice in law, is guilty of a crime. The precise question now has been several times decided, viz.: that one illegally voting was bound and was assumed to know the law, and that a belief that he had a right to vote gave no defense, if there was no mistake of fact. No system of criminal jurisprudence can be sustained upon any other principle. Assuming that Miss Anthony believed she had a right to vote, that fact constitutes no defense if in truth she had not the right. She voluntarily gave a vote which was illegal, and thus subject to the penalty of the law.

Brushing aside all of Selden's excellent reasoning, Hunt concluded: "Upon this evidence I suppose there is no question for the jury and that the jury should be directed to find a verdict of guilty."

Alarmed, Selden switched tactics to Hunt's own position on jurisdiction. Since the standards of eligibility for voting are set by the state, a decision about the right to vote "is out of the jurisdiction of the United States Courts and of Congress." Thus, "the whole law upon that basis, as I understand it, is not within the constitutional power of the general government, but is one which applies to the States. I suppose that it is for the jury to determine whether the defendant is guilty of a crime or not."

Selden appealed once again to the court not to prevent the jurors from considering his professional advice, and the fact that the election inspectors had also concluded Anthony had a right to vote. The jury had a right to act on the law itself by finding a general verdict of guilty or not guilty:

The court has listened for many hours to an argument in order to decide whether the defendant has a right to vote. The arguments show
the same question has engaged the best minds of the country as an
open question. Can it be possible that the defendant is to be convicted for acting upon such advice as she could obtain while the
question is an open and undecided one?

Hunt shot back: "You have made a much better argument than
that, sir."

Selden ignored this. "As long as it is an open question, I submit
that she has not been guilty of an offense. At all events it is for the
jury."

But Hunt would listen to nothing. He was the lord in this courtroom, and he was the law. To allow the jury to fulfill its constitutional
role would be to deny him his lordship's prerogative. He would, therefore, have to prevent the jury from exercising its absolute right to deliver a general verdict on the law by exploiting the weapons of surprise
and the jurors' ignorance of their true, constitutional powers.

I cannot charge these propositions of course. The question, gentlemen of the jury, in the form it finally takes is wholly a question or
questions of law, and I have decided as a question of law, in the first
place, that under the Fourteenth Amendment which Miss Anthony
claims protects her, she was not protected in a right to vote. And I
have decided also that her belief and the advice which she took does
not protect her in the act she committed. If I am right in this, the result must be a verdict on your part of guilty, and therefore I direct
that you find a verdict of guilty!

The courtroom gasped. Selden jumped up: "That is a direction no
court has the power to make in a criminal case."

Snubbing him, Hunt directed the clerk. "Take the verdict, Mr.
Clerk!"

The clerk addressed the jury: "Gentlemen of the jury, hearken to
your verdict as the court has recorded it. You say you find the defendant guilty of the offense whereof she stands indicted, and so say you
all."

The jurors were paralyzed and failed to respond; Selden tried to
rescue them. "I don't know whether an exception is available, but I
certainly must except to the refusal of this court to submit those propo-

sitions, and especially to the direction of the court that the jury should find a verdict of guilty. I claim that it is a power that is not given the court in a criminal case."

Selden demanded that the clerk poll the jury, but Hunt shut him out. "No, gentlemen of the jury, you are discharged." It had happened so quickly and was so precisely timed as to suggest careful rehearsal,

Throughout the entire trial, the twelve jurors had uttered not a word, but as they recovered from their shock they were surrounded. Quizzed by the defense and the press, the jurors expressed anger, frustration, and outrage. Most of them complained it was not their verdict at all, and they had not challenged the clerk because they were uncertain about their power to do so.

Nonetheless, it was clear that the majority sentiment on the panel would have been to exonerate Anthony. It is very likely that Anthony would have been acquitted unanimously had this jury, even though skewed by the method of selection, been able to deliver its own verdict. At any rate, we can be certain she never would have been convicted. In the event of a hung panel, the division would have been heavily one-sided in Anthony's favor. The effect would have been almost the same as acquittal since the prosecution would have had greater difficulty in retrying her. If just a single juror had been well enough informed to know that he could have spoken up, Hunt would have been overridden and his "guilty" verdict vetoed. The power of the jury is supreme in the courtroom, and "guilty" must be unanimous. But jurors must first know they have this power and must exercise it. The atmosphere in the courtroom had thoroughly intimidated them. Hunt, a skilled veteran of courtroom artifice, knew which tricks to pull, and when and how to pull them.

Hunt had now altered the entire character of the trial. No longer was the issue women's suffrage; now the question had become which held the greater authority: the thrice constitutionally guaranteed right to trial by an impartial jury, supported by every state constitution which, in composite, declared that "The right to trial by jury shall remain inviolate forever and secured to all," or the dictatorial whim of a single member of the Fraternal Order of the Black Robe, even though a member of the nation's highest court.

Many newspapers across the country which did not support the women's cause nonetheless condemned Hunt. The Rochester *Democrat and Chronicle* termed it "a grand over-reaching assumption of authority" by a man who believed "he is scarcely lower than the angels so far as personal power goes." The New York *Sun* attacked Hunt for offending "one of the most important provisions of the Constitution. The right to trial by jury includes the right to a free and impartial verdict." Otherwise the jury would be "twelve wooden automatons, moved by a string pulled by the hand of the judge."

The Utica *Observer,* although approving Hunt's interpretations of the Fourteenth Amendment, nonetheless condemned his seizure of jury power. He had "outraged the rights of Susan B. Anthony." The *Legal News* of Chicago charged Hunt with committing a worse offense against the Constitution than had Miss Anthony by "voting illegally" for "he had sworn to support the Constitution and she had not."

The Canandaigua *Times* editorialized that despite Miss Anthony's "crime," there "is a serious question" as to the propriety of a proceeding whereby the proper functions of the jury are dispensed with. "If this may be done in one instance, why may it not be done in all?"

The *New York Times* and the San Francisco *Chronicle,* on the other hand, sneered at Anthony for having gotten herself convicted, as if she were to blame, and approving her just reward. They made no comment about Hunt. *Harper's Weekly* was nastier. The issue of July 5, 1873, seemed to revel in its comment that "Miss Anthony has at length come to grief at the hands of the law." Hunt was not criticized. A cartoon in *Harper's* depicted her as the stereotypical schoolmarm, sourfaced, prissy, devoid of charm or humor. Anthony was actually quite the opposite. A pleasant, compassionate woman of outgoing personality, she had an attractive appearance in spite of the misfortune of uncoordinated eyes. This did not affect her sight, but explains why her photographs are almost always in profile.

Now that the verdict had been recorded (and the official record lists this, however improperly, as a conviction by jury), Judge Hunt felt safe in allowing the jury to hear from Susan Brownell Anthony herself. No longer referring to her as the "defendant," he ordered her to stand up: "Has the prisoner anything to say why sentence shall not be pronounced?"

"Yes, your honor," she replied. "I have many things to say, for in your ordered verdict of guilty you have trampled under foot every vital principle of our government. My natural rights, my civil rights, my political rights, my judicial rights are all alike ignored. Robbed of the fundamental privilege of citizenship, I am degraded from the status of citizen to that of a subject; and not only myself individually, but all of my sex are, by your honor's verdict, doomed to political subjection under this so-called form of government."

This was more than Hunt had bargained for: "The court cannot listen to a rehearsal of arguments the prisoner's counsel has already consumed three hours in presenting."

But Anthony would not be stopped. "I am not arguing the question, but simply stating the reasons why sentence cannot, in justice, be pronounced against me. Your denial of my citizen's right to vote is the denial of my right of representation as one of the taxed, the denial of my right to a trial by jury of my peers. . . ."

"The court cannot allow the prisoner to go on."

"But your honor will not deny me this one and only poor privilege of protest against this high-handed outrage. Since the day of my arrest last November, this is the first time that either myself or any person of my disfranchised class has been allowed a word of defense before judge or jury. . . ."

"The prisoner must sit down—the court can not allow it. . . ."

"All of my prosecutors, from the eighth ward corner grocery politician who entered the complaint, to the United States Marshal, Commissioner, District Attorney, District Judge, your honor on the bench, not one is my peer, but each and all are my political sovereigns; and had your honor submitted my case to the jury, as was clearly your duty, even then I should have just cause for protest, for not one of those men was my peer; but native or foreign born, white or black, rich or poor, educated or ignorant, awake or asleep, sober or drunk, each and every man of them was my political superior; hence in no sense my peer. . . ."

Hunt interrupted: "The court must insist—the prisoner has been tried according to the established forms of law. . . ."

"Yes, but by forms of law all made by men, interpreted by men, administered by men, in favor of men and against women; and hence your honor's ordered verdict of guilty against a United States citizen for the exercise of that citizen's right to vote, simply because that citizen was a woman, not a man. But yesterday the same man-made forms of law declared it a crime punishable with $1,000 fine and six months' imprisonment to give a cup of cold water, a crust of bread, or a night's shelter to a panting fugitive as he was tracking his way to Canada. . . ."

"The court orders the prisoner to sit down. It will not allow another word."

But she got in a few more. Since the court had denied her justice, "failing even to allow a trial by jury not of my peers, I ask not leniency at your hands but the full rigors of the law."

"The court must insist . . ." and Anthony sat down.

"The prisoner will stand up." She did. Then the judge ordered: "The sentence of the court is that you pay a fine of one hundred dollars and the costs of the prosecution."

"I shall never pay a dollar of your unjust penalty. And I shall earnestly and persistently continue to urge all women to the practical recognition of the old revolutionary maxim that 'resistance to tyranny is obedience to God.' "

Judge Hunt then revealed his own doubts about whether justice had been done. Having worked himself into an equivocal position, his order was equivocal. He directed: "Madam, the court will not order you committed until the fine is paid." This was a curious order, based possibly on the ground that he feared reversal and reprimand had he jailed her. Nor did she ever pay the fine, nor was she ever imprisoned, Hunt had protected himself. The lack of punishment apparently did save him from censorship. As for Anthony, since she never paid the fine or actually suffered an injury, she had no grounds for appeal.

The next morning Selden returned to court to ask for a retrial, but the adversary before whom he was compelled to make his appeal was the same as the one who had created the need to appeal—Judge Hunt. Selden began:

> The trial of this case commenced with a question of very great magnitude—whether by the Constitution of the United States the right of suffrage was secured to female equally with male citizens. It is likely to close with a question of much greater magnitude—whether the right of trial by jury is absolutely secured by the federal Constitution to persons charged with crime before the federal courts.

He related to the court the events of the trial and the stunning effect on the jury and that:

> no juror spoke a word during the trial, from the time they were impanelled to the time of discharge. The jurors have been merely silent spectators of the conviction by the court. They have had no more

share in her trial and conviction than any twelve spectators who have sat by during the trial. If such course is allowable in this case, it must be equally allowable in all criminal cases, whether the charges be for treason, murder or any minor grade of offense which can come under the jurisdiction of a United States court; and as I understand it, if correct, substantially abolishes the right of trial by jury.

Selden cited the Constitution, adding that "the response to the question, guilty or not guilty, must come from the jury, must be their voluntary act, and cannot be imposed by the court. The court has no right to anticipate the verdict by an expression of opinion calculated so to influence the jury to take from them their independence of action.

"With what jealous care the right of trial by jury in criminal cases has been guarded by every English-speaking people from the days of King John, indeed from the days of King Alfred is known to every lawyer and to every intelligent layman." Selden described how in a recent New York murder trial a juror had become ill and, by stipulation, the trial had continued with eleven jurors to a conviction. The court of appeals, however, returned the case for retrial, as "even by a showing of consent" by the defendant, eleven did not constitute a proper jury. There could never be fewer than twelve.

Despite Selden's rational argument and the validity of his constitutional appeal, Hunt did the expected. He denied retrial. Nor was Anthony ever able to appeal to a higher court.

Consider this: had a true jury verdict been given, it is almost certain that the right of women to vote would have been recognized as inherent and constitutionally protected beginning that afternoon of June 17, 1873, by edict of a relatively homogeneous jury of twelve men, probably all white and relatively stable financially. But because of a judicial imperative and judicial petulance, American women were forced to struggle for forty-six more years to win that recognition in the Nineteenth Amendment.

The drama now shifted to the three inspectors of election, and that very afternoon, before the same judge but with different jurors, likewise unidentified, John Van Voorhis took over the defense. These preselected jurors had been forced to sit in the courtroom to witness the entire Anthony trial for the purpose of intimidating them.

The account of the jury trial of Beverly W. Jones, Edwin T. Marsh, and William B. Hall is the subject of the next chapter.

10

"She, Then and There, Was a Person of the Female Sex, Which She Well Knew!"

O n the very same Thanksgiving Day in 1872, when Susan B. Anthony and fifteen other women were arrested for illegal voting, the three young inspectors of election in Rochester's eighth ward, Beverly W. Jones, Edwin T. Marsh, and William B. Hall, were also taken into custody, charged first with registering the women who were "not . . . entitled to be registered" being "of the female sex, contrary to the form and statute of the United States of America . . ." and, second, with receiving the votes "of certain persons, and not then and there entitled to vote . . . knowingly and willfully . . . with force of arms . . . against the peace of the United States of America and their dignity."

Along with the women, the three inspectors journeyed the two hundred miles to Albany for their January 16, 1873, indictments and were ordered to stand trial on June 18 in Rochester, later switched to Canandaigua, the day after the Anthony trial. On that June afternoon, the three submitted themselves to twelve previously selected male Ontario County jurors, whose identities have not been preserved. Despite the show of disrespect to them, these twelve anonymous citizens were to share the responsibility of determining a philosophical issue which had been troubling many highly placed legal authorities for many years. They had been forced to agonize, under judicial order, as witnesses through Anthony's trial held the previous day and ending that same morning.

Youthful attorney John Van Voorhis of Rochester, who had assisted in the defense of Susan B. Anthony, was now to defend the inspectors on his own. Defendant William B. Hall again protested his involvement on the ground that he had never supported the registration of the women, but Hunt ignored his plea. Van Voorhis opened by raising a jurisdictional question.

The trial was being conducted in a federal court before a federal judge and jury under an act of Congress. However, Congress had no power to pass laws for the punishment of inspectors of election, who were elected under the laws of the State of New York. The inspectors were state officers and, therefore, if they were prosecutable they could be prosecuted only under state law in a state court. Congress had never defined qualifications for voters in any state, and had passed no registry law. Nor could the national legislature do this. An 1870 law did define as a crime "knowingly and willfully [to] receive the vote of any person not entitled to vote." Punishment for violating this law would be a fine of five hundred dollars, imprisonment up to three years, "or both."

Moreover, the indictments did not identify that an offense had been committed, Van Voorhis pointed out. The defendants were charged only with having "received the votes. What they did with them does not appear. Any bystander who had received these votes could be convicted under this indictment as well as they," he explained. However, Hunt passed this by without taking any action.

United States Attorney Richard Crowley, prosecuting the case himself, limited his evidence to establishing, in rather lengthy and repetitive detail, that the three inspectors had entered the names of the women in the register; that they filed the register with the city clerk who, under summons, brought the document to court to show the jury. He then presented the stipulated evidence that the inspectors had given ballots to the women, and later received them, presumably marked. When Van Voorhis tried to answer that the voting had been done in good faith and belief, and, therefore, at worst, it was an innocent error, Crowley objected to this "as immaterial." Hunt sustained the objection to prevent Van Voorhis from producing centuries of precedents firmly establishing that willful intent is a necessary element to elevating a mere mistake into a crime.

Van Voorhis called as his first witness Beverly Jones, who testified that he at first balked at registering Miss Anthony because it was "contrary to the Constitution of the State of New York." Anthony, he said, did not claim rights under state law but under the new Fourteenth Amendment, and asked if he had read it. Jones said he had, and Miss Anthony started to read the amendment to him when "Mr. Daniel J. Warner said . . ."

Crowley interrupted. "It is entirely immaterial what either Wagner or Warner said," and Hunt followed his lead: "I don't see that that is competent in any view of the case." Hunt then asked Jones directly: "Was your objection to registering Miss Anthony on the ground that she was a woman?" to which Jones replied "It was contrary to the Constitution of the State of New York, on the grounds that she was a woman."

Van Voorhis asked him to tell what occurred then, and Jones began again: "Mr. Warner said . . ."

"Objection!"

"Sustained. I don't think that is competent what Warner said," Hunt commanded, even though Warner's official role was to guide the less experienced inspectors.

Van Voorhis appealed: "The district attorney has gone into what occurred at that time, and I ask to be permitted to show all that occurred at the time of the registry."

"I don't think that is competent. I don't think it is competent to state what Wagner or Warner advised."

Van Voorhis protested. He merely wanted "to show what was said and done at the time Miss Anthony and the other ladies registered."

Hunt was unmoved: "I exclude it."

"Does that exclude all conversations that occurred there with any persons?"

"It excludes anything of that character on the subject of advising them. Your case is just as good without it as with it."

"I didn't offer it in view of the advice, but to show precisely what the operation of the minds of these inspectors was at that time, and what the facts are."

"It is not competent."

Van Voorhis, frustrated, shifted to election day. He wanted to show the jury that the women had folded their ballots before giving them to the inspectors, preventing them from knowing whether they had actually voted.

Van Voorhis then asked Jones: "In receiving those ballots did you act honestly in accordance with your sense of duty, and in accordance with your best judgment?"

"I did."

"Did anyone present challenge the voting?"

"Miss Anthony was challenged by a bystander and I told her she would have to swear her ballot. I presented her the Bible and administered to her the preliminary oath, which she took. I turned to the gentleman that challenged her and asked him if he still insisted on his challenge; he said he did; I told her she would have to take the general oath, and she took it." Jones explained that this procedure was used for every challenge.

Inspector Edwin T. Marsh took the stand, and when he was asked if upon receiving the votes he had acted honestly and according to the best of his judgment, he replied: "I most assuredly did."

Hall was not called, but Susan B. Anthony was. Although Hunt had found her incompetent as a witness in her own trial, he allowed her to testify for the inspectors, but she at first demurred. "I would like to know if the testimony of a person who has been convicted of a crime can be taken."

"They call you as a witness, madam."

Van Voorhis asked if she would "state what occurred at the board of registry when your name was registered."

"That would be very tedious, for it was full an hour."

"State generally what was done."

"Objection!"

Hunt then queried her. "You presented yourself as a female, claiming that you had a right to vote?"

"I presented myself not as a female at all, sir. I presented myself as a citizen of the United States. I was called to the United States ballot box by the Fourteenth Amendment, not as a female but as a citizen, and I went there."

This fragment of testimony was quite enough for Hunt. He cut Anthony off, although he did accede that all three inspectors had "acted honestly and in accordance with their best judgment."

Van Voorhis then addressed the jury. Since the women had taken oaths, if the inspectors had rejected their votes, they would thereby have been subject to criminal charges for not accepting their ballots. He cited a recent appeal from conviction where the court said that "the inspectors have no authority by statute to reject a vote" after the oath had been taken. This decision had been written by Henry Selden while still a judge: "The course required by the statute to be pursued where the right of any persons to vote is challenged cannot be reconciled with any discretionary power of rejection invested in the inspectors [who] have no discretion left to them in such a case . . . nor can they act upon their own opinion or knowledge."

Hunt permitted Van Voorhis to continue for some time, letting him cite several other decisions. Van Voorhis concluded: "All that I have quoted from the English cases and our own is to show that malice must be proven to make out the offense, is expressly contained in the statute under which this indictment is framed. The words are 'knowingly and willfully' . . . and willfully means contrary to a man's own conviction. Here is a total absence of any pretense of malice. It is conceded that the defendants acted honestly and according to their best judgment. They are not lawyers nor skilled in the law. They had presented to them a legal question which, to say the least, has puzzled some of the ablest legal minds of the nation. If they can be convicted of crime, a test must be imposed upon them which no judge in the land could stand. The defendants must be discharged by this court."

Crowley then rose to deliver his closing, but before he could speak, Hunt offended propriety and the courtroom.

"I don't think it is necessary for you to spend the time in argument, Mr. Crowley. I think upon the last authority cited by the counsel there is no defense in this case."

Rejecting again his constitutionally assigned role of judicial impartiality, Hunt enlisted himself on the prosecutorial team. He would in effect deliver the prosecutorial closing, augmenting its influence upon the jury with the impressive authority of a black judicial robe. He would negate all of Van Voorhis's propositions and authorities. "Under the laws of this state as it stands," he directed, "under no circumstances is a woman entitled to vote. When Miss Anthony, Mrs. Leyden and the other ladies came there and presented themselves to offer their votes, when it appeared they were of the female sex, the power and authority of the inspectors was at an end. In that view of the case, is there anything to go before the jury?"

Fearing a reprise of the offense against Anthony, Van Voorhis almost shouted: "Yes, Your Honor."

"What?"

"The jury must pass upon the whole case and whether the defendants acted willfully and maliciously."

"It is too plain to argue that."

"There is nothing but circumstantial evidence."

"Your own witness testified to it."

"But 'knowingly' implies knowing that it is a vote for representative in Congress."

"That comes within the decision of the question of law. I don't see that there is anything to go to the jury."

Alarmed, Van Voorhis would block a second seizure of a jury's exclusive power to deliver the verdict in a criminal case: "I cannot take Your Honor's view of the case, but of course must submit to it. We ask to go to the jury upon this whole case, and claim that in this case, as in all criminal cases, the right of trial by jury is made inviolate by the Constitution—that the court has no power to take it from the jury."

Hunt appeared to yield. "I am going to submit it to the jury. Gentlemen of the jury: This case is now before you upon the evidence as it stands, and I shall leave the case with you to decide."

"I claim the right to address the jury," Van Voorhis protested.

"I don't think there is anything upon which you can legitimately address the jury." But Hunt found there were some things upon which he himself could legitimately address the jury, which amounted virtually to dictating convictions.

"I decided in the case this morning, which many of you heard, probably, that under the law as it stands, the ladies who offered their votes had no right to vote whatever. I repeat that decision, and I charge you that they had no right to offer their votes nor the inspectors of election ought not [*sic*] to receive them. I charge you that they are liable in this case. But instead of doing as I did in the case this morning —directing a verdict—I submit the case to you with these instructions, and you can decide it here, or you may go out."

In desperation Van Voorhis pleaded: "I ask Your Honor to instruct the jury that if they find these inspectors acted honestly, in accordance with their best judgment, as you have conceded they did, they should be acquitted."

"I have expressly ruled to the contrary on that, gentlemen. That makes no difference."

"And that in this country . . . under the laws of this country . . ."

"That is enough . . . you need not argue it, Mr. Van Voorhis."

Stumbling over his own words, Van Voorhis proceeded hastily: "Then I ask Your Honor to charge the jury that they must find the fact that these inspectors received the votes of these persons knowingly, and that such votes were votes for some person for members of Congress, there being in the case no evidence that any man was voted for for member of Congress, and there being no evidence except that secret ballots were received, that the jury have a right to find for the defendants if they choose."

"I charge the jury that there is sufficient evidence to sustain the indictment upon this point."

"I ask Your Honor also to charge the jury that there is sufficient evidence to sustain a verdict of not guilty."

"I cannot charge that."

Defeated, Van Voorhis turned to sour sarcasm: "Then why should it go to the jury?"

"As a matter of form."

"If the jury should find a verdict of not guilty, could Your Honor set it aside?"

"I will debate that with you when the occasion arises." What Hunt meant by this is not clear, because a "not guilty" verdict by a jury closes the issue permanently. Hunt could not set it aside lawfully as there can be no "debate" or appeal. But with a judge as arbitrary as Hunt, who could tell what?

Hunt pressed the jurors for quick convictions. "Gentlemen, you may deliberate here, or retire as you choose."

The jurors resisted. They would retire, so Hunt desired to punish them. Although it was not yet five o'clock, and the jurors had eaten nothing nor had taken any break since before noon, he would imprison them in the jury room by recessing the court until 7:00 P.M., probably so that he could have his own dinner. He would offer no comfort to the jurors.

Nonetheless, when the court reassembled at seven, the jurors showed they had continued to resist. "Have you agreed of your verdict?"

The foreman, unidentified, was reported to have "replied in the negative."

Irritated, Hunt pressed them: "Is there anything upon which I can give you any advice, gentlemen, or any information?"

"We stand eleven for conviction and one opposed."

Hunt drove into the resistant juror: "If that gentleman desires to ask any questions in respect to the question of law, or the facts in this case, I will give him any information he desires."

The unidentified juror was too petrified to come forward.

Hunt pushed harder. "It is quite proper, if any gentleman has any doubt about anything, either as to the law or the facts, that he should state it to the court. Counsel are both present, and I can give such information as is correct."

One of the jurors, probably the lone dissenter, timorously demurred: "I don't wish to ask any questions."

Hunt then delivered his *coup de grâce*. Without making any arrangements to feed the jurors or to provide them with accommodations of any kind, he flew into the face of the Eighth Amendment's prohibition against cruel and unusual punishment. He hinted that he would confine the jurors to their dismal jury room all night, imprisoned as if they themselves were convicted criminals. He laid a specially heavy burden upon the conscience of the lone dissenter by placing full responsibility upon him for an overnight ordeal for all twelve: "Then you may retire again, gentlemen. The court will adjourn until tomorrow morning." He banged his gavel and got up from the bench. The jury was taken out.

We are left to imagine the scene in the jury room—did eleven distraught men turn against the sole obstacle to their release? and if so, how savagely? Facing the prospect of twelve dismal hours without food or water and possibly without plumbing facilities, sleeping on a hard floor—just because of one stubborn person! Did the eleven or any among them threaten him? The record does not tell us. At any rate, ten minutes were as much as the conscience-stricken dissenter could withstand, and who can fault him? Possibly expecting something like this, the court had not actually disbanded. The jurors were brought back and the court reassembled.

The clerk called their names (without preserving them for us) and asked: "Gentlemen, have you agreed upon your verdict?"

"We have," shouted the foreman.

Lumping the three defendants together and the counts against them all in one, the clerk demanded: "How say you. Do you find the prisoners at the bar guilty of the offense whereof they stand indicted, or not guilty?"

The foreman replied: "Guilty."

Van Voorhis demanded the jurors be polled, and Hunt felt safe in allowing it. Each juror responded that it was his verdict.

Can this be called a true jury verdict? Obviously it was not. Although we can never know what the true verdict of this jury would have been, we can be certain, based on post-trial comments, that several jurors would have stood for acquittals outright. At least we can be assured that there would have been no convictions. If the jurors, or some of them, had been fully informed as to their powers, or that they could have objected to Hunt's pressuring them, they would have blocked the forced verdicts. Or what would the verdicts have been if Hunt had at least accommodated them comfortably overnight?

Too often jurors do not know the limitations of judicial power, in the face of the intimidating character of a black robe, and that the judge cannot force upon them his opinion of either facts or law. Since to convict requires unanimity (a vital protection against injustice), if this jury had not been unanimous either way, the practical effect would have been acquittals, as it would have been difficult for Crowley to try the defendants again.

The next day Van Voorhis moved for a new trial for the three men on the ground they "were substantially deprived of the right of trial by jury. The instructions of the court to the jury were imperative, and equivalent to a direction to find a verdict of guilty. The jury was not at liberty to exercise its own judgment." Not surprisingly, Hunt denied the motion, although he did allow comments by defendants Jones and Marsh. Jones was forceful: "Your Honor has pronounced me guilty of a crime; the jury had but little to do with it. For the past four years I have acted conscientiously, faithfully and according to the best of my judgment and ability. I did not believe I had a right to reject the ballot of a citizen." But having been convicted, he would submit to punishment. "If it is to vindicate the law that I am to be imprisoned, I willingly submit to the penalty."

Inspector Marsh then charged the judge: "So far as I knew, the question of woman suffrage had never come up in that shape before. We were in a position where we could take no middle course. Decide which way we might, we were liable to prosecution. We were expected, it seems, to make an infallible decision inside of two days of a question in regard to which some of the best minds of the country are divided. I believed then and I believe now that we acted lawfully. The verdict is not the verdict of the jury."

Hunt sentenced all three to pay fines of twenty-five dollars apiece and the costs of the prosecution; but, like Anthony, and under the advice of many prominent persons, they refused to pay, and to "allow process to be served." Their plight received such widespread national attention that a United States senator, Benjamin Butler, declared that "the President will remit the fines if they are pressed too far."

And indeed they were pressed too far. Humiliated by the defiance of all four defendants, Hunt on February 26 of the following year, 1874, ordered the three men seized and imprisoned. As soon as Anthony learned of this, she rushed to the jail, urging them to hold out and promising to work for their early release.

She barely rested for the next five days, lecturing, going to newspapers, preparing an appeal to Grant for pardons, and collecting bail money. On March 2 she returned to the jail with sixty-two dollars for their bail, and succeeded in having them released. On that same day she received a telegram from Butler advising that Grant had arranged a pardon and remission of the fines. During their five days in prison, the inspectors became celebrities, received hundreds of callers, and were served bountiful meals brought to them daily by the women whose votes they had accepted. Upon their release, they were widely feted, and when they ran for reelection as inspectors at the next term they were returned to office by a large majority—of male voters. Even William B. Hall was reelected. Ironically, nothing is said about the public reception of the abused jurors in either case.

Anthony was never pardoned because she was never jailed, nor did she ever pay the fine. Judge Selden did appeal to both Houses of Congress for remission of her fine, basing his claim on the precedent of publisher Matthew Lyon, who, in 1797, had been imprisoned and fined one thousand dollars upon his conviction under the Alien and Sedition Acts. His fine had been refunded with interest to his heirs. However, the reviewing committees in both Senate and House rejected Anthony's appeal by narrow margins, without considering the chief basis for the claim—denial of trial by jury.

Twenty-four years after the trials, Van Voorhis reflected on the abrogation of jury rights. In 1897 he observed: "If Miss Anthony had won on the merits, it would have revolutionized the suffrage of the country, and enfranchised every woman in the United States. There was a prearranged determination to convict her. A jury trial was dangerous, and so the Constitution was openly and deliberately violated.

"The Constitution makes the jury, in criminal cases, the judges of the law and of the fact," he said. "The mandate of the Constitution is that no matter how clear or how strong the case may appear to the judge, it must be submitted to the jury," and if the judge controls the jury, as Hunt did in both trials, "he himself is guilty of a crime for which impeachment is the remedy."

Van Voorhis was expressing the official policy declared by the U.S. Supreme Court in 1794. Our first Chief Justice, John Jay, had written in *Georgia* v. *Brailsford* (3 Dallas 1) that it is the obligation of the jury to disregard an inequitable law and nullify it: "The jury has a right to judge both law as well as fact in controversy." It cannot be expected that any of the jurors in either trial would have heard about the Jay decision; but if even one had been informed and acted on his knowledge, he could have overcome Hunt's high-handedness. And had there been no convictions, as Van Voorhis assessed, women's right to vote would have been effectually recognized on an equal basis with men's in 1873. No constitutional amendment would have been necessary. Two juries, despite being composed exclusively of white males, probably upper class, acting in conscience, understood that the right to vote was inherent in citizenship. Forty-six years of pain and struggle to achieve the artificial endowment-by-permit embodied in the Nineteenth Amendment would have been eliminated. Which demonstrates the supremacy of jury power over all other branches of government and as the principal safeguard of the people's liberties!

By his judicial arm twisting, Hunt was actually attesting to juror integrity and superior authority. Albeit backhandedly, he was acknowledging that the free jury can effectively "bind down government in the chains of the Constitution," to use Jeffersonian phraseology. Restraint by jury is exercised by the jury nullifying whatever law offends their sense of equity. The blockade set up by government against this is to keep the jurors ignorant and to intimidate them. Thus Hunt exploited his position by intimidating these two juries.

Nonetheless, Van Voorhis had faith enough to believe that if Anthony had been able to appeal to the Supreme Court, the decision would have been to order a new trial. The question would not have been the right to vote but the right to trial by jury. And Hunt would have had to disqualify himself. But since she had not been held in custody nor paid a fine, she had suffered no loss, and was therefore ineligible to make a habeas corpus appeal.

After the two trials, Hunt returned to the U.S. Supreme Court to hear the appeal in 1874 of Mrs. Janet Minor of St. Louis. She had been denied a ballot at a local election, and the denial had been upheld by intermediate courts, bypassing jury review. Her lawyer-husband, Francis, pled the case for her. Hunt sided with the majority in determining that although Mrs. Minor was a citizen, this did not of itself entitle her to enjoy the franchise.

Hunt did not remain on the dictionary-defying Supreme Court very long. He was so seriously incapacitated in 1879 he was unable to fulfill his obligations on the court, and was asked to resign. He refused, however. Since he had not been on the court for ten years, he would not receive a pension substantial enough to satisfy him. For three years he remained obdurate until Congress, under pressure to get rid of Hunt and not having grounds to impeach him, yielded. In 1882 he was granted full retirement benefits.

Hunt's record on the court was undistinguished, except for a single instance which blazed as brilliantly and fleetingly as a Red Devil skyrocket. Ironically it was his defense of the right to vote—of a man to be sure, but of a black man!

In response to the spread of Ku Klux Klan intimidation of Negroes who tried to vote, Congress, in May 1870, passed the "Enforcement Act," the purpose of which was to protect the right of black *men,* at least, by imposing severe penalties for night riding or for interfering in any manner with their right supposedly guaranteed by the Fifteenth Amendment. Two inspectors at a municipal election in Kentucky had refused to receive and count the vote of William Garner, a black man. Although the inspectors were indicted, the trial court prevented Garner from bringing his case before a jury by dismissing the indictment. First-level appellate courts also blocked a jury hearing, effectively invalidating parts of the Enforcement Act and weakening any chance of protecting the black voter.

The case reached the Supreme Court in 1876 under the title *United States* v. *Reese* (92 US 214). Eight justices persisted in refusing to allow Garner to go before a jury, and brushed aside any censure of KKK night riding. Chief Justice Morrison R. Waite wrote the majority opinion: "The Fifteenth Amendment does not confer the right of suffrage upon any one," he reasoned. It merely "prevents the States or the United States . . . from giving preference, in this particular, to one citizen of the United States over another on account of race, color, or previous condition of servitude." Although the second section of the Fifteenth Amendment authorized Congress to enforce "by appropriate legislation," Waite rationalized curiously that the appellant "has not been contended, nor can it be, that the amendment confers authority to impose penalties for every wrongful refusal to receive the vote of a qualified elector."

The Chief Justice declared that the imposition of penalties could apply "only when the wrongful refusal . . . is because of race, color or previous condition of servitude." The Enforcement Act (although it was apparently intended to do just that) had not, in Waite's convoluted view, limited penalty provisions to race, but "in general language was broad enough to cover wrongful acts without as well as within the constitutional jurisdiction. . . ." Therefore, he concluded, "to limit this statute in the manner now asked for would be to make a new law. . . . This is no part of our duty." (This is hypocritical, since the court consistently makes what is called "case law" in defiance of the constitutional caveat limiting to Congress alone the power to write true law.)

The single dissenter, the one judge to rise in support of universal (male at least) voting rights, was this very same Ward Hunt! In a far-ranging dissent, he argued that the limitation of the act to cases of wrongful refusal on the basis of race was amply provided for in the first two sections of the act, and was clearly incorporated into the penalty provisions of the third and fourth sections. He supported his reasoning by two points. First, the third and fourth sections made punishable certain acts denying the right of or hindering a citizen from voting "as aforesaid," relating specifically to racial discrimination. Second, Hunt found himself to be "better satisfied with this construction of the statute when, looking at the Senate debates at the time of its passage" he found:

> First, that attention was called to the point whether this act did make the offence dependent on race, color or previous condition; second, that it was conceded by those having charge of the bill that its language must embrace that class of cases; third, that they were satisfied with the bill as it then stood, as it now appears in the act we are considering.

The Fifteenth Amendment, he said, was intended for the benefit of all citizens, in all elections, state and federal. In particular Congress had meant to confer upon the freedmen all political rights possessed by white inhabitants upon all "citizens of the United States; the subject was the right of these persons to vote, not at specified elections

. . . but the right to vote in its broadest terms," and therefore the sections of the Enforcement Act which guaranteed voting rights to them were constitutional. The actions of state officers in denying suffrage to Negroes were tantamount to state action and subject to federal restraint. Hunt concluded with the somber observation that the majority's opinion brought "to an impotent conclusion the vigorous amendments on the subject of slavery."

After his skyrocket had burned itself out, Hunt, like it, fell to the ground. Within that same year the Supreme Court heard another black voting rights case. Here the white defendants were indicted for conspiracy to threaten or intimidate a citizen from voting in Louisiana. Chief Justice Waite used the excuse that the defendants were only exercising their right of free assembly, which antedated the Constitution and thus the indictment was fraudulent. As in the Reese case, the black victims were denied a jury trial (*Cruikshank* v. *United States,* 92 US 542). In this instance, Hunt reversed his former position by joining the majority.

After six years of ill health, in 1886 he was delivered up to receive the retribution of the Great Jury in the Sky.

Part 6

IN SEARCH OF AN
IMPARTIAL JURY

11

MURDER IN HAYMARKET SQUARE, CHICAGO, 1886 AND 1887

O n June 26, 1893, Illinois governor John Peter Altgeld called his secretary of state, William H. Hinrichsen, into his office and announced: "This morning I am going to pardon unconditionally Fielden, Schwab and Neebe. Do you think this is a good policy?"

Hinrichsen was alarmed. "I do not!" he protested.

But the governor had already made up his mind. He struck the desk with his fist: "It *is* right!" he declared.

Witnessing this interchange was Chicago banker Edward S. Dreyer, who was an active member of the Amnesty Committee pressuring the governor to issue the pardons. Altgeld had been studying the cases of the three men who termed themselves "anarchists" for the six months he had been in office. Samuel Fielden and Michael Schwab had been sentenced to hang, and Oscar W. Neebe to be imprisoned for fifteen years for crimes which Altgeld was convinced they had never committed. For indeed they had not.

Altgeld regretted that he could not also pardon Albert Parsons, August Spies, George Engel, Adolph Fischer, and Louis Lingg; they were already past pardoning. The first four had been hanged on November 11, 1887, in as clumsy a spectacle as was ever staged (their nooses had been tied so loosely that instead of their necks being snapped instantly, they were suspended for eight excruciating minutes while being strangled to death). More precisely, they were murdered by judicial directive born of prejudice.

As for the impetuous Lingg, the youngest of the eight, to escape public humiliation he had blown himself up the day before by exploding a homemade bomb in his cell. He had not done a complete job, however. With ironical hypocrisy, the court that had condemned him rushed in doctors to save Lingg's life for the next day's hanging. They did not succeed; he died during the afternoon.

For Altgeld, as he knew it would be, the pardons were virtual political suicide. He became "one of the most reviled men in America." Even Theodore Roosevelt called him "a friend of the lawless classes [who] condones and encourages the most infamous of murderers."[1] Many another in high places had advised Altgeld not to issue the pardons which went against positions taken six years earlier by every member of both the Illinois and United States Supreme Courts—and by a "jury" of twelve men who were the original condemners.

Altgeld did it, he told a reporter from the *Chicago Tribune,* because "I have done what I thought was right, and if my action was right, it will stand in the judgment of the people."

The governor published a statement. He had not pardoned the three because they had been punished enough, as he was urged by some to do, or for expediency, or out of magnanimity. For if they had "had a fair trial, and nothing has developed since to show that they are not guilty of the crime charged in the indictment, then there ought to be no executive interference, for no punishment under our laws could then be too severe."[2] Altgeld was freeing them because they had not been lawfully convicted; because the evidence unmistakably showed that they were innocent of the crimes for which they had been charged; because they had been "railroaded"; because presiding judge Joseph E. Gary had "conducted the trial with malicious ferocity"; and especially because the "jury" that had convicted them had been "packed," and thus was not a true jury.[3]

On August 20, 1886, the twelve-man panel had pronounced all eight defendants guilty of murdering seven policemen and injuring many others when a bomb exploded among police ranks invading a rally in Haymarket Square, Chicago, on the night of the previous May 4, to demand that the rally disperse.

Until the police broke in, the labor-sponsored rally had assembled peaceably, although some of the speeches were provocative (but except for a stand-up comic whose success is measured by the number of laughs per minute, a speech is not truly a speech unless it does provoke somebody). The outdoor rally was breaking up anyway as it was after ten o'clock and a light rain had started to fall. The reason for the rally was to press for reducing the then twelve-hour workday to eight hours. "The right of the people to assemble in a peaceable manner to consult for the common good" is a "chief political right," Altgeld stated in his *Reasons for Pardoning*.[4] Who actually threw the bomb, as even the prosecution admitted, was not known then, nor, despite considerable speculation, has ever been determined. But this much is certain: none of these eight professed anarchists was guilty or linked to the bomb thrower—nor was a ninth, who had fled abroad to escape prosecution.

Why could not any of the seven members of the illustrious Illinois high court in their 267-page apology for their opinion in the case[5]— probably the longest ever written by them—have seen this? Why did all eight judicial deities (one vacancy) sitting on their Washington thrones, intellectuals all, boasting such members as Chief Justice Morrison Waite, who authored the opinion, and justices John Marshall Harlan and Joseph P. Bradley, refuse to accept it? Only a year earlier, Bradley had written the much acclaimed *Boyd* v. *U.S.* decision in defense of the Fourth and Fifth Amendments' protections of the sanctity of personal papers, and against warrantless searches.

Most critically, why had not the jury stopped the gross injustices as they were beginning?

The jury had not stopped them, as this chapter reveals, because it was not a true jury. Merely to assemble a panel of twelve "gentlemen," as I cannot repeat too often, is not necessarily to assemble a jury. The primary characteristic of a jury, as intended by our Constitution and history, is *independence*: the complete freedom of these representatives of all the governed to review any act of government and express in good conscience their consent or disapproval. This panel of twelve did not in any way meet that standard. It had been packed, stacked, controlled, pressured—and indeed so thoroughly manipulated by judicial prosecutor Gary as to render the trial a travesty, drawn out for two hot Chicago summer months in 1886. In reviewing this story, I start at the end and move forward.

But first a preface on the characters of the defendants, and on the terms "communism," "socialism," and "anarchism," because these words were loosely used during the trial. The three terms conjure up visions of wild-looking, unkempt, heavily bearded men; near-mad, bomb-throwing terrorists. Except possibly for Louis Lingg, these men did not remotely fit the stereotype. They were, on the whole, intellectual, highly literate, and scholarly; at home in upper-level academia; highly principled family men in their thirties and forties who were deeply and passionately troubled by the chasm between the extreme wealth of capitalist owners and the abject poverty of underpaid workers who supported them—and of the laws and government institutions which consistently favored the former over the latter. Could men of such high ideals support a government which suppressed every attempt by labor to improve the living conditions of their families?

Albert Parsons was perhaps the most vocal and best-educated of the eight. On October 8 and 9, 1886, following his conviction on August 20, he addressed the court in an eight-hour plea for a new trial. Referring to the railroad strike of 1877, he described the plight of workers at that time seeking better working conditions:

> I see the streets of Chicago, as was the case last winter, filled with 30,000 men in compulsory idleness; destitution, misery and want upon every hand. . . . Then on the other hand I see the First Regiment . . . practicing a street-riot drill for the purpose of mowing down these wretches when they come out of their holes . . . to be slaughtered in cold blood . . . to butcher their fellow men when they demand the right to work and partake of the fruits of their labor.[6]

All these men wanted, Parsons said, was "a little more pay . . . to get their hungry children bread." A typical response came from the governor of Pennsylvania who taunted them with Marie Antoinette let-them-eat-cake disdain: "Give them a rifle diet for a few days and see how they like that kind of bread."[7] Parsons was the last of the eight men to spend three days pleading not so much to the unbending Judge Gary, as to literally the whole world. He spoke the longest.

I question whether these men were true "anarchists," which means believing in no government at all. They were, in fact, ardent supporters of the principles of the United States Constitution which they invoked several times during their trial. Parsons maintained that their prosecutors were "the real anarchists" because they defied the law of the Constitution and deprived the defendants of the protections and freedoms intended to be guaranteed therein. "We stand upon the Constitution of the United States," Parsons declared in his non-anarchistic, emotional plea,[8] expressing views more akin to Jeffersonian and Madisonian philosophy of a limited "government chained down by the Constitution" than to anarchy.

In the first of the eight post-conviction appeals for retrials on October 7, August Spies had defined "anarchism" as "a free society without kings or classes—a society of sovereigns in which the liberty and economic equality of all would furnish an unshakable equilibrium as a foundation and condition of natural order."[9] This is in the spirit of James Madison's feeling that if men were angels there would be no need for government.

The defendants' professed antipathy was not to government as proposed by our Founding Parents but to the prostitution of it foisted upon the working classes by powerful business interests which could virtually buy public officials. This was the era of the "robber barons," when working men and their families were, in effect, slaves of business owners. Theirs was a time when the development of new labor-saving machinery caused men to be thrown out of work by management more interested in bookkeeping accounts than human lives. No attention was given to adjustment and rehabilitation, leaving many workers in desperate conditions.

To oppose a "government" unconcerned with the plight of its people by suppressing the principal source of its own wealth—labor and the products resulting thereof—is not truly "anarchism." Nor could it be either "socialism" or "communism." These terms are the opposites of "anarchism," implying rigid governmental control of human lives. Whatever, as the trial developed the original charge of murder devolved into a question of semantics and the fearsomeness of linking highly charged and misunderstood terms irrationally together; neither court nor prosecution would attempt to define or explain the terms for the jurors.

There was no logic in selecting any of these eight men for victimization, and even less in joining them together. They chanced by fate to be within easier reach for capture than any other group of eight. They did not all know each other, some of them meeting for the first time in the courtroom when the trial began. It was impossible for them to have been conspirators.

Except for Parsons, all of the defendants were foreign born, which made it possible to stir up xenophobic prejudice against them. Worse, six of them had emigrated from Germany, a country not in good favor at the time, and they had not become citizens; they spoke German and read the Chicago-published German-language newspaper, *Arbeiter-Zeitung,* as well as the English labor paper, *The Alarm,* edited by Parsons. Fielden was English.

The intensity of prejudice against foreigners can be measured by the emotional reaction of the very first issue (October 1887) of the presumably calm, scholarly *Columbia Law Times,* the journal of Columbia University Law school, New York. In endorsing the convictions, this journal referred to Parsons as "an American by birth, we regret to say,"[10] and equated foreign birth with traitorism. But Parsons was more than American-born. He dated his ancestry back five or six generations, making him purer than any son of the American Revolution.

What the Haymarket affair was really about was breaking up the labor movement. On the day before the May 4 rally, there was a strike at the McCormick Harvester plant in Chicago, during which strikebreaking police shot four men dead. No action was taken against these officers, although there was no question about the identity of the shooters.[11] The next night, when seven policemen fell, government took a different view. If the culprit could not be found, there were plenty of available scapegoats to accuse.

The chief obstacle to swift justice was the requirement that the trial be by jury. This could not (at least in form) be avoided. In a situation such as this, where evidence was weak and largely circumstantial, the risk of acquittal by a truly impartial, randomly selected jury would be a disaster too great to chance. It would be necessary to control the panel tightly. The energy, the time and money invested by the government, court, and big business in securing a dominated jury actually was a testimonial in reverse to the basic honesty of jury trials, and a back-handed compliment to its potential as the "grand bulwark of all liberty."

No sooner had Altgeld become governor in January 1893, than he was pressured to grant the pardons. But he would not do so at once, there also being great pressure upon him against leniency. Also he wanted to be sure. When Altgeld did become sure he was unwavering, as he made clear in his 63-page *Reasons for Pardoning.* First was the question of jury "packing":

The record of the trial shows that the jury in this case was not drawn in the manner that juries usually are drawn; that is, instead of having a number of names drawn out of a box that contained many hundred names, as the law contemplates shall be done to insure a fair jury and give neither side the advantage, the trial judge appointed one Henry L. Ryce as a special bailiff to go out and summon such men as he, Ryce, might select to act as jurors. This is always a dangerous practice, for it gives to the bailiff absolute power to select a jury that will be favorable to one side or the other.[12]

The record shows, Altgeld continued, that Ryce:

boasted while selecting jurors that he was managing this case; that those fellows would hang as certain as death; that he was calling such men as the defendants would have to challenge peremptorily and waste their challenges on, and that when their challenges were exhausted, they would have to take such men as the prosecution wanted.[13]

This meant that by the time the defense had exhausted all the peremptory challenges permitted them, they were still faced with a panel in which every member "stated frankly that he was prejudiced." The defense counsel called the attention of Judge Gary to the fact that Ryce was producing only candidates predisposed to conviction; that he had confined his pool to clerks, merchants, and manufacturers, without allowing a single workingman on his panel. Gary refused to heed this objection.

Altgeld cited an affidavit sworn to by a rejected juror, Otis S. Favor, "one of the most reputable and honorable business men of Chicago." Favor had offered his statement to the previous governor, Richard J. Oglesby, on November 7, 1887, only four days before the scheduled executions, swearing that while he had "no sympathy with anarchy," he came forward because of his "interest as a citizen in the due administration of the law, and that no injustice should be done under judicial procedure."[14]

Favor confirmed defense accusations against Ryce, in that he and other persons had heard Ryce say: "I am managing this case . . . and know what I am about. These fellows . . . are going to be hanged as certain as death." Oglesby shelved the affidavit. His greater interest was to win a popularity contest. In the last weeks before the executions, Friday, November 11, this governor was literally bombarded by petitions, pleas, and demands from thousands of persons; from celebrities of the day to men on the street; from business, government, and labor leaders from around the world coming down on the sides of both clemency and "letting the law take its course." In one week alone, Oglesby received petitions for mercy with forty thousand signatures, but they were not enough to satisfy his insecurity as to where his greater popularity lay.

He tried to shift responsibility for commuting the sentences of the seven condemned to death to life in prison. (Neebe was not to be hanged.) First, he would humiliate them by forcing them to plead for their lives by making a kind of apology. Parsons, Fischer, Lingg, and Engel refused to be cowed. They were not guilty and had nothing to apologize for. Spies, Fielden, and Schwab did plead, but three days later Spies recanted; he wrote the governor asking that he alone be hanged to stand for all seven. Particularly great pressure was put upon Parsons to plead, but he remained adamant. Only thirty-eight years old with a wife and two adored and adoring children, he refused to "grovel before the authorities nor flinch if that fatal moment should come."

Finding no rescue from his dilemma in this direction, Oglesby then turned to some fifty Chicago businessmen. If they approved clemency he would grant it, and many of them did. To him it was not a matter of right or wrong but a popularity issue; it was a question of numbers. Retail magnate Marshall Field, however, was opposed and he was the most influential of all. So, when Field came out against clemency, many of the fifty capitulated. They feared that by opposing him, their businesses and social interests would suffer. Thus at the last moment Oglesby commuted the sentences of only Schwab and Fielden.

Governor Oglesby had been sought out as a desperate hope after the United States Supreme Court had refused to take any action at all by rationalizing that they had no jurisdiction, thus allowing the decision of the Illinois Supreme Court to stand.[15]

Officially, the appeal from the Illinois court was for a "writ of error"; but, as chief justice Morrison Waite wrote with icy detachment, "writs of error to the state courts have never been allowed as of right," and it is the duty of the applicant to ascertain from an examination of the record of the state court "whether the case on the face of the record will justify the allowance of the writ." A writ of error, according to

Bouvier's Law Dictionary, is "issued out of a court of competent jurisdiction directed to judges of a court of record commanding them to examine the record in order that some alleged error in the proceedings may be corrected." The defendants did not have an automatic right to appeal on grounds of a writ of error; they had to prove that the record of the state court contained errors.

Such a writ, Waite continued,

> ought not to be allowed if it appears from the face of the record that the decision of the federal question which is complained of was so plainly right as not to require argument, and especially if it is in accordance with the judgment of this court in similar cases.[16]

Waite saw the Bill of Rights as applying only to the federal government, not to the states.[17] But the Preamble declares that the Bill is "declaratory and restrictive." Eight of the ten amendments are limitations specifically upon the federal government—Congress *cannot* commit certain offenses against persons and property. The states are not mentioned because Congress cannot legislate for sovereign states. This was a major reason why our Founders originally did not want a Bill of Rights: not to identify a right would appear to mean exemption from the enumerated prohibitions. Thus, for example, if an order is issued to father A to stop beating his children, father B would not be prohibited since he is not named in the order. Because Congress is identified as being restrained from making a law respecting the establishment of religion, by the reasoning of Waite's court the states are not restrained. Waite turned his attention to a challenge by the condemned men to "the validity of the State of Illinois, under and pursuant to which the trial jury was selected and impaneled, on the ground of repugnancy to the Constitution of the United States, and the state court sustained the validity of the statute."[18]

The defendants also charged that they had been compelled to be witnesses against themselves; that they were denied equal protection of the laws, contrary to the Fourteenth Amendment; and that other offenses had been made against them.

To answer, the court delivered high-toned declarations: "The particular provision of the Federal Constitution, under which the right, privilege or immunity is claimed, or to which the state law is repugnant, need not be indicated upon the record; but it suffices to make a general claim of protection under the Constitution of the United States."[19]

To decide if a federal question was involved, the judges would consider the opinion of the Illinois supreme court, and in this case it was found that "the state courts adjudicated that Illinois Statute authorized the impaneling of jurors with a preconceived and present opinion as to the guilt of the petitioners; and accepting that construction as conclusive, the United States Supreme Court may hold that the Act is unconstitutional and void, [and] constitutionality must be determined by its natural and reasonable effect."[20]

Following his reasoning is like watching a tennis ball bouncing back and forth over the net. First Waite is on one side and then the other. He issued a series of declamations:

> Constitutional provisions for the security of person and property should be liberally construed, [and] a uniform current of decisions . . . that one on trial . . . was entitled to an impartial jury; and that if a proposed juror admitted upon his voir dire that he had a fixed or firm opinion touching on the question of the prisoner's guilt . . . such person was not impartial.[21]

The right to a speedy and public trial by an impartial jury was "inviolate," Waite wrote, and then bounced over the net. The court reviewed the *voir dire* inquisitions of two controversial jurors as representative of all.[22] Theodore Denker, twenty-seven, the third juror impaneled, was a shipping clerk who was reported by Avrich to have said before the trial that "the whole damn crowd ought to be hanged."[23] The Supreme Court did not acknowledge having heard this statement, nor several others by seated jurors as recounted in Mrs. Parsons's biography of her husband, first published in 1889; for example, juryman John B. Greener, who believed indictment by a grand jury implied guilt; juryman Andrew Hamilton's feeling that someone had to be made an example of; and the felicitous selection as jury foreman of one Frank S. Osborn, a salesman for none other than the fearsome Marshall Field.[24]

Waite quoted from the inquisition of Denker by chief prosecutor, Julius S. Grinnell: **Q:** "Have you formed an opinion upon the question of the defendants' guilt or innocence?" **A:** "Yes." **Q:** "Have you expressed that opinion?" **A:** "Yes." **Q:** "Is that opinion such as to prevent you from rendering an impartial verdict in the case?" **A:** "I think it is."

"At this stage of the examination he was challenged for cause," but Grinnell posed a leading question to Denker: "If you were taken and sworn as a juror in this case, can't you determine the innocence or the guilt of the defendants upon the proof that is presented to you here in court regardless of your having any prejudice or opinion?"[25]

Denker picked up the cue: "I think I could." Prosecutor-Judge Gary then not so much asked a question of Denker as put the answer to him: "Can you fairly and impartially try the case and render an impartial verdict upon the evidence as it may be presented here and the instructions of the court?" And Denker replied dutifully: "Yes, I think I could."

Grinnell and Gary wanted "damn-crowd-ought-to-be-hanged" Denker on the jury so badly that they pushed until he had provided an opening large enough for Gary to overrule the cause challenge. Although this evidence was presented to the Supreme Court, Waite maintained that Denker did not have "a fixed or firm opinion touching on the question of the prisoners' guilt" quite firm enough to be "not impartial."

Waite then reviewed the examination of the last juror chosen, Harry T. Sandford, twenty-five, a voucher clerk for the Chicago and Northwestern Railroad and former petroleum broker in New York. When asked if he had a prejudice against the defendants, Sanford replied: "Decided."

Here, too, would be the juror Grinnell and Gary wanted: "Do you believe that would influence your verdict in this case? Would you try the real issue of murder, or would you try the question of socialism and anarchism, which really has nothing to do with the case?" Sandford replied: "Well, as I know so little about it in reality at present, it is a pretty hard question to answer."[26]

Grinnell then suggested an easy answer to his next question: "If you should be selected as a juror in this case, do you believe that, regardless of all prejudice or opinion which you now have, you could listen to the legitimate testimony introduced in court, and upon that and that alone render and return a fair and impartial, unprejudiced and unbiased verdict?"[27]

Without hesitating, Sandford replied: "Yes."[28] With this show of hypocrisy, the defense challenged Sandford for cause, but Gary waved it aside: "The juror is qualified in my opinion." By this time, July 16, three weeks after jury selection had begun on June 21, the defense had used all allowed peremptories, and since cause challenges had to be judicially approved, they were stuck with Sandford. Nonetheless, in Waite's view, Sandford's response was enough for him to approve Gary's decision to retain him. His "impressions were not such as would refuse to yield to the testimony that might be offered, nor were they such as to close his mind to a fair consideration of the testimony," he said, and Sandford was qualified within the standards set by an Illinois statute. Waite quoted that statute: (Sec. 14 Chap. 75, Revised Statutes of Illinois, titled "Jurors"):

> the fact that a person, called as a juror, has formed an opinion or impression based upon rumor or upon newspaper statements . . . shall not disqualify him . . . if he shall, upon oath, state that he believes he can fairly and impartially render a verdict therein in accordance with the law and the evidence, and the court shall be satisfied of the truth of such statement.[29]

These justices paid no heed to Ryce's manipulative jury packing; nor did Waite explain how he could reconcile this position with earlier constitutional eloquence on juror impartiality. Waite issued a convoluted apology:

> A jury is generally understood to mean . . . twelve men impartially selected. . . . If a juror's mind is preoccupied with an opinion upon the case to be tried, that, upon principle and by all the cases, incapacitates him as a juror . . . the writ of error is a writ of right. . . . "Due process" means consistency with common law right. There must be an impartial jury . . . a juror must be indifferent [and it is a denial of due process to be] tried by a packed jury.[30]

Continuing, Waite found grounds to reverse this reasoning:

> Upon the trial of the issue of fact raised by a challenge to a juror in a criminal case on the ground that he had formed and expressed an opinion as to the issues to be tried, the court will practically be called upon to determine whether the nature and strength of the opinion formed are such as in law necessarily to raise the presumption of partiality. . . . The finding of the trial court upon that issue ought not to be set aside by a reviewing court unless the error is manifest. . . . It must be made clearly to appear that upon the evidence the court

ought to have found the juror had formed such an opinion that he could not in law be deemed impartial.[31]

The case must be one in which it is manifest the law left nothing to the conscience or discretion of the court. If such is the degree of strictness which is required in the ordinary cases of writs of error from one court to another in the same general jurisdiction, it certainly ought not to be relaxed in a case where, as in this, the ground relied on for the reversal by this court of a judgment of the highest court of the State is, that the error complained of is so gross as to amount in law to a denial by the State of a trial by an impartial jury to one who is accused of crime.[32]

Detaching themselves now from the urgency of only nine days remaining, the justices, through Waite, coolly pronounced stern judgment, devoid of humanitarian sentiment:

We are unhesitatingly of the opinion that no such case is disclosed by this record. . . . Being of the opinion, therefore, that the federal questions presented by the counsel for the petitioners, and which they say they desire to argue, are not involved in the determination of the case as it appears on the face of the record, we deny the writ![33]

Thus did the court conclude that attorneys for the condemned men had not shown that the state court had committed any error in accepting the jurors as impartial, and disposed of "Constitutional provisions for the security of person and property [being] liberally construed," and "The particular provision of the Federal Constitution, under which the right, privilege or immunity is claimed, or to which the state law is repugnant [not needing to] be indicated upon the record," a "general claim of protection under the Constitution of the United States" being sufficient.

By refusing to intervene, and being unable to see "a federal issue for the Supreme Court," the justices became accomplices in the murders about to be committed. Yet Altgeld, reviewing the same juror records, was firm in the opinion that basic constitutional issues had been violated, and that the jury was well stacked.

Two months before this, the Illinois supreme court had also snubbed the defense plea against juror bias, using substantially the same reasoning. In that unanimous decision (*Spies et al.* v. *The People of Illinois,* 122 Ill. 1), the judges declared that the Illinois statute quoted by Waite was "not obnoxious to the objection [of seating a juror] that it is in violation of that clause of the [Illinois] constitution which guarantees to the accused party in every criminal prosecution a speedy trial by *an impartial jury*" (p. 10, italics in original).

To rub it in, the court added: "A judgment of conviction in a criminal case will not be reversed for errors committed in the trial court in overruling challenges for cause to jurors, even though the defendant had exhausted his peremptory challenges, unless it is further shown that an objectionable juror was forced upon him and sat upon the case, after he had exhausted his peremptory challenges" (pp. 10–11). In its 267-page analysis this court could not find a single instance of forcing an objectionable juror upon the defense, despite Ryce, Denker, Sandford, and Gary's (according to Altgeld) "malicious prosecution."

For the three weeks of jury selection, 981 talesmen were subjected to inquisition. Each side was entitled to twenty peremptory challenges per defendant, totaling 160; the defense was compelled to use all of theirs as Judge Gary kept denying challenges for cause no matter how obvious the bias. The prosecution, by comparison, chose to use only fifty-two. The original panel summoned had been exhausted by the first week without a juror seated, mostly because of defendant protests. It was then that Gary resorted to the rare practice of seeking assistance from the prosecution-biased sheriff to prescreen candidates, a procedure of questionable lawfulness.

Special bailiff Henry Ryce, as Altgeld describes in his *Reasons for Pardoning,* boasted that if he found a talesman who was "lukewarm, or was opposed to conviction, he would of course not summon him." In this way he was able to shape the *venire* dispatched to the courtroom which contained "ten or twelve men that would be sure to hang those fellows."[34]

Jury stacking never changes. Six centuries before Haymarket, a thirteenth-century English sheriff reported to his mayor, doubling as presiding judge in a trial, that he was

> proud to say it will be an excellent jury for the Crown. I myself have picked and chosen every man on the panel. I have spoken to them all, and there is not one whom I have not examined carefully, not only as to his knowledge of the offense wherewith the prisoner stands charged; but of all the circumstances from which his guilt can be collected, suspected or inferred. . . . I should ill have performed

my duty if I had allowed my bailiffs to summon a jury haphazard, and without previous ascertaining the extent of their testimony. Never had any culprit a better chance for a fair trial.[35]

A century after Haymarket, the National Jury Project (NJP) pioneered what it calls the "science" of jury "consulting." Their "science" differs from Ryce and the thirteenth-century sheriff only by its added hypocrisy. The NJP has contrived an ingenious camouflage which they euphemistically call creating the "best possible courtroom conditions." Unlike Ryce and that ancient sheriff, these twentieth-century jury packers eschew personal contact with individual jurors. They go behind jurors' backs to study personal histories and records.[36]

For example, the NJP disguises the function of its consulting services behind such pedantic language as "to identify patterns of response [by] incorporating social science factors . . . and addressing the structural and case-specific issues that are important to effective jury selection [to provide] a proven advantage in securing the best possible courtroom conditions."[37] In English that means: "getting ten or twelve men who would be sure to hang those fellows."

Rushing in to cultivate the fertile field which the NJP has been tilling since the 1970s are probably four hundred or more firms nationally selling very high-priced jury-packing services to provide wealthy clients with "proven advantages." It should be obvious that "jury consultants" dedicate themselves to destroying the ideal of juror impartiality, and place a premium on wealth. A "proven advantage" is no guarantee of winning the verdict, but does guarantee destroying the institution of trial by jury.

The Illinois court devoted 100 pages to stating the case and lawyer summaries, followed by 167 pages deciding that the trial was as pure as could be.

Reviewing the inquisition of the jurors as the higher court and Altgeld were to do, the seven members of the Illinois court could see no imbalance between prosecution and defense in that each started with the same number of peremptory challenges. Altogether there were 750 challenges for cause and 212 peremptories, which, adding the twelve finally selected, totaled 974—leaving seven of the 981 unexamined. This was enough for the judges to discount defense complaints that the jury was packed:

We can not reverse [Judge Gary] for errors committed . . . in overruling challenges for cause to jurors, even though the defendants exhausted their peremptory challenges unless it is further shown that an objectionable juror was forced upon them and sat upon the case. . . .[38]

That is, word for word, the amazing lead-in which this judicial panel gave for its later vindication of Gary's outrageous partisanship.

After studying the suggestive questions put to Sandford to induce him to respond yes to the final question: "Do you believe that if taken as a juror you can try this case fairly and impartially?" the seven brethren compartmentalized their thinking:

It is apparent that the opinion of the juror was based upon rumor or newspaper statements, and that he had expressed no opinion as to the truth of such rumors or statements.[39]

By such self-deception, the Illinois judges shut out all consideration of how often Gary had overruled legitimate cause challenges by the defense. One situation related by Altgeld was prospective juror Rush Harrison, who had admitted on his *voir dire*: "I feel that these men are guilty; we don't know which; we have formed this opinion by general reports in the newspapers. Now, with that feeling, it would take some very positive evidence to make me think these men were not guilty. . . ." To remove Harrison, the defense was forced to use one of its rapidly diminishing peremptories. Altgeld reviewed several other cases, which explain why the defense ran out before Sandford entered the jury box.[40]

The peremptory challenge, as a rule, is the most pernicious device for packing juries. The *voir dire* process leading to challenges is an invasion of privacy and personal security and a warrantless seizure of persons, houses, papers, and effects, which the courts refuse to acknowledge. The only function of the challenge is to build bias into the panel: two sides compete, thus making the procedure a contest to determine which side is the more skillful packer. It is deceitful to pretend that the objective is anything else.

However, when one side is confronted with only prescreened candidates, the opposing side is pushed in self-defense to examine and challenge. But this is not usually effective. A better plan is to "challenge the array," or reject the entire panel without *voir dire,* and start over with a new panel selected at random.

The Illinois judges inexplicably ruled that Sandford's prejudices were not "strong and deep"; his dislike of "socialists, communists and anarchists" did not mean he could not judge fairly. And so "we cannot see that the trial court erred in overruling the challenge for cause of the twelfth juror."[41]

Altgeld observed that Ryce had "carried out the threat that Mr. Favor swears to. Nearly every juror called . . . had formed and expressed an opinion . . . that he was prejudiced against" the defendants.[42]

Parsons in his post-conviction plea tried to bring to Gary's attention how severe the imbalance was. He reviewed the examinations of several jurors challenged for cause by the prosecution, which challenges Gary allowed. One of these was a juror named Hammill, who was asked: "Do you believe in Socialism, Anarchism or Communism?" Hammill answered: "Some of the principles I believe in." **Q:** "Do you believe in capital punishment, or hanging for murder?" **A:** "I do not." **Q:** "Do you believe in self-defense?" **A:** "Yes, sir." **Q:** "Then, don't you believe that society has a right to protect itself?" **A:** "Not to take a life."

That was enough for rapacious prosecutors. Off went Hammill on a cause challenge, which neither of the reviewing courts paid much attention to.

Parsons asked jurors several constitutionally offensive and intrusive questions: "Do you believe in the enforcement of the law?" "Do you believe that society has a right to protect itself by law?" "Have you any sympathy for any person or class whose object is the overthrow of the law, or whose object is to overthrow law and government by violence?"[43]

If the answers were not satisfactory to the prosecution, Gary raised no barrier to cause challenges. Thus was Grinnell able to hang on to far more peremptories than he ever needed.

But jury packing was not the only device for controlling the verdict. Altgeld put a question to himself: "Does the proof show guilt?" and answered it: "The state has never discovered who it was that threw the bomb . . . and the evidence does not show any connection whatever between the defendants and the man who did throw it."[44] He quoted Gary's reasoning upon overruling a defense motion for a new hearing following the jury verdict. Gary had said:

> *The conviction has not gone on the ground that they did have actually any personal participation in the particular act which caused the death of* [police officer] *Degan, but the conviction proceeds upon the ground that they had generally, by speech and print, advised large classes of the people, not particular individuals, but large classes, to commit murder, and had left the commission, the time and place and when, to the individual will and whim, or caprice, or whatever it may be, of each individual man who listened to their advice, and that in consequence of that advice, in pursuance of that advice, and influenced by that advice somebody not known did throw the bomb that caused Degan's death. Now if this is not a correct principle of the law, then the defendants of course are entitled to a new trial. This case is without precedent; there is no example in the law books of a case of this sort.*[45] (Italics in original)

Altgeld contested Gary's "legal principle," and, to whatever extent the defendants might have "advised" a disciple to commit murder (and it is uncertain that any one of them, let alone all, did) and that murder was then committed, it is manifest that such evidence would be so unreliable that the whole case would never have even been brought into court originally, much less reach trial stage.

The questions of who threw the bomb was not a jury issue as long as it was known that he was, or they were, none of the eight defendants. Gary surmised: "It is probably true that Rudolph Schnaubelt [the ninth suspect who fled the country to escape prosecution] threw the bomb!" He presented no evidence to support this assumption; however, Schnaubelt was not on trial. In instructing the jury, Gary said:

> The gist and pith of all is that if advice and encouragement to murder was given, if murder was done in pursuance of and materially induced by such advice and encouragement, then those who gave such advice and encouragement are guilty of murder.[46]

Fifteen judges on two supreme courts refused to censure Gary's convoluted reasoning, or his disdain for the principle of "reasonable doubt."

Gary was loose with his definition of "circumstantial evidence." *Black's Law Dictionary* says it is "Testimony not based on actual personal knowledge or observation of the facts . . . but upon other facts from which deductions are drawn. . . . Process of decision by which court or jury may reason from circumstances known or proved, to establish by inference the principal fact."

Gary refused to follow this definition. He wrote his own specially tailored, suggestive definition. Circumstantial evidence, he told the jury,

> is the proof of such facts and circumstances connected with or surrounding the commission of a crime charged as tend to show . . . guilt or innocence . . . and if those facts are sufficient to satisfy the jury of the guilt of the defendants beyond a reasonable doubt, then such evidence is sufficient to authorize the jury to find the defendants guilty.

He continued: it "is as a matter of law . . . just as legal and just as effective as any other evidence,"[47] and "a conspiracy may be established by circumstantial evidence the same as any other fact, and that such evidence is legal and competent for that purpose."[48]

As to Gary's definition of "conspiracy," this was, in the opinion of the defense, the most "vicious" of all. "If these defendants, or any two of them," Gary told the jurors,

> conspired together with or not with any other person or persons to excite the people or classes of the people of this city to sedition, tumult, and riot, to use deadly weapons against and take the lives of other persons . . . in pursuance of such conspiracy, and in furtherance of its objects, and of the persons so conspiring publicly, by print or speech, advised or encouraged the commission of murder without designating time, place or occasion at which it should be done . . . then all of such conspirators are guilty of such murder whether the person who perpetrated such murder can be identified or not . . . nor does it matter whether such advice and encouragement had been frequent and long continued or not, except for determining whether the perpetrator was or was not acting in pursuance of such advice and encouragement and was or was not induced thereby to commit the murder . . . and all such conspirators are guilty of murder.[49]

He failed to suggest how the jurors could identify this "little man who wasn't there" and to what extent his nebulous presence may have resulted in his being "advised and encouraged" by an uncertain conspiracy, and "influenced" thereby to commit a dastardly act, but it didn't matter anyhow,

> if there was such a conspiracy, how impracticable or impossible of success its end and aims were, nor how foolish or ill-arranged were the plans for its execution, except as bearing upon the question whether there was or was not such conspiracy.

How Gary could hold in thrall all fifteen supervising judges at higher levels who were constitutionally obliged to guard against mental sleight of hand is not explainable, but somehow he did. Chief Justice Waite forever disgraced his reputation—as indeed they all did—by falling under Gary's spell and declaring that the trial judge's "instructions" to the jury "will not be found to be so general in character as it is claimed to be, if its language is carefully analyzed and considered in connection with other instructions given for the State."[50]

Flaunting his position and intoning with false erudition, Gary mesmerized a compliant jury with a stretched-to-transparent definition of "reasonable doubt." Doubt, he said, would arise only from evidence introduced, not from something missing or unknown. If the evidence wasn't there, as the actual culprit was not, the jury was not to question why. This judge would place the burden on the defense to prove innocence rather than upon the prosecution to remove doubt.[51]

With all this, Gary still would not chance the risk of at least one noncompliant juror. So when the defense proposed several "reasonable doubt" instructions for him to read, he refused, and the jurors never heard the following advice (and again none of the fifteen higher judges chose to censure his censorship of it):

> . . . in order to convict these defendants, [the jury] must not only find that they entered into an illegal conspiracy, and that the Haymarket meeting was an unlawful assembly in aid of such conspiracy, but that in addition thereto the bomb by which Officer Degan lost his life was cast by a member of the conspiracy, in aid of the common design, or by a person outside of said conspiracy, aided and abetted by all or some one of those defendants . . . any one or more of these defendants not found beyond a reasonable doubt to have been a member thereof, and who is or are not proved beyond a reasonable doubt to have been present at the Haymarket meeting, or who, if

present, did not knowingly counsel, aid, or abet the throwing of the bomb . . . such defendant or defendants you are bound to acquit.[52]

The Illinois Supreme court righteously declared that Gary had "properly refused" that instruction "because it told the jury that the defendants" not present at Haymarket should be acquitted in spite of a state statute declaring that defendants are guilty "if they advised and encouraged the murder to be committed, although they may not have been present."[53]

Another instruction withheld by Gary would have informed the jurors that if the conspiracy of the defendants had been "to bring about a change of government for the amelioration of the condition of the working classes by peaceful means, if possible, but if necessary to resort to force," and that the Haymarket meeting had been organized only for that purpose, and that the bomb "was thrown by a person outside of said conspiracy and without the knowledge and approval of the defendants . . . the court instructs the jury that they are bound to acquit the defendants."[54]

But even if the defendants had "unlawfully conspired" and "the Haymarket meeting was an unlawful assembly," the jury would nonetheless be obliged to acquit unless the jurors should agree that the defendants had aided and abetted the unknown thrower of the bomb.[55] Gary also would not tell the jurors that the fact that the defendants "may be Socialists, Communists or Anarchists" was immaterial. However, to the judges on the state supreme court, being an "anarchist may have been a proper circumstance to be considered."[56]

To keep the jurors from being too reasonable about "reasonable doubt," Gary cautioned them:

> The rule of law which clothes every person accused of crime with the presumption of innocence, and imposes upon the State the burden of establishing his guilt beyond a reasonable doubt, is not intended to aid any one who is in fact guilty of crime to escape, but a humane provision of law, intended, so far as human agencies can, to guard against the danger of any innocent person being unjustly punished.[57]

He agreed to deliver one caution requested by the defense:

> The burden is upon the prosecution to prove by credible evidence, beyond all reasonable doubt, that the defendants are guilty as charged . . . it is the duty of the jury to acquit any of the defendants as to whom there is failure of such proof.[58]

The higher court judges were apparently willing to accept this caution as balancing enough to keep them from being disturbed by whatever else Gary did as an instructor in the law, but Altgeld was appalled. Referring to how Gary's definitions of "circumstantial evidence," "conspiracy," and "reasonable doubt" conflicted with such an occasional caution as this one, the governor wrote in his *Reasons for Pardoning*: "In all the centuries during which government has been maintained among men, no judge in a civilized country has ever laid down such a rule before." He found that Gary's excuse for it was that "the prosecution, not having discovered the real criminal, would otherwise not have been able to convict anybody."

Gary himself was appalled—but not until after the executions. Too late, he admitted that his charge was "contrary to all legal precedent."[59] But he qualified his self-criticism with the excuse that because the case was unprecedented, it required an unprecedented ruling from the bench. If Gary had "strained the law" a bit, he should be "commended not criticized."[60]

There is no record that Gary received any kind of commendation for murdering five innocent men and keeping three more in jail for an extended period, but neither is there record of at least so much as an official reprimand, let alone anything as drastic as impeachment. Altgeld did what he could. He accused "prominent police officials" of terrorizing "ignorant men [witnesses] . . . threatening them with torture if they refused to swear to anything desired," and bribing prosecution witnesses. According to him, Gary had

> conducted the trial with malicious ferocity and had forced all eight men to be tried together where the evidence would be more confusing, rather than in separate trials; that in cross-examining the state's witnesses he confined counsel for the defense to the specific points touched on by the state, while in the cross-examination of the defendant's witnesses, he permitted the state's attorney to go into all manner of subjects entirely foreign to the matters on which the witnesses were examined in chief; also that every ruling throughout the long trial on any contested point was in favor of the state, and fur-

ther that page after page of the record contained insinuating remarks made by the judge in the hearing of the jury, with evident intent of bringing the jury to his way of thinking; that these speeches, coming from him, were much more damaging than any speeches from the state's attorney could possibly have been; that prosecutor Grinnell often took his cue from the judge's remarks.[61]

Henry David, who studied the case extensively, corroborated Altgeld's conclusions. He found that Gary was in league with the prosecution by consistently favoring Grinnell in his rulings and permitting the introduction of inadequate evidence, if it were hurtful to the defendants.[62]

At the behest of both prosecution and defense, Gary did a surprising thing: he suggested to the jurors that they had power to act on the law, telling them on one occasion that they "are the judges of the law as well as the facts in this case." This is a truth which practically every twentieth-century judge flees from in abject terror and panic, but knows he cannot honestly deny since it is a quality inherent in the fact of the people's sovereignty over government. But in advising the jurors of this truth, Gary laid upon them a burden so heavy as effectually to negate its usefulness. If they chose to judge the law, he warned, the jurors should be able to "say upon their oaths that they know the law better than the court itself. . . . Before assuming so solemn a responsibility, they should be assured that they are not acting from caprice or prejudice," but are controlled "from a deep and confident conviction that the court is wrong and that they are right."[63] Worded in this way, his advice confounded an uncertain jury.

The power of the jury to act on the law means not that they "know the law better than the court," but that they have the option of determining if the law is equitable, if it is fair to the people and their rights. It is the power to evaluate the law in question and to nullify or declare void any government action which the jurors find offensive. Gary apparently was pushed to discharge a judicial obligation, and after doing so to dispose of it by intimidating the legal novices from considering the primary question: "Is the law fair?"

As these chapters have shown, juries have answered by overturning laws establishing state religions; laws restricting freedom of expression and of peaceable assembly; laws prejudicial to women and minorities; and, in general, laws supporting tyrannical governments.

None of these juries has professed to "say upon their oaths that they know the law better than the court itself," simply that the law is bad, or unfair, or restrictive of liberty. And when the juries have done this, they are juries of conscience—juries that sense what is fair play and rate fair play above legalisms.

Jury nullification came up a second time when Gary declared that the "jury in a criminal case are the judges of the law and the evidence, and have to act according to their best judgment of such law and the facts." In this instance, however, the charges were multiple murder and bomb throwing, and nullification of a law declaring random murder criminal is hardly controversial. Nullification would apply against Gary's "as a matter of law" definitions of "conspiracy," "circumstantial evidence," and "reasonable doubt," and to aiding and abetting unknown persons.

To cover this, the defense got Gary to say: "The jury have a right to disregard the instructions of the court," but he again vitiated its effect by repeating his caution: "provided they can say upon their oaths that they believe they know the law better than the court."[64]

Whether the jurors considered this advice or were subdued by the burden placed upon them is not apparent from the results, but they are reported to have determined the verdicts in relatively quick time— barely three hours to consider the mass of evidence concerning eight defendants. Half of this time, as estimated by David, had been spent considering the fate of Neebe, the only defendant the jurors did not sentence to death.[65] The court had adjourned at 3:30 on the afternoon of August 19, a Thursday. *American State Trials* reports blandly that "the jury retired and the court adjourned."[66] Where the jurors retired to is not indicated, but that they had been "sequestered" in "comfortable" accommodations throughout the entire period was alluded to only once by juror James H. Brayton, a school principal, upon discharge. He told Gary that he had been "deputed to the only agreeable duty that it is in our province to perform, and that is to thank the Court and the counsel for the defense and for the prosecution for all your kindly care to make us as comfortable as possible during our confinement."[67]

However, the jurors did not deliver their verdict that day. They were held, presumably comfortably, overnight. By 8:30 on the morning of August 20, more than a thousand persons had thronged the sidewalks before the Criminal Court building. The entrance was blocked by a cordon of police; all police stations were guarded and the police reserves were being held in readiness. Admission to the courtroom was limited, and at least forty-eight policemen guarded the prisoners.

Every juror was solemn as he entered the courtroom; the defense sensed what the verdicts would be. The faces of the eight defendants were drained with anxiety, although Schwab, Parsons, and Engle affected calm. At exactly ten o'clock, Gary addressed the court: "All spectators, every one, except the officers of the Court, must be seated and every one must preserve absolute silence. Gentlemen, have you agreed upon your verdict?"[68]

Foreman Osborne (Marshall Field's delegate), responded: "We have." He handed a paper to the clerk, who read: "We, the jury, find the defendants August Spies, Michael Schwab, Samuel Fielden, Albert R. Parsons, Adolph Fischer, George Engel and Louis Lingg guilty of murder in the manner and form as charged in the indictment, and fix the penalty as death.

"We find the defendant Oscar W. Neebe, guilty of murder in manner and form as charged in the indictment, and fix the penalty at imprisonment for fifteen years." The jury was polled. The defense moved for a new trial, and Gary postponed a decision until October 7. At that time he granted each defendant an opportunity to address the court, which they all did, his only generosity being to allow full voice for each, and to sit in feigned attentiveness for the three days while they spoke.[69] Their speeches were highly emotional, intellectual appeals to an insensitive judge who ignored them; he had made his decision before the verdict was in.

Spies, speaking first, charged that they had been convicted "by a jury picked out to convict," and that State's attorney Grinnell and police captain Bonfield were guilty of "the heinous conspiracy to commit murder."[70] All of them professed that they were convicted not of murder but by prejudice against the labor movement, and from fear of the word "anarchy."

Gary, responding on the final day, stated that the addresses were directed not so much at him, but "said to the world; yet nothing has been said which weakens the force of the proof or the conclusions therefrom upon which the verdict is based." He showed not only that he had heeded nothing, but that he knew the verdicts of the controlled jury were foregone. He showed himself eager to schedule so early an execution date as December 3—later postponed, through appeals, until November 11 of the following year.

Haymarket goes down as a black mark against trial by jury because it is classified as a jury trial. But it was more like a distorted misrepresentation of a model which is then misused to stand for the species from which the model was drawn. The defendants hardly had a chance, considering the panel of twelve men foisted upon them to take the form of a "jury." The argument is sometimes made that the *voir dire* process is necessary to eliminate such jurors as Denker and Sandford. Except that will be neither the result nor the solution. A jury selected without refinement at random from the widest possible community base could conceivably include a Denker and possibly a Sandford also, but it would also include jurors whose pretrial views reflect a varied range of opinions, even polar opposites. The ten more moderate jurors would temper the extreme, and might knock the bigotry entirely off. While the result in Haymarket might not have meant acquittals, there would have been no convictions either. A hung jury is not to be sneered at. For an anecdotal example of such a situation is provided by the two trials of the Sweet brothers in Detroit, 1925–26, recounted in chapter 8.

NOTES

1. Paul Avrich, *The Haymarket Tragedy* (Princeton, N.J.: Princeton University Press, 1984), pp. 421–25.

2. John Peter Altgeld, *Reasons for Pardoning Fielden, Neebe and Schwab* (1893), p. 5.

3. Henry David, *History of the Haymarket Affair* (New York: Russell & Russell, 1936), pp. 495–500.

4. Altgeld, *Reasons for Pardoning Fielden, Neebe and Schwab,* pp. 40–41.

5. In *Illinois Reports* 22.

6. *The Accused and the Accusers,* Leon Stein and Philip Taft, eds. (New York: Arno and The New York Times, 1969), pp. 108–109.

7. Ibid., p. 109.

8. Ibid., p. 104.

9. Ibid., p. 6.

10. *Columbia Law Times* 1 (October 1887): 18.

11. *The Accused and the Accusers,* introduction.

12. Ibid., pp. 6–7.

13. Ibid.

14. Altgeld, *Reasons for Pardoning Fielden, Neebe and Schwab,* pp. 8–9.

15. The court performed their artful dodge, as recorded in *United States Report,* 123 (November 2): 80.

16. Ibid.
17. Ibid., p. 81.
18. Ibid.
19. Ibid., p. 82.
20. Ibid.
21. Ibid.
22. Ibid., pp. 87–90.
23. Avrich, *The Haymarket Tragedy,* p. 266, quoting *Life of Albert R. Parsons,* Lucy E. Parsons, ed., 2d ed. (Chicago, 1903).
24. Ibid., p. 267.
25. *United States Report,* pp. 87–88.
26. Ibid., pp. 88–89.
27. Ibid., p. 89.
28. See also *American State Trials,* 12:22.
29. Ibid., p. 23.
30. *United States Report,* pp. 83–84.
31. Ibid., p. 90.
32. Ibid.
33. Ibid., p. 91.
34. David, *History of the Haymarket Affair,* p. xiii.
35. Palgrave, Merchant, and Friar, pp. 127–29.
36. National Jury Project, *Jurywork* (New York: Clark Boardman Co., 1979; rev. 1983).
37. From an advertising flyer to the 1983 edition of *Jurywork.*
38. Illinois decision, p. 258.
39. Ibid.
40. Altgeld, *Reasons for Pardoning Fielden, Neebe and Schwab,* pp. 20–21.
41. Illinois decision, p. 264.
42. Altgeld, *Reasons for Pardoning Fielden, Neebe and Schwab,* p. 24.
43. *The Accused and the Accusers,* pp. 162–63.
44. Altgeld, *Reasons for Pardoning Fielden, Neebe and Schwab,* p. 35
45. Ibid., p. 36.
46. *American State Trials,* 12: 260.
47. Ibid., p. 266.
48. Ibid., p. 265.
49. Ibid., p. 264.
50. Ibid.
51. David, *History of the Haymarket Affair,* p. 309.
52. *American State Trials,* 12: 272.
53. Ibid.
54. Ibid., pp. 272–73.
55. Ibid., p. 273.
56. Ibid., p. 275n.
57. Ibid., p. 267.
58. Ibid., p. 269.

59. Avrich, *The Haymarket Tragedy,* p. 277.

60. Ibid., pp. 277–78, quoting Lucy Parsons, *The Famous Speeches of the Eight Chicago Anarchists,* 2d ed. (Socialist Publishing Society, 1910).

61. Altgeld, *Reasons for Pardoning Fielden, Neebe and Schwab,* p. 62.

62. David, *History of the Haymarket Affair,* p. 306.

63. *American State Trials,* 12: 268.

64. Ibid.

65. David, *History of the Haymarket Affair,* pp. 315–16.

66. *American State Trials,* 12: 275.

67. Ibid., p. 277.

68. Ibid., pp. 275–76.

69. Their speeches are recorded in several publications, first by the Scholastic Publishing Society in Chicago in 1886; more recently in *The Accused and the Accusers*; also in *American State Trials,* 12:277–311.

70. *American State Trials,* 12: 277.

12

WHEN IS A JURY NOT A JURY?

THE TRIALS OF THE SONS OF VICTOR HUGO, 1851, AND ÉMILE ZOLA, 1898, PARIS, AND A COMMENTARY ON HIS SERVICE AS A JUROR BY ANDRÉ GIDE, 1913

No one anywhere raised a question about the legitimacy of the verdict. Although it had been almost universally condemned throughout the world, and even by a minority of Frenchmen, as an outrage against justice, as bigotry and as suppression of freedom of the press, the validity of the decision by the jury was not challenged. Certainly not by the French opposition, which accepted it on its face no matter how vehemently critical it was of the conduct of the trial; nor by any observer in Europe no matter how closely the trial was followed; nor even in England or the United States, where trial by jury had been held sacrosanct for centuries was there uncertainty that, no matter how unjust, the verdict had been lawfully delivered.

When presiding Judge M. Delegorgue announced in the Assize Court of the Seine on February 23, 1898, that the jury had found novelist Émile Zola guilty of very loose charges of offending the French government and in particular several prominent army officers, he let loose maddened supporters of the verdict to riot all over France, while a minority of Zola sympathizers fell into despair. The coolest, the most unruffled of all was Zola himself. The verdict was what he had expected, and he had achieved his primary goal of creating worldwide attention.

The jurors were not polled; they did not need to be, nor could they have been in the courtroom uproar. They had reached their decision in

315

only thirty-five minutes following fifteen days of trial; they had been out long enough to do hardly more than select their foreman and, without allowing time for discussion or deliberation, taken probably but a single written vote. The tally has been reported variously as eight for conviction to four for acquittal, or seven for conviction to five favoring acquittal—the most slender of margins.

And no one in the world is reported to have challenged the validity of such a verdict that, whatever was the count, it was not unanimous. Neither the *Times* of London nor the *New York Times,* each of which had been carrying lengthy news stories daily, reported the sharp division, let alone suggested immorality in legally enshrining uncertainty. They reported only that Zola had been found guilty—by verdict of a jury! The *Encyclopaedia Britannica,* in its article on Émile Zola, noted that Zola had been "condemned" without giving recognition that a jury had been involved at all.

When in 1791, the newly organized post-revolutionary government had begrudgingly complimented its great rival across the channel by acknowledging the superiority of the English trial by jury over the monarchical court established by Louis XIV in 1670, the Constituent Assembly decided that acknowledgment was condescension enough. The legislature was impelled to resist "a servile imitation" of the English system even while rebelling against the absolutist monarchy they had just overthrown. The wording of the 1670 statute may not have been so bad on the surface, in that it had prescribed for the judiciary to lean over backward to favor the accused at trial to avoid unjust convictions. But this was not followed in actual practice when good laws get twisted without proper supervision or accountability. How could the new government satisfy the desire for fairness without genuflecting too deeply before Anglicanism?

France had had little experience with trials by jury, and that anciently. From the twelfth to the fourteenth century there had been a system of "popular justice" wherein disputes were settled by assemblies known as *mallus,* or Hundred Court, presided over by an elected judge who sat with the tribal elders and freemen. This was followed by a system called *scabini,* where a royal, hence elitist, appointee sat with seven or more nobles in both civil and criminal trials.

During the feudal period, the local courts were controlled by the lord of the domain, with his vassals acting as advisers; and when a vassal was brought to trial he was judged by his equals, a privilege not extended to persons of lower social standing. While there was a relationship to trial by jury in that decisions were rendered by panels of nonprofessionals, it was somewhat distant.[1]

Proponents of the post-revolutionary French jury also looked to "free America" as a model where the jury was "the only humane system of practice." In France "we can not do better than adopt it without delay," recommended one adviser speaking to the Constituent Assembly in 1789, although delay there was for two years. This advocate also suggested "ameliorating [the jury system] in certain details."[2]

The jury had its detractors as well: "This new institution cannot be in any respect in accord with our Ordinances and our present form of examination. It has appeared to us to be necessary to recast everything so as to form a complete and harmonious system."[3] There was considerable judicial apprehension that jurors would respond "not on facts" but by "misguided conscience . . . permeated by revolutionary passion . . . [and become] the judgment of a collection of ignoramuses [producing] shameless acquittals."[4]

But the proponents were able to overcome these doubts and win out—in September 1791, anyway. The Assembly adopted the first law establishing trial by jury in criminal cases, or the French interpretation of it. Certain "ameliorating details" were applied by a clumsy hand touching up a masterwork. First, the legislature rejected the civil jury entirely; this would keep the criminal jury "always in peril," a fear expressed by Alexis de Tocqueville in his *Democracy in America.* Second, only nine members of the panel were to be drawn from the citizenry; the other three would be professional magistrates, or "assessors," to sit with them in deliberations and vote, in order to dull the excesses of ignoramuses shamelessly eager to bring in acquittals. Clearly this was antithetical to the free juries of England and America. And then, of course, simple majority verdicts were accepted. Thus, whenever the three elitist assessors favored one side, this would require a minority of only four "citizens" to make a "majority."

But that was not the end to the "ameliorations." The basic *venire* from which the nine were drawn was refined: nobody under age thirty or over seventy was taken; only citizens entitled to vote were eligible, and there was an elitist character to voting entitlement. The resulting limited number of eligibles was enrolled in a special register which was sent to the local "attorney-general syndic," who would draw out at random two hundred names to form the general jury list for the succeeding specified period.[5] Thus this official would be able to screen out, or at least reduce, the number of "ignoramuses."

The court was then empowered to give directions "intended to enlighten the jury, to concentrate its attention, and to guide its judgment but . . . not to restrain its freedom. The jury owe to the judge respect and deference."[6] In sum, while the jury was given permission to go out to swim, it was not to go near the water!

Despite these trammels, there apparently turned up within a very short time enough ignoramuses so badly misguided by conscience as to recklessly dip a toe into the water. But in 1793 the Reign of Terror had descended with such overpowering ferocity that it wiped out the jury and many other institutions that had been organized in the hope of bringing liberty to France. The panels were reshaped as commissions which discarded the form "and committed murder by wholesale, refusing even the aid of advocates to the accused."[7]

When the Terror had passed, a new campaign began to reestablish the jury. Arguments against it were the same as anywhere else: judges were "true peers of the accused," and "have what the jurors have not, study, knowledge and experience of affairs."[8] Jurors would tend to be ignorant and inexperienced, guided by fears, hesitations and passions, and a general desire to shun service. The workingman was not sufficiently "enlightened," nor had he time or leisure to serve. The middle classes, regarding service as burdensome, would in effect yield by default and allow the judicial "peers" to take over. In 1808 Napoleon asked seventy-five judges for their opinions regarding reestablishing the jury. Thirty declared against revival, twenty-two favored, and twenty-three refused to express an opinion. Napoleon's response was to swing his influence toward those favoring, and the jury was reinstituted, although burdened with the same liabilities. The government retained control over the formation of the basic panels by restricting the roster of eligible electors to membership in special classes such as military and naval officers, physicians, notaries, lawyers, and others "of respectable status." Jurors were given judicial "instructions," and were discouraged from acting on the law; to the extent there were intrajury discussions, it can be expected that the novice jurors—already a select lot—would be too often influenced and intimidated by the three seasoned "assessors."

Nevertheless, in the pattern of independent jurors everywhere, those who did slip through the refining sieve transgressed the strictures placed on them often enough, as Forsyth tells us, so that it became "notorious that [jurors] do regard and are influenced by, the amount of punishment which the law affixes to a crime . . . and the greater the penalty is, the more difficult it is for them to agree among themselves upon the question against the prisoner. . . ."[9]

"But this is by no means peculiar to France," Forsyth observed. "It is the instinct of human nature . . . the same occurs in England, and must be the case wherever juries exist . . . it teaches the lesson that penal laws must not be too severe, so as to revolt the sense of the people; otherwise they will be rendered nugatory by verdicts of acquittal."[10]

Esmein also gave high marks to the French jury in action in the face of all its handicaps. "The jury, before it had been twenty years in existence, victoriously resisted the opposition of Napoleon's terrible will . . ." and was a "corrective . . . independent of political power."[11] Though the nine jurors were "ignorant, undisciplined, full of prejudices," apparently there were enough times when they (perhaps sometimes with the support of one or two magistrates) were "not dependent upon any authority and the citizen does not feel really safeguarded unless he has perfectly independent judges when his liberty or his life is in the balance."[12]

Thus there was the age-old conflict between the people and government which, then as now, pushed to reduce the panels to subserviency by what Forsyth calls "this all-absorbing spirit of state-meddling."[13] The laws governing the operation of the jury were changed frequently in France during the nineteenth century, but nonunanimity was a constant. For a short period the division was set at nine to three, and at others at eight to four, but most frequently at seven to five. Even today, the "courts of assize are composed of three professional magistrates and nine jurors," and an eight vote majority convicts.[14]

That the so badly contorted French "jury" (if the term is not incorrect) should bring in any verdicts of conscience at all is more to the credit of jury trials than that it is discredit that French "juries" succumbed as often as they did to sanction some terribly tragic results. When Louis-Napoleon was named president in 1848 for a single four-year term, he began a program to ensure his permanency; he executed a *coup d'état* in 1851, and in the following year declared himself Emperor Napoleon III. Among his tactics was control of the press, which brought him into a continuing battle against French newspapers, until he was deposed in 1870. Many editors were charged and would have to be convicted; juries would have to be controlled largely by terror.

In May of 1851, before the *coup,* a young editor, aged twenty-four, was brought up on charges, according to the London *Times,* of having "flung" in his newspaper *L'Événement* an "outrage . . . on the courts, the law officers, and the jury" which had condemned to death a defendant in a murder trial. The *Times* quoted excerpts of his editorial in its issue of June 14, 1851:

> Four days ago, in the public square of a town of France, in presence of the sun and of civilization, the law, that is to say, the divine and holy fire of society, took an unhappy man, who struggled and shouted, seized him by the neck, by the arms, and by the legs, dragged him by the hair, and tore the skin from his body, in order to drag him to the scaffold. What had this man done to society? He killed some one. What has society done to this man? It martyred him.

The editorial condemned capital punishment, accused the government of being "forgetful of the Gospel," and demanded that the attorney general resign his position. The youth with the temerity to write so boldly was Charles Victor Hugo, all the more vulnerable for being the son of Victor Hugo, who was himself out of favor with Louis Napoleon. But exactly what he was accused of doing is not quite clear. The London *Times* limited its description of the charge to an "outrage"; Hugo biographer Joanna Richardson dug no deeper than to say that the son was "showing disrespect to the law."[15] Another Hugo biographer, Matthew Josephson, referring to the June 14 editorial, reports that Charles was "indicted for a strong article attacking the government for the execution of a prisoner, and attacking the institution of capital punishment generally";[16] but where was the crime? Charles Hugo's own biographical sketch in the *Dictionary of Biography, Past and Present* avoids identifying the charge against him, saying only that he was "condemned" for it, without reference to trial by jury.

Indeed, Charles Hugo's "crime" was no more than his having offended Louis Napoleon. Victor Hugo's biographers gloss over the trial even though Hugo himself defended his son. They likewise slough off any reference to a jury. The same London *Times* of June 14, 1851, referred to above, described, on the other hand, "the judge and jury who found him guilty and condemned" him, but did not report the split within the jury, nor how the judge was involved in the verdict. Instead, the London paper inappropriately limited commentary to finding fault with Charles's editorial as "sickly sentimental" to "inspire compassion for the criminal and horror for those who 'martyrized' him"—which may or may not be justified criticism; but again, where was the crime? It is surprising that the *Times,* in the face of its familiarity with the long history of trial by jury in England, offered no commentary on the fact of trial on so flimsy a base, to say nothing of the inequity of nonunanimity. Charles was sentenced to six months' imprisonment and fined five hundred francs.

Victor reassured his son:

> My son, you receive this day a great honor. You are now worthy to combat, to suffer, perhaps, for the great cause of truth. From this day forward you enter the true manly life of our time. . . . Be firm in your convictions, and if you want an incentive to strengthen your faith in progress, your belief in the future, your religion for humanity, your execration for the scaffold, your horror of irrevocable and irresponsible penalties, think that you sit where [other great martyrs] sat.

Forsyth rated this as one example of the jury becoming a "pliant instrument" of "state-meddling" in political prosecutions.[17]

Charles's younger brother, François-Victor, was not deterred from criticizing the government, and was similarly charged in September. His jurors-cum-magistrates also succumbed, or at least seven of them did, the division not reported. François suffered a harsher fate: nine months' imprisonment and a fine of two thousand francs. Victor Hugo was very supportive of both sons, praising them for their resistance and visiting them almost daily until they were released.

Another French newspaper, the *Presse,* commented on the two trials, quoted in the London *Times* on September 18, 1851:

> The *Événement* appeared yesterday before the Court of Assizes of the Seine, presided over by M. Perrot de Chezelles. The *Événement* was suspended. The responsible editor of the journal M. Paul Maurice, was condemned to nine months' imprisonment and 3,000 fine. The author of the article, M. François Victor Hugo, was condemned to 2,000 francs and nine months' imprisonment. M. Victor Hugo has only two sons; . . . they had the same cradle, and will share the same

dungeon. . . . The *Événement* will then have four editors in prison. Where will the government stop in this path?

The *Times* then listed thirteen other newspapers all "condemned," presumably by the French form of juries. "In a short time we shall be obliged to employ as extracts from inviolable writers what we dare not write ourselves. Such is the state in which the liberty of the press stands in France on the 15th of September, 1851." However, the *Presse* did not blame the split-verdict system as being at fault, apparently not seeing that otherwise few if any editors would have been convicted.

Forsyth attributed this "unhappy" state to two causes: "first, that the government has influence in the selection of jurymen; and secondly, that freedom of political discussion is neither properly understood nor sufficiently valued in France."[18] He quoted a French jurist who had criticized the French system as

a magnificent frontispiece before the rubbish of despotism; [a] deceitful monument, whose aspect charms but freezes with terror when we penetrate into it. Under liberal appearances, with the pompous words, jury, public debates, judicial independence, and individual liberty, we are gradually conducted to the abuse of all these things, and to the contempt of all our rights. An iron rod takes the place of the wand of justice.[19]

Forsyth feared, as did de Tocqueville, that the lack of a civil jury would keep the criminal jury "always in peril."[20] The people "have been brought up in habits of servile dependence upon the will of the government," which explains why "French juries actively seconded the government in its attacks upon the liberty of the press, and thus have conspired with it against their own freedom."[21]

But there is another reason for the apparent anomaly. There is no doubt that the jury in any shape, if left to itself, is antagonistic to arbitrary power. Hence, in all continental nations where it has been introduced, the governments have endeavored to retain some influence over its decisions by entrusting the formation of the primary lists of the jurors, out of whom the particular twelve are to be selected, to their own officers . . . [to] paid servants of the government.[22]

When *Événement* was ordered suspended on September 17, there was published the very next day "another journal, precisely similar in appearance and in principles . . . out of the same office under a title which, with the exception of a single letter, was the same—the *Avènement.*" This journal published a letter from Victor Hugo himself, and "the jury brought in a verdict of guilty without extenuating circumstance," against the editor who had accepted full responsibility for publishing it.[23]

The severity of Napoleonic law against the liberty of the press was commented upon by what was then called the New York *Daily Times* in one of its earliest issues, No.153, on March 15, 1852:

> The extreme severity of the law on the Press creates a deeper disaffection than any measure of the present Government, though it is in logical accordance with the rest of its policy. If a legislative body should be composed, as it tells the people it must be, only of the out-and-out supporters of Government; if as its accredited organs also say, parliamentary discussion is bad, and a parliamentary opposition an unmixed evil, extra parliamentary discussion and a free press can be little better. The law, put in its full force, must reduce the political press to the merest echo. . . .

Disregarding so severe a law, another French newspaper dared to write that in spite of the frequency of jury convictions of the press, "if any man were to call for the suppression, or even temporary suspension of that guarantee [trial by jury] those who would cry out loudest against such an attempt would be the very journals which have suffered most."[24]

Forty-seven years later, a different kind of tyranny skewed jury composition. In the trial of Émile Zola, it was the tyranny of a lynch mob whose sheer numbers enabled it to rule not by right but by power to threaten because it was a majority. The madness of this majority-rule democracy would have been successfully deflected had the French not superstitiously dreaded creating "a servile imitation" of the way things were in England and the United States: shunning unanimity in favor of the majority verdict.

Impetus for the charges against Zola was an "Open Letter to the President of the Republic" published in *L'Aurore* on January 13, 1898.

An oversize banner headline shouted: "J'ACCUSE!" In his letter, Zola accused many high French military officers of corruption in the companion courts-martial of army Captain Alfred Dreyfus in 1894 and Major Marie-Charles Esterhazy, the latter just concluded. Dreyfus had been convicted on false evidence and intentional misidentification of handwriting on a traitorous paper called the *bordereau* (memorandum). However his real "crime" was being a Jew in a country almost as anti-Semitic as Nazi Germany a generation later. Dreyfus was stripped of honors and rank and sentenced to years of exile and solitary confinement on tiny Devil's Island. Esterhazy, the true author of the *bordereau,* not being a Jew, was acquitted "on orders" by his corrupt court-martial board only two days before, January 11. The miscarriage was so glaringly obvious to Zola (and all the world) that he threw himself into action immediately.

Ironically, Zola was somewhat anti-Semitic himself, as his novels revealed. Yet he was able to look beyond his own prejudice to appreciate that there was more at stake than the condemnation of an innocent man. The integrity of the French nation rested on this issue, as well as justice and truth, as was evident from worldwide negative reaction to the two trials. If he ignored the larger issues now, Zola would lose respect for himself. But he had to confront a myopic military and government, so insecure in their dictatorial rigidity that they could not survive against criticism or the possibility of having committed even a benign, unintentional error, let alone deliberate malice.

Zola's "Open Letter" exploded upon a public unprepared for it. Neither Zola nor the publishers of *L'Aurore,* Georges Clemenceau and Ernest Vaughan, could have foreseen the sensation it caused. Over 300,000 copies were sold before noon on the day the paper was issued, January 13. Thousands of copies were burned by army sympathizers in a futile effort to suppress it, but the gauntlet had been thrown down to President Félix Faure.

Zola was blunt and direct with his accusations. He not only consciously defied the restrictive press laws of 1881 which would make defaming the government a crime; he brazenly cited them, and dared the generals to prosecute. He began "J'Accuse" by outlining the basis for the Dreyfus "Affair." Then he identified the generals and charged them, in one case, of "having been the diabolical artisans of the judicial error and . . . of grotesque and culpable machinations"; in another, "of mental weakness"; in a third of "stifling" evidence of Dreyfus's innocence, and "of an outrage against humanity"; of "having conducted an inquest which is vile . . . of the most monstrous partiality; of "having composed deceitful and fraudulent reports"; of "an abominable" press campaign to distract attention from the real issues, and:

> Finally, I accuse the first [Dreyfus] Court Martial of having violated the law in convicting a defendant on the basis of a document kept secret, and I accuse the second [Esterhazy] Court Martial of having covered up that illegality on command by committing in turn the juridical crime of knowingly acquitting a guilty man.

He then cited the press law "which punishes offenses of slander. And it is quite willingly that I so expose myself . . . I have but one passion, one for seeing the light, in the name of humanity. . . ."[24]

The first need of the government was to obtain a "co-operative" judge to control the evidence the jury would be allowed to hear. M. Delegorgue was described by one reporter of the Dreyfus Affair as being "well-fed, chubby," and "pleased to be presiding judge of a case of world interest." He knew he would be under army pressure to "admit or suppress those facts which form the judgment of the jury. . . ."[26] What would be suppressed was evidence regarding corruption in the Dreyfus trial; only Esterhazy's evidence would be introduced.[27] This would create a serious handicap for the defense because the Dreyfus evidence was needed to prove corruption in the Esterhazy trial.

One complaint which neither prosecution nor defense could register was violation of the "speedy trial" trial requirement. In less than four weeks, on February 7, the court was ready for trial. The jurors which Delegorgue and his two judicial associates picked out somehow escaped the burden of chaperoning magistrates—all twelve had been drawn from the citizenry. Their names and addresses were published "by *Le Petit Journal* and other scurrilous prints," as reported by Zola biographer Ernest Alfred Vizetelly.[28] Publication would enable an intimidating public to contact and threaten them, as indeed it did. However, neither the London nor New York *Times* carried their names, nor did Zola biographers, although Alan Schrom identified them individually by occupation. Vizetelly writes that "numerous threatening letters were sent to these men, intimating that vengeance would follow if they should dare to acquit 'the Italian.' "[29] (Zola's mother was French, his paternal grandfather Italian.)

The panel was selected without incident on the first day; the homogeneous group (all white men, of course) consisted, according to Schrom, of three small merchants, a roof builder, a copper worker, a clerk, a landlord, a tanner, a seed salesman, a metal worker, a market gardener, and a cloth merchant.[30] Whether by accident or design, the judges managed to keep off the panel men of education, professionals, and intellectuals. Seven were laboring men, or lower-level employees; the four merchants and the "landlord" may have held some property. They cannot be stereotyped, nor can we conclude that the division within the jury would have been different had the panel been more diverse. We can know only that whoever they were at least four if not five had the stamina to withstand the pressure put upon them, and hold for conscience and freedom of the press.

French trials did not conform to American standards. In the United States the prosecution presents its case first, followed by defense cross-examination of witnesses. When the prosecution rests, the defense proceeds. However, the French, shunning slavish imitation, refused to adopt this order. A more grievous fault, virtually heretical by traditional American-English standards, was that the accused was tried under a presumption of guilt, and was thus compelled to "prove" innocence. (Neither the London nor New York *Times* called attention to this pivotal failing.)

Thus the defense carried a much heavier burden than in the United States, and this burden was many times compounded when war minister General Billot, one of the generals accused by Zola, arbitrarily decreed that "Chiefs and subordinates are above such outrages: the opinion of Parliament, the country and the Army has already placed them beyond reach of attack."[31]

The chief prosecutor, Attorney-General Edmond van Cassel, began his opening by warning that discussion of Dreyfus was not relative to Zola. Even the name "Dreyfus" could not be mentioned. He told the jury that they were limited to determining only if Esterhazy had been acquitted "on orders." Delegorgue obediently directed that no Dreyfus evidence could be set before the jury.

For his defense counsel, Zola had wisely selected a brilliant thirty-eight-year-old attorney, Fernand Labori, who responded by telling the jury that he was "not much astonished, Gentlemen, at the difficulties which Monsieur Zola meets in this affair, and I expect that this incident, which is the first, will not be the last." Defiantly he addressed the cases of Dreyfus and Esterhazy as inseparable as they were essentially one and the same. Both officers had been prosecuted for the same crime of treason, and the crucial document at both trials had been the same *bordereau*:

> . . . it would be hardly possible for us to prove the guilt of Major Esterhazy and his acquittal in obedience to orders, if at the same time we did not have the right to prove the innocence of ex-Captain Dreyfus.

From the beginning, Delegorgue showed himself to have been well chosen from the government's view. In effect, he was an active member of the prosecution. Critical to Zola's defense was the production of almost a hundred witnesses, many of them hostile, actually pro-prosecution witnesses whom van Cassel would have subpoenaed under the American system. Labori needed them in effect for cross-examination, and Delegorgue conspired to block their appearance. To start, Billot was relieved from responding to his summons; then former president of the alleged "republic," Casimir-Perier, wrote the court that "I am unable to enlighten justice . . . constitutional responsibilities would impose silence upon me."

The officer accused by Zola of the Esterhazy cover-up, Lieutenant-Colonel du Paty de Clam, declined "the honor" of appearing because "I am bound by professional secrecy," which was the same excuse used by Captain Lebrun Renault. Major Ravary declared: "My presence at the trial would be absolutely useless. I therefore abstain from appearing." Mademoiselle Blanche de Comminges sent a doctor's certificate excusing her. General Mercier, whom Zola had called "an accomplice" suffering from "mental weakness," informed Delegorgue that he had received authorization from General Billot not to appear. And even Major Esterhazy, despite being a central figure, sent an arrogant refusal: "It is plain . . . that in this trial the object of M. Zola is . . . to reverse by revolutionary method the decree of acquittal rendered in my favor on January 11. . . . I consider that I am not obliged to respond to M. Zola's summons."

Labori was infuriated. He shouted at the court: "All these witnesses seem to imagine that they constitute a caste apart, and that it is permissible for them to rise above the law, above justice itself, and personally appoint themselves judges as to whether or not they are useful witnesses in a trial . . . we insist and we protest."

When Mme. Lucie Dreyfus appeared, Delegorgue refused to allow her to speak, and Zola leaped to his feet:

> I demand to be allowed the same rights accorded to thieves and murderers. They can defend themselves, summon and question witnesses, but every day I am insulted in the streets; they break my carriage windows, they drag my name through the mud, and the gutter press treat me like a crook. I have a right to prove my good faith, my integrity and my honor. . . . I appeal to the integrity of the jurors. I make them judges of the situation in which I am placed, and I entrust myself to them.

Labori then tried to reintroduce the Dreyfus case: "Monsieur Zola has made two assertions. He has asserted that the court-martial of 1894 convicted in the person of ex-Captain Dreyfus, an innocent man, by illegal methods."

"He is not prosecuted for that," Delegorgue replied, and ordered Mme. Dreyfus not to testify.

"Will you permit me then, Monsieur le Président, to ask in our common interest, what practical means you see by which we may ascertain the truth?"

The puppet judge retorted: "That does not concern me."

Zola jumped to his feet to complain that the case was confined to just fifteen lines of "J'Accuse." "These things I declare unworthy of justice . . . I do not place myself above the law, but I am above hypocritical methods!"

"Bravo," shouted Labori, clapping his hands.

Later that day defense witness Louis Leblois was just beginning to speak when Delegorgue broke in. Labori protested the interruption as violating courtroom procedure. Delegorgue replied sarcastically: "Permit me, Maître, I suppose that the court is entitled to question the witnesses."

"It is not entitled to interrupt."

"I did not interrupt. I simply asked him for indications on a point."

Labori retorted: "the Code of Criminal Examination authorizes witnesses to give their testimony without interruption and to be questioned after their deposition is finished."

Former President Casimir-Perier was summoned in spite of his earlier refusal to testify. He was sworn, but declared that "duty" prevented him from telling the whole truth. To every question Labori asked, Delegorgue broke in: "The question cannot be asked!"

Labori tried a "critical question": was the former president "aware that at a certain moment a secret document was laid before the court-martial in the Dreyfus case, outside the proceedings of the trial and without the knowledge of the accused?"

"The question cannot be asked," Delegorgue directed.

Zola jumped up again: "Is it understood, then, that no attention is to be paid to the word 'illegality' contained in the complaint? Then why was it included in the first place?"

Delegorgue again was arbitrary: "The court has rendered a decree on that point. There can be no testimony regarding the thing previously judged."

There followed a completely illogical dialogue between Labori and the judicial sycophant in which the latter consistently blocked any response by the witness to Labori's incisive questions: "You cannot ask that question . . . the question will not be put."

Labori "put" it anyway: "As to the Dreyfus case and that of Ester-hazy, they are connected only indirectly with the Zola case."

Delegorgue stonewalled, and coined a classic inanity: "There is no Zola case!"

Before the third day of trial had ended, its tenor had been established. The defense was frustrated for the full fifteen days of the trial's duration so that the jury received only bits and portions of the defense testimony, and the meager amount was squeezed out under difficulty. Not long into the trial Labori appealed directly to the jurors:

> The proof we wish to show you is so striking that our opponents are making efforts to prevent its becoming known. Nevertheless, if it is necessary, I will declare it alone, without witnesses. If I fail, Dreyfus will remain in the gallows, where he was placed by a law expressly made for him.[32]

This address was followed by "violent protests." Indeed, even while the jury was being selected there were demonstrations outside and around the courtroom. Zola was hissed, and his carriage attacked, with shouts of "Conspuez Zola!" ("Spit on Zola!") One man who shouted "Vive Zola" was seized by the crowd and hustled away. Many of these demonstrations were conducted within the presence of the jurors.

Zola also protested:

We know everything concerning the Dreyfus case, but it is impossible to describe the pressure to impose silence upon the men who are able and ready to reveal the truth. Our documentary evidence is not even looked at, and our witnesses have refused to testify or have been ordered to be silent. There is no room for doubt. There is no question nor possibility of a question. The facts are clear and absolutely beyond denial, but the authorities refuse to allow us to produce our evidence and then hold up the feebleness of our cause to the derision of the public.[33]

When another witness was called, Delegorgue admonished him: "I warn you that I cannot let you say a word of the Dreyfus affair."[34]

The witness protested: "It seems to me essential for enlightening the jury to give them cognizance of that correspondence."

"It is not possible," commanded the judge. When Labori asked for "full light" to be thrown on the case, Delegorgue retorted: "The witness must, according to law, depose and not read his evidence."[35]

In contrast to the hostility surrounding him, Zola received support from the intellectual and artistic world. Upon first arriving at court he was presented with more than four hundred telegrams from all over the world. One telegram was signed by more than a thousand legal and literary celebrities; another was from a group of Catholic priests.

Zola asked the judge what was the maximum penalty he would have to suffer if convicted. He was told six months. "If truth could but emerge from this trial, I would willingly take six months more."

But Delegorgue's cooperation with the prosecution made getting at the truth difficult, or perhaps because of it, truth was, from time to time, arrived at through the back door. Labori quizzed several army officers in succession, but the judge repeated his refrain: "The question will not be put." Commandant Fornizetti was directed to make no reference to the Dreyfus case; Major Paty du Clam pleaded "professional secrecy" to avoid interrogation.

To overcome judicial bias, Labori often addressed the jurors directly. After six more witnesses were prevented from answering, the *New York Times* of February 11 reported a reverse effect in the courtroom: the proceedings had become "mirthful," making it "impossible not to be convinced that Dreyfus was convicted on a secret document." (A century and a half earlier Andrew Hamilton had advised the jury in John Peter Zenger's trial that "the suppressing of evidence ought always to be taken for the strongest evidence." If the *Times* reporter could see through the cover in the Zola case, some of the jurors might have been responding in the same way, to help account for the split verdict.)

But the Dreyfus evidence was not all that Delegorgue would exclude. On another day, when handwriting expert Paul Meyer was testifying, and Labori asked that three other handwriting experts who had testified on the *bordereau* in the Esterhazy trial be brought to confront him. The judge forbade it: "They are bound to professional secrecy."

"But, Monsieur le Président, I beg of you," pleaded Labori.

"No, no, they were right."

"I insist."

"No. I have said no."

"But I have to ask a question."

"You shall not ask it."

"Oh, Monsieur le Président, it is an interesting one."

"It is useless to shout so loudly."

"I shout because I need to make myself heard."

"You cannot ask that question. The Court must keep out of the debate anything that would uselessly prolong it. I say that this is useless, and it is my right to say so."

"But you do not even know the question."

Nevertheless, witness Meyer was able to slip into the record that the *bordereau* was in Esterhazy's handwriting, and later Labori managed to get before the jury the testimony of two other handwriting experts that Esterhazy had indeed written the traitorous document, Dreyfus was innocent.

On the tenth day of trial Delegorgue denied permission to Labori to cross-examine one of the generals accused by Zola.

"You do not have the floor. The incident is closed."

"Excuse me, Monsieur le Président."

"You do not have the floor," the judge repeated angrily, and ordered the clerk to "bring in Major Esterhazy."

Labori ignored this: "I have some questions to ask the witness."

"This was an incident outside the trial. You do not have the floor."

"I ask for the floor."

"I do not give it to you."

When Esterhazy did come to the stand, Delegorge again frustrated Labori. The major responded: "I shall not answer these questions," and Delegorgue supported him.

Albert Clemenceau, the brother of Georges, the future president of France, and attorney for *L'Aurore* publisher M. Perrenx, brought to trial with Zola, broke in: "How is it that one cannot speak of justice in a courtroom?" The judge replied irrationally: "There is something above that—the honor and safety of the country."

It was hardly necessary for van Cassel, presumably the chief prosecutor, to participate in the trial at all. Indeed, he was silent throughout most of it, since Delegorgue was performing that function so well for him. But van Cassel did deliver a closing address to the jury, full of anti-Semitic references to Dreyfus as "a Jew who belongs to a rich and powerful family." He blamed Zola for instigating violent street demonstrations that continued throughout the trial, a perverse accusation in that the demonstrations were on the prosecution's side, against Zola.

Van Cassel portrayed the army as "the image of the country," and to attack the generals was an "unpatriotic campaign. No, it is not true that a court-martial has rendered a verdict in obedience to orders. It is not true that seven officers have been found to obey anything other than their own free and honest conscience. You must condemn those who have outraged them, gentlemen of the jury. France awaits your verdict with confidence."

Another burden was placed upon the jurors when the generals warned them that they would all resign if they acquitted Zola. Surely this was jury tampering as it carried a hint to the demonstrators to riot. Zola charged that the threat was a directive to convict.[36] Delegorgue, of course, did nothing.

After fifteen days of trial, this jury of "small shopkeepers and artisans," in the words of Nicholas Halasz,[37] retired. The twelve men had been "attentive, bewildered by the parade of so many generals, celebrities and renowned speakers. They remained awestruck to the end."[38]

Zola and his friends, twelve in all, were apprehensive. If the jury did acquit, they feared that none of them would survive the day. Yet in spite of everything, four, more likely five of the unsophisticated jurors possessed the stamina to hold to conscience and principle, giving credence to the high assessment of the jury by Forsyth and Esmein. They had taken the position of Labori and Andrew Hamilton: excluded evidence is the most critical evidence. Perhaps several of the seven or eight of the other jurors agreed with the principle but were cowed by fear of personal attack.

This was substantiated by the next day's skeptical view of the verdict in the *New York Times.* The reporter wired his editor that the jury had agreed "days ahead on the verdict . . . due to threats." He did not, however, question the legality of nonunanimity. The London *Times* on the same day wrote that on the jury's return "they gave as their verdict that M. Perrenx, as the publisher of the *Aurore,* and M. Zola, as the writer of the article, had been guilty of defamation of the Paris Court-Martial," without reporting the division. (The *New York Times* added a pre-high-tech-era sideline which sounds quaint a century later: "The court was lighted by electricity, which revealed the face of every person.")

For his part, Zola declared that he was "a victim of mob violence, official cowardice and a grand miscarriage of Justice."[39] Yet he took the verdict calmly.

A split decision, of course, would not have held under a true jury system. In the United States the jury would have remained deadlocked unless one side would have been able to swing the other over. If not, and it would have been difficult with so wide a split as this, there would have been no verdict. The trial would have ended with a hung jury, and would have remained that way unless there were a second trial. Since we have no information regarding the characters of the individual jurors, or whether any of them were interviewed or spoke about the trial afterward, we can never know for sure how they were influenced. We know only that "the jury system" cannot be blamed for this obvious gross miscarriage of justice.

Albert Clemenceau did characterize the jury as composed of "twelve trembling citizens" who made "the law bow before the saber."[40] Upon conclusion of the trial he reflected, probably with a touch of ironic relief, upon the earlier concern of Zola's friends: "Had Zola been acquitted, not one of us would have come out alive."[41]

As it was, there was violence enough, so viciously anti-Semitic as to set a precedent for the Nazi Kristallnacht a generation later— crowds racing through the streets jeering at Jews, smashing store windows, invading Jewish-owned shops, and besieging and breaking into synagogues.

Although the verdict had not been unanimous, the foreign press's indictment of it as "French madness" nearly was. Even the Russian press obliquely condemned the tyranny of czar Nicholas II by decrying the French verdict as symbolizing "the decadence of people hypnotized by the terror of truth . . . justice is called the right of the strongest."[42]

The London *Times* editorialized that "Zola's true crime had been in daring to rise to defend truth and civil liberty"; the *Daily Mail* found "France . . . disappearing from the list of civilized nations," and one American newspaper wrote that "The French Republic cannot and should not live if a military caste, Jewish devourers, or a mob of students can put it in a hysterical state impelling it to trample underfoot the freedom of its citizens."[43] Where the legality of the verdict was "suspect," it was not on the basis of nonunanimity, for it had been "duly delivered."[44]

Labori immediately filed an appeal with the High Court of Appeal where a judge of higher integrity, Chambereaud, sat as judge advocate. Joining in the appeal was an aging battler for law and justice who had stood against Louis-Napoleon half a century earlier. Attorney General Manau, now eighty, argued that the defenders of Dreyfus such as Zola were "neither traitors nor sell-outs, but the honor of the country." He was disgusted with the anti-Semitic furor, and read into the record the Biblical precept: "Thou shalt not follow the multitude and do evil and when thou shalt speak at a trial, thou shalt not proceed so as to pervert the law." The appellate judges spent two days thinking things over, and on April 2 a divided court gave Zola a fifty-eighth birthday present by overturning the conviction.[45]

This decision brought the High Court judges under attack as being "in the service of Jewry" and one of their number, because his name, Loew, sounded Jewish although he was an "Alsatian Protestant," was denounced as a "German Jew." The venerable Manau was declared falsely to be an undercover German whose speech had been "shameful . . . obscene." The military judges of the Court-Martial met on April 8 to consider if they should proceed with a second trial. By a vote of five to two they decided to refile, but to restrict the charges to a single sentence of the Zola letter: "A Court-Martial has just dared to acquit Esterhazy on command, a supreme offense to all truth and all justice. . . ." They also decided to move the trial from Paris to Versailles because the army was more in evidence there and could better dominate the jury. The hearing was set for May 23 so as not to detract from a national election on the 22nd.[46]

On that day Fernand Labori objected to the move on the ground that the Versailles Court of Assizes was outside the area of jurisdiction. He was turned down, but the court postponed the second trial to July 18. Zola now faced a dilemma. If the Assize court would not allow him to present his evidence based on the whole of "J'Accuse," it would be almost impossible to prove the truth of his accusations before what was expected to be another panel of "twelve trembling citizens." And even if they did win the verdict, they feared that would set off new and worse rioting.

Labori advised Zola that in the event of a further rebuff on July 18, he should "default." When on that date this did happen, Zola got up from the defendant's bench and walked slowly through the crowd and out of the courthouse. As he passed, he had to endure vile shouts and slanders about his loyalty to France, based on his father being part Italian and part Greek.

In a kind of remake of *A Tale of Two Cities,* Zola fled to London without delaying even to pick up a change of clothes. He lived in exile in England for eleven months under an alias, but was victorious in the end. On June 4, 1899, he received word that he had stirred up enough turmoil to win a "revision" of the Dreyfus trial, which later ended in overturning that conviction and restoring Dreyfus's rank and honors.

There was no need now for Zola to undergo a second trial or a second jury, for he had succeeded in his objective of exposing the truth without serving any jail time.

The philosopher and novelist André Gide spent twelve days as a trial juror serving on several short cases in Paris in May and June 1912. He recorded his experiences the following year in a small book titled *Recollections of the Assize Court.*[47] "What struck me most during these sittings," Gide wrote in his introduction, "was the conscientiousness with which every one, Judges, Counsel and Jurymen, carried out their tasks."[48]

Later, Gide revised some of his recollections by showing suspicion of the motives of judges who conducted their trials to influence the jurors: "The manner in which the Judge puts his questions, in which he aids and favours a certain witness, be it unwittingly, in which conversely he embarrasses and hurries another, soon informs the Jury of his personal opinion. How difficult it is for the Jurors not to be influenced by the Judge's opinion . . . a clever Judge can do what he likes with the Jury."[49]

Gide qualified this assertion by finding that jurors did act independently, and were not always malleable. He relates one example of a jury acquitting "not because there was any doubt of [the defendant's] guilt, but because the Jury considered that there was no call for a sentence in this trifling matter . . . several of them were indignant that the time of the Court should be taken up with such bagatelles, which, they said, happened daily everywhere." Acquittal was by a majority.[50] He related other instances of jury resistance to judicial domination:

> It is not necessary to be highly educated in order to be a good Juryman, and I know certain "peasants" whose judgment was more sane than that of many intellectuals. Nevertheless, I am surprised that people who are entirely unaccustomed to mental work are capable of concentrating their attention for the length of time necessary here, often for hours on end.[51]

Still today the French government continues to fear juries by straitjacketing them and limiting the areas of jurisdiction. Not only is there no civil jury, but by a law passed as late as July 21, 1982, the right to jury trial is withdrawn in many criminal cases, such as those involving the security of the state, terrorism, treason, spying, and "other infringements of national security."[52]

Which leaves what? The Machiavellian form without real substance.

NOTES

1. Andrew West et al., *The French Legal System* (London: Format Publishing, 1992), pp. 5–10.
2. A. Esmein, *History of Continental Criminal Procedure* (London: John Murray, Publishers, 1914), p. 408.
3. Ibid., p. 411.
4. Ibid., p. 466.
5. Ibid., pp. 414–15.
6. Ibid., p. 416.
7. William Forsyth, *History of Trial by Jury* (New York: Lenox Hill Publishers, 1878), p. 296.
8. Esmein, *History of Continental Criminal Procedure*, p. 466.
9. Forsyth, *History of Trial by Jury*, p. 305.
10. Ibid., pp. 305–306.

11. Esmein, *History of Continental Criminal Procedure*, p. 563.

12. Ibid., pp. 563–64.

13. Forsyth, *History of Trial by Jury,* p. 307.

14. René David, *French Law* (Baton Rouge: Louisiana State University Press, 1972), pp. 39–46, and *The French Code of Criminal Procedure*, Gerald L. Kock, trans. (London: Sweet & Maxwell, Ltd., 1964), pp. 8–11.

15. Joanna Richardson, *Victor Hugo* (New York: St. Martin's Press, 1976), p. 112.

16. Matthew Josephson, *Victor Hugo* (New York: Doubleday Doran and Co., 1942), p. 320.

17. Forsyth, *History of Trial by Jury,* p. 307.

18. Ibid., p. 309.

19. Ibid., pp. 309–10.

20. Ibid., p. 354.

21. Ibid., p. 360.

22. Ibid., p. 361.

23. Reported in the London *Times,* September 27, 1851.

24. London *Times,* September 23, 1851, quoting the *Journal des Débats,* one of the censored newspapers.

25. From "J'Accuse," as quoted in Jean-Denis Bredin, *The Affair: The Case of Alfred Dreyfus* (New York: George Braziller, Publisher, 1986), pp. 248–49.

26. Nicholas Halasz, *Captain Dreyfus* (New York: Simon and Schuster, 1955), p. 138.

27. F. W. J. Hemmings, *The Life and Times of Émile Zola* (New York: Charles Scribner's Sons, 1977), p. 164.

28. Ernest Vizetelly, *Émile Zola: Novelist and Reformer* (1904), p. 450.

29. Ibid.

30. Alan Schrom, *A Biography of Émile Zola* (New York: Henry Holt and Company, Publishers, 1987), p. 177.

31. Ibid.

32. Quoted in the *New York Times,* February 8, 1898.

33. Ibid.

34. London *Times,* February 9, 1898.

35. Ibid.

36. Halasz, *Captain Dreyfus,* p. 154.

37. Ibid., p. 139.

38. Ibid.

39. *New York Times,* February 24, 1898.

40. Bredin, *The Affair,* p. 268.

41. Ibid., p. 270.

42. Ibid., p. 272.

43. Ibid.

44. Ibid., p. 279.

45. Ibid., pp. 300–301.

46. Ibid.

47. André Gide, *Recollections on the Assize Court,* English-language ed. (London: Hutchinson and Co., 1913).

48. Ibid., p. 7.

49. Ibid., p. 120.

50. Ibid., pp. 8–9.

51. Ibid., p. 123.

52. John Bell, *French Constitutional Law* (Oxford: Clarendon Press, 1991), pp. 316–17.

Afterword

"THEY'RE COMING TO GET YOU!"

*H*aving read the various accounts of juries in this book, you can be reassured in knowing that, although they are true, fortunately for you, they all happened to someone else. The excitement you may have experienced, the tortures you had to suffer, were vicarious. You have always been able to return safely to your own bed and the comfort of your daily routine.

Except for one gnawing thought: jury duty is something that can happen to anybody, even—a terrifying prospect—to you. If it should, there could be another story, one you would write yourself. Or should I say, *when* it does, as it will (or perhaps already has). How do they find you? What can you expect? Why pick you when there are so many other people? You can't condemn anybody to death!

Among the reasons for the success of the jury is that it is Abraham Lincoln's "government of, by and for the people" in action. (We should put less stress on getting out the vote and more on getting out the jury, because it is the truer voice of the people, exerting a surer and faster impact on government and public policy.) While there are certainly excusable situations that prevent many people from serving on juries, you can, by this time, appreciate the need for universality. And the duty to serve on a jury can't be universal without you. (You won't admit it, but down deep you're eager to serve: it makes you feel important and helps you escape the routine in your life that has grown a little humdrum by now.)

First, how do they get your name? Procedures vary among jurisdictions, but the most widely used sources are voters' registration lists.
They might, for example, take a random draw of every fifty-seventh
name to form the basic jury *venire*. However, so many otherwise eligible citizens are not on the voters' lists (often deliberately to avoid
being called), that in recent years many jurisdictions have added the
names of those who hold automobile operators' permits and who are
at least of voting age. Some jurisdictions go by property ownership;
some accept volunteers. Some take names from telephone books. Any
single list tends to discriminate because it excludes those not on the
list, and many lists (property owners, license holders, etc.) are skewed
toward wealth.

If we can escape discrimination only by universality, we confront
a troublesome paradox. If we are to be "secure [in] the blessings of liberty to ourselves and our posterity" (we being the "posterity" our
Founders had in mind when they wrote the Preamble to the Constitution), the government will retain minimal information about us, and
keep very few lists. The more lists the more easily government can
keep close watch over us, and the easier it is to become dominant over
us. It must be the other way around—an open government without secrets and we, the governed, keeping close watch over those who
govern us.

The paradox arises because our chief defense against an all-pow-
erful government is trial by jury. If we are to form juries, somebody,
if not the government, has to have access to the sources for jurors and
the authority to issue calls from those sources. Therefore, there is a
need for some kind of list, however odious. If there were no lists, we
could not summon jurors; without juries the government would not be
restrained from, among other offenses, compiling endless lists exposing all manner of private information. We therefore find ourselves
as a civil society in a Gordian knot that cannot be resolved by an impatient Alexandrian blow!

Would we escape both knot and paradox if we used volunteer
juries? On the surface this might seem to be an answer, but in practice
it is shown to be just the opposite. Volunteer juries do not represent the
community in cross-section, which is the essential character of a true
jury. Most people won't volunteer (would you?) and those who do represent narrow interests; moreover, they would tend to become professionals, serving repeatedly, which immediately makes it *not* a jury.

Such panels favor government. Where volunteer or selective panel systems have been tried—one form being the elitist "blue ribbon jury"—the results are disasters. However, even these panels manage to return verdicts of conscience often enough to frustrate their sponsoring tyrannies. Examples are a series of "seditious libel" trials in eighteenth- and nineteenth-century England—practically all of them related to freedom of speech and of the press—where select "special juries," chosen by the courts on the basis of presumed pro-conviction biases, nonetheless returned conscience acquittals more than half the time; and slavery trials in the pre-Civil War American South where whites returned a surprisingly greater number of verdicts sympathetic to blacks than we might suppose.

But the paradox extends further. While procedures vary among federal, state, and municipal districts, your initial contact may be by letter, but not necessarily a "summons." More than likely its tone will be a tad condescending. There may be a questionnaire with it, together with a reference to a legal authority "requiring" you to answer the questions, and, more significantly, to be summoned. The notification may assume authority by declaring: "You have been selected to serve as a juror . . ." or "By order of the presiding judge, you are directed to appear . . ." or "You are summoned" followed by a threat of punishment if you do not show up. The letter may list qualifications for jury service, as well as acceptable grounds for excusal.

The contradiction we meet here is that government, as servant, cannot compel the sovereign citizen to do anything he or she does not wish to do, as long as that citizen does not intrude upon the rights of another person. Thomas Jefferson observed: "A wise and frugal government, which shall restrain men from injuring one another, shall leave them otherwise free to regulate their own pursuits." To compel attendance is a matter of "involuntary servitude," an unequivocal prohibition of the Thirteenth Amendment. But "voluntary jury servitude" does not work. It might be rationalized that if you don't respond, you are causing injury to another person by denying him his "inviolate" right to a jury trial, even threatening the entire institution. Therefore we may consider this to be the exception to Jefferson's frugal government standard.

Nonetheless, by justifying this exception on the ground that so lofty an end excuses a lesser means, we could be opening the way to unlimited "color of law" exceptions which put on the sheepskin of lawfulness to conceal the illegal wolf. And the paradox remains that the jury—the *randomly selected, nonvolunteer jury*—is the great bulwark against runaway government.

Thus there must be a balance. An officer of the trial court could continue to issue jury *calls* (as opposed to "summonses") without assuming a power that does not constitutionally belong to him. The citizen, on the other hand, must understand his moral duty to respond as an obligation of citizenship greater than voting. He must not be deceived as to the underlying voluntary nature of the call, but impressed that the survival of our American republic depends upon his serving. Which now implies that a certain element of compulsion is needed to achieve the essential cross-sectional character. I am troubled to know how to prescribe this balance. Upon responding, however, the "compelled/volunteer" places himself under jurisdiction of the court to the extent of fulfilling what is in effect a contractual obligation.

The problem involves a "conflict of rights" and the "weighing of competing interests," wherein the lesser right or interest yields to the stronger. A California Court of Appeals considered such an issue in an October 1996 case relating to the jury *voir dire* (*People* v. *Duran*, 96 *Daily Journal* DAR 12785):

> The jury is a cornerstone of our nation's judicial system. The inviolate right to trial by jury is guaranteed by the Constitution. As a matter of public policy, the integrity of our jury system must be carefully safeguarded. The continuing viability and vitality of the jury process depends upon public support and participation. . . .

A serious threat to encouraging "public support and participation" comes from:

> The increasing scrutiny being placed on prospective jurors [making] it more difficult to obtain willing participants in this vital civic duty. . . . Few would quarrel with the proposition that the willingness of people to serve on a jury would be chilled by the knowledge [of becoming subjects of scrutiny].
>
> Our jury system also depends upon adherence to the public policy which discourages harassment of jurors. . . .

But the unanimous decision of the judicial trio in *People* v. *Duran* covers up the deliberate and malignant feature of harassment, and evades the question of the most discouraging forms of harassment: the humiliating questionnaire and *voir dire*.

The same three judges, however, chose to "recognize the importance of *voir dire* in obtaining impartiality," and would not suggest eliminating all scrutiny, only what they termed "increasing scrutiny," without providing any measure to help us understand the difference between acceptable scrutiny and that which "increases." *Voir dire*-style scrutiny is acceptable if it doesn't "increase"—as long as we know where to start. But this premise is wrong. The function of scrutiny—indeed its only function—is to destroy impartiality and randomness. And if scrutiny destroys impartiality, this removes the rationale for *voir dire* entirely and leaves no space for any scrutiny.

Taking California jury law as generally representative, we find legal support for hypocrisy. Section 191 of the Code of Civil Procedure starts out with a high-minded exposition: "The Legislature recognizes that trial by jury is a cherished constitutional right [*sic*], and that jury service is an obligation of citizenship. It is the policy of the State of California that all persons selected for jury service shall be selected at random . . . from a representative cross-section of the population of the area" and that they have an obligation to serve.

However, this is debased in practice. California citizens are told they are "required" to answer the questions "in accordance with Section 196" of the Code. This section would empower "the jury commissioner or the court [to] inquire as to the qualifications of persons on the master list" and "may require any person to answer, tender oath, orally or in written form all questions as may be addressed" to him or her. Anyone who fails to respond "may be summoned to appear. . . ."

Section 205 additionally would empower the jury commissioner to "require a person to complete a questionnaire" and the court could later "require" the juror to respond to more questions. The letter and laws ignore the disturbing implication that answering means becoming a witness against oneself. This violates the Fifth Amendment's protection against involuntary disclosures. How, then, can 205 exert any authority? The apology is that you are not "incriminating" yourself by answering, which is perplexing because the word "incriminating" was not written into the Constitution. "Incriminating" appears nowhere, except in judicial allocution. The broader term "witness against oneself" means that you cannot be "required" to give any information you do not choose to give. Its incriminating or harmless nature has nothing to do with it.

The questionnaires delve into personal lives and take on "under color of law" forms of being legal "demands," which, of course, they cannot be. You fulfill your obligation as an American citizen by serving, period. Long before the Constitution was even a dream, monarchs knew they had to defer to that natural proposition. The courts are limited to knowledge of your name and the judicial district where you reside but not necessarily your home address, that you are at least eighteen years old, that you understand English, that you are physically and mentally able to withstand the rigors of jury duty, and that you are not an active partisan in the trial at hand. Nothing else. Absolutely *nothing else!* But you are free to express anything else you wish voluntarily.

The necessity of honoring the "inviolate" jury as a "cornerstone of our nation's judicial system" outweighs what probably is "reluctant" rather than "involuntary" servitude under "conflict of rights." But there is no rights conflict in refusing to submit to *voir dire* and scrutiny by questionnaire.

Despite protestations to the contrary, the courts lie when they tell us they seek "fair and impartial jurors." No euphemism is warranted to soften that accusation. The real function is to stack the jury with individuals who are biased to the respective side, hoping that the outcome can be foretold. The primary desire of each side is to "win," and so the goal is the properly biased jury. There is no interest in fairness or impartiality. The Constitution says nothing about "fair and impartial" jurors anyway. The phrase in the Sixth Amendment is "impartial *jury*" and there is a difference. The jury approaches impartiality when it is composed of a mixture of varying interests and partialities which tend to moderate each other during free, uninhibited discussion in the jury room; diversity is best attained through unmolested random selection of the original panel.

After the jury for O. J.'s civil trial had been picked, and before the actual hearing began, experienced trial observers were content to accept, as having met constitutional standards for "impartiality," a panel skewed to favor the plaintiffs. It is clear that a skewed panel is by definition not impartial, and therefore not only does not meet constitutional standards, but does not meet them by conscious and deliberate intent. That the trial did end with a plaintiffs' verdict does not prove that the panel was or was not skewed, although the plaintiffs' jury pickers would like to boast that, by having successfully skewed it, they offended the Constitution. The O. J. example is more dramatic but no different than most trials committing similar criminal violations less publicly to demonstrate the hypocrisy of trial procedure.

There is one school of legal thinking that teaches that the most important part of a trial is jury selection, because the outcome is determined by the bias built in. If this is true, it is a greater hypocrisy to continue with the actual trial. As soon as the jury is sworn, the court should announce the verdict which everybody knows, and dispense with the spectacle. Of course this isn't true, but it points out that the objective of sometimes spending weeks offending hundreds of American citizens is to snub constitutional caveats.

"Color of law" questionnaires have been used with impunity for so long that they are now thought to be unchallengeable. The questions in both the criminal and civil trials of Simpson, while more extensive than most, were not atypical. They demanded information about private family life, occupation, education; newspapers and magazines subscribed to, television and radio programs heard; personal friends and their occupations; and memberships in clubs and associations, including political and religious affiliations. Other intrusions covered hobbies, ways of spending leisure time, personal opinions; suits for nonpayment of bills, drinking habits, and, for women, whether they had ever had abortions or used "intra-uterine devices." And judges wonder why "the willingness of people to serve" is "chilled"!

In trials where questionnaires are used, the juror candidates, after returning them, will wait for weeks, perhaps months, for a second letter which may be a "summons" to appear at court at a specified day and time. They may or may not remind a juror that he did not answer all the questions. The juror might call attention to the issue by challenging the authority of the summons, but since trial by jury is so entrenched as a "cornerstone" of constitutional republicanism, essential to freedom—the country *needs* him—it might be wiser to accept one's fate and fight on a more certain front.

Section 214 of the California code dictates that when a jury is required, "the Court may make an order directing a trial jury to be drawn . . . ," and Section 225 empowers the sheriff or marshal "to summon the persons named therein to attend the court . . ." and that "any trial juror who fails to appear" shall be resummoned, and if he still fails shall be subject to "attachment or fine" (Sec. 238). If there is a scheduling problem, the juror can ask for a postponement which will likely be granted with a new summons date.

At the courthouse you will be treated with minimal courtesy more or less "bestowed." (There are exceptions, as there are to all generalizations.) You will be directed to a rapidly filling "Juror Assembly Room" with few conveniences: a lounge area, perhaps with magazines and newspapers strewn about; a TV area; and food and beverage vending machines, which you'll have to put money into. This is an insult. To encourage citizen participation, the courts should at least provide a snack bar, free telephone privileges, transportation, and parking. Some jurisdictions may do so, but in many the accommodations are harsher.

At some point a court official will call for your attention and read a short lecture about "civic duty." You may also be given a pamphlet. What the clerk says and what's in the court-approved pamphlet are probably, in part, misleading. The procedure is under the direction of judges who will want to impose their authority over you; they will describe your "duties" so as to keep you submissive. They will tell you that the jury is restricted to determining what the facts are, and that you are to take the law as the judge "instructs" you. By now you know that the ultimate and highest power of the jury is to evaluate the law. They will prepare you to accept the *voir dire* with docile resignation.

When they call you to be examined, you will face a dilemma. Do you answer questions that make you a witness against yourself, or do you refuse to answer and risk being cited for contempt of court and possibly jail for a few hours? Not much of a choice! A third alternative, which is probably no more than a stall, might be to toss a few questions back. Very often you will be asked first "Are you married?" or "Who are the members of your immediate household?" to which you can reply with a deferential question: "Just before I answer that question, sir (or ma'am), may I ask you something?"

"Surely. How may I help?"

"If I tell you who lives with me, is this not invading the sanctity of my home? Isn't there something in the Constitution about that?"

You have given the judge a severe jolt. He'll have to answer, and how he does depends on how seriously he is discomposed. Perhaps: "Yes, that is true, but we're not invading your home here. We're trying to get a fair jury to try this case, and in order to do that we must know if you would be a good juror for this type of case. Not every juror is a good juror for every trial."

"Well, I can understand you want a fair jury, but how does who I live with affect my ability to be fair? Are you saying that only a married person can be fair, or unmarried, or if I live with my brother, or what? I do not understand."

"No, we're not saying that. It's your total personality and experiences."

"I suppose that's true, but at the same time isn't what happens inside my home highly personal? Isn't it still a sanctity-of-the-home thing? and possibly embarrassing to some people if not to me?"

"We're not trying to embarrass you, but the defendant here is on trial for his life, and it is all important that we have jurors who can look at the issue impartially, and that's why we ask these questions."

"Yes, but at the same time the court reporters there are taking down every word for the public record, which means that everything I say can be broadcast all over the world."

"If there is something embarrassing we can go into chambers and discuss it there."

"I'm not saying there's anything embarrassing—except it would seem to me to be embarrassing enough to say there was something embarrassing. And doesn't it go in the public record anyway?"

You may not get this far, but however far you do get you will have put the judge on the spot by challenging his actions. Obviously, he won't like this. The judge wants to control the courtroom completely, and won't appreciate having his authority questioned. Everyone else genuflects before him; he expects you to do the same. He may add, as some judges do, that there is no constitutional issue covering you as a prospective juror. He may insist upon your answering him. If you continue to resist, you may risk contempt. The charge is false since it cannot be contempt to invoke our basic law. Even if wrongly invoked, part of freedom is a right to be honestly wrong. Nonetheless, judges do not accept such challenges with grace, as San Francisco judge Ollie Marie-Victoire did not when I questioned her. "You invoke your constitutional rights [*sic*] and march straight to the county jail." (She should have known there is no such thing as a "constitutional right." All rights are *inherent* and with us from birth. The Constitution merely recognizes rights, enumerating just a few of them, but protects all.)

"But how can the Constitution not cover me? Are there times in this country when the Constitution doesn't work? I'm only trying to get myself straightened out."

"I've already told you. We need to get a fair jury, and that's what we're trying to do. I'm going to direct you to answer the question, and if you refuse I will cite you for contempt. Once again: Who are the members of your immediate household?"

The few times when jurors have continued to resist have resulted in contempt charges. In my own case, Marie-Victoire threatened contempt, ordered me off the jury, and had my name stricken from the jury rolls, which, by the way, is illegal. When I challenged this, I was nominally reinstated, but I will never know if my name came up again. Many years later I was once more summoned, but never got further than the general assembly room.

In Texas, juror candidate Dianna Brandborg refused to answer several *voir dire* questions she regarded as too personal; the judge charged her arbitrarily with contempt and, without giving her an opportunity to be heard or defend herself (a sacred right), jailed her for three days and fined her two hundred dollars. Attorney Rick Hagen defended her without charge and won a landmark decision supporting her claim to privacy (*Brandborg* v. *Lucas,* 4:94CV228, E. D. Texas).

Another attempt to inject integrity into the trial would be to question the honesty of jury selection. When the judge explains that the object is to seek a fair jury, if you are hardy enough you might ask: "Are you really? Doesn't each side want to win the case, and if so, is each really not looking for jurors biased in its favor and not being fair at all?"

This will be another jolt to the court because, of course, it is true. If you press any further you will not only risk contempt, but the judge may declare a mistrial, alleging that you have "tainted" the other jurors. That shouldn't concern you. You may notice solemn-faced individuals, at the elbows of opposing counsel, whispering in their ears. These may be "jury consultants" who are charging exorbitant rates precisely to aid the litigants (with the judge's acceptance) to find a receptive jury, thus negating the judge's protestations about seeking fairness. Truth will be on your side but custom and might are on theirs, and too often might wins the first round. Truth suffers, but sooner or (more often) later, it conquers. To conquer eventually, truth needs its defenders, its martyrs. Revelations like these are intended to speed a conquering truth.

Unless you have drawn that rare commodity, a judge actually dedicated to keeping faith with his oath to uphold the Constitution, you will now face contempt. Only if there are enough jurors, each one as knowledgeable as you, will there be any hope of winning. If you happen to be on a big-profile case covered by the world's news media, being written up may console you in your jail cell—together with knowing you have struck a blow in defense of freedom and the American republic and made history. What price a clear conscience? Freedom is not free! It has to be fought for over and over again.

Taking a different stand, if you want to be on the jury, the blander, the briefer your responses, the more affably given without any semblance of concealment, the more you may help your chances, whereas defiance will alienate. But you cannot be sure and they may want to toss you anyway. At which point, if you're bold enough and have nothing (except contempt) to risk, you might challenge the judge as you had not before, by referring to the declared ideal of "random selection." Since by random selection you got there in the first place, ask the judge if he is attempting to shape the jury by making a nonrandom, arbitrary rejection of you.

I'm sure you can tell yourself how the judge is likely to react. It was when I challenged Marie-Victoire that she ordered six bailiffs to escort me out.

If you do survive this ordeal and get on the jury anyway, you won't be allowed to hear all the evidence. From time to time one side or the other or the judge will cry out: "I object." To withhold evidence from the jury is suspect, as I pointed out previously. If the goal is truth, the only way to uncover it is to examine every factor which leads to it. Otherwise, no matter how convincing all the rest, there will be doubt because you cannot tell how influential the missing evidence would be. What is so important that one side wants you to know it and the other side is so desperate to keep it from you? Recall Andrew Hamilton's advice in John Peter Zenger's freedom of the press trial in 1735: "I will beg leave to lay it down as a standing rule in such cases, *that the suppressing of evidence ought always to be taken for the strongest evidence.*" When the judge keeps evidence from the jury, he has taken control of you and the trial.

Present-day evidence that Hamilton was correct is an estimate by Reverend Jim McCloskey of Centurion Ministries in Princeton, New Jersey, that "there are about as many innocent persons in the nation's jails as there are pigeons in the park," many having been convicted by juries. He attributes the miscarriages to the conscious suppression of the "strongest evidence," to tainted testimony, to unreliable witnesses, to misidentifications of defendants offered by prosecutors deliberately intending to mislead the jurors. One of the convicted innocents is former Black Panther Elmer "Geronimo" Pratt, jailed from 1970 to 1997 on a murder charge because jurors never heard vital evidence in his behalf. In 1996, several jurors, learning of the deceptions, signed affidavits testifying that at the 1972 trial, "We we were victims. We were pawns of the government. We were set up."[1]

Another example featured four Virginia jurors who, eleven years after convicting Joseph Payne of murder in 1985, pleaded with Governor George Allen to save Payne from death by lethal injection because they, too, felt they had been deceived. *U.S. News and World Report* reported in its July 8, 1996, issue that fifty-nine death row inmates had been rescued in the preceding twenty years when legal aid centers in twenty states exposed false convictions by deceived juries. How many other convicted persons have not had access to such assistance?

In Pratt's case, an indifferent court system delayed correcting the error for more than a year, but with the dedicated assistance of Reverend McCloskey and Centurion, a court is expected to review the case and possibly will have released him by mid-1997, just past press time for this book, but twenty-seven years late for Pratt! Centurion devotes its entire limited resources to rescuing innocents, and to date has saved seventeen persons, and as of this writing is working on twenty more cases.

Dr. Sam Sheppard of Cleveland was convicted in 1954 by a jury from which exculpatory evidence was withheld. He was acquitted in 1966 by a second jury which was "allowed" to hear the evidence.

Once impanelled, the jury will also be admonished about the fact-law issue, the judge "protesting too much" and too often that you must take the law as he *dictates* it. He will ignore the fact that what has made the juries I have written about great is that they rejected such dictation from the bench, and followed conscience by casting out what they considered to be unjust law, compared with juries who accepted the judge's reading and caused catastrophe. Every judge knows the jury is the last authority in determining the proper law. This was dramatically (and hypocritically) admitted by a California Court of Appeals in April 1997.

When the jurors in a trial asked the judge if the defendant, charged with receiving stolen property was subjected to the particularly harsh "three strikes sentencing scheme," the judge refused to tell them that it was a "three strikes" case, fearing that if the jurors knew, it would "encourage them to exercise their power of 'jury nullification.' " Early in the trial of *The People* v. *Charles W. Nichols* (97 *Daily Journal* DAR 4539) the judge cautioned the defense not to tell the jurors the punishment was twenty-five years' imprisonment. Later the jurors sent a note to the judge: "Is the defendant part of the three strikes and you're out?" The judge dodged: "You have given us a note. Sometimes we can answer them and sometimes it's not the appropriate thing to do. If you don't get an answer, you're not supposed to speculate what the answer might have been or make guesses. I do want to remind you again that in your deliberation, you're not to discuss or consider the subject of penalty or punishment. That subject must not, in any way, affect your verdict. You do have to live with the information that we give you folks here in this room."

The problem troubling the black-robed brotherhood is that when jurors know they have a three strikes case, they often acquit a guilty defendant because a quarter century's incarceration is too severe. Judges protect themselves by not giving jurors this information. The appellate court approved the trial judge's decision because the jurors' question was "an implicit request for guidance regarding the jury's power to ignore the evidence . . . because it was important to the jury's decision as to whether it should exercise its power of jury nullification. Although the jury has 'undisputed power' to ignore the evidence and the law and to acquit if that is what it chooses to do, the courts have not required trial judges to instruct on this power" (p. 4543). The appellate judges reviewed a bit of nullification history showing that the existence of this power is unquestioned, but jurors are not to be told of it "as a matter of course: What makes for health as an occasional medicine would be disastrous as a daily diet. The fact that there is widespread existence of the jury's prerogative, and approval of its existence as a 'necessary counter to case-hardened judges and arbitrary prosecutors' does not establish as imperative that the jury must be informed of that power. Instructing on power of jury nullification 'may achieve pragmatic justice in isolated instances, but we suggest the more likely result is anarchy' " (p. 4543, quoting from *U.S.* v. *Dougherty,* 473 F2d 1113,1136; and *People* v. *Dillon,* 34 Cal 3d 487–88).

These judges brazenly continued their amazing confession: "The California cases, while recognizing the jury's 'undisputed power' to acquit regardless of the evidence of guilt, reject suggestions that the jury be informed of that power, much less invited to use it," quoting from *People* v. *Honeycutt* (20 Cal 3d 150, 157). The court found further support for endorsing official deception by citing the 1983 *Dillon* decision of the California State Supreme Court. Whereas Justice Otto Kaus wrote a minority opinion that trial judges must tell the jurors the truth when they ask about nullification, every one of his six colleagues on that court "expressly rejected it" (p. 4543).

"Thus, in California, trial courts are not required to instruct on the power of jury nullification even if the jury asks whether it has that power. In sum, the trial court did not err when it refused to inform the jury this was a three strikes case or that the jury had the power to 'nullify' the verdict."

For contrast, here are some declarations from the past:

"It was impossible [that] any matter of law could come in question till the matter of fact were settled and stated and agreed by the jury, and of such matter of fact they were the only competent judges" (Lord Chief Justice Mathew Hale, 2 Hale P C 312, 1665).

"You [i.e., the jurors] have the right to take upon yourselves to judge both law as well as fact in a controversy" (from our first Chief Justice, John Jay, in *Georgia* v. *Brailsford,* 3 Dallas 1, 1794).

In 1771 a young John Adams wrote: "It is not only [a juror's] right, but his duty . . . to find the verdict according to his own best understanding, judgment, and conscience, though in direct opposition to the direction of the court."[2]

"It is the settled law that the jurors are judges of the law and the facts" (*Anderson* v. *State,* 42 Ga 9, 1871).

"The jury has the power to bring in a verdict in the teeth of both law and facts . . . the jury were allowed the technical right, if it can be called so, to decide against the laws and the facts" (*Horning* v. *District of Columbia,* 254 US 135, 1920).

And more recently, the California Court of Appeals notwithstanding:

The jury has an "unreviewable and irreversible power . . . to acquit in disregard of the instruction on the law given by the trial judge. The pages of history shine upon instances of the jury's exercise of its prerogative to disregard instructions of the judge . . . ," or so ruled the District of Columbia Circuit Court in *U.S.* v. *Dougherty* in 1972 (473 F 2d 1113, 1139, 1972).

The jury has "the undisputed power to acquit, even if its verdict is contrary to the law as given by the judge and contrary to the evidence" (*U.S.* v. *Moylan*, 417 F2d 1002, 1969).

Once again we may refer to Lord Chief Justice Vaughn's support of the nullification verdict given by the Bushell jury when acquitting William Penn, cited at length in the first chapter of this book.

In sum, being a good juror means to be guided by the honesty of your conscience as your very best "inner policeman." It means also that the courts must operate in good conscience. To acknowledge the necessity of compelling attendance by nonvolunteer jurors does not justify abuse and mistreatment. And maybe if jurors were paid the nominal minimum wage from the time they arrive at assembly rooms until they are dismissed, whether they actually serve or not, judges would then be more reluctant to summon overly large numbers of people.

Jurors, who are the real sovereigns in the courtroom, should be treated with full respect by court clerks and support personnel—even by judges—and not subjected to the indignity of excessive scrutiny. And, equally important, no facts relevant to the case should be withheld from them.

I cannot repeat too often the outstanding lesson of history: when jurors receive *all* the evidence, when they are informed of their full powers, when they are left to themselves, when they are free of outside influences, and when there are twelve of them together—in short, when they are *independent*—they almost invariably prove that they are the ultimate guardians and defenders of the people's liberties.

It seems that power shared briefly with others, all of whom are unaccustomed to it, tends to ennoble and thus to keep our rights secure.

NOTES

1. *San Francisco Chronicle,* March 28, 1996.
2. *Yale Law Journal* (1964): 173.

BIBLIOGRAPHY

CHAPTER 1: THE FATHER OF OUR COUNTRY

Beaven. *The Aldermen of the City of London.*

Blackstone, Sir William. *Commentaries on the Laws of England.* San Francisco: Bancroft-Whitney Co., 1915–16.

Bushell, Edward. *The Case of Edward Bushell et alia.* Ca. 1670.

"Bushell's Case," 1 Freeman 2, De.Term S. Mich., 1670; references found in *English Reports* 84 1112–15; 86 777–78; 89 2–6; 124 1006–16.

Campbell, John Lord. *The Lives of Chief Justices of England.* London: John Murray, 1849.

Cobbett's State Trials. Vols 1–10. London, 1809.

Forsyth, William. *History of Trial by Jury.* London: J. W. Parker & Son, 1852

Foss, Edward. *A Biographical Dictionary of the Judges of England.* London: J. Murray, 1870.

Howell's State Trials. Vol. 5, p. 444: *Trial of John Lilburne.*

Lady Newdigate. *Cavalier and Puritan in the Days of the Stuarts.* London, 1901.

Penn, William. *An Appendix by Way of a Dialogue between a Barrister and a Juryman, Asserting Claims of Juror against the then Cur-*

rent Doctrine Decrying Their Authority. London, 1670; also *Howell's State Trials*, 1014.

Penn, William. *The People's Ancient and Just Liberties Reasserted. . . .* London, 1670. Reprint Lawton Kennedy, San Francisco, 1954.

———. *Truth Rescued from Imposture*. London, 1671.

Pepys, Samuel. *The Diary of Samuel Pepys*. Edited by Henry B. Wheatley. London: G. Bell & Sons, 1928.

"A Person of Quality." *Guide to the English Jury*. London, 1682.

Spooner, Lysander. *An Essay on Trial by Jury*. 1852

S. S. (Samuel Starling). *An Answer to the Seditious and Scandalous Pamphlet, entitled "The Tryal of W. Penn and W. Mead. . . ."* London, 1670.

Stubbs, William. *The Constitutional History of England*. Oxford: Clarendon Press, 1880.

———. *Trial by Jury—the Birth-Right of the People of England*. Oxford: Clarendon Press, 1880.

The Tryal of Wm Penn and Wm Mead for Causing a Tumult. Edited by Don C. Seitz. Boston: Marshall Jones & Co., 1919.

Whitebrook, J. C. *Edward and John Bushell, Puritans and Merchants*. London, A. W. Cannon & Co., 1915.

CHAPTER 2: IT IS MY ROYAL WILL AND PLEASURE . . . !

Churchill, Winston S. *The New World*. New York: Dodd, Mead & Company, 1966.

Howell's State Trials. The Trial of the Seven Bishops, 4 James II 183, 1688.

Jones, J. R. *The Revolution of 1688 in England*. New York: W. W. Norton & Co., Inc., 1972.

Keeton, G. W. *Lord Chancellor Jeffreys and the Stuart Cause*. London: MacDonald, 1965.

Macaulay, Thomas Babington. *History of England from the Accession of James II*. Chicago: Belford,Clarke & Co., 1848.

Wiener, Joel H. *Great Britain, The Lion at Home*. New York: Chelsea House Publishers, 1974.

(See also the general histories of English law listed in the bibliography to chapter 1.)

CHAPTER 3: WHAT IT TAKES TO BE A GOOD CZAR

Baring, Maurice. *The Mainsprings of Russia*. Edinburgh: Thomas Nelson and Sons, Publishers, 1914.

Bergman, Jay. *Vera Zasulich, A Biography*. Stanford, Calif.: Stanford University Press, 1983.

Berman, Harold J. *Justice in Russia*. Cambridge, Mass.: Harvard University Press, 1950.

Broido, Vera. *Apostles into Terrorists*. New York: The Viking Press, 1977.

Feifer, George. *Justice in Moscow*. New York: Simon and Schuster, 1964.

Footman, David. *The Alexander Conspiracy*. La Salle, Ill.: A Library Press Book, 1974.

Graham, Stephen. *Tsar of Freedom, The Life and Reign of Alexander II*. New Haven: Yale University Press, 1935.

Kucherov, Samuel. *Courts, Lawyers and Trials under the Last Three Tsars*. New York: Frederick A. Praeger, 1953.

LeRoy-Beaulieu, Anatole. *The Empire of the Tsars and the Russians*. New York: G. P. Putnam's Sons, 1903.

Lincoln, Bruce. *Autocrats of All the Russians*. New York: The Duke Press, 1981.

Maxwell, Margaret. *Narodniki Women: Russian Women Who Sacrificed Themselves for the Dream of Freedom*. New York: Pergamon Press, 1990.

Mosse, W. E. *Alexander II and the Modernization of Russia*. London: The English Universities Press, Ltd.

Thaden, Edward C. *Russia Since 1801*. New York: John Wiley and Sons, Inc., 1971.

New York Times, issues of February 1878.

Westwood, J. N. *Endurance and Endeavour, Russian History, 1812–1980*. Oxford: Oxford University Press, 1981.

CHAPTER 4: PRACTITIONERS OF THE DETESTABLE ARTS

American State Trials. Vol. 1, pp. 514ff.: *The Trials of Bridget Bishop et alia.*

American State Trials. Vol. 5, pp. 85ff.: *The Trial of Thomas Maule.*

Boyer, Paul and Steven Nissenbaum, eds. *The Salem Witchcraft Papers.* New York: Da Capo Press, 1977.

Criminal Trials. Scotland, 24 Jac. VI, 1591, pp. 242ff.

Ewen, C. L'Estrange. *Witch Hunting and Witch Trials.* New York: Barnes & Noble, 1929.

Gragg, Larry. *The Salem Witch Crisis.* Westport, Conn.: Praeger.

Hansen, Chadwick. *Witchcraft at Salem.* 1969.

Naipar, Barbara. Trial for Witchcraft, 1591: *Criminal Trials* 24 Jac. 242.

Nevins, Winfield S. *Witchcraft in Salem Village in 1692.* Boston: North Shore Publishing Co., 1892.

Robinson, Enders A. *Salem Witchcraft and Hawthorne's* House of the Seven Gables. Bowie, Md.: Heritage Books, Inc., 1992.

Rosenthal, Bernard. *Salem Story . . . Reading the Witch Trials of 1692.* Cambridge, Mass.: Harvard University Press, 1993.

Sergeant, Philip W. *Witches and Warlocks.* New York: Benjamin Blom, Inc., 1972.

Starkey, Marion L. *The Devil in Massachusetts.* Garden City, N.Y: Doubleday and Co., 1961.

Stevens, Winfield S. *Records of Salem Witchcraft, Copied from the Original Documents.* Roxbury. Mass.: W. Elliott Woodward, 1864.

Upham, Charles W. *Salem Witchcraft.* Williamstown, Mass.: Corner House Publishers, 1971. Originally published 1867.

Williams, Selma R. *Riding the Nightmare.* New York: Atheneum, 1978.

Woods, William, ed., *A Casebook of Witchcraft.* New York. G. P. Putnam's Sons, 1974.

CHAPTER 5: "THE GREATER THE TRUTH, THE GREATER THE LIBEL"

Alexander, James. *A Brief Narrative of the Case and Trial of John Peter Zenger.* Edited by Stanley Nider Katz. Cambridge, Mass.: The Belknap Press, Harvard University, 1963.

American State Trials. Vol. 16, p. 1: *The Trial of John Peter Zenger for Libel, New York City, 1735.*

Aymer, Brandt, and Edward Saggarin. *A Pictorial History of the World's Great Trial.* New York: Crown Publishers, 1967.

Colden, Cadwallader. *Letters and Papers of Cadwallader Colden, 1749–1755.* New York: New York Historical Society, 1937.

Howell, T. B. *A Complete Collection of State Trials.* Vol. 17, p. 676: *The Trial of John Peter Zenger.*

Levy, Leonard W. *Emergence of a Free Press.* Oxford: Oxford University Press, 1985.

Rutherfurd, Livingston. *John Peter Zenger, His Press, His Trial.* Gloucester, Mass.: Peter Smith, 1963

New York Times, April 24, 1953.

(Additional sources for information on the Zenger trial appear in almost any publication on the subject of freedom of the press, etc., but they are repetitive of or corroborative with primary and the sources identified above.)

CHAPTER 6: ALIEN AND SEDITION ACTS TRIALS, 1798 TO 1800

American State Trials. Vol. 10, p. 774: *The Trial of Thomas Cooper*; p. 813: *The Trial of James Thompson Callender*; p. 676: *The Trial of William Duane et alia*; p. 687: *The Trial of Matthew Lyon.*

Austin, Aleine. *Matthew Lyon, "New Man" of the Democratic Revolution, 1749-1822.* State College, Penn.: Pennsylvania State University Press, 1987.

Brant, Irving. *Impeachment, Trials and Errors.* New York: Alfred A. Knopf, 1972.

Burleigh, Anne Husted. *John Adams.* New Rochelle, N.Y.: Arlington House, 1969.

Campbell, Tom W. *Two Fighters and Two Fines.* Little Rock, Ark.: Pioneer Publishing Co., 1941.

Cappon, Lester J. *The Adams-Jefferson Letters.* Chapel Hill: University of North Carolina Press, 1959.

Dauer, Manning J. *The Adams Federalists.* Baltimore: The John Hopkins University Press, 1968.

Hudson, Edward G. *Freedom of Speech and Press in America.* Washington, D.C.: Public Affairs Press, 1963

Miller, John C. *Crisis in Freedom.* Boston: Little, Brown and Co., 1951.

Peabody, James Bishop, ed. *John Adams, A Biography in His Own Words.* New York: Newsweek, 1973

Proffat, John. *A Treatise on Trial by Jury, including Questions of Law and Fact.* San Francisco: Sumner, Whitney and Co., 1877.

Rehnquist, William H. *Grand Inquests.* New York: William Morrow and Co., 1992.

Schachner, Nathan. *Thomas Jefferson, A Biography.* New York: Appleton-Century-Crofts, Inc., 1851

Shepherd, Jack. *The Adams Chronicles.* Boston: Little, Brown and Company, 1975

Smith, James Morton. *Freedom's Fetters, The Alien and Sedition Laws and American Civil Liberties.* Ithaca, N.Y.: Cornell University Press, 1966.

The Trial of Samuel Chase. New York: Da Capo Press, 1970.

Warfield, E. D. *The Kentucky Resolutions of 1798.* New York: G. P. Putnam's Sons, 1894.

Wharton, Francis. *State Trials of the United States during the Administrations of Washington and John Adams.* Philadelphia: Carey and Hart, 1849.

CHAPTER 7: LAWS DO NOT MAKE PEOPLE FREE, PEOPLE MAKE LAWS FREE

Birney v. *Ohio,* 8 Ohio 230, 1837.

Campbell, Stanley W. *The Slave Catchers, Enforcement of the Fugitive Slave Law, 1850–1860.* Chapel Hill: University of North Carolina Press, 1968.

Catterall, Helen Tunnicliff. *Judicial Cases concerning American Slavery and the Negro.* New York: Negro Universities Press, 1937.

Cheek v. *State,* 38 Ala 227.

Coleman, J. Winston. *Slavery Times in Kentucky.* Chapel Hill: University of North Carolina Press, 1940.

Commonwealth v. *Aves,* 35 Mass 193, 1836.

Cooley. *Blackstone's Commentaries on the Laws of England.*

Cover, Robert M. *Justice Accused: Antislavery and the Judicial Process.* New Haven: Yale University Press, 1975

Crandall against *Conn.,* 10 Conn 339, 1834.

Cushing, John D. "The Cushing Court and the Abolition of Slavery in

Massachusetts: Notes on the 'Quock Walker Case.' " *American Journal of Legal History* 5 (1961): 118.

Dave v. *State,* 22 Ala 23, 1853.

Engerman, Stanley L., and Robert William Fogel. *Time on the Cross: The Economics of American Negro Slavery.* Boston: Little, Brown and Co., 1974.

Fehrenbacher, Don E. *The Dred Scott Case: Its Significance in American Law and Politics.* New York: Oxford University Press, 1978

Finkelman, Paul. *Slavery in the Courtroom.* Washington, D.C.: Library of Congress, 1985.

———. *Statutes on Slavery.* New York: Garland Publishing Inc., 1988.

Forsyth, William. *History of Trial by Jury.* New York: Burt Franklin, 1875. Reprint New York: Lenox Hill, 1971.

Genovese, Eugene D. *Roll, Jordan, Roll: The World the Slaves Made.* Cambridge, Mass.: Pantheon Books, Harvard University Press, 1965.

Graham v. *Strader et alia,* 44 Ky 173, 1844.

Higginbotham, A. Leon, Jr. *In the Matter of Color: Race and the American Legal Process, the Colonial Period.* New York: Oxford University Press, 1978.

Howard, Warren S. *American Slavers and the Federal Law, 1837–1862.* Westport, Conn.: Greenwood Press, 1976

Hudson v. *State,* 34 Ala 1859.

Litwack, Leon F. *North of Slavery: The Negro in the Free States, 1790–1860.* Chicago: University of Chicago Press, 1961.

Lucid, Robert, ed. *The Journal of Richard Henry Dana, Jr.* Cambridge, Mass.: The Belknap Press, Harvard University, 1968.

Martin v. *Everett,* 11 Ala 375, 1847.

Moore, George H. *Notes on the History of Slavery in Massachusetts.* New York: D. Appleton and Co., 1866.

Morris, Thomas D. *Free Men All: The Personal Liberty Laws of the North, 1780–1861.* Baltimore: The Johns Hopkins University Press, 1974

Nash, A. E. Keir. "Fairness and Formalism in the Trials of Blacks in the State Supreme Courts of the Old South." *Virginia Law Review* 56 (1970): 64.

Pease, Jane H. *The Fugitive Slave Law and Anthony Burns.* Philadelphia: J. B. Lippincott Co., 1975.

Prigg v. *Pennsylvania,* 41 US 539, 1842.

Respublica v. *Blackmore,* 2 Yeats (Pa) 234, 1797.

Scott, John Anthony. *Hard Trials on My Way.* New York: A. A. Knopf.

Sellers, James Benson. *Slavery in Alabama.* Tuscaloosa: University of Alabama Press, 1950.

Spooner, Lysander. *An Essay on the Trial by Jury,* 1852. Reissued by Arizona Caucus Club, Mesa, Ariz.

State v. *Jones,* 5 Ala 666 1843.

Stewart, James Brewer. *Holy Warriors, The Abolitionists and American Slavery.* New York: Hill and Wang.

Stroud, George M. *Sketch of Laws Relating to Slavery in the Several States.* Philadelphia: Kimber and Sharpless, 1827.

Taylor, Joe Gray. *Negro Slavery in Louisiana.* Baton Rouge: Louisiana Historical Association, 1963.

Tillman v. *Chadwick,* 37 Ala 317, 1861.

Turnipseed v. *State,* 6 Ala 664, 1844.

United States v. *Hanway,* 26 F Cas 105, 1851.

Wiecek, William M. *The Sources of Antislavery Constitutionalism in America, 1760–1848.* Ithaca, N.Y.: Cornell University Press, 1977.

Winchendon v. *Hatfield,* 34 Mass 123, 1808.

Wright against *Deacon,* 5 Pa 62, 1819.

Wroth, L. Kinvin, and Hiller B. Zobel, eds. *Legal Papers of John Adams,* Vol 2. Cambridge, Mass.: The Belknap Press, Harvard University, 1965.

CHAPTER 8: A MAN'S HOME, A MAN'S CASTLE

Aptheker, Herbert, ed. *Writing in Periodicals Edited by W. E. B. Du Bois, Selections from The Crisis, 1911-1925.* Millwood, N.Y.: Krauss-Thompson Organization, Ltd., 1983.

Buchanan v. *Warley,* 245 U.S. 60, 1917.

Corrigan v. *Buckley,* 299 F 899, 1924.

Corrigan v. *Buckley,* 271 U.S. 323, 1925.

Darrow, Clarence, *The Story of My Life.* New York: Charles Scribner's Sons, 1932.

Fine, Sidney. *Frank Murphy, the Detroit Years.* Ann Arbor: University of Michigan Press, 1975.

Hays, Arthur Garfield. *City Lawyer.* New York: Simon and Schuster, 1942.

Hays, Arthur Garfield. *Let Freedom Ring.* New York: Da Capo Press, 1937.

————. *Trial by Prejudice.* New York: Covici, Frelde Publishers, 1933.

Jensen, Richard J. *Clarence Darrow.* Westport, Conn.: Greenwood Press, 1992.

Pond v. *People,* Mich Reports, 1860, p. 175.

Stone, Irving. *Clarence Darrow for the Defense.* Garden City, N.Y.: Doubleday, Doran & Co., 1941.

Weinberg, Kenneth G. *A Man's Home, A Man's Castle.* New York: The McCall Publishing Company, 1971.

CHAPTERS 9 AND 10: TRIALS OF SUSAN B. ANTHONY AND THE INSPECTORS

An Account of the Proceedings on the Trial of Susan B. Anthony, and the Inspectors of Election, 1872. Reprint New York: New York Times Publishing Co., 1972.

American State Trials. Vol. 3, p. 5: *Trials of Susan B. Anthony and of the Inspectors of Election.*

Anthony, Katharine Susan. *Susan B. Anthony.* New York: Russell & Russell, 1954.

Chamberlin, Everett. *The Struggle of '72 & the Issues & Candidates of the Present Presidential Campaign.* Chicago: Union Publishing Co., 1872.

DuBois, Ellen Carol, ed. *Correspondence, Writings, Speeches of Elizabeth Cady Stanton and Susan B. Anthony.* New York: Schocken Books, 1981.

Gage, Matilda Joslyn. *The United States on Trial, Not Susan B. Anthony.* Reprints of her speech in Rochester and Canandaigua preceding the trials, 1873.

Harper, Ida Husted. *The Life and Work of Susan B. Anthony.* Indianapolis: The Hollenbeck Press, 1898.

Kutler, Stanley I. *Justices of the United States Supreme Court, 1789–1969.*

Stanton, Elizabeth Cady, ed. *The History of Woman Suffrage.* New York: Fowler & Wells, 1887.

"Susan B. Anthony's Vote." *Harper's Weekly,* July 5, 1873.

Women in America. *Judge Hunt and the Right of Trial by Jury.* Manchester, N.H.: Arno Press.

CHAPTER 11: MURDER IN HAYMARKET SQUARE

American State Trials. Vol. 12, p. 1: *The Trial of the Chicago Anarchists,* 1886.

Atkinson, Charles Milner. *Jeremy Bentham, His Life and Work.* New York: August M. Kelley, Publishers, 1969.

Altgeld, John Peter. *Reasons for Pardoning Fielden, Neebe, and Schwab.* State of Illinois Printing Presses, 1893.

Avrich, Paul: *The Haymarket Tragedy.* Princeton, N.J.: Princeton University Press, 1984.

Bentham, Jeremy. *The Elements and Art of Packing as Applied to Special Juries.* New York and London: Garland Publishing Co., 1978.

Columbia Law Times. Vol. 1. New York: Columbia University Press, 1887.

David, Henry. *The History of the Haymarket Affair.* New York: Russell & Russell, 1936.

In the Matter of August Spies, et al., 123 U S Reports 80, 1887.

National Jury Project. *Jurywork.* 1983.

Parsons, Albert. "An Appeal to the People of America." New York: Columbia University Library, 1887.

Parsons, Lucy. *The Famous Speeches of the Eight Chicago Anarchists in Court,* 2d ed. Socialist Publishing Society, 1910.

Spies, August, et al. v. *People of the State of Illinois. Illinois Reports* 122 (1887): 1.

Stein, Leon, and Phillip Taft, eds. *The Accused and the Accusers.* New York: Arno Press and the *New York Times,* 1969.

CHAPTER 12: FRENCH TRIALS

(I used several sources on French juries, particular covering the trials of the Hugo brothers and Émile Zola. Much of the information was overlapping, and quotations from one source often duplicated that of the others.)

Andrews, Richard Mowery. *Law, Magistrates, and Crime in Old Regime Paris, 1735–1789.* Cambridge University Press, 1994.

Bell, John. *French Constitutional Law.* Oxford: Clarendon Press, 1992.

Bredin, Jean-Denis: *The Affair: The Case of Alfred Dreyfus.* New York: George Braziller, 1986.

David, René. *The French Legal System.* New York: Oceana Publications, 1958.

Dictionary of Biography, Past and Present. Detroit: Gale Research, 1974.

Esmein, A. *A History of Continental Criminal Procedure.* London: John Murray, 1914.

Forsyth, William. *History of Trial by Jury.* New York: Burt Franklin, 1875. Reprint New York: Lenox Hill, 1971.

Gide, André. *Recollections of the Assize Court.* London and Melbourne: Hutchinson & Co., Ltd., 1913.

Halasz, Nicholas. *Captain Dreyfus, The Story of Mass Hysteria.* New York: Simon and Schuster, 1955.

Hemmings, F. W. J. *The Life and Times of Emile Zola.* New York: Charles Scribner's Sons, 1977.

Josephson, Matthew. *Victor Hugo.* Garden City, N.Y.: Doubleday, Doran & Co., Inc., 1942.

Kock, Prof. Gerald L. *The French Code of Criminal Procedure.* London: Sweet & Maxwell, Ltd., 1964.

Moriarty, Gerald P., trans. *The Paris Law Courts.* London: Shelley and Co., Ltd., 1893.

Nixon, Edna. *Voltaire and the Callas Case.* New York: The Vanguard Press, Inc., 1961.

Paleologue, Maurice. *The Dreyfus Case.* New York: Criterion Books, 1957.

Richardson, Joanna. *Victor Hugo.* New York: St. Martin's Press, 1976.

Schrom, Alan. *A Biography of Émile Zola.* New York: Henry Holt and Company, 1987

Tocqueville, Alexis de. *Democracy in America.* New York: A. A. Knopf, 1945.

West, Andrew, et al. *The French Legal System, an Introduction.* London: Fourmat Publishing, 1992

INDEX

367